Harlem Crossroads

Harlem Crossroads

❖

Black Writers and the Photograph
in the Twentieth Century

Sara Blair

PRINCETON UNIVERSITY PRESS
PRINCETON AND OXFORD

Library of Congress Cataloging-in-Publication Data
Blair, Sara.
Harlem crossroads : black writers and the photograph in
the twentieth century / Sara Blair.
p.   cm.
Includes bibliographical references (p.   ) and index.
ISBN-13: 978-0-691-13087-3 (hardcover : alk. paper)
ISBN-10: 0-691-13087-6 (hardcover : alk. paper)
1. American literature—African American authors—History and criticism.
2. Politics and literature—United States—History—20th century. 3. African Americans—
Intellectual life—20th century. 4. Photography—United States—History. 5. Photography—
Philosophy. 6. Harlem (New York, N.Y.)—History. 7. Modernism (Literature)—
United States. 8. African American aesthetics. I. Title.
PS153.N5B563 2007
810.9′358—dc22   2006100313

British Library Cataloging-in-Publication Data is available

Title page photograph: Danny Lyon, Hattiesburg, Mississippi, 1964. Magnum Photos.

This book has been composed in Minion with Mona Lisa display

Printed on acid-free paper. ∞

press.princeton.edu

Printed in the United States of America

1   3   5   7   9   10   8   6   4   2

for Jonathan Freedman
and for Ben and Miriam

Contents

Illustrations

Acknowledgments

This book has taken shape over more years than I care to recall, and a number of institutions and places have given it shelter and growing room. It began in earnest soon after my arrival in Ann Arbor, where it was nurtured by two remarkable departmental chairs, Lincoln Faller and Sidonie Smith. A generous grant from Michigan's Office of the Vice President for Research (OVPR), enabling me to travel to archives from New York to Los Angeles, Tucson to Ottawa, and many points between, allowed me a freedom of discovery and invention without which this work could never have taken shape. The welcome award of a 2005–6 National Endowment for the Humanities grant, supplemented by a Michigan Humanities Award, made the book's completion possible (or, as my daughter Miriam would say, really real). In the final stages of the process, generous subventions from the Department of English and OVPR enabled me to make the photographic materials so central to my thinking, and my dream life, available to my readers; for that opportunity I am grateful.

Above all, I feel lucky in my indebtedness to my colleagues at Michigan, whose boundless intellectual energy, cheerful rigor, and downright chops never fail to impress me. Paul Anderson, Carol Bardenstein, Kerstin Barndt, Jay Cook, Gregg Crane, Jonathan Freedman, Kevin Gaines, Sandra Gunning, June Howard, Kader Konuk, Joanne Leonard, Julian Levinson, Joshua Miller, Phil Pochoda, David Scobey, Patricia Yaeger, Magdalena Zaborowska, and Rebecca Zurier read, conversed, parried, commented, and traded resources in ways that have immeasurably strengthened this work and made it immensely more fun to pursue. Special thanks are due to Alan Wald, whose scholarly range is matched only by his eagerness to share his extensive collection of radicalia, and to Larry Goldstein, who at an early stage offered me the opportunity to coedit a special issue of the *Michigan Quarterly Review*, and thus begot my regular forays into the gallery world. My graduate students in recent courses on visuality and U.S. modernism and the image in theory and practice may find observations in these pages that reflect our conversations; I am grateful to have had the opportunity to work through with them, if not inflict on them, ideas central to the project. Special thanks to Jennifer Sorenson (at the outset) and Angela Berkley (at the eleventh hour), who provided shrewd, omnicompetent research assistance when I needed it most; I look forward to reading their work in print in the not too distant future.

During the years in which this book grew, one home away from home has been the Bread Loaf School of English, whose peerless director, Jim Maddox, graciously allowed me to offer courses on modernity and the image-world in spite of their eccentricity to his program. For attentive interest in my work and lively conversation about its possibilities, I am grateful to Isobel Armstrong, Michael Armstrong, Dare Clubb, Harry Elam, Michele Elam, Dixie Goswami, Jennifer Green-Lewis, Lucy Maddox, Margery Sabin, Robert Stepto, Bryan Wolf, and Michael Wood; I am also indebted to my Bread Loaf students, who always help me see familiar objects anew. Caroline Eisner offered welcome irony and much-needed technical assistance in a setting in which a stray bolt of lightning, or the occasional miscreant beaver gnawing on a power line, could send a day's work into permanent oblivion. At the Middlebury Museum of Art, Emmie Donadio made it possible for me to mount an exhibition of photographs during the summer of 2006, for which I am grateful (not least because it clarified the mysterious work curators do). While at Bread Loaf, I was regularly struck by the dissonance between the subject of my work and the bucolic landscape in which, for successive summers, I pursued it. But the oscillation between Ripton, Vermont, and 135th Street, Harlem, was far from unpleasant, and bracingly productive.

In an important way, this book is also the product of numerous travels and forays (if not one-night stands) in other departments. It got a significant boost early on at the Tri-College American Studies seminar, to which Gus Stadler was kind enough to invite me to present; the comments of participants— especially Kim Benston—were of considerable moment to what came after. Lively respondents to presentations for the Oxford American studies faculty at the Rothermere American Institute (thanks to Ron Bush), the University of Chicago's Americanist faculty seminar, the University of California–Irvine, SUNY–Buffalo, and Williams College contributed significantly to the ongoing work. Fellow participants at the 2004 Flair conference at the Harry Ransom Center—especially Mia Carter, Susan Stanford Friedman, Michael North, and Marianna Torgovnick—gave me new insight and frames of reference. I was particularly fortunate to find myself on a panel at the 2004 American Studies Association, reprised by invitation at the NEASA "Sightlines" conference in 2005, with Joseph Entin, whose observations on photo-text helped me to re-think my own; Maren Stange, who offered a host of bracing suggestions and generous, judicious counsel about access to archives and image makers; and Laura Wexler, whose acuity as a respondent refocused my readings and made them considerably better. From early days in Charlottesville, I am indebted for perspicacity and friendship to Alison Booth, Rita Felski, Clare Kinney, and Elissa Rosenberg. At large, in the vast yet close space we call the profession, I have been the recipient of aid and comfort from Rachel Adams, Bill Brown, Wai Chee Dimock, Jennifer Fleissner, Jacqueline Goldsby, Gordon Hutner, Catharine Jurca, Arlene Keizer, Cristanne Miller, Ross Posnock, Shawn Michelle Smith, Eric Sundquist, Michael Szalay, Alan Trachtenberg, Kenneth Warren, and Cindy Weinstein. Further along in the process, I found myself completing the manuscript in the environs of Williams College; special thanks to Karen Swann, Anita Sokolsky, and Stephen Tifft for making my stay there so pleasurable. The serendipity of meeting and conversing with Marcellus Blount, Erina Duganne, Cecilia Hirsch, Anthony Lee, John Limon, Carol Ockman, and Bernie Rhie made Williamstown a special kind of crossroads for me.

As I hope the pages that follow attest, a good deal of the pleasure of this work resulted from my experiences in archives, museums, galleries, and other kinds of places in which texts and images come, sometimes unwittingly, to rest. For expert, attentive aid in locating and using archival materials, I am grateful to Dr. Alice Lotvin Birney and Maricia Battle at the Library of Congress; Cynthia Young at the International Center for Photography; Cyndie Campbell at the National Gallery of Canada; Amy Rule and Leslie Calmes at the Center for Creative Photography; Joseph Struble at George Eastman House; Vicki Harris at the Laurence Miller Gallery; Patricia Willis at the Beinecke Library; Leslie Hein at the Nebraska State Historical Society; Kendra Greene at the Museum of Contemporary Photography; Michael Shulman at Magnum Photos; and James Martin at the Richard Avedon Foundation. Among the institutions whose archives were crucial to my work, I am grateful to staff at the Schomburg Center for Research in Black Culture, the Howard Greenberg Gallery, the New York City Municipal Archive, and the New York Public Library; Bruce Silverstein at Silverstein Photography; and Norma Stevens at the Richard Avedon Foundation (in whom, it must be noted, the scholarly world lost a truly great editor). For their enthusiastic responses to my queries and their generosity in sharing the rich resources of the Addison Gallery of American Art, I am grateful to Julie Bernstein and Allison Kemmerer, and look forward to continuing work with them. Thanks also to Carl Chiarenza, Willie Gregory, Albert LaFarge, Gerard Pellison, Alan Thomas, and Doug Wixson for bracing suggestions in correspondence and conversation. Of special moment were the responses of photographers who shared their work and experience. Dawoud Bey traded thoughts on Ellison, documentary, and his own Harlem portfolio at a key moment; Oscar Palacio helped me rethink relations between documentation and expressive modes. The opportunity to work with Richard Avedon was the great serendipity of this project; he was as generous and acute as he was legendary (although to my son Ben's regret I never did meet the beekeeper).

For permission to reproduce images I am grateful to the Richard Avedon Foundation, John Callahan, Ted Croner, Fanny Ellison, the estate of Louis Faurer, David Heath, William Klein, Helen Levitt, Danny Lyon, Lorna Simpson, the Aaron Siskind Foundation, Donna Mussenden VanderZee, Toby White, and Julia Wright. Parts of chapter 3 previously appeared in *The Cambridge Companion to Ralph Ellison* and in the spring 2005 issue of *Raritan*, to whose editors—Ross Posnock and T. J. Jackson Lears, respectively—I am grateful for goodwill and a gimlet eye. As the book lurched toward completion, the anonymous yet inimitable readers for Princeton University Press, the attentions of the ever-vigilant Hanne Winarsky and Terri O'Prey, and the remarkable talents of Madeleine Adams and Jane Lincoln Taylor made it immeasurably better. First, last, and always there to steady it and to make possible the sometimes wayward, sometimes urgent forays into the wider world on which it depended, has been Jonathan Freedman. This book is for him, and for Ben and Miriam, who always let me go and always call me home.

Preface

❖

One chilly November afternoon, as I was browsing through the finding aid for Ralph Ellison's papers at the Library of Congress, I noticed a series of brief entries indicating the existence of a photographic archive that supplemented Ellison's abundant written record. Because his images were housed in another section of the Library and required a new set of permissions to examine, I was disinclined to pursue this lead. It was, after all, November, and I thought I was writing a chapter focused on a larger body of representations of Harlem after the Renaissance, destined to appear as part of a book titled *The Places of the Literary*. Ellison's published work and manuscripts offered plenty of material for thinking about that issue. Why look any further?

But curiosity won the day and, some months later, I found myself in the pleasant viewing room of the Library's Prints and Photographs Division. Ushered to a work station, offered a light table and a pair of shapeless white gloves, I watched as a Library staff member wheeled out a trolley with five large cardboard boxes. "Here it is," she said. "Go to." Inside those boxes, arrayed (sometimes jumbled) in folders and envelopes and plastic sleeves, were a range and variety of images I found no less than stunning. As I made my way through this trove, I began to understand Ellison, that singular and exemplary figure, in a new way: as a writer whose engagements with visual objects—particularly photographs—profoundly shaped his self-imagination and practice. Photography, it struck me, was hardly a hobby or a side line for Ellison. It was a resource for his imaginative and intellectual self-construction as rich as jazz, or even literature itself.

This was not, however, the end of my discoveries. On a subsequent visit, I came across the portrait photograph with which chapter 3 begins: the image, much handled and creased as if to fit inside a wallet (where Ellison had indeed kept it), of Richard Wright, sporting his own considerable camera in hand. Encountering that photograph, I felt something very much like what Roland Barthes describes at the opening of *Camera Lucida* as he finds himself looking, via a photograph, on eyes that have looked on the eyes of Napoleon: in the presence of an irreducible expression of being and history. The fact of Wright offering himself both as photographer and as subject thus to be imaged, kept ready to hand by Ellison at the outset of his career, exhorted me; there was an untold story about black writers and the photograph as an expressive object and a form of social agency. After several sessions with Ellison's images, it was clear that my narrative about Harlem after the Renaissance would have to expand and refocus itself considerably to explore this possibility—and so it did. The presence of Wright's talismanic image in Ellison's archive led me, in best Ellisonian fashion, both back to earlier figures and forward to succeeding ones, in whose work I found rich confirmation of the power of the photograph for writers who simultaneously negotiated racial imperatives, the hard facts of everyday postwar life, and the rich possibilities of struggle with expressive form.

The resulting book tries to bring this untold story to light and to argue its importance for American literary history, photographic history, and the rapidly shifting cultural field in the twentieth-century United States. Throughout, I have aimed to see photographic practice and objects anew—or rather, to see them not in terms of critical traditions that frame photography as myth or as disciplinary regime (as does so much important work on photo history), or even as a mode of knowing what Jean-Luc Nancy calls "la réalité de la pensée" (a phenomenological approach currently being explored to theoretical rather than historical effect), but rather as they appear to have made sense and suggestion in particular contexts of encounter for various writers, from the pages of America's picture magazines and the organs of the radical left to specialized photo journals, state-sponsored archives, private galleries, and the Museum of Modern Art.

This focus on writers and the literary field has, of course, yielded a very different sort of emphasis than that produced by work in photo history. Until recently, the emphasis of that discipline has fallen on distinctive institutional structures (state agencies, the mass press, museums) and ideological frames (New Deal liberalism, cold war state building, aestheticism) for image production and circulation. Although that view is critical—in every sense of the word—to any understanding of the uses of photography in American modernity, it has certain blind spots. Producing, in effect, its own kind of segregation, it has left the kinds of engagements and crossings with which I am concerned more or less invisible. When Langston Hughes worked (sometimes simultaneously) with photojournalists, documentary agencies, and some of the most celebrated art photographers of the postwar era, his interest was hardly contained by the rubrics of the picture press, or the state archive, or the exhibition gallery; when Richard Wright took up his own camera in service of photo-text production in New York, Chicago, and Africa, he was enabled as much as constrained by the institutional forms of postwar image making. Ditto Ralph Ellison, making documentary images for the mass press and portrait photos of fellow authors on his day job as he wrote *Invisible Man*, all the while studying the work of postwar photographers who were altering possibilities for understanding subjective experience and the social landscape. For these and other writers, the photograph itself, as it moved fluidly across vastly different informing contexts and sutured itself to a kaleidoscopic array of projects, frames, and fields, was a rich site of experience and response. Breaching boundaries of production and reception, wrenching images from instrumental contexts for their own uses, the work of these writers defies the settled logic of institutional reading; it becomes visible only when viewed in broader cultural and social frames.

By way of focusing on their engagements and on the place of the work they produced in the labile field of photography, I take Harlem as a point of departure. The story I tell begins with an introductory account of how photography came to Harlem—that is, how Harlem became, after the Renaissance and at the inauguration of a new era of the mass image, a signally important proving ground for photographers testing the possibilities of new stylistics and new relations to their subjects. Quite differently from images made under the auspices of the storied Farm Security Administration photo project, or commandeered by purveyors of visual experience and consumer modernity such as *Life*, certain projects for documenting Harlem in the wake of its "first great" riots (which I consider in chapter 1) predicated themselves on the fraught history of looking in that place, and on the residual histories and afterlives of Harlem as America's black metropolis, a distinctive site of social encounter. These projects, I argue, inaugurated an alternative vector of documentary imaging, site-specific and self-conscious, to which a host of writers were attuned.

Successive chapters consider some of these writers and their responses to the photograph in more detail. Chapter 2 addresses Wright's work with the Farm Security Administration archive, work that founded an African American tradition of photo-text and became a powerful resource for his own late work in the context of African independence movements on problems of imaging modernity. In chapter 3, I detail Ellison's sustained investment in photographic materials and stances, particularly with reference to *Invisible Man*; that landmark novel is, I argue, essentially a photo-text that suppresses its own informing visual referents. Baldwin's life- and career-long interest in producing photo-texts is the subject of chapter 4. Studying his ongoing collaborations with the photographer Richard Avedon, I argue for their value in exposing (to use the obvious word) a distinctive social history—that of Jewish and African American crossings—that informs the development of documentary imaging in the United States, and I consider the culmination of this work in a photo-text that both explodes and brilliantly exploits the stylistic conventions of the form. Addressing a more literal context of explosion, chapter 5 takes up the photo-text and documentary engagements of Lorraine Hansberry, Chester Himes, and John Oliver Killens in the context of a hardening skepticism among Black Power and Black Arts advocates about the image as a tool of white America. Each of these writers, I show, engages with documentary archives (or in Himes's case tropes) so as to negotiate their own commitments and self-representations, not least to negotiate the imperatives of identity thinking. The book closes with a coda focused on Toni Morrison and her uses, as novelist, editor, cultural critic, and instantly recognizable spokeswoman, of documentary archives and images. Close attention to them makes visible the real force of the novel *Jazz*—surprisingly, her only novelistic representation of the Harlem Renaissance—and provides a useful frame for looking back at the crossroads history I explore.

   The motif of the look back inevitably suggests the Orpheus myth, or rather the problem for any visual accounting of this era of a longstanding emphasis, in African American studies and in cultural studies more generally, on music as the privileged, uniquely authentic expressive form. In what follows, I address this problem in specific contexts. More broadly, what I frequently missed in writing this book was the sense of a many-voiced dialogue, on the order of the one that has defined jazz studies for at least a decade, about the complex forms and uses of photography (and more broadly of visual texts or culture) as it circulates through various communities, especially in twentieth-century contexts, and occasions changing responses. All the more powerful, then, has been the work of scholars (among them Geoffrey Batchen, Anthony Lee, and Shawn Michelle Smith) who have begun laying the groundwork for such a conversation. It is my hope within these pages to have done justice to their example, and to have contributed in some way to the rising interest in the photograph and visuality across a wide array of disciplines, from American studies and literary studies to rhetoric, cultural history, and anthropology. Although the lack of a stable disciplinary home for work on images creates structural challenges for anyone seeking to address different histories of response, it also offers a singular opportunity for rethinking the social and experiential relations between images and history, and the effect (as Alan Trachtenberg has so influentially put it) of images as history. Collectively, the writers I engage have a great deal to suggest not only about their own interests and practices, or about consequential crossings between literary and photographic production. They also challenge latter-day readers to consider how photographs and visual experience might occasion varied kinds of critical reflection in the ambit of a still-elusive modernity. Finally, the literary does have its places and its place in this work, not least in offering a rich field on which to stake new ways of looking back.

Harlem Crossroads

◈

Introduction

A Riot of Images:
Harlem and the Pursuit of Modernity

◈

On March 20, 1935, readers of newspapers across the United States were greeted with news of an unprecedented event: the outbreak the previous evening in black America's cultural capital of what the elder statesman Adam Clayton Powell wryly called Harlem's "first great riot."[1] As Powell recognized, what made the event a "first" (if not "great") was its inversion of the structure, omnipresent in a burgeoning American modernity at least since Reconstruction, of white-on-black violence.[2] If the widespread destruction of white-owned Harlem property that ensued was not exactly payback for decades of white aggression and mob violence from Brownsville, Atlanta, and Houston to Tulsa and Springfield, Illinois, and many points between, it was a form of notice to white America that the old dispensations had become a thing of the past. Powell's sense not just of history but of precedent being made—"first" implies iterations to follow—is prevalent in journalistic documentation of the event, particularly in its prominently featured photographs. How is this new fact of American modernity to be imaged and, by implication, managed or imagined?

In considering that question, we might usefully focus on one widely reproduced image of the 1935 outbreak, an image at once representative and suggestive (figure I.1). The photograph features a paddy wagon full of African Americans (all those visible are men; some are obviously injured) who have been taken into police custody. Shot at point-blank range, exploiting in its handling of light and tonality a certain shock effect, the image nonetheless conveys

Figure I.1. Injured Rioters in a Police Patrol Wagon, Harlem, 1935. Corbis.

something of the social complexities attendant on its making. Tightly framing its subjects with the receding horizontal lines of the vehicle's interior and the diagonal patterning on the doors' protective grillwork, the composition emphasizes the orderly containment of black men's bodies in postures of resignation and distress; note the formal regularity established in the play of the men's folded hands and headgear. Absent a directive caption, the shot tenders uncertainty about their status; they are booked as looters but imaged, at least potentially, as victims. Yet in the context of an interwar mass readership (presumptively white), this uncertainty is itself pointed. Whether its subjects are read as criminals or potential objects of sympathy, the image emphasizes the power of modern social agencies—not least the documentary camera—to manage social disorder.

In connection with this image we might usefully consider a second, similar yet strikingly different in effect (figure I.2). It too was shot by an anonymous photojournalist and circulated widely in the mainstream and African American presses; it too can fairly be said to represent the visual record from which it is drawn: eyewitness photographs of the second "great riot" in Harlem on

Figure I.2. Harlem Riot, Arrest of Looters, 1943. Corbis.

August 2, 1943.[3] This time (Powell was prescient), the civil unrest was extensive, resulting in multiple fatalities and millions of dollars in damage to white-
owned businesses; it brought home the raw fact of persistent social inequality
heightened by wartime mobilization.[4] But the context of escalating retributive
or social action seems curiously at odds with the tenor of the photograph.
Indeed, absent explicit captioning or textual accompaniment, and in spite of
the prominence of nightsticks, a viewer encountering this image might understandably fail to identify its subject as violent social disorder.

In lieu of bloody or bandaged men in postures of submission, an attractive
young woman smiles openly at the camera, part of a group of style-conscious
women balancing boxes of hosiery and other consumer goods (one shopping
bag is emblazoned with the logo "Modesse") as they are escorted by police. If
their destination is presumably once again the paddy wagon, the affective logic
has shifted considerably; in a parody of gallantry, one of the officers appears
to assist his detainee with her packages as they cross the street. This difference
is not, however, entirely an effect of the shot's focus on women. The photographic record of the 1943 outbreak contains its share of more-predictable riot
images (burning cars, injured passersby), but it also includes a host of others

Figure I.3. Boys Wearing Looted Formal Wear, August 2, 1943. Corbis.

in which groups of adolescent boys and young men parade insouciantly in looted blond wigs, or in top hats and tails vastly too large, in the mode of Harlem's signature zoot suit (figure I.3).[5] Perhaps it would be hasty to call such gestures revolution, and perforce they would not, in 1943, be televised. But they were clearly being made available, even self-consciously staged, for photographic observers.

How might we account for the differences in cultural logic implied by these images? The most powerful social fact registered in the 1935 "great riot," as in its documentation, was the end of the Harlem Renaissance era; in the wake of its cartwheeling, high-flying optimism, and of the economic expansiveness that underwrote it, remained only the sobering realities of what residents north of 110th Street called the Raw Deal.[6] And when "thousands of curious white visitors thronged Harlem's sidewalks" on the evening after the 1935 outbreak, according to a *New York Times* report, their racial tourism was no longer predicated on the kinds of engagement, however problematic, associated with the heyday of the Renaissance. Now, "visitors" were mainly on hand to view the shocking evidence of seething unrest, communist agitation, and racial retribution, in a landscape "alive with resentful Negroes."[7] Years before any recognition of the second ghetto as such, Harlem was taking shape, in image and in fact, as a new kind of urban space and icon: inner city, social underground, a complex legacy and a representational challenge.[8]

The most striking photographs of the 1943 event can be said to suggest an awareness of the growing role of the image in this transformation, and of the changing contract between the documenting camera and its subjects, particularly in Harlem.[9] However determined to strike a blow against white ownership of local trade and the blatant fact of unequal treatment in housing and employment, Harlem citizens who took to the wartime streets were enacting their desire for a share in American modernity for a host of watching eyes. Throughout the frenzied hours of disorder, the heart of Harlem—the broad boulevard of Seventh Avenue—served as the runway for a variety of "surreal" tableaux;[10] in effect it became "a ridiculous fashion show"—"the most colossal Negro picnic ever seen"—whose participants onlookers were invited to record.[11] In this encounter, agency photographers, photojournalists, and amateurs alike confronted a new kind of social spectacle and fact; Harlem became the occasion for what we might call a riot of images, conspicuously new in tone and affect. They premised a newly iconic Harlem, at once metonymic of America's modernity and revelatory of its social failings. And in so doing, they instanced the growing power accorded the camera as a mode of documenting and knowing America—and no less of belonging to it.

The images of Harlem riot, the riot of Harlem images, thus implicate—as they helped propel—a broader cultural shift of central moment to the readings that follow. Between 1935 and 1943, America was giving birth to a full-blown image culture, largely experienced and transacted in the definitive genre of the era: documentary. Although the origins of documentary image making were of much longer reach, the national ascendancy of that genre—which may be defined for my purposes as the attempt, commercial or socially conscious, to record the events, affective life, material culture, or local practices of specific communities—began in earnest in the United States in the mid-1930s, at about the moment of Harlem's first riot.[12] That moment also marked the advent of a differently explosive phenomenon, the so-called Leica revolution: the development of high-quality, portable 35 mm handheld cameras, roll film, and lightweight flash equipment that enabled rapid and sequential shooting under uncontrolled or quickly changing conditions (like those prevailing during civil unrest).[13]

These technological breakthroughs not only shifted the ground of the photographic encounter, lifting it out of the studio and onto the street; they also, as I will argue in more detail later, significantly altered the ontology of the photographic image, which was no longer premised on a cult of memorial or the mode of nostalgia. Relocated to the wayward, anonymous thoroughfares of the city, at a moment of sharply heightened interest in the material circumstances of ordinary Americans, the portable camera became the privileged apparatus for documentary—and more broadly social—seeing. By the mid-1930s, photographic images produced on site in urban venues had played a part in the visual archive for almost three-quarters of a century. But the advent of the new portable technology within this specific social context, where it was being shaped to a host of liberal-managerial and commercial uses, significantly altered the terms and potential meaning of the documentary image.[14] Training itself on the epochal realities of everyday life, photography framed them for national consumption and meditation, and thereby powerfully shaped modern American sentiment, class relations, racial regimes, and national ideals.

What one historian calls the "dramaturgical" quality of the 1943 Harlem outbreak is, in other words, powerful testimony to the gathering power of visuality, and in particular of the documentary photographic record, in the interwar period.[15] Indeed, the two "great riots" can be seen to bookend a series of events that chart the spreading reach of the photographic image as an ideological vehicle and as an aesthetic object. In November 1936, the media tycoon Henry R. Luce shrewdly capitalized on the new photographic technologies to found "an entirely new publishing venture": the "picture magazine," exemplified by the wildly successful weekly *Life*.[16] Within a year and a half of its launching, the journal had achieved an unprecedented circulation of seventeen million readers, all seduced by its distinctive cocktail of news, gossip, and spectacle—what the critic Bernard DeVoto shrewdly called "equal parts of the decapitated Chinaman, the flogged Negro, the surgically explored peritoneum, and the rapidly slipping chemise."[17]

For the first time in media history, the photograph, or what Luce called "the photographic essay"—the conjoining of "naturalistic," "unposed," "honest" images with narrative analysis, oral testimony, and directive captions—had become the essential engine of mass communication.[18] The cover of *Life*'s inaugural issue featured an image by the documentary photographer Margaret

Bourke-White (a monumentalizing shot of an early New Deal success, the Fort Peck dam in Montana) that launched the journal's visual style and catapulted Bourke-White herself to meteoric fortune. A few months later, in collaboration with the writer Erskine Caldwell, Bourke-White published a photo-text documentary volume titled *You Have Seen Their Faces*. It became an instant sensation and the model (and antimodel) for a spate of photo-text books featuring documentary images, including the modernist classic *Let Us Now Praise Famous Men* (1941). Meanwhile, in 1935, Rexford Tugwell, the director of the quintessential New Deal agency later called the Farm Security Administration (FSA), had formed a special "historical" unit to create a photographic archive of forgotten Americans—and of the federal rehabilitation projects that were, thanks to liberal ideology, bringing "relief" to the displaced, the poverty-stricken, the illiterate, and the unfed. Over the next five years, picture magazines such as *Fortune, Life, Look, Today*, and *Nation's Business* as well as innumerable garden-variety national and regional journals became voracious clients of the FSA and other photo archives. By 1940, the FSA's Historical Section alone was placing some 1,406 images per month in such commercial vehicles.[19]

As even this brief sketch suggests, and as photo historical scholarship has emphasized, documentary image making under the sign of modernity not only penetrated to but defined the coalescing realms of mass media, New Deal state building, and postwar consumerism. No wonder that it played such a significant role in shaping the responses of Harlem's inhabitants to their own political disenfranchisement and social marginality. What is surprising—or as yet unacknowledged—is the degree to which real and iconic Harlem shaped the development and uses of documentary, not only as a photographic practice but as a set of representational possibilities, both visual and literary. The evolving interests of documentary practice in all its forms were varied, and its practitioners were fluidly positioned on a cultural field encompassing radical socialism, nation building, Stalinism, and every other socially conscious stripe. But they shared to a remarkable degree an interest in Harlem as a site of encounter, an emblem of the challenge of representing American modernity. In the wake of the 1935 riot, at the moment of photography's ascendancy as a cultural agency and a form of art, Harlem became a photographic proving ground. The self-taught, left-leaning members of the New York Photo League worked there regularly beginning in the mid-1930s; the picture press founded by Luce also predicated its power to slake a definitively modern thirst for sensation on its ability to provide viewers with a gallery of images to which Harlem is literally central: "Farmer faces, mining faces, faces of rugged individualists, Harlem faces, hopeful faces, tired old faces, smart night club faces . . .—the faces of the U.S."[20] Throughout the 1940s and 1950s and beyond, for socially conscious, photojournalistic, and experimental photographers alike, Harlem remained a special provocation, a site that afforded charged visual opportunities, spectacles, evidence, found objects, and decisive moments.

Harlem after its first great riot—which is to say, Harlem after the Renaissance—thus profoundly shaped representational practices and conventions at midcentury, in photographic texts and beyond, as image makers, writers, and others sought to explore its everyday life in the name of marketable shock, making it new, or making social change. For some of these observers, the appeal was not (or not only) the scandal of conditions on the ground north of 110th Street. To be sure, the hard facts of daily life in Harlem—site of the most densely populated housing tract in Manhattan, the highest rates of infant mortality in the city, and a structural unemployment rate that was, even during the Depression, significantly higher than that of any other population or community—were of precisely the sort to attract liberal-managerial zeal.[21] But for certain observers, Harlem as a photographic proving ground offered a unique opportunity to meditate on the very conditions of documentary encounter: what powers accrued to the camera and the photographer's gaze; what kinds of social transactions produce a documentary text, and how they are represented, aestheticized, or repressed within it; how the drive for formal nuance and complexity serves or negates the representation of human and social being.

These opportunities to test the limits and possibilities of documentary knowing, now a primary agency of modern American social life, arose in the face of Harlem's distinctive histories as a site of racial and cultural encounter, indelibly inscribed both in everyday practices and in the built landscape. In a landmark text of the Renaissance moment, *Black Manhattan* (1930), James Weldon Johnson had noted that "the history of New York" might be traced as "the name of Harlem has changed from Dutch to Irish to Jewish to Negro."[22] The texture of this transformation—of its survivals and afterlives, its residual and palimpsestic effects—was even more variegated than Johnson suggests. Well beyond the turn of the century and into the Depression, the streets, structures, and facades of Harlem bore marks of its earlier life as an immigrant enclave, most prominently for German and Eastern European Jews but also for Italians, Puerto Ricans, and other diasporites, migrants, and refugees, whose presence and practices produced a distinctive "kaleidoscope" effect.[23] If the earliest histories of displacement (that of the Manhattan indigenes by Dutch settlers, and the latter by English arrivals) remained invisible, definitively modern forms of contact and appropriation shaped the very streetscape; thus the architectural historian Michael Henry Adams has commented that Harlem's thoroughfares, preserving the tangible record of its various communities, resemble "the image produced by two facing mirrors: a reflection of a reflection of a reflection."[24]

The historical record, not to mention a growing body of recent scholarship, suggests the relative ease with which America's others assimilated to whiteness by learning to discriminate against or to appropriate the culture of their black neighbors, tenants, and employees. But Harlem subjects nonetheless negotiated the mutual mediations or "reflection[s]" of race, ethnicity, and origin unique to their home place on a daily basis. Lino Rivera, the youth whose supposed beating by police in 1935 was made the emblem of African America's exclusion from social promise (and the justification for unrest), was the son of Puerto Rican immigrants; when throngs of reporters sought comment from his family, they found themselves outside an apartment on Manhattan Avenue, just south of the infamous flats area around Saint Nicholas Park and markedly west of the "separate" neighborhood of Spanish Harlem.[25] Two months later, when Benito Mussolini's troops began bombing Ethiopia, Lenox and Seventh Avenues were tense with "patriotic skirmishes" between black residents and those of Italian descent; a local school, P.S. 178, became a battleground for the two Harlem populations, on which it evenly drew.[26] Among the objects of spectatorial interest during the 1935 riot were "the words the Chinese laundryman painted on his window when the Negroes were breaking windows of all the white business places . . .—'Me colored too.' "[27] Throughout the interwar period, one of the most active branches of the Workman's Circle or *Arbeter Ring*, a Jewish workers' union committed to progressive social action, was the Number Two branch in Harlem. Hardly the usurious Jewish landlords of Harlem lore, its members remained committed to cross-racial politics founded on a shared experience of tenement life.[28] After the Renaissance, at the inception of the reign of documentary, Harlem constituted a special kind of crossroads. It exemplified both the cultural moment of Americans of African descent and the shifting facts on the ground of the mutual mediation—however cautious, limited, and economically one-sided—of American racial and expressive cultures.

The growing traffic at that crossroads, for black and white and other Americans, for literary and photographic figures, and for competing views of American modernity, is what I seek to explore. I begin with a rising interest among photographers, after the 1935 outbreak, in Harlem as a provocative site for documentary meditation on race, usable histories, and the value of culture. At its best—that is to say, its most self-conscious—that interest recognized and explored its continuities with the Renaissance moment. The most responsive white—or other-than-black—photographers working in Harlem made central to their evolving aesthetics the troubling legacy of slumming and appropriation that framed their engagements with post-Renaissance culture. In so doing, they created their own vectors of entry into mainstream culture; they also irrevocably altered the terms of the documentary enterprise, and negotiated the competing legacies of formalism and socially conscious art in innovative ways. From across the color line, Harlem by the early 1950s had become an enabling resource for the first generation of African American documentarians, tenaciously seeking to counter the drag of the Renaissance as a model and burden, the uplift-inflected conventions of Harlem portraiture (exemplified by the commissioned studio work of James VanderZee and Morgan and Marvin Smith), and a voluminous archive of exploitative or deadening images of black life.[29] In the decades following the 1935 outbreak, through the turbulent reach of the New Deal and wartime state, Popular Front activity, the liberal consensus, cold warriory, civil rights activism, black nationalism, and more, black and white and other image makers responded variously to local urgencies, competing aesthetics, and one another. Aaron Siskind, the practitioners of the New York Photo League, Roy DeCarava, Henri Cartier-Bresson, Helen Levitt, William Klein, Don Charles, and many others thus came to make images in and about Harlem that tested or resisted foregone conclusions about race, progress, and modernity as they evaded unitary politics and critical accounting.

This work, I show, increasingly influenced and involved literary figures who would become canonical—in no small part through the results of their as yet unexplored interests in photography. Although engagements with photography and photo-text were hardly limited to one side of the color line, it is startlingly evident that virtually every African American writer of national significance during the postwar period engaged directly with the archives, practices, and effects of documentary photography. Richard Wright confronted the nearly fatal success of his own breakthrough novel, *Native Son*, by producing a photo-text document in collaboration with the FSA photographer and bureaucrat Edwin Rosskam, and he continued, over the course of his fitful career, to try to harness documentary conventions and image making to the changing shape of the postwar novel as he struggled to move it beyond the limits of protest. Although his planned overtures to and contacts with such storied photographers as Levitt and Lisette Model never materialized in textual collaborations, they attest to the continuing power of postwar images as a model for his work, and help account for his production and the place of images in his final turn to globalist politics and the genre of travelogue.

Likewise, although an early collaboration between James Baldwin and Richard Avedon on a planned Harlem project failed to produce a text, it set the terms by which each figure began to explore competing legacies of formalism and activism, modernist and documentary concerns, within his developing art. Baldwin's engagement with documentary imaging enabled his formulation of an aesthetics of witnessing, and shaped the plangent, often controversial uses he made of a personal and collective past in the autobiographical mode. More specifically, the social histories implicated in the conjunction of a son of Harlem and another of bourgeois Jewish strivers powerfully framed their eventual production of the photo-text volume *Nothing Personal* (1964). And, to take perhaps the hardest case of all, Ralph Ellison: long understood as a profound (if not exemplary) skeptic of images and the power of visuality, Ellison was in fact himself a professional photographer living in Harlem while he wrote *Invisible Man*. Read against the as yet unexplored archival evidence of his interests in documentary and postwar photography, that novel frames itself as a photo-text that suppresses its own visual referents and analogues, so as to harness the affective power and stances of postwar photography to the postwar novel.

Without these writers, the canon of American literature at midcentury is unthinkable. Without their engagements with photography, I argue, their work as we know it would have been impossible.[30] Reading them, and other figures, through their photographic engagements—which have remained essentially invisible within literary and cultural history—we arrive at an altered understanding of the literary field at midcentury, and of photography as a practice and cultural resource. Although the writers I address developed quite different responses to the challenge and possibilities of photography, they exemplify a larger movement whose uneven arc I mean to trace: from Harlem, which came to shape representational conventions associated with documentary in all its forms, to the varied, often restive, work of writers seeking to probe the "surreal" landscape of postwar America and the riven legacies—modernist, socially conscious, naturalist, absurdist, protest-ant—of their craft.

As this summary suggests, my account is neither a systematic history of documentary or photographic practices nor an exhaustive study of literary engagements (black, white, or other) with the photographic image. Rather, I focus on specific collaborations—or, to return to a key figure, crossings—that instance the unacknowledged power of photography as a resource for literary figures. In turn, these crossings provide evidence for a variety of claims at work throughout the book: for the uses (rather than merely the power) of visuality in African American culture; for the history of exchanges between

Jews and African Americans (on which more later); for the mutual implication of the novel and the photograph in the tenor of American public life at mid-century and beyond. Taking Harlem as crossroads and lens, exploring the intersection of literary and photographic practices that evolve from the cultures and institutions of documentary, my work takes up precisely where canonical readings—most notably, Alan Trachtenberg's magisterial *Reading American Photographs* (1989)—leave off: at the very moment when documentary culture and the inauguration of the mass image-world create a new set of conditions for visual production and experience, and a new resource for writers—particularly black writers—attuned to the rhythms of national life.[31] Reading these writers reading (and in some cases making) American photographs, I offer new accounts of their practices and achievements. And those accounts have implications for our understanding of the uses and significance of photography, in particular, and of visual culture at large.

Neither my method nor my local arguments will be uncontroversial, so it would be well for me to outline the various lines of approach in the disciplines I engage, and at whose intersection, not unlike that of a Venn diagram of overlapping fields, I situate my work. Among the most influential scholars of a previous generation of photo historians, the reigning wisdom on documentary photography (particularly that of the New Deal era) has been correctively critical—attuned, that is, to the ways in which documentary practices enabled the promotion of state agendas and corporatist values, the control of ever greater sectors of the citizenry, and the criminalization of socially marginal or deviant figures (most conspicuously African Americans).[32] In the field of American studies, this corrective view has had special purchase; indeed, any exceptionalism with respect to U.S. contexts has served only to redouble skepticism about the photograph as an imposed mode of seeing, a means of "testing, confirming, and constructing a total view of reality."[33] This may in part be because critical emphasis has fallen on photography as a nineteenth-century cultural formation, rooted in the historical logic of its inceptions and earlier uses. In some of the most provocative and influential recent readings in the field, photography has been powerfully sutured to pre-twentieth-century nation-building projects. The rapidly growing image repertoire, it has been persuasively argued, was instrumental in reshaping national identity after the Civil War as normatively masculine and white; photographic portraiture, in all its guises and practices, is shrewdly seen to have assisted at the birth of the modern middle-class subject by shaping a new cultural good—interior selfhood—on which exclusionary citizenship was increasingly founded.[34] Likewise, the practice of photography by elite nineteenth-century women, as both a profession and a visual regime, is richly shown to have enabled the formation of a domestic front that drew its social power from the logic of imperialism.[35] Ironically, the very historical acuity of these readings—their insistence on the deep embeddedness of photographic meaning and practice in specific social contexts—has underwritten a free-floating skepticism about visuality at large. In the wake of this body of work, photography itself threatens to become newly evidentiary: not of historical or social processes, but of its own complicities and dangers. The result is that photography in its broadest cultural resonances and aesthetic effects is writ as "not democracy"—rather its betrayer and scourge.[36]

In the field of African American studies, scholars of black cultural production have redoubled such vigilance about the implication of photography in failed or false democracy. With ample justification, they have fastened on deep, enduring histories of surveillance, appropriation, and a disciplinary gaze that "congeals" black bodies as it "arrest[s] representation at the threshold of human being."[37] For many critical readers of African American culture who do address photography, its most salient effect in black life has been its production of lynching images, an archive whose existence owes its life to the participation—or at weak best, the studied neutrality—of the camera in the face of brutal murder.[38] More broadly, the centrality of music and oral expression in black culture has produced a persistent emphasis on what we might call the sonic at the expense of the visual. For key readers in the field throughout its developing life, from Henry Louis Gates, Houston Baker, and Kimberly Benston through Paul Gilroy and beyond, all black arts aspire to the condition of music: African American, and indeed American, modernity is embodied by the figure of "the blues musician at the crossing"; the possibility of black diasporic modernity is fundamentally "heard to be a matter of music."[39] (Not for nothing has the visual culture scholar Michele Wallace dissented by proclaiming: "I am at war with music.")[40] In the ongoing study of African American culture, photography has been—with certain sharp objections—framed as a blunt instrument or coercive tool, a merely instrumental source of evidence or an irrelevance to meaningful critical practice.[41]

These variously disciplinary readings are powerful, necessary, and foundational to any alternative claims, including my own. Beyond their frames of reference, however, are the undeniable facts that photography has had a life and afterlives beyond the specific social and institutional contexts in which it first took shape and that it has historically galvanized a wide range of oppositional and affirmative practices in the very communities it functioned to segregate, disenfranchise, or render invisible. The writers I address engage variously with photographic precedent, becoming both avid consumers of images (in mass circulation, on exhibition, and in archives) and producers of new ones—even, perhaps, of new kinds of images, or at least of images aware of the expressive and cultural designs of changing photographic agencies. Their responses should, I argue, figure prominently in the exploration of what a recent anthology calls "photography's other histories."[42] Committed to that exploration, my work aims to contribute to a rising interest across disciplines in the modalities of the visual as grounds for consequential engagement with social history and experience.[43] More distinctively, I aim to educe the powerful crossing between—the mutual mediation of—twentieth-century literary and photographic practices, in the generation of new stylistics and cultural stances alike.

In the exploration of that crossing, I attend closely to another of consequence to histories of image making. Photography, as I show in more detail later, has a life belonging explicitly to the twentieth century in the United States, when the small-camera revolution, following on the felt effects of industrial growth, great and lesser migrations, and diaspora, radically altered the possibilities for documentary image making—and not only in technical or formalist ways.[44] Canonical photo history emphasizes the forms of middle-class slumming and ethnographic curiosity enabled by portable cameras from the advent of street photography in the later nineteenth century (particularly by the first Kodak models of the 1880s); it thus obscures a signal shift in the practice and uses of site-specific imaging from the mid-1930s on.[45] This shift implicates not only the social relations in which photography takes part, but changing conceptions of the very being or ground of the photographic image, and the possibility of dissenting and affirmative responses founded in them.

Far from the socially privileged, middle- or leisure-class subjects of canonical study, the vast majority of U.S. practitioners in the wake of the Leica revolution and the Harlem riot were amateurs, autodidacts, immigrants, refugees, or inhabitants of tenements, uptown or down. More to the point, they were also overwhelmingly Jews: not quite white, or only provisionally white in the racial economy of interwar America. The startling preponderance of immigrant and first-generation Jews on the field of documentary from its inception as a distinctly modern agency—a preponderance so marked, one photo historian has noted, as to make that field "difficult to imagine without them"—has only recently begun to attract scholarly attention.[46] Their presence was a necessary if not sufficient condition to the evolution of documentary as a labile genre committed, in its most generative strain, to the marginal and forgotten as subject matter and to the purview of the outsider or the alienated as a point of stylistic departure.[47]

In response to their growing body of Harlem-inflected work, black writers and intellectuals were drawn into collaboration with Jewish (aka "downtown" or socially conscious) photographers on documentary projects, resistance to its effects, and redefinition of its terms and uses. They were, of course, responding to the oppressive reach and power of the photographic archive and its representations of black Americans. But they also responded to the varied possibilities embodied by the photograph as an agency, record, and cultural form. In so doing, they embraced what the cultural anthropologist Christopher Pinney calls "photographic affirmation and revelation," in a moment when photography became a "locally appropriated medium" in a widely consequential way.[48] My book does not essay a full-fledged study of Jewish and African American relations on the field of culture, in the manner of recent work by Eric Sundquist, Jeffrey Melnick, and others. But it does explore those relations in an array of photographic contexts, offering an alternative to the identitarian readings of Jewish imaging that currently hold sway, and arguing for the shaping force of this social history on the ongoing life of the photograph, of documentary, and of the literary field.[49]

In fact, I argue, the matrix of immigrant experience, tenement culture, and documentary stylistics is crucial to the emergence of a new conception of the image, a new reading of its ontology that compels the engagement of black writers, underlies the expressive experiments they conduct, and bespeaks the value of those experiments for readings of photography and visual culture. As photographs of the "great riots" in Harlem suggest, the very lability and promiscuity of the modern camera endowed its images with multiple, simultaneous lives: as a form of evidence, a mode of sensation, a call to arms, a considered aesthetic artifact. These alternative logics are worth noting in some detail. Temporally speaking, the riot images—which we can understand as representative of the full range of documentary and photojournalistic production of the epoch—proclaim both "this was real" (i.e., they are evidentiary) and "you are there" (they trade in sensation). But they are hardly predicated on the kinds of truth claims—absolute fidelity to truth of character, uncanny veracity—long associated, both in their historical moment and among critical readers afterward, with earlier nineteenth-century photographic technologies.[50] Nor do they offer themselves up with the elegiac effect so influentially described by Roland Barthes: that "superimposition" of reality onto what has passed, such that the photograph above all proclaims the status of all its subjects as the "That-has-been," exposing to us only what is "already dead."[51] No longer produced or circulated in contexts predicated on these daguerrean, characterological, or elegiac effects, images of the riot era self-consciously partake in a new regime, what *Life*'s first picture editor aptly called "the quick nervousness of pictures."[52]

This logic of "nervousness" multiplied not only the state-building, disciplinary, or coercive effects of photography. It transformed the image itself as an object in flux, promiscuously available for commerce, protest, and art. Even as a veritable flood of photojournalistic or otherwise documentary images conditioned viewers to consume the world (usually with unearned sentiment or indifference), the entry of cultural outsiders onto the photographic field shaped other uses of sympathy, distance, and alienation. Perhaps the most purposive account of this felt transformation is given by Lisette Model. Forced, as the daughter of a prominent Viennese Jew, to flee twice from the advances of Hitler's Reich—first from Austria, and then Paris, for New York—she took up photography, like so many interwar figures, in response to the exigencies of fascism and imposed exile. I will have occasion to discuss in more detail her profoundly influential photographic practice and its links with the work of writers such as Wright and Ellison. Here I want to focus briefly on her offices as a teacher of documentary photography in postwar New York, to suggest how close attention to the twentieth-century contexts of photographic production might alter our sense of possible traffic in the image and of its social implications.

For photo historians (among others), the single most misleading feature of photographic practice—and of documentary in particular—is what Allan Sekula calls "the folklore of photographic truth": the implied claim that the image is a neutral, objective copy or artifact of an object or event in itself, irrefutably real.[53] Yet that presumption was systematically challenged by photographers of the postwar era, working to redefine the uses of documentary imaging. In unpublished teaching notebooks associated with her legendary courses at the New School (attended by, among others, Diane Arbus), Model defines the development of documentary with reference not to the picture "Industry"—Luce and his minions—but what she calls "the mind guided camera." The purpose of the latter is definitively not "to reproduce or imitate nature" (i.e., to embrace fidelity or photographic mimesis) but "always to express the actual state of human understanding of the world and life."[54] Central to this notably subjectivist view of photographic work is the key argument—revisited throughout Model's lecture notes—that the photograph should be understood neither as a replica nor as an indexical trace of the objects it pictures. Rather, "in spite of the fact that [the] image represents streets, houses, people," it is "merely an *analogy* of the physical world around us."[55]

Here, Model's conception—in effect a manifesto—veers sharply from the emphasis on the indexicality of the image that undergirded state-sponsored documentary. Instead, her language echoes the thinking of Charles Saunders Peirce, who understood the photograph as simultaneously indexical and iconic: an object both symptomatic of the world beyond it and linked to that world through a resemblance not innate, but forged in perception and experience.[56] As a leading experimental practitioner and a figure who embodies the condition of displacement, Model firmly insists on the latter relation. Functioning as an "analogy"—that is, a likeness in incidentals of visual semblance between modes of experience otherwise categorically unlike—the photograph presents us with familiar aspects of our social world only to demand that we confront what is unknown, mysterious, or otherwise obscured by our conventions for inhabiting it ("We are surrounded by thousands of images. Most of them [are] invisible because we are blinded by routine").[57] For Model, the photograph in the era of the mind-guided image, braced against nostalgia and the allure of unmediated reality alike, is both a "projection" of the material world and a way of exploring its underlying social relations. "An immaterial [version] of what surrounds us," the image as such "makes it possible" for the viewer "to be receptive" to social and existential verities "project[ed]" within it.[58] Thus limned, Model's account of the ontology and effects of the photograph literally underlines its difference from received notions in the New Deal documentary context. Against the skepticism generated by commercial and state-sponsored photojournalism's claims to objectivity and social mastery, she poses consequential possibilities for forms of curiosity, uncertainty, and serendipity. In her vision, the photograph is reframed as an occasion for probing "the effects of the actual state of human understanding," and a tool for making usable histories and self-consciousness ("Photojournalism Search; to know oneself").[59]

This brief for photography is powerfully inflected by social dislocation. To the extent that it accounts for postwar photographic practice, it begins to suggest why so many black writers of the 1930s and beyond would find in the camera and its objects a model, a resource, and an analogue. At their most self-conscious, their engagements with the camera anticipate the recent counterargument of the photographer Jeff Wall, who has declared (contra Sekula) that there are not one but "two myths of photography. One is that it tells the truth. The other is that it lies."[60] African American writers at midcentury engage both views, refusing to resolve them. Responding to the forms and limits of socially conscious and New Deal art, the afterlives of modernism and the Harlem Renaissance, and the matrix of postwar social movements, writers at the crossroads of these epochal projects are simultaneously drawn by postwar photography's postures of outsidership and self-scrutiny, and by the deep history of uses and misuses of the image. Mining photography's range of effects—analogy, sympathy, shock, intimacy, distance, the conferral of dignity, alienation—they seek to harness its varied agencies to the fraught but heady contexts of midcentury culture. When they remake the form of the novel to explore the existential effects of poverty, invisibility, or rapid social change; work to bend the shape of received narrative forms to the energies of shifting social experience; struggle with the black writer's burden of authenticity: in these and other aims, writers in the ambit of photography test the powers of their art in a landscape increasingly shaped by visual texts and visuality. They also test those powers in the ambit of Harlem, originating source and productive resource for a riot of representational stances, icons, and styles. Between the Renaissance and Black Arts, modernism and the second ghetto, grew and flourished the Harlem to which I now turn, crossroads for writers, the photograph, and an American modernity aborning.

Chapter One

Documenting Harlem: Images and Afterlives

❖

S ometime in 1936, in the wake of the first "great riot," a public school-
teacher-turned-photographer named Aaron Siskind received an invitation to collaborate on an "extensive cultural analysis" of black Harlem,
still in the throes of the Depression and emerging as an icon of the newly
intransigent ghetto.[1] The invitation came from an African American sociologist and Harlem resident named (so he claimed) Michael Carter. Siskind ac-
cepted. Leading a team of eight photographers, he worked in concert with
Carter and a cast of players representing institutions from the 135th Street
Branch library, the National Urban League, and the church of Father Divine
to funeral homes and the Apollo Theater. Together they spent some three years
producing an influential yet elusive photo-text titled "Harlem Document."
Although the project was never published in full in its intended form, its images—particularly Siskind's—circulated widely, from the *Daily Worker* to the
New York Times, from the Harlem Y to the San Francisco World's Fair.[2]

"Harlem Document" exemplifies, and helped inaugurate, a distinctive history of crossroads engagements. Practically speaking, it appears to have been
founded on a sleight-of-hand. Carter, who represented himself as a professional sociologist interested in analysis of the effects of poverty and segregation, was in fact a journalist named Milton Smith, employed by the *Brooklyn
Eagle* to cover the Negro beat and Harlem. He eventually parlayed his contacts
with black celebrities (including Richard Wright, whom he interviewed and
photographed for the *Eagle* in 1945) into freelance work for *Parade*, stints at

the *Afro-American* and *Ebony* (for which he worked as a photojournalist, creating his own picture stories), and a career in what he called "interracial public relations."[3] Eager for the hustle, or at least the main chance, Smith appears to have played a game all too familiar in the context of Renaissance-era Harlem. Masking himself in the authority of liberal social science, he sought, and gained, access to institutions of representation and print. But Smith's strategic masquerade had perhaps unintended effects, and they mark "Harlem Document" as a definitively post-Renaissance project. Smith would later note that he had "completely dropped the 'Michael Carter' crap" and was hard pressed "to find reasons for having adopted [it] in the first place."[4] Premising the joint study of Harlem on a Renaissance-inflected logic—what David Levering Lewis calls "patient manipulation"—Smith set in motion a close, sustained collaboration with a remarkable afterlife, one that helped revise the possibilities of documentary representation itself.[5]

In what did such revision consist? "Harlem Document" (and a closely linked project, "The Most Crowded Block in the World") was hardly unique in recording urban poverty or black disaffection.[6] During 1936–39, the years in which the "Document" was produced, images of both were becoming iconic, in the era's defining styles of radical muckraking, New Deal propaganda, and *Life*-style photojournalism. But the "Document" distinguished itself from their logic of exposure by seizing on a powerful opportunity that Harlem uniquely afforded: the chance to address the conditions of production for its own representations. Against the drift of Smith's initial logic (and perhaps of his initial "sociological" contributions to the "Document"), Siskind's images meditate on the racial practices and fantasies embedded in Harlem, writ as a social space generated by the interplay between poverty and promise, uplift and drift, authenticity and appropriation. Increasingly, his photographs belie the avowed purposes of documentary: the call to action, pure "verism," fidelity to social facts.[7] They thus test the limits and possibilities of documentary as the era's dominant cultural genre. Marshaling the duality of Harlem as a poetic resource, Siskind's images create a space for more complex, meditative engagement—not only but not least by white viewers—with the failures of America's defining ideals and the role of culture in redressing them.

The question of the social uses of documentary has itself been the subject of extensive documentation. In visual history, cultural studies, and scholarship on liberalism alike, documentary of the 1930s has been painstakingly studied in relation to New Deal statism, the rise of corporate culture, and the emerging disciplines of public relations and consumer management. But most studies of what has been called the documentary decade have foregrounded institutions of New Deal image making proper: the FSA's Historical Section; the photography divisions of the Federal Writers' Project, the U.S. Department of Agriculture, and other federal agencies; the visual apparatus of the Works Progress Administration's (WPA's) popular state guidebooks.[8] Dwelling on the enormous archive of agency images of the sharecropping South, the Dust Bowl West, and the dislocation of Americans within them, such readings mirror the projects they historicize: they have largely been, as Nicholas Natanson puts it, "absent a central fact of twentieth-century black experience," migration to the city and the diasporic cultures of black urban centers.[9]

Alternative views of documentary imaging are opened in a reading that foregrounds Harlem as a site that shaped photographic practice (and, through it, forms of social response). Siskind's images are a useful point of origin for such rereading; to an appreciable degree, they register the role that Harlem plays in shaping a postriot, post-Renaissance response to urban America—and to the era's definitive project, the articulation of a manageably diverse, indigenous American culture.[10] In the production and the afterlives of "Harlem Document" we can trace the context on which both depend: the history of Harlem as a site of black and white investments and of black-and-tan cultures, thoughtfully engaged as a resource for a new kind of image making. Read in this context, the "Document" asserts itself as a founding project in a post-Renaissance genealogy of photo-texts that confront the power of images in black and white. In turn, their redirection of the documentary ethos opened representational and expressive possibilities to which literary figures, in the moment and long beyond, would become self-consciously indebted.

"The so-called documentary picture left me wanting something": Siskind and the "Document" Aesthetic

How is "Harlem Document" different from other "documents"? To address that question, we might well begin with a photograph by Siskind from a previous project pursued in New York's infamous haunt of down-and-outers, the Bowery (figure 1.1). One of a small number that survives from Siskind's early work, the image already typifies his photographic ethos. Shot from the rear at the middle distance, it features two men whose posture and dress, as well as their entry into a transients' hotel, suggest resignation (but not, it should be argued, defeat). Pausing at the threshold of the flophouse, eschewing frontality or any kind of direct contact with its subjects, the image seems far less interested in sociological analysis or the kind of willed sympathy we associate with

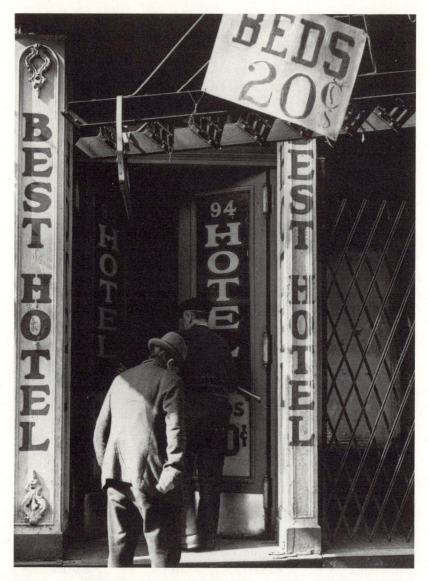

Figure 1.1. Aaron Siskind, Untitled, from "Dead End: The Bowery," ca. 1935–36. Aaron Siskind Archive, Center for Creative Photography. By permission of The Aaron Siskind Foundation.

New Deal image making than with the elusive, haunting quality of its subjects' human being. The formal structure of the image has been strikingly shaped to focus on that being, both displaced and heightened by the insistence of the framing signage ("Best Hotel Hotel Hotel Best Hotel"), the rhythmic patterning of the hotel's security gate, and the geometric exactitude of the shadow that slices neatly across the nearest subject's torso, as if the latter were as depthless as the picture plane itself, too insubstantial for the cast shadow to bend to its volume. In a place made infamous as "the home of the defeated, the derelict and the thief," and in the context of documentary conventions designed to "revea[l] the familiar, dismal conditions of tenement life," Siskind's shot resonates as another kind of image, human rather than analytic; it is conceived not to anchor a news story, didactic response, or party line but rather to probe the life of social beings, and the uses of the camera for promoting their recognition as such.[11]

I highlight this image from the Bowery project because such images—or rather, the presumptions they encode—led directly to Siskind's work in Harlem. At the time of Smith's invitation, Siskind was leading a documentary production unit called the Feature Group within the storied New York Photo League, and the Group had already begun three modest projects—not only "Dead End: The Bowery," but also "Portrait of a Tenement" and "Park Avenue North and South."[12] All were conceived and executed as photo-essays, or assemblages of photographic images and text; that mode defined the commercial aspirations of the picture magazine, the radical uses in European contexts of photomontage, and the managerial liberalism of FSA publications alike. But Siskind's Feature Group evolved a documentary practice that distinguished itself from all these modes. In their work, the collective discipline, work rhythm, and unifying themes were inseparable; all revolved around the life-worlds of the tenement and ghetto street. If, like other photo-documentarians, they imaged the stark limits of Franklin Delano Roosevelt's democratic vistas, their interest was focused not on evidence of deprivation or failure but on the everyday social exchanges in which such limits were actively experienced.

It was presumably these assumptions about documentary imaging that moved Smith/Carter to seek collaboration with the Feature Group in Harlem. Countering a prominent culture of agitprop, free of the specific imperatives of projects shot to work scripts for the FSA, Siskind directed his coworkers to eschew "the literal representation of a fact" in favor of "a growing concentration of feeling."[13] Against the dominant images of both commercial and muckraking photojournalism—"pictures all clichés of the men-at-work type"—he insisted on "the detailed exploration" of "the special case."[14] As critics have frequently noted, the tenement images of the Feature Group bespeak the limited technical skills of its journeymen members. But they move purposively toward the kind of distinction for which Siskind aimed.

In practical terms, that achievement depended on collaborative on-site work that Siskind called "preparation in excess": extensive research, note-taking, "visits to the scene, . . . casual conversations [with subjects], and more formal interviews—talking, and listening, and looking, looking."[15] Yet in spite of his pedagogic insistence on a research protocol that would appear to have accorded with Smith/Carter's "sociological" stance—an insistence on "dig[ging] out the facts and figures" as the ground for image choices—Siskind had rejected the tenets of agency-sponsored documentary from the moment he picked up a camera.[16] As his working notes and published statements make clear, he flatly opposed the reigning emphasis on objectivity as key to the management of American modernity and difference.[17] Rather than aim for "the literal representation" of social fact, Siskind self-consciously set out to "make pictures to express a predetermined idea"—pictures, that is, whose aesthetic and social power ensued from their refusal of allegorical meaning, their reference "limited" to the specific exchanges and conditions that produced their subjects, and themselves.[18] Intrinsic to Siskind's photos and those he guided the Feature Group in making, in other words, is some representation of the mediating power of the documentary image maker, some reflection of or on the camera's choices and interests.

What Siskind insists on describing as "exercises in realism," then, have a conflicted relation with the dominant 1930s genre of the photo-story.[19] Such tension—a resistance to the directives of New Deal photographic ideology encoded within the structure and visual rhetoric of images—has been said to mark the work of more familiar, and more celebrated, New Deal image makers such as Walker Evans and Ben Shahn.[20] But Siskind's Photo League images differ radically from this FSA work in one crucial way. Their exploration of the tension between formal and social imperatives, between mediation and documentation, is predicated on their embeddedness in the sites of experience and exchange to which they bear witness. The FSA's iconic images—Lange's weary migrant mother (figure 1.2), Arthur Rothstein's bleached steer's skull in the wasted Badlands (figure 1.3), Evans's grim and blighted and far from redemptive Bethlehem (figure 1.4)—record a studied distance from the subjects of their documentation, perhaps inevitable in the work of leftist culture makers invading the domains of Western landowners, Southern sheriffs, union organizers, evicted tenants, and black sharecroppers subject to Jim Crow. While the most powerful of these images make a virtue of necessity,

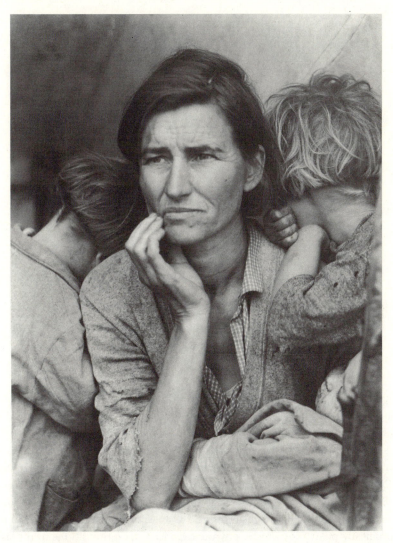

Figure 1.2. Dorothea Lange, Destitute Pea-Pickers in California, 1936. Farm Security Administration/Office of War Information Collection, Library of Congress.

their austerity is not in the end fully chosen. At best, they register respect for the limits of the camera as an agency foreign to the social world it documents or exposes.[21]

By contrast, the downtown images of Siskind and the Feature Group emerge organically from a world its practitioners knew and inhabited—indeed, a world whose social history spawned the very practices in which they were

Figure 1.3. Arthur Rothstein, Bleached Skull of a Steer, South Dakota, 1936. Farm Security Administration/Office of War Information Collection, Library of Congress.

engaged. The origin of twentieth-century documentary photographers (and photography) in New York's downtown, specifically on the Lower East Side, was a definitive fact in the evolution of photo-text practices and aesthetics. Siskind himself was a first-generation American born of Russian Jewish parents; like vast numbers of the generation described by Alfred Kazin and Irving Howe, he came out of the tenement culture of the Lower East Side and Browns-ville, graduated from City College, and followed the beaten path to culture making via the study of English (his field as an elementary schoolteacher) and specifically poetry (of which he wrote significant quantities). One of his last photographic projects was a series of images created to accompany the verse of that perennial immigrant and radical hero, Walt Whitman. His profile is typical of the Feature Group, whose members included Lucy Ashjian, Morris Engel, Beatrice Koslofsky, Jack Mendelsohn (later Manning), Jerry Friedma-cher, Dick Lyon, and Sol Prom. His colleagues were, that is, overwhelmingly the children or grandchildren of Eastern European Jewish émigrés, citizens of tenement culture who had been attracted to the Photo League via the left ferment of the Lower East Side.

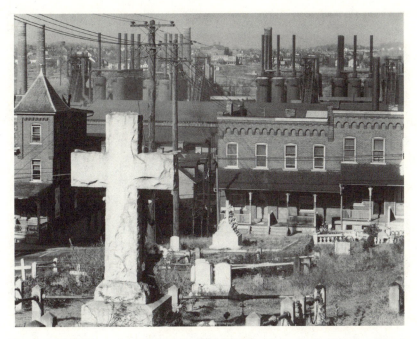

Figure 1.4. Walker Evans, Graveyard and Steel Mill, Bethlehem, Pennsylvania, 1935. Farm Security Administration/Office of War Information Collection, Library of Congress.

It was from the ever-expanding East Side that the League drew the vast majority of its small membership during the 1930s, and in which it was housed throughout its existence, initially on Fourteenth Street and later in a second-floor walk-up on East Twenty-first. The tight, reticulated networks of ghetto culture making, in the words of one observer, "stamped the League physically and culturally."[22] The very premises in which the Feature Group met to plan projects, discuss technical issues, produce enlargements, and collaborate on layouts and textual material was a "dilapidated old townhouse" with "grimy stairs," peeling walls, and encrustations of filth, and members quipped that they "could always tell a visitor" by his willingness "to grab the banister"—as opposed to the regulars, who "didn't touch a thing we didn't have to."[23] By 1947, the Photo League, along with the Communist Party, the Civil Rights Congress, and the Veterans of the Abraham Lincoln Brigade, was among the first organizations blacklisted by U.S. Attorney General Tom C. Clark—a dubious distinction occasioned not only by the League's left-leaning work but by the ethnic origins of its members.[24] What Clark and his minions identified as an intrinsic or organic relation between the Photo League and socialist, radical,

Figure 1.5. Lewis W. Hine, Midnight at the Bowery Mission Bread-line in the Old Days of Depression, 1909. George Eastman House.

and leftist subjects (in both senses of the term) was, in fact, the basis of Siskind's documentary aesthetic. Privy firsthand to the raw material of Depression-era photojournalism—evictions, foreclosures, strikes, protests, hunger marches, and work actions—Feature Group members were free both to exploit and to meditate on their dual status as social participants and photographic observers of the city's locked-out generation.[25]

The kind of "realism" for which Siskind strove under these conditions has been both celebrated and critiqued, but never fully framed in the context of the Feature Group's indigeneity to the life-worlds it began by documenting. Their initial project was the Bowery study, which was "easy," in Siskind's assessment, in demanding little in the way of formal research; he and his fellow Group members "just worked outdoors," trolling the familiar thoroughfare to make images of down-and-outers, flophouse residents, prostitutes, and other locals.[26] By 1936, the Bowery already had a long history as a photographic site for bourgeois shock and management, codified by Jacob Riis, nuanced by Lewis Hine, and updated in the police-blotter style of Weegee (figures 1.5, 1.6).[27] Siskind's images confront and oppose that history; they forestall "easy" assimilation of their subjects, either as photographic figures or as the objects of a social gaze. Even his apparently more conventional images of down-and-

Figure 1.6. Weegee (Arthur Fellig), Shorty, the Bowery Cherub, New Year's Eve at Sammy's Bar, 1943. Collection of the International Center of Photography, New York. © Weegee/International Center of Photography/Getty Images.

outers reject such framing conventions. Carefully differentiated via the conventions of portraiture and the power of the middle distance—in the texture of worn socks, the hard-luck tale told by the once-smart hat, the culture of waiting recorded in the shape of folded hands—Siskind's Bowery dweller is neither readily classifiable in progressive taxonomies nor clearly located on the New Deal political landscape. He is almost unimaginable as a federal "rehabilitation" client; he is hardly glorified as a heroic proletarian; the camera's mode of framing such subjects, conspicuously austere and decidedly formalist, rebuffs victimology. Thus viewed, Siskind's fellow downtowners become denizens of American modernity's dead ends, recognizable yet far from intimate. To them has been restored both the hard-won truths of the bread line and bindlestiff and the mystery of social circumstance.[28]

Such studied distance can be the purview only of culture makers working on home turf. It becomes even more palpable in the Feature Group's second project, for which Siskind made the majority of images, the "Portrait of a Tenement." Siskind was careful to adhere to his own developing documentary principles, insisting on research, interviews, and detailed discussion of the intended arc of the photo-essay. But a shared experience of tenement culture and local history clearly underpinned the venture. As he later admitted, "We made the portrait really by just 'coming on' to the building down the street," moving "up the stairs" to do "a complete study of this little family, three people, sort of foreign born, living in a very clean, sparse sort of house."[29] Refusing to specify the kinds of details so dear to avid consumers of documentary, Siskind blurs the social identity of his subjects. Does "sort of foreign born" mean the subjects are first-generation yet ethnically marked Americans—like himself? that they are speakers of Yiddish or another tongue who would seem "foreign" to gentile culture makers? Even as he raises such questions, Siskind insists on the precision with which the everyday living conditions of the subjects are captured by the camera's eye: in "sparse" detail, "very simply," "each room" at a time.[30]

Siskind's descriptions of the Feature Group's early photo-stories resonate with tensions encoded in the images themselves: between strangeness and intimacy, the foreign and the known, interiority and social landscape. To underscore the centrality of these tensions to his aesthetic, Siskind consistently distances the Feature Group's mode of embedded production from the guerilla point-and-shoot of the FSA (the latter an outgrowth not only of the outsider status of its itinerant photographers but of matériel shortages and tiresome administrative procedures).[31] Asked retrospectively about the power of FSA images as models for the Group's early documentary work, Siskind disingenuously replied: "I don't remember the FSA pictures [of the time] at all."[32] In fact, FSA images were widely circulated at the Photo League during the later 1930s; Walker Evans, Arthur Rothstein, and Dorothea Lange had sustained contact with the League and its members, and FSA aesthetics were instrumental in shaping a documentary pedagogy within the League's activities.[33] But Siskind's disingenuousness is revealing. Unlike agency-mandated projects— what the FSA staff photographer Jack Vachon called "same old hash"—the Feature Group's Bowery and tenement portraits were decidedly not the work of outsiders entering a local space with a brief to document the need for technocratically managed change.[34] Nor did they cultivate the shrill outrage of professional muckrakers, or the slick professional's eye for commercially viable images of the common man. Working on known territory in a shared social context, Siskind and the Feature Group achieved a distinctive visual rhetoric marked simultaneously by earned knowledge and psychic distance.

Here, the importance of the Feature Group's early documentary projects to the imaging of Harlem comes into sharper focus, intersecting squarely with Harlem's fraught history as a site of racial encounter. The preoccupation of vast numbers of black metropolitans with the mass photographic record, in which two centuries of viciously, casually, and romantically racist notions of black personhood were being codified with terrifying power on an unprecedented scale, has been studied in considerable detail.[35] For all its changing contours, the anxiety of image was perhaps the most enduring legacy of the Harlem Renaissance. But the stakes, in the divisive and violent climate of social agitation and centralized reform, were exponentially higher. How to turn a face to the world (and increasingly, the cameras) that will "help the Negro," as one irate *New York Amsterdam News* reader put it, rather than "bring our race down"?[36] What with communist proselytizing and the imperatives of the New Deal (both framing African Americans as hapless premoderns, ripe for Party leadership or state management), Harlem residents of the late 1930s felt what one prominent journalist called "a desperate need for [images] which would help build the community rather than sensationalize it."[37] Although Harlem was becoming one of several U.S. centers for black photographers, the latter had emerged during the Renaissance out of a commercial studio tradition dependent on uplift modes; its most distinguished practitioners, James VanderZee and Winifred Hall Allen, were generally dismissed during the decades after the Renaissance as purveyors of an overly stylized, white-mimed gentility.[38] Not until the 1950s would black, Harlem-based photojournalism— the regular appearance of black photographers' images in both mainstream and African American publications—be a matter of regular fact. Yet photography constituted "a necessity" in the era of dispossession, "the central instrument by which blacks could disprove" white America's iconic representations.[39]

In inviting Siskind and the Feature Group uptown to create a photo-story that would help "build community," Smith/Carter clearly bowed to another necessity, seeking plausible collaborators with access to funds, agencies, and venues for publication. But his choice is nonetheless pointed. Siskind had quit the original Soviet-linked New York Photo League and joined the reorganized group in 1936 only on condition that he be free from all Party or activist duties, allowed to focus solely on teaching and "work"; he remained vigilant about the exploitation of Feature Group images by radical organs with a penchant for "forcing pictures out of context."[40] Insisting on a "very quiet and very formal" documentary style, Siskind resisted the sensationalism and condescension of what none other than Roy Stryker, chief of the Historical Section of the FSA, called "the goddamn newspaper pictures."[41] In Siskind and the Feature Group, Smith/Carter identified a usable instrument for the ongoing project of black image management. But he also found something more: the possibility of collaboration between photographers and subjects who were located, alternatively and simultaneously, within and without the framing contexts—tenement culture, progressive uplift, the radical left—that initiated their contact.[42]

Responding self-consciously to his own status as a framing outsider, the fact of a partially shared social landscape, and the history of white looking in Harlem, Siskind probes the aesthetic and cultural consequences of the documentary mode with unprecedented effects. His ethos was enabling for the Feature Group, but it would also prove a valuable precedent to later African American photographers working to free themselves of the twin burdens of America's image archive and the ongoing imperative to represent the race. Incorporating into his practice an awareness of the specific challenges of Harlem as a photographic site of encounter, Siskind works to chart a representational territory bounded by the sensationalist exposé, the uplift profile, the racial picturesque, and the mass media spectacle. Within that space, black self-representation and white image making come into uneasy yet productive contact, and the genre of documentary resists instrumentality, posing open-ended questions about its viewers' habits of encounter with their own occluded history.

For the most part, scholars of "Harlem Document" have focused on the instability of the text, which existed in two basic forms: as a traveling exhibition and as a now lost book maquette. They have painstakingly recounted the evidence for Smith/Carter's original narrative for the project, discussing the meaning of its images within his familiar categories of interest—"labor, religion, health, housing, crime, recreation, society, and youth"—and in relation to his captions and frameworks, heavily laced with statistical fact.[43] This work challenges reception histories in which individual images have been aestheticized at the expense of social intentions, and needfully emphasizes the collaborative aims of the Feature Group and its work with Harlem residents. But it fails to account for the way in which the instability of the "Document" itself became a resource for Siskind's work. Not until 1981 would Siskind publish a selection of his Harlem images in book form. The very partiality and belatedness of the text—which Siskind, stressing its continuity with the earlier project, titled *Harlem Document: Photographs, 1932–1940*—are instructive.[44] Initially resistant to his publisher's request for a "Document" book, Siskind agreed to allow his images to be paired with contemporaneous oral histories and other material gathered in Harlem by Federal Writers' Project staff, including Ralph Ellison, Dorothy West, and Vivian Morris. Rather than a betrayal of the Feature Group's collaborative process, as one prominent critic contends, Siskind's decision to jettison Smith/Carter's quantitative narrative can be read as an attempt to replace the shopworn mode of documentary as exposé with an aural collage of voices—ice vendor, jump-ropers, union man, lay preacher, sex worker, and so on—speaking from within their varied places in the community. Retaining the frame of Smith/Carter's original narrative trajectory, the *Harlem Document* denies it an instrumental shape. Yoked to vernacular voices, freed of numbing statistical fact, Siskind's Harlem images achieve something closer to their original dual aim: exploration of the space in which their subjects register a complexly mixed experience of modernity, and an insistence on documentary practice as a form of encounter with that reality.

That the revised version of *Harlem Document* registers the dependence of Siskind's work on the space that generates it is clear from the moment we open the text, even before a narrative framework has been erected. The frontispiece to the volume pairs two images clearly chosen to reflect the Janus faces of Harlem, its histories of resourceful self-determination and betrayed possibility. The images also suggest the doubleness of the documentary enterprise conducted across color lines by a photographer negotiating the uneven effects of his presence. The first, reproduced without title or caption, features an aproned man whose accouterments would make him recognizable to Harlemites as a follower of the popular cleric Father Divine (figure 1.7). Leaning out of an oversized window, he holds aloft a pie as he gazes at an unseen object outside the image frame; hanging below the windowsill is a hand-lettered sign that reads, "Peace Home Cooked Meals 10 & 15¢." Shot from a distance with a flattened depth of field, the image creates the effect of legibility; specific

Figure 1.7. Aaron Siskind, Untitled, from "Harlem Document," ca. 1937–40. Center for Creative Photography. By permission of The Aaron Siskind Foundation.

details of dress, the battered quality of the sign, the texture of the ornamental stone facade of the building, are equally in focus. At the same time, a certain wariness about the camera's approach is recorded via composition. The framing device of the railing, slightly blurred in the foreground, marks the separation of the viewer from the subject, just as the subject's posture of incomplete frontality denies the satisfaction of direct address. Nonetheless, the image bespeaks a certain confidence in linked, if not shared, enterprises. The subject's literal gesture of uplift, placed within Harlem's ongoing spiritual and entrepreneurial cultures, heightens the viewer's sense of emergence from interiority (here, a literally unfathomable space) into the open air. Yet that emergence is productively elliptical. Black self-determination is served up, but not for the viewer or camera. With Siskind's characteristic use of a frame within the frame, the camera insists on its constructive role in composing the image, even as it marks a respectful distance from the life-world it registers.

This essentially affirmative version of Harlem uplift, *Harlem Document*, and the relations between them is undermined by the image we encounter on the verso page. Also presented without a caption, it effectively inverts the compositional and spatial effects of the initial photograph (figure 1.8). Positioned not on the street but at the entry to an unevenly lit interior, the camera looks through an open doorway toward a shadowed vestibule, where its subject— clad not in white but in black, facing not toward but away from the viewer— stands in a posture that suggests neither uplift nor motion but stasis. The brightly lit chandelier visible in the first photograph is echoed here in the stark, unlit overhead fixture; depth of field, flattened to create relative monumentality in the first image, has been restored to maximize the effect of distance from the subject, who appears all but absorbed by the expressionistic play of shadow and light. Also notable (especially in contrast with the bright clarity of the preceding image) are myriad scratches and scrapes marring the surface of the interior's doorways and walls and even the texture of the subject's coat; the image cultivates ambiguity about whether these marks belong to the material site or to the photographic negative, or both.[45] Yet this is no mere exercise in the manipulation of technical elements. Pausing at this particular juncture, the camera invites us to meditate on the quality of the gaze that would look beyond the threshold, even as it recognizes its subject's ultimate illegibility in "objective" or quantifying terms. The possibility of shared social space, preserved in the initial photo in the form of economic exchange, has been seriously troubled here; the image arouses, only to forestall, the reader's desire for assimilation of its social content through imaginative contact with its subject.

Figure 1.8. Aaron Siskind, Untitled, from "Harlem Document," ca. 1937. George Eastman House. By permission of The Aaron Siskind Foundation.

These twinned images construct a carefully wrought frame for Siskind's documentary aesthetic. In so doing, they both remember and depart from the aims of the original project. The vast body of "Harlem Document" images was designed either to further Smith/Carter's narrative arcs about the conditions of life and labor, accompanied by his strenuous quantifications—"Such squalor as that shown above is not isolated, but depressingly typical. A quarter of a million people live in 8,902 dwellings, half of which were built before 1901"[46]—or to extol the achievements of black culture makers within institutions they organized and controlled. If the Group collectively felt that "the point was lost" with respect to racism and poverty on the one hand or black self-empowerment on the other, photographs were restaged and retaken.[47] While Siskind's choice of images for *Harlem Document* retains this dual interest in the material life-world and in black self-determination, it alters their significance. Here they resonate not as matters of quantifiable fact—and thus of administrative redress or progressive nation building—but as occasions for an ethos of suggestive restraint, through which America's post-Renaissance metropolis might be vouchsafed productive representation, and white Americans made party to that process. While Smith's rhetoric bristles with activist indignation, Siskind embraces a willed passivity, hazarding its misrecognition as voyeurism or merely formalist detachment.

Inaugurated in the tenement projects as a tension between familiarity and distance, embeddedness and austerity, this aesthetic achieves its fullest expression in Harlem, responding to modes of white image making in the black metropolis so as to broaden its range of effects. Reckoning with the looming history of "the early 1920s," the work of white predecessors in Harlem who "exploited whatever exotic manifestations" the culture of striving black folk provided, Siskind emphasized to Feature Group members that "this job" posed specific documentary challenges.[48] "Caution[ing]" them to bracket their earned "knowledge about the subject" as well as any sense of a shared material or social history, he enjoined his collaborators "to become as passive as possible," "to let the facts fall away and at the crucial moment" of photographic encounter "to permit the subject to speak for itself."[49] The pair of images chosen to introduce and frame *Harlem Document* retrospectively honors Siskind's understanding of the limits of the camera's entry into black worlds within worlds as the generative condition of the documentary enterprise.

What begins in the tenement and downtown images, then, as a willed distance from familiar cultural landscapes becomes in *Harlem Document* a more complexly measured distance, an invocation of Harlem as a series of uneasily shared or contested spaces in which alternative experiences of New Deal social life and the myriad aspects of American modernity can be confronted. *Harlem Document*'s twinned opening images are exemplary in this respect. Elliptical angles, the studied use of light and shadow, the creation of tense or broken sight lines: these formal elements register not an absence of shared history but a form of contact between the camera and its subjects that has been rendered partial and unstable. Frequently locating itself at sites of entry into social spaces—kitchens, dressing-rooms, union halls—into which it has been invited yet not assimilated, Siskind's camera refuses the frontality of both Renaissance and New Deal visual modes and troubles the play of gazes. While his Bowery and downtown subjects are often withdrawn, lost in thought, or incapable of looking back, the eyes of his Harlem subjects are differently unavailable; unaverted, aware of the camera's presence, they rarely choose to meet its gaze. Neither victims nor minstrels, they forestall unearned recognition, quantification, and racial truisms alike.

That Siskind wills this austere relation to his subjects is made clear by his camera choices and working mode. Unlike many of his FSA counterparts and the majority of photojournalists whose careers were staked on "'candid camera' work," Siskind never pursued Feature Group projects with 35 mm cameras—defined, in a 1936 article in Hearst's *Fortune*, as instruments for "photograph[ing] . . . people when they don't know they are being photographed."[50] Fundamental to Siskind's aesthetic was the refusal of such power and the seeking of consent, however partial or skeptical. Toward that end, he worked in Harlem with cumbersome 4 × 5 and 5 × 7 view cameras, essentially light-tight boxes that oblige the operator to compose the image on a viewing glass before shooting. The complex loading requirements of these cameras, and their use of individual film holders or plates rather than roll film, resulted in far fewer images, demanded a high degree of commitment to a particular shot, and made it virtually impossible to work quickly or journalistically.[51] But this was precisely the point. Lugging his bulky equipment around Harlem, carefully positioning his tripod, disappearing beneath a focusing hood to compose his work shot by shot, Siskind would have been highly visible—what we might call beholden: a figure of nineteenth-century imaging technologies rather than an emblematically modern image maker with a camera so portable it lets the photographer "sho[ot] from the hip . . . and g[e]t your man."[52] Siskind's writings make it clear that he was committed to the aesthetics as such of the large-format camera, with its extraordinary fidelity to visual detail at various ranges. But he was no less committed to a photographic practice that implied—even required—an active awareness of social context and of its shaping role in image production.

No wonder, then, that documentary byplay—the problem of the look and the look back—accrues such resonance in *Harlem Document*. Forty-some years after the fact, the volume offers a collage of images and texts so as to comment retrospectively on the framing conditions for the presence of the Feature Group—downtown Jewish leftists, first-generation children of the ghetto striving to make claims on America—in Harlem. Structural to the text is a series of voices commenting on that presence. Harlem had been, until a race-panicked sell-off of the early 1900s orchestrated by black entrepreneurs, an immigrant enclave, to which downtown tenement Jews (including most of Siskind's fellow photographers) had both personal and collective connections: Siskind himself had lived during his teens on 134th Street, and later taught school at P.S. 179, on West 101st Street.[53] In the volume's opening text, we encounter the oral history of Clyde "Kingfish" Smith, the "Heigho fish man" covering northern Manhattan, who remarks the differences required in his performances in black and Jewish blocks: "In the Jewish neighborhood they appreciate the rhyming and the words more, while in the colored neighborhood they appreciate the swinging and the tune, as well as the words" (HD, 13). His history ends with a transcription of his peddling call:

> I can't go home 'till all my fish is gone.
> Stormy weather.
> I can't keep my fish together,
> Sellin 'em all the time.
> . . . I don't see why
> You folks don't come and buy
> Stormy weather, Come,
> Let's get together,
> Sellin 'em all the time.

In an apparent afterthought, Smith remarks: "I wouldn't sing this one in a Jewish neighborhood. They don't know the tune and they couldn't appreciate the song" (HD, 17).

The "tune," of course, is the monumental American standard "Stormy Weather," penned by composer Harold Arlen—né Hyman Arluck in none other than a "Jewish neighborhood"—in 1932; it was first sung at Harlem's notoriously segregated Cotton Club by Arlen's colleague, a new girl singer who went on to make it a vehicle for international stardom across the color line: Lena Horne. In the context of Feature Group production, Smith's offhand comment opens the territory of Harlem as a space of nested ironies, where appropriation and collaboration, blues authenticity and pop commercialism,

Figure 1.9. Aaron Siskind, Untitled [Our Own Community], from "The Most Crowded Block in the World," ca. 1940. George Eastman House. By permission of The Aaron Siskind Foundation.

folk recognition and capitalist exchange, and Jewish and African American relations with whiteness all jostle and interpenetrate.[54] Siskind's choice of an accompanying image can be read as a response to the social claims of Smith's call. Facing the last page of the transcribed interview is a portrait of another vendor, the proprietor of the Our Own Community Delicatessen, leaning genially against the doorframe of his store (figure 1.9). His casual posture—rumpled apron, crossed legs, relaxed demeanor—disrupts the formal regularity of the image: diamond tiles patterned along the facade and entry, wine bottles and canned goods stacked in careful pyramids, the linear sectioning of the composition. Too, the figure's folk singularity and the details of signage contend with capitalist standardization ("Enjoy Pepsi-Cola Healthful and Refreshing"). Intrinsic to this play of cultural realms is the presence of Siskind's camera, which invokes the characteristics of the large-format genre to mark its studied distance. Readable neither as a traditional portrait nor as an example of what the Feature Group called "casual pictures"—shots intended to document the life-world of "people walking and talking in the streets"—the image borrows from the conventions of both genres to register the social transaction that produced it, a transaction predicated precisely on questions of embeddedness ("delicatessen" indeed), contact, and the limits of "our own community."[55]

Harlem Document can thus be seen to riff on Smith's succinct parting shot. If the fishman's swinging rhythms make sense "only in a colored neighborhood" (HD, 17), the documentary work that engages them is possible only in Harlem. Throughout the text, as its subjects comment trenchantly on the presence of white folk (and of those ambiguously white folk, Jews) in Harlem, their histories are paired with images that raise questions about the kind of collaboration and sufferance that produced them. Surviving records from the Feature Group's extensive minutes and work assignment logs show that Siskind was particularly interested in producing images pertaining to Harlem nightlife. His vastly greater technical expertise surely came into play on this assignment; the apprentice work of Feature Group members was routinely found to be "underexposed to such an extent as to render [their shots] useless"—a problem that shooting under real-time, available-light club conditions would have exacerbated.[56] But Siskind's images suggest a more intrinsic logic. To a far greater degree than the work of his Feature Group colleagues—or even that of African American photographers such as Morgan and Marvin Smith and Robert H. McNeill, who produced images of Harlem nightlife for commercial purposes—his work in entertainment venues foregrounds the play of competing modernities staged in those sites.[57] Here, white bourgeois worship of the so-called primitive is entangled with black Americans' changing relations to the forms of diaspora culture; the commercialization of black expressive genres is inseparable from African American negotiations of Euro-American modes, and the camera partakes self-consciously in both.

The commitment of these images to, and their departures from, the Feature Group's aims are instructive. Determined "to show the contribution of the Negro to American music," the collective agreed "that a picture of white people going to the Appollo [*sic*] Theatre to hear Negro musicians would be the best" visual representation of the case.[58] But the body of work that Siskind produced in response to this imperative resonates with nothing like its naively celebratory intent, or even with a straightforwardly ironic response. Making use of the "muddy" working conditions of Harlem clubs and theaters, Siskind sought to register the dynamism and drive of jazz and jive.[59] He framed them not as "frenzied" manifestations of racial primitivism or oppression—keywords in ongoing Feature Group discussions—but as quintessential cultures of an emergent American modernity.[60] At the same time, his shots trouble the assimilation of club performers both as entertaining bodies and as objects of photographic scrutiny.

Within *Harlem Document*, that aim is accomplished with the inclusion of a small portfolio of nightlife images, apparently made at the Lenox Avenue club Barron's. That this body of images posed hermeneutic problems within the Feature Group is a matter of record. When Siskind presented his initial shots, "the group did not seem to be able to come to any decision about them"; finding them "keyed too low," they shelved the images in order to compare them with others to be taken by Jack Mendelsohn, who typically worked with the lightweight, automated Rolleiflex camera and would thus bring to the table more conventionally "dramatic" images.[61] For six months, Feature Group members debated the merits of Siskind's club photos; he was asked to reprint for "dark tones that were deeper and richer" and to rethink lighting that "left some parts [of the club interiors] too dark." In the end, certain images were judged technically "adequate" for presentation.[62]

But another reading of these photographs in the context of *Harlem Document* would acknowledge the logic of failed distinctions, of insufficiently crisp tonalities. A key example is the culminating image in a four-photo sequence placed dead at the center of the text, in its only thematic montage (figure 1.10).[63] Shot from overhead, presumably from the cheap seats of a balcony, without strobe, pinspot, or other additional lighting, the image initially strikes the viewer as both cluttered and empty, indecisive with respect to its own visual economy. On closer examination, however, the acute angle of presentation, the awkward figure placement, and the disruptive verticality of the composition make suggestive sense.

Structurally, the image is organized around a series of triangular elements: the alcove in which smartly dressed white club clients lounge, whose vertex opens out on the trio of male dancer and light-skinned black chorines awaiting their number; the adjacent triangular mass of the bandshell, on which a trio of jazzmen play, partially screened from the audience by stage elements and the body of the featured dancer. In terms of visual rhetoric, these triangles create a series of triangulated relationships that freight the image with tension. The display of black female nudity confirms the urbane sophistication of the white female viewers, even as it unsettles their implied claims (for which the watching women's cigarettes are a metonymy) to erotic and social freedom. The knowing gazes of the black performers in the wings, unseen by the club

Figure 1.10. Aaron Siskind, Untitled, from "Harlem Document," ca. 1937. George Eastman House. By permission of The Aaron Siskind Foundation.

audience, counter white spectatorial privilege with an alternative take on modernity, an ironic distance from the culture industry's production of race. Simultaneously, the segregation of dark-skinned black men behind the dancer's shawl—an improvised DuBoisian veil—confronts the photo's viewer with the dynamics of the color line, the invisibility of black cultural labor, and the self-consciousness with which Harlemites manipulate the codes of metropolitan urbanity. Crucial to this multiplicity of tensions are both a failure to make precise tonal distinctions—skin color and social grouping are rendered unreadable, decidedly unnaturalized—and a measured insistence on the play of gazes across social and photographic space. Among the legible eyes in the club interior, it is those of the white female patron that look back at the camera, and thus at the viewer (presumptively white), implicating both in the unsettling recognition of the histories on which their social power is predicated.

No wonder that the Feature Group and other documentarians would find such work ambiguous or elusive. While Smith/Carter and others disputed the narrative placement of the project's thesis—"which is that conditions in Harlem should be improved"—Siskind insisted that "the important thing was not our thesis but our attitude toward" it: a productive self-consciousness about the entanglement of documentary motives with the particular conditions of Harlem contact and production.[64] That concern translates throughout *Harlem Document* into a studied emphasis on social contexts that resist legibility in the progressive terms of the original enterprise. One shot sometimes referred to as "Girl by Dressmaker's Dummy," originally linked with typical Smith/Carter narratives (eviction; lost job; youth labor; the destruction of black family life), appears in *Harlem Document* without any such didactic framing context (figure 1.11). Absent its influence, the camera is free to exploit the ambiguous effects of the middle distance to suggest the lived experience of such social realities for its adolescent subject. Dwarfed by the dummy—an emblem for her straitened economic prospects, her possible links with craft traditions, her entry as a modern woman into the mode of consumer, and her potential future as a contestant for the attentions of men—she stands awkwardly at the threshold of a troubling sea-change. The image's placement in the text, between transcriptions of children's jump-rope rhymes—"Chicken in the car / Car wouldn't go / Chicken jump out / The car went slow" (34)—and the oral history of a showgirl—"I been doin this for goin on two years now, hoping an wishing that some day I'll get a break and be somebody" (45)—reinforces our sense of this trajectory. Visually, the subject's posture rhymes with the stance of the African statuette placed carefully atop the massive pile of clothes and furnishings dominating the foreground; the question of its psychic relevance and symbolic resonance—ancestral or art object? souvenir? religious icon?— is raised by the photo's insistence on the acute unevenness of black urban modernity. Such complication of social fact is achieved, again, by Siskind's way of foregrounding the role of the camera. Uncertain of the logic by which this space is framed—not that of the exposé, or the consensual portrait, or the pictorialist view—the viewer is denied the comforting affirmation of a modernity whose social and psychic complexities might be mastered.

Figure 1.11. Aaron Siskind, Untitled [Girl by Dressmaker's Dummy], from "Harlem Document," ca. 1938. Center for Creative Photography. By permission of The Aaron Siskind Foundation.

Figure 1.12. Aaron Siskind, Untitled [Man Sleeping on Bed], from "Harlem Document"/"The Most Crowded Block in the World," ca. 1939–40. Center for Creative Photography. By permission of The Aaron Siskind Foundation.

Like a number of the images chosen for *Harlem Document*, this shot of the adolescent girl shows an unusual sensitivity to the gendered quality and implications of metropolitan spaces. But it is Siskind's images of black men, mirrored, framed, negotiating the camera's gaze, that prove most powerful as an analogue for the work of Harlem image makers in his wake. Among the most widely reproduced (and controversial) of the images from the "Document" is an untitled shot often referred to as "Man Sleeping on Bed" (figure 1.12); it has been offered as evidence both of the "projection, voyeurism, . . . fantasy, and desire" that inform the documentary gaze and as a "case in point" of the possibilities of white image making imaginatively in tune with black social experience.[65] Perhaps most notable, however, is an aspect of the image absent from both readings: its focused meditation on the possibilities and limits suggested by the camera's presence in this overdetermined space.

The dominant effect of the shot, obviously, is irony. Its subject appears to be asleep, his body turned away from the eyes of the pinups and iconic figures that look down on him in a chilling parody of recognition. Yet irony is the generative means, rather than the end, of the image's effects. The subject's unself-conscious repose exposes the turgid artificiality of the studio glamour shot and "candid" celebrity portrait; his posture communicates the effect of withdrawal from watching eyes, rather than unself-consciousness or an embrace of their banal erotic modes. Once again, image placement speaks volumes: on the facing page of *Harlem Document* begins the oral history of a former organizer of rent parties and their associated sex trade—a juxtaposition that amplifies the ambiguity of the black male subject's relations to mass-mediated white eroticism. Indeed, the psychic distance between Siskind's Harlem subject and Hollywood's constructions of libido—note the central spread, "Holy Terror of Hollywood!"—is so pronounced as to suggest that the deepest misidentifications are enacted here not by the sleeper but by the viewer who encounters him, within a photographic space that acknowledges its continuity with the dream-world of the picture magazines. Announcing a commitment to the realm of the oneiric, the image refuses the legibility of didactic interest; we fail to read this subject by understanding him as victim of a nightmare from which he can never awaken. With equal force, the image forestalls the legibility of the progressive ideal: no amount of social engineering could address the kind of social embeddedness registered here. The mirror on the wall, empty of reflection, is no crystal ball; it offers no resolved image of its subject's self-understanding or of the agency of documentary imaging in recording it.

With this image and others of its moment, Siskind reaches the limits of the documentary enterprise in and in response to Harlem. Shot in 1940 during Siskind's last collaborative sessions there, "Man Sleeping on Bed" is contemporaneous with a body of work that diverged sharply from the Feature Group's mode, eschewing human subjects for the exploration of what Siskind called "objects in a setting."[66] Roundly criticized by Photo League members, these new images—of destroyed buildings, of the spaces inhabited by religious communities and their architectural forms—increasingly committed to an ethos of abstract expressionism; they embraced a decidedly formal "ambiguity" and "conflict," transforming vernacular landscapes into diffusely expressionist modes, creating tensions between familiar objects and their use as vehicles for subjective expression.[67] Critics have usually understood this body of work as a radical departure from Feature Group collaboration; a few dissenters have read it as imaginatively continuous with "Harlem Document."[68] But neither its rupture from nor its continuity with documentary practice can be credited without fuller consideration of the role of Harlem in the evolution of Siskind's work.

In an account of the photographic epiphany that redirected his work, Siskind describes his attempts during the early and mid-1940s to shoot rock photographs—large-format compositions that used geological formations to experiment with Cubist juxtaposition, found landscapes, and expressionist modalities. Central to these images was the way "these rocks hovered over each other," "pushed against each other," with the energy of "what I call contiguity. Then I felt I had gotten something that was unique."[69] If the resulting images moved beyond Siskind's ethos of restrained engagement with human life-worlds, it was nonetheless "documentary": "It was a document of my philosophy, a projection of my philosophy, and I was able to do it without distorting [the found landscape] too much."[70] Documenting, in other words, the essential process of photographic encounter—now stripped of social text, crystallized as the "experience" that brings together "the objective world" and "the sheet of paper on which" its representation "will be realized"—Siskind insisted on the meaningful unassimilability of the world before the camera's eye.[71]

These, then, are the key terms of Siskind's new credo: "contiguity," ambiguity, the "wiping out [of] real space" so as to "shift from description to idea."[72] If they define an expressionist—a decidedly postobjective—sensibility, they can nonetheless be seen to evolve from his commitments as a documentary photographer in post-1935 Harlem. Restrained contiguity on the grounds of a partially shared, contested landscape; engagement with a range of affective responses that refuse to be reduced to a unitary meaning; the evacuation of a "real space" of legible modernity in favor of the oneiric space of social memory and psychic encounter: these aims are learned on the ground, conditioned by the multiple life-worlds of Harlem and the manifold effects of its histories of cultural encounter. It is surely no accident that Siskind left Harlem, Feature Group collaboration, and progressive-style documentary in one fell swoop. However successful in dictating the terms of their reception and uses, his "Harlem Document" photographs define the limit of documentary as a resource for implicating America's social histories of looking and naming. In the final incarnation of the "Harlem Document" images as a visual response to the call of the archive, we can perceive their original aim: the creation of spaces of existential reverie that resist incorporation into modernity's evolving social logics for managing modernity.

In received histories of photography, Siskind's turn from Harlem and documentary camera work to his real calling—an abstract expressionism that would influence such artists as Jackson Pollock, Willem de Kooning, and Franz Kline—remains a footnote to, or at best a harbinger of, a zeitgeist shift. Under pressure of red-baiting and postwar anomie, the story goes, social realism packed up and left town, superseded by an abstract expressionism "utterly devoid of social content."[73] Like the Harlem Renaissance a decade before it, the work of socially conscious documentary is understood to come to a crash-

ing halt, rendered irrelevant (even anachronistic) by the swiftly morphing social contexts of liberal modernity. To a significant degree, this broadly drawn
picture of postwar culture making shores up a color line that has long domi-
nated histories of visual culture. Making a commitment to abstraction the
benchmark of avant-garde sensibility and postwar relevance, it obscures the
afterlives of documentary practice among African American image makers, for
whom socially referential work continued to be not only a cultural imperative
but a productive strategy for rethinking signifying logics inherited from Euro-
American modernism.[74] Siskind's final images of Harlem might serve as a point
of departure for the generation of an alternative genealogy. Referential yet
verging onto the territory of the nonobjective, formally self-conscious yet committed to the found material landscape, the *Harlem Document* images can be
read as a bridge to postdocumentary representations of black culture that also
emanate from the lived realities of Harlem. Linked neither by party line nor
by the rubric of influence but by their riffs on embeddedness in that social
space, the two bodies of work sketch an alternative trajectory for documentary
as a genre of response to social experience—and as a resource for other respondents, particularly literary figures, to the urgencies of postwar America.

"Visions, Dreams, and a Few Nightmares": Roy DeCarava and the Afterlives of Documentary

A key figure of this postdocumentary dispensation is the Harlem-based African
American photographer Roy DeCarava, whose work is typified by the 1950
image "Two Women, Mannikin's Hand."[75] Its mode of implication chimes
suggestively with that of Siskind's work (for example, in "Girl by Dressmaker's
Dummy"). In both shots, prosthetic bodies give menacing form to the realities
of economic survival and the psychic toll of racial iconography and de facto
segregation. Like Siskind's subject, the eponymous women of this photograph
are at once exemplary urban subjects cloaked in anonymity and figures of a
spiritualized power; they emanate a haunting expressivity in the face of modernity's menacing dislocations. The contrasts between the images are marked but
also instructive. The calculated distance of Siskind's camera from his subject's
inwardness—the recognition of an unbridgeable experiential gap buttressed
by race—brings the complex nearness and contemplative detachment of De-
Carava's image into sharper focus. Whereas Siskind's late documentary work
invites viewers who are, like himself, outsiders into a space of "breathing
room," asking them to meditate on the social implications of their acts of

reading, DeCarava's camera insists on a taut proximity that mesmerizes as it troubles.[76] The tactile qualities of the hair and skin of the subject in profile, the beautifully modeled drapery of her companion's headscarf, register in lyrical contrast to the mannequin's artificial hand; its painted talons are washed to disturbing pallor by a harsh light accentuating the mechanical joint, transforming it into an emblem of dismemberment. White and black, nature and *nature morte*, fashion and lived practice, the mass-produced and the intimately human: the disparities implied are all the more resonant, all the less secure, for being so resoundingly familiar.

Such carefully wrought, powerfully realized tensions are exemplary of DeCarava's Harlem work. Beginning his professional life as a painter and serigrapher, DeCarava committed to the camera as his medium in 1947 (a resonant moment in the development of photographic practice). For the next half-dozen years he focused on making photographs of the people and spaces of Harlem, a choice dictated in part by accessibility. Born in Harlem Hospital in 1919, DeCarava grew up playing stickball on its bustling streets, attended the Harlem annex of Textile High School and the storied Harlem Art Center, apprenticed as a printmaker through a WPA project in Harlem, studied at the George Washington Carver Art School, and remained vitally active in community projects reflecting the cultural bravado of Harlem at midcentury.[77] But DeCarava's belonging to Harlem has in a specific sense been overemphasized. If, as Peter Galassi asserts, DeCarava "had only to be himself to see Harlem from within," he also conceived of his early work there as an opportunity for creating a new aesthetic with and for the camera, one that combined meditative distance with palpable intimacy.[78] With this complexly wrought stance, DeCarava evaded the programmatic thrust of postwar cultural politics centered in Harlem. Drawing on realism and expressionism, referentiality and abstraction, formalism and vernacular codes, DeCarava amalgamated and transformed them, and in the process expanded the possibilities for the camera as an instrument of cultural response.

Exemplifying this aim is DeCarava's successful 1951 application for a Guggenheim Fellowship, the first awarded to an African American photographer. Although much has been made of the idiom of racial celebration it deploys— the text of his proposal, one critic claims, "could have come from the pen of Langston Hughes"[79]—DeCarava's statement cannily deploys the rhetoric of site work, which is not so much rejected as hijacked in service of an interpretive frame that yokes elements of Black Arts, socially referential, expressionist, and nonobjective practices. His goal, DeCarava writes, is "to photograph Harlem through the Negro people," with a psychic plenitude intended to displace scientific exhaustiveness for good: "Morning, noon, night, at work, going to work, coming home from work, at play, in the streets, talking, kidding, laughing, in the home, in the playgrounds, in the schools, bars, stores, libraries, beauty parlors, churches, etc."[80] These apparently casual categories riff pointedly on the sites elaborated by Smith/Carter in "Harlem Document," Roy Stryker in his FSA shooting scripts, and hosts of other New Deal culture makers, generated by managerial interest. By contrast, DeCarava's rubrics are constructed from the perspective of everyday practice, designed so as to yield images that will "show the strength, the wisdom, the dignity of the Negro people." If that rhetoric chimes with the intentions of the Feature Group in its work on storefront churches, black unions, and race leaders (to say nothing of the idiom of marching blacks), DeCarava decisively rejects the "documentary or sociological stance" that has governed the iconography of black America in favor of what he underscores will be an artistic rendering, "a creative expression"—as he would elsewhere put it, an artistic "expression of self," shaped in the service of "lasting beauty."[81]

Yet DeCarava's aestheticism, itself a repudiation of the demand for socially conscious work from black artists, is undergirded by the promise of an insider's view, "the kind of penetrating insight and understanding of Negroes which I believe only a Negro photographer can interpret." That claim in turn implicates something other than the celebration of blackness, however defined. Embracing the rhetoric of universalism that marked the broader postwar turn to abstraction, DeCarava aims to "revea[l] the roots from which spring the greatness of all human beings" at the same time that he offers a hermeneutic object for those bound experientially by racial history. In a canny double entendre, he claims, "I want to heighten the awareness of my people."[82] At stake, across color lines and aesthetic ideologies, are both the visibility and the self-consciousness of black Americans as complexly located subjects of modernity, negotiating the panoply of its terrors and pleasures.[83] Throughout DeCarava's career, these imperatives remain linked. In dialogue both with vernacular and folk idioms and with the visual languages of modernism and expressionism, committed to social activism yet insistent on photography as "a law unto itself," with the power to "change [the subject], reshape it in an image which expresses both the object and something of myself," DeCarava fluidly negotiates cultural imperatives whose context, stage, and point of departure could only be Harlem.[84]

The body of work DeCarava generated during the early 1950s—unprecedented in its scope, intimacy, and embeddedness in a specific life-world—resulted in his first and best-known book: a 1955 collaboration with fellow

Harlemite Langston Hughes titled *The Sweet Flypaper of Life.* Their partnership was inaugurated by DeCarava, who may have been emboldened to contact Harlem's elder statesman by the popularity and timeliness of Hughes's long-running sketches of Harlemite Jesse B. Semple, or "Simple"[85]; in any case, the joint venture was heady and mutually beneficial. *Flypaper* sold more than 35,000 copies, many if not most to African Americans, and as biographer Arnold Rampersad notes, "no book by Hughes [alone] was ever greeted so rhapsodically."[86] But that very success created certain structural problems for DeCarava. Hughes's accompaniment to his selection of 140 of DeCarava's Harlem photographs, an entirely fictive narrative, was voiced by an imaginary protagonist, the matriarch Mary Bradley. Hughes, however, sequenced and paced the text with an eye toward refuting several decades of sociological and documentary gospel on Harlem poverty, crime, and psychic disintegration—as in the monitory statistics of Smith/Carter, whose effect Siskind rejected for the latter-day *Harlem Document.* The resulting photo-story, whose recreation of extended family life was so convincing as to obscure its own fictionality, was read by critics as a signal instance of the form it sought to overturn.

Yet such misreading may be less willful than latter-day critics have implied, to the extent that it presumed certain documentary engagements on the part of DeCarava's collaborator. For Hughes, an emblematic figure of racial celebration Renaissance-style, the production of *Flypaper* extended a long experience of working in photographic and photojournalistic modes. Hughes's Simple sketches had appeared regularly (and would continue to appear, for some twenty-three years in total) as columns in the *Chicago Defender*; and the appeal of the latter as the nation's most influential black newspaper was greatly enhanced by its canny use of images (including those featured weekly in "The Defender News Reel," combining the conventions of photojournalism and vernacular imaging).[87] These contexts lent Hughes's accounts of the bar-stool conversations between his Northern-educated first-person interlocutor and the streetwise, mother-witty, Southern-born Simple—" 'If you want to know about my life,' said Simple as he blew the foam from the top of the newly filled glass the bartender put before him, 'don't look at my face, don't look at my hands. Look at my feet and see if you can tell how long I been standing on them' "—a documentary flavor.[88] Just as the famed street life and crime scene photos of street haunter Weegee enhanced the reportage of the left-leaning *PM*, the graphic and photographic context for Hughes's sketches enhanced the vernacular rhythms of his characters' exchange. In effect, the original venue of the Simple sketches obscured the boundaries between fiction and the kind of vernacular reportage associated with WPA fieldwork (like the observations recorded by Margaret Walker and Ralph Ellison in Harlem and linked to Siskind's photographs in *Harlem Document*). So heightened was the documentary or reality effect of Hughes's pieces that, shortly after they first appeared in 1949, the *Chicago Defender* began receiving large volumes of mail "addressed only to Simple, as if his creator were superfluous—or a fiction himself."[89]

Beyond the vernacular cadences of Simple, Hughes brought to the making of *Flypaper* hands-on experience with documentary and photojournalistic production. As early as 1934, Hughes was spending significant time with the man who would become the most storied photojournalist of the documentary era, Henri Cartier-Bresson; Hughes had invited the photographer to stay with him in Mexico City, and accompanied him on the photographic forays that led to some of Cartier-Bresson's most celebrated work. Based on that work, Hughes wrote a brief essay (unfortunately never published) on the power of documentary imaging to produce what he called "pictures more than pictures," at once aesthetically arresting and capable of "comment upon the social order that creates" the imaged lives.[90] Back home in Harlem, during the same year in which Simple was born, Hughes began collaborating with Griffith J. Davis, his former student, fellow rooming-house tenant on West 127th Street, and the first photographic stringer for *Ebony*, black America's answer to *Life* magazine. Together Hughes and Davis produced a short series of pieces on such familiar photojournalistic topics as the Harlem Church for the Deaf, the backstage hobbies of storied Harlem entertainers, and the gap between tenement conditions and expressive culture in black Atlanta.[91]

Although Hughes apparently soon tired of such work—hardly a challenge for an internationally acclaimed poet, dramatist, lyricist, novelist, and memoirist—the experience of producing documentary photo-text would prove useful. During the summer and fall of 1955, as he worked to assemble the photographs for *Flypaper*, Hughes was also choosing and responding to images for a massive illustrated volume titled *A Pictorial History of the Negro in America*, on which he collaborated with the former WPA employee and acclaimed children's writer Milton Meltzer.[92] The *Pictorial History* may have fallen short of its goal of providing an image "of every famous and important Negro from Nat Turner . . . to . . . Ralph Bunche," but it was hardly the kind of potboiling Hughes had undertaken for *Ebony*—less hustle or piecework than article of faith.[93] Everywhere throughout the *Pictorial History*, as it covers the experience of black Americans from the first settlements through the gathering civil rights movement, Hughes's belief in the power of the image—particularly the photograph—to render visible and to dignify its subjects is bedrock and self-evident.

Nor was Hughes uninterested in photo-text as a vehicle for more-challenging experimentation with the kinds of stories that might be told about Harlem and black modernity. Sometime in 1950, Hughes approached documentary photographer Marion Palfi with his own design—down to page layouts and specific photo choices—for a photo-text collaboration on Harlem. Palfi, an émigré who had fled European fascism in 1940 and found her calling as a socially conscious image maker, was well known to Hughes. Her portraits of him figured prominently in her first U.S. exhibition in 1945; he was among her "dearest friends" and her most important "guide" in the U.S. context, and it was through Hughes that Arna Bontemps came to use Palfi's portraits in his own pictorial who's-who of black America, *We Have Tomorrow* (1945).[94] Titled "Ups and Downs," Hughes's manuscript plan not only anticipates the kinds of practice-based categories DeCarava would generate for his Harlem work, it proposes specific photographic subjects and sites in which to address them. Hughes's categories range from the sublime ("Jazz," "Artists," "Motion," "Pictures") to the absurd ("Bathrooms," "Aprons," "Muscles," "Beards"), but the point of such hierarchies is to frame them as continuums within the Harlem context, where the lowest and most reflexive expressive act—the wearing of the zoot suit, the display of a photo torn from the pages of a cheap mass magazine, the street dwellers trading rhythms on an upturned washtub—has a direct, vital, and organic relation to its iconic and "high" Harlem counterpart, from Joe Louis's sartorial splendor and Jacob Lawrence's paintings to Duke Ellington's suites and the concert music of Marian Anderson.[95] Hughes framed his own contribution as an "explanation" for the structural premise that, at least in Harlem, "Nobody is up as long as the other is down."[96] Staking this conclusion—itself, one might argue, a synthetic restatement of Hughes's radical, Renaissance, Popular Front, and postwar engagements—on the power of documentary images, Hughes bids to reclaim the everyday life of Harlem for affirmation and sustaining social practices. In so doing, he reflects on and extends his own iconic status as a Harlem writer, whose art in effect documents an organic culture from within.

Hughes's iconicity as a spokesman for black vernacular culture, along with his efforts to promote African American visibility via the image, almost certainly shaped the reception of DeCarava's early work. But that work itself took documentary conventions as a point of conceptual departure, and they remained a touchstone for DeCarava's elaboration of an alternative practice intensely conscious of its representational precedents. From the beginning of his career, DeCarava was committed to the use of available light, without flash or other enhancements; during the 1940s and early 1950s, that stance was revolutionizing the work of postwar photographers such as Robert Frank, W. Eugene Smith, and Louis Faurer, who harnessed documentary stylistics to the exploration of more-intimate subject matter, new social landscapes, and more-nuanced expressive modalities.[97] DeCarava also committed exclusively to the small-camera format, eschewing panoramic, precisely detailed observation in favor of the small camera's implied spontaneity and found (rather than orchestrated) subjects. Since the advent of the Leica revolution, the handheld camera had allowed for the kind of expressionist and surrealist effects associated with the work of Cartier-Bresson—its acknowledged master (and an acknowledged influence not only on Hughes but also on DeCarava). Yet such effects were bound up, in the very work Hughes had observed, not only with referentiality but with the force of a certain social consciousness and with documentary idiom. To the extent that DeCarava's work registered its own ambitions to transform the expressive capacities of the medium, it inherited documentation as a legacy and an antecedent. Quite apart from Hughes's cultural standing or modes of generating a fictive voice, such doubleness is embedded in DeCarava's early work. No less a figure than Edward Steichen—the highly influential photographer whose images spanned pictorialism, "straight" documentation, and beyond, and since 1947 the director of the Department of Photography at the Museum of Modern Art—began collecting DeCarava's work for the museum's fledgling art photography collection, even as he chose four of DeCarava's *Flypaper* images for inclusion in the museum's 1955 documentary exhibition, The Family of Man.[98] Indebted by necessity, and with the force of creative exploitation, to the history and power of documentary, *The Sweet Flypaper of Life* set the stage for DeCarava's decades-long struggle to be understood as the originator of a post-, anti-, or meta-documentary form.

In this specific way, DeCarava's early Harlem work can be linked to Siskind's images at the conclusion of "Harlem Document": both seek to displace the documentary rhetoric of objectivity with an affective complexity understood as the product of subjective response. The link appears more plausible with respect to another of DeCarava's projects in 1955, the opening (in his home on West Eighty-fourth Street) of A Photographer's Gallery (APG), one of only two institutions in New York City then devoted to the exhibition and sale of photographs as fine art. DeCarava was firm—even adamant—about APG's presumptions; in a statement of intentions, he wrote, "It is a gallery that values the single photograph on its merits alone, not how well it fits into a picture sequence, not because the subject is an important figure, or of news value, but because the subject is important to the photographer and will result in a photograph of lasting beauty."[99] In another decisive statement, DeCarava asserted: "A photographic print is the end in itself, a law unto itself, to be hung on a wall and to be lived with and enjoyed."[100] Nothing could be further from the uses of FSA—or even Photo League—output, so promiscuously sutured to the graphic or do-gooding designs of liberal reformers and the picture magazines, exploited as evidence or illustration, consumed or made evidentiary and then discarded.

It was, nonetheless, photographers trained in the Photo League's documentary conventions whose work DeCarava chose to exemplify APG's aesthetic aims. The inaugural exhibition at the gallery showed nineteen photographers, all but one belonging to what the *New York Times* reviewer Jacob Deschin called the "documentary school."[101] Deschin singled out for notice the work of Lou Bernstein, who perfectly fit the mold of Siskind's Feature Group collaborators. Born on the Lower East Side, later identified with the Jewish neighborhood of Williamsburg that became his signature subject, Bernstein brought his training at the Photo League in the heyday of the feature groups to bear on an evolving practice of street documentary, in images wedding clarity of resolution and detail with nonobjectivity. Siskind had modeled for students the practice of exploiting relations to the social context of image making as a shaping resource; in work like Bernstein's, that practice vitally informed the embrace of subjective documentary. Among other photographers APG exhibited were Dan Weiner, a Photo Leaguer with close ties to Walker Evans and Cartier-Bresson as well as Siskind (and later a key influence on the subjective documentary aesthetic of Gary Winogrand); Leon Levinstein, a student of Sid Grossman at the Photo League, whose work there focused in part on Harlem; and Ralph Eugene Meatyard, whose inscrutable, haunting images of masked children and decrepit landscapes in his native Kentucky were first shown just prior to his appearance at APG, in a 1956 exhibition that juxtaposed his work with Aaron Siskind's.[102]

From the perspective of these entanglements, DeCarava's Harlem work can be seen to take up where Siskind's belated *Harlem Document* leaves off: at the threshold of the oneiric, where alterity and self-knowledge are entangled and inevitably racialized; at the boundary—so consequentially marked, in Harlem—between outsidership and belonging, where respectful distance becomes intimate stillness, an ethos of "invisibil[ity]" and "wait[ing]."[103] Siskind's work has rarely been read in conjunction with DeCarava's, and then only to suggest that they inhabit sharply discontinuous worlds: white and black, socially conscious and subjectivist, New Deal and civil rights era.[104] But despite acute differences in shaping contexts, and the determinative difference of race as a structural feature of their site work, there is an important point of contact emphasized by these dissimilarities. Both photographers use their relations to the space of Harlem to generate a socially implicated image making, exploiting the conventions of documentary even as they seek to move beyond them.[105]

Among DeCarava's earliest photographs and those published in *Sweet Fly-paper*, his domestic portraits of Harlem rank-and-file—working men and women like Sam and Shirley Murphy, Joe and Julia James—are often considered the most original and powerfully charged, in that they "fill a gaping hole in the world's image of Harlem" and "its image of itself."[106] But DeCarava framed his affectionate shots of Harlem's private spaces with ambitious, self-referential images of storefronts, sidewalks, and streets. In them, what Sherry Turner DeCarava has identified as the defining elements of DeCarava's work—reflections on human scale in the built (and ghetto) environment; dynamic rhythms produced through tonal subtlety, composition, and thematic elements; an unprecedented richness of implication in the use of light and shadow—come most powerfully into play. Not least, these hallmarks function as a visual language for exploiting the history of Harlem as an iconic space. Deliberately referencing both the documentary archive and rhetorics of black uplift only to render them insufficient, DeCarava paves a middle way between referentiality and lyricism, race-centered and generic integrities, a modernism of form and one of social action.

An exemplary image from this body of work is "117th Street" (1951).[107] Here, DeCarava alludes to his own developing body of work, in which the mesmerizing visual rhythms and tonal effects of "wall space" have already become pronounced, marking its departure from the documentary archive.[108] With remarkable purposiveness, DeCarava refuses the purview of frontality or proximity, forestalling both the obvious intimacies of the insider's camera and a detachment that registers as journalistic. Instead, DeCarava transforms the vacant lot, that longstanding trope in documentary site-work for urban blight and for the power of progressive modernity to redeem it. Here, the ghetto wasteland becomes a proscenium on an epic scale, directing our gaze not only to the lyrical movement and activity of inhabitants and passersby but to the presence of what the sociologist Jane Jacobs famously calls eyes on the street. In DeCarava's rendering, the instrumental space of urban renewal becomes the foreground we occupy, a vantage point from which the dynamism and rootedness of black life in Harlem are palpable yet detached from constraining racial specificity. Boarded windows, discarded newspapers, the detritus of urban life—all have their place in the scene, but the epic scale of the image refuses them psychic or social centrality. The very massiveness of the urban facades comprising the stage set before us lends interest—and more: agency—

to the human figures they all but enclose. Lit with a mysterious beneficence that imbues their movements with purpose, these subjects participate in a drama at once social and existential, beyond the realm of the merely spectacular or documentary.

Yet with all its universalizing aspirations, the power of this image depends for its full effect on locatedness, on the intimacies of place as the context for social experience. That there should in the early 1950s be such a vacant lot on 117th Street, or anywhere else in Harlem, is hardly a matter of surprise. During the postwar period, scores of "neighborhood revival" programs involving federal, state, and private agencies transformed the area between 110th and 155th Streets into a giant construction and demolition zone, awash in rubble and soot. But Harlem residents would have recognized the street DeCarava images as a notorious site for sociological inquiry and for civil disturbances, including looting and arson during the August 1943 riots. Throughout the postwar era, 117th Street remained an emblem of blight and a target of urban renewal. In 1947, New York's Urban League chose for an "experimental" project on housing conditions the blocks of buildings on 117th and 118th Streets between Fifth and Lenox Avenues; city inspections over the course of three days there resulted in 1,807 reports of serious code violations in some 564 tenements, well known to be "filthy, rat-infested, and in a shocking state of disrepair."[109] As late as 1964, when Harlem activists staged a rent strike based on the city's lack of enforcement among slumlords of housing codes, the focus of their activity—and that of photojournalists covering the event—was the same block of tenements on 117th.[110]

DeCarava's "117th Street" acknowledges as it transmutes this history. Among the half-obliterated graffiti marked on the brick facade that forms the backdrop of the image, the lettering "P U S" is clearly visible, hinting at an infection in the urban organism, hidden beneath its facades. All the more extraordinary, then, is DeCarava's alchemy, which transforms the iconic Harlem street into a site of affective plenitude, on a scale that confirms its subjects' psychic and social complexity by fully engaging the viewer's own. Decisively nonobjective in its aims, "117th Street" achieves its stylized effects via a practice akin to Siskind's postdocumentary ethos: "wiping out real space," framing it as the ambient space of affective process and response.[111] For both photographers, the history of Harlem as a dual, nested space—at once material and symbolic, oscillating among promise and penury, racially charged fear, pride, and desire—enables such a transformation. Siskind's work marks the limits of progressive culture making by reflecting on its entanglement with the mutually mediating histories of ghetto Jews and the black metropolis. Too specific, too limited to his own agency to serve as an influence or even a formative anti-model, his work is nonetheless continuous with DeCarava's response to the post-Renaissance problem of framing black modernity, via the mediation of experiential histories and documentary codes.

Perhaps no single DeCarava image in his Harlem portfolio educes this problem of framing more powerfully than the 1950 photograph "Gittel," which might well be set in dialogue with Siskind's photograph "Our Own Community."[112] Most immediately, "Gittel" records the intimate details of an urban landscape marked, even haunted, by a history of contending ownerships, whose social tensions resonate not in a safely distant past but in the intricate texture of everyday life. The image teems with signifiers: the battered board in the left foreground, announcing the services of "Morris Gittel General Insurance Broker"; the notice crudely painted on a concrete pillar for Gittel's services as "Notary Public," complete with the classic pointing hand; the gilded lettering of Gittel's plate-glass window, supplemented by cardboard placards listing services in English and Spanish. At the still center of this commercial collage stands a woman in profile, draped in a black cloak and scarf, her eyes shielded by dark sunglasses. Erect and apparently motionless, framed by the assertive thrust of concrete and marble pillars, she appears to subsist in a zone of quietude cut off from the instrumental necessity of Gittel's modernity, with all its narratives of loss and dislocation: fire, eviction, "riesgos" and "robo," "birth certificates" for recent arrivals "born in the South." Urban sentry, muse, black priestess, the hooded woman embodies a set of claims unutterable in the idioms of insurance, notarizing, or bourgeois self-recognition, yet recognizable only in the context of this psychically charged space—"our own community" no longer, now a collage of alternative modernities. Like Siskind's use of white pinups in "Man Sleeping on Bed," DeCarava's framing of the woman offers no readily legible contrast—between, say, Jewish and black or commercial and folk presences in Harlem—but instead a series of mysterious metonymies and juxtapositions. Occupying the central space of the image, which is simultaneously the crossroads of America's urban diasporas, the unnamed woman embodies DeCarava's aesthetic. Her presence conjoins an existentialist take on social invisibility, black spirituality, and a profoundly suggestive formalism tempered by social connotation.

A comparative reading of "Gittel" suggests the complexity of its participation in photographic idioms after documentary, and the power of Harlem as an organizing site for their negotiation. DeCarava's emphasis on signage reprises the structural paradoxes of Walker Evans's work, in which the handmade and the mass-produced, artisanal integrity and technological power, are made not only to signify as elements of a socially conscious practice, but also to figure the unique agency of the camera as emblem and recorder of New Deal social life. But, committed to a similarly "straight approach," DeCarava evades Evans's distanced irony.[113] Rooted in Harlem, participating in its urban tableaux, DeCarava's images achieve their psychic richness and affective power by refusing to abandon either racial affirmation or claims to universalism: they make human practice and social fact mutually constitutive. The complexity of DeCarava's Harlem photographs is at once found and metaphoric; it figures both the resourcefulness of black expressive cultures and the power as such of his aesthetic framings and meditations.

DeCarava's work thus exemplifies the transformative power of Harlem as an iconic site for documentary photography, and more broadly for visual modernism, in their robust afterlives. Read in conjunction with Siskind's work, his early images make visible a history of photographic response to Harlem as a site of contact, misrepresentation, and exchange—a history in which the modernist will to formalism or reverie and the imperatives of social engagement alike are implicated. At large, the conjunction of these very different Harlem documents clarifies the ongoing power of photography as a resource for cultural and imaginative response to the very depredations and misrepresentations the mass image has imposed. During the production of *The Sweet Flypaper of Life*, DeCarava wrote privately that "the time will come when photography will cast aside its literary crutch"—the framing contexts, captions, journalistic accompaniment, and reportage that comprised the photo-essay, the photo-text, even *Flypaper* itself—"and stand on its own feet as a legitimate means of expression."[114] If the fate of photographic images continued to be mixed in the postwar era, their value to the "literary" was sharply in the ascendancy. Read in concert, Siskind's and DeCarava's work in Harlem opens a view onto the labile possibilities of the image for writers intent on harnessing its effects to their evolving work. Their documents make visible a history of writing for and against the photograph as a provocation and an emblem, a bearer of history and a social burden. In this history, borne out in the unlikeliest texts and careers, black writers live the afterlives of modernism, the novel form powerfully shapes the social landscape, and the photograph becomes the secret sharer of the word.

Chapter Two

From *Black Voices* to *Black Power*: Richard Wright and the Trial of Documentary

In May 1937, as Aaron Siskind and the Photo League's Feature Group were collaborating on "Harlem Document," the twenty-eight-year-old Richard Wright—a mainstay of radical and progressive circles in Chicago, and a published writer who had been singled out for praise not only in *New Masses* but in the *New Republic*, the *Saturday Review of Literature*, and the *New York Times*—arrived in New York with forty dollars in his pocket and the borrowed clothes on his back.[1] Although his move to Harlem was only one in a series of increasingly far-flung migrations from his birthplace in Natchez, Mississippi, it launched and defined Wright's career as a novelist—indeed, *the* novelist of the New Deal, Popular Front, problem-and-protest era. Ten months later his first book, *Uncle Tom's Children*, was published to ringing acclaim, on the strength of which Wright received the Guggenheim Fellowship that allowed him to complete *Native Son*. Scholars have assiduously detailed the activities in the densely overlapping circles of Harlem, left intellectual culture, and New Deal projects that enabled these achievements. What has remained obscure, however, is the degree to which Wright's engagements with the world of New York publishing, the Communist Party apparatus, and fellow New Deal writers were also an education in—we might call it an exposure to—the possibilities of documentary photography as a resource for his work and self-fashioning.

Indeed, Wright's move to Harlem inaugurated a kind of hyphenation; throughout his subsequent career, his stylistics, political commitments, and writerly aspirations were yoked to the conduct of the documentary image.

Such a reading dissents sharply from received accounts of Wright, which tend to focus narrowly on *Native Son* as his representative, singularly successful text, exemplifying his radical distrust of documentary conventions (and, more broadly, of all visual culture). In a recent reading, Maurice Wallace has argued that the unitary, even obsessive, thrust of that novel is its concern with a "picture-taking racial gaze that fixes ... black male subjects within a rigid and limited grid of representational possibilities," and in the process certifies "the primacy of the picture"—in particular the documentary photograph, with its apparently incontrovertible truth claims—"over the person in the white mind."[2] According to this reading, any subsequent interest on Wright's part in photography as an aesthetic model or cultural practice must be either wholly negative or pathetically self-deluding: the camera, as *Native Son* clearly shows, not only lies, but "enframes," "paralyz[es]," "arrests" black male subjects, who can only "will to survive the visually inflected problematics of race and manhood in American culture."[3]

The issue of Wright's engagements beyond *Native Son* will be the focus of the account that follows; first, I want to counter this reading by suggesting how Wright's career-making text anticipates them. If the failure of Bigger's opportunity, and even subjectivity, is predicated on visual practices, it is crucial to note that his fragile efforts of self-consciousness also take effect on the grounds of image making and a willed contestation of its powers. With respect to his initial police interrogation at the Dalton house, the narrative notes, "They wanted him to draw the picture and he would draw it like he wanted it. . . . In the past had they not always drawn the picture for him?"[4] Later, Bigger is quick to intuit that the "impersonal" stance of photojournalists is far "more dangerous" than the open animosity of the police; working the very iconography of the empty-headed Negro that their labor perpetuates, he concentrates on composing himself for the men who wield cameras and bulbs and "flas[h] their lightning" at him (187, 200). Even his tracking of the tightening police cordon (and thus his impending doom) around Chicago's South Side via late-edition newspapers, with their increasingly prominent photographs, creates the space for his experience of a certain will to power (228). "Eyes . . . wide," Bigger embraces the hysterical fury of the sensationalist picture press; its very framings of his criminality occasion "a smile that was half-leer and half-defiance" and his first full-fledged affirmation of will: "I—I did it!" (229, 230).

This is not to contest the force of Wright's critique of racism as a visual operation, but rather to mark his investment in Bigger *as* a sometime contestant—however fatally ill-matched—on the visual field. By critical consensus, what turns out to be *Native Son*'s account of embattlement over the making and use of images is the most bracing, most successful arc of the novel as such. When Bigger Thomas surrenders to the pursuers who "gras[p]" and "dra[g]" his body amid roars of "'Kill 'im!' 'Lynch 'im!' 'That black sonofabitch!'," his final assertion of agency is a steady refusal to avail himself of, or submit himself to, visual experience (253). Pushed through the trapdoor of a tenement roof, he "closed his eyes"; as his capturers haul him, head "drumming," down long flights of steps, he "shut his eyes and tried to lose consciousness" (253). And in the closing image of Book Two, as his capturers place him in the posture of crucifixion in the freshly fallen snow amid "an array of faces, white and looming," Bigger's "eyes closed, slowly, and he was swallowed in darkness" (253). What Wright withdraws from the closing section of the novel that follows is the possibility of any look back—a possibility that, I will argue, structures the claims of his photo-textual work and of his evolving self-understanding as a black (and ultimately transnational) intellectual.

In other words, what a reading of Wright's ongoing relations with visual histories and practices demands is not emphasis on the evacuation of Bigger's agency (which is incontestable) but on the fact that any agency Bigger might achieve necessarily expresses itself as a kind of image making. (Even his brutal murder of Bessie entails such activity: brick in hand above her prone and sleeping body, "he had to stand here until that picture" of his recent experience "came back"; afterward, with the very detachment of the photographers who have shot him, he "turn[s] to Bessie again and thr[ows] the light" of his flashlight "upon the face of blood and death" [222, 223–24].) To the extent that *Native Son* implies the inevitable victimization of black Americans (especially black men) as objects of a photo-ethnographic gaze, the burden of Wright's work beyond the novel is to counter the force of such inevitability. Wright's career after *Native Son* can be read, at least in part, as an attempt to revisit—if not correct—any implication by that novel of a categorical failure of visual agency, and of the look back as a representational strategy and social stance. To read *Native Son* as determinedly antivisual is to suppress or ignore the fact that its author would begin, just months after its publication, a collaborative photo-text project predicated on his intentioned use (and even his own production) of documentary images. The resulting volume would prove to be an enduring model for African American writers in his wake—and more: it allowed Wright, at a critical juncture, to make trial of photo-text as a genre liberated from the racial and representational constraints epitomized by his own landmark novel.

That Wright was unusually attuned to both the force and the possibilities of visual practices is apparent from the raw materials of his life story, which read as a tantalizing array of proto-symbols for knowing, visibility, and optical play. One of his earliest memories, by his account, involves the eight-year-old Wright falling from his perch on scaffolding outside his family's rooming house in Jackson, where he had been conducting what one biographer calls "his career of voyeurism"—that is, peeping in on the comings and goings in a brothel in a neighboring flat.[5] Likewise, as Wright recalls it in the first-person introduction to *Uncle Tom's Children*, "The Ethics of Living Jim Crow," his first full-time employment, at age sixteen, was in the Jackson workshop of an interstate concern called the American Optical Company, which produced precision lenses. That context is also framed as his induction into the racial regime Wright called simply "the dread."[6] In response to his request that they honor the owner's agreement that Wright be instructed "in the mechanics of grinding lenses," his two coworkers—both white—brutalized him until he agreed to walk off the job immediately.[7] Some months later, Wright's eventual flight from Jackson—for Memphis, a larger branch of the optical company, the famously borrowed library card, and his ensuing "conversion" to literature and radicalism—was financed by criminal enterprise framed by visual experience; Wright's travel was staked by the proceeds from the resale of movie tickets stolen during his stint as a ticket-taker in the only theater in Jackson open to black patrons.[8] If, as the biographer Michel Fabre argues, this scheme inaugurated the trope of writer as criminal for Wright, it also sutured his authorial self-declaration to visual contexts and practices, creating a powerful if elusive link between them.

Such a link is already visible in tentative form in Wright's earliest published work. The broad arc traced by the fictions of *Uncle Tom's Children*, from racially terrorized, irremediably lonely adolescence to heroic and collectivist action, rhymes with another tentative movement: from the optical lens as an index of white surveillance and labor denied in "The Ethics of Living Jim Crow," through the invocation of sanctified witnessing—"The Bible says testify whut yuh see n speak whut yuh know"[9]—in "Fire and Cloud," to the dynamics of a mutual gaze between son and mother as she resists the terrorist tactics of their murderers at the conclusion of "Bright and Morning Star." Notably, Wright's gathering interest in the gaze and the look implicates them as an instrument not only of terror or racial surveillance but also of black self-assertion: in the latter story, the elderly mother who sacrifices herself to protect a gathering coalition of black and white communists wields both the gun with which she kills the sheriff's informant and an unflinching "loo[k] at the white faces of the men" who have come to suppress such activism at all cost.[10]

The interest there embodied, in visuality as a weapon, generative trope, and resource for the self-made African American novelist, is Wright's distinctive contribution beyond *Native Son*. And that contribution is critically shaped by, and in an important sense maps, his experience as migrant, celebrity, and perennially marginal figure in metropolitan Harlem. Wright never became a Harlem writer in any of the sustained versions of that persona adopted by his competitors and successors. But Harlem was the crucible in which his awareness of the signifying possibilities of the documentary photograph took shape, the site where a purposive engagement with documentary image making was made generative for his work. At that crossroads for political and aesthetic enterprises, Wright discovered new meanings and uses for the photographic image and the witnessing eye, not (or not merely) as symbolic objects but as contested social practices, rich in implication for the midcentury novel.

Indeed, to retrace Wright's steps in the interlude between his arrival in Harlem in May 1937 and the publication of *Native Son* in March 1940 is also to map his growing engagement with visual culture, and in particular the documentary camera. On his arrival, Wright supported himself by serving as the director of the Harlem bureau of the *Daily Worker* (a perhaps inflated title; in actuality, he was the lone reporter-editor assigned to "Negro affairs"). By all accounts he was an unspectacular journalist; the two hundred plus articles he churned out during his six-month stint were straitened both by Party politics and by his own disinclination to cover small-scale events. But the experience introduced Wright to journalism from the inside, at the very moment when visual and first-person reportage of dramatic events—the trial of the Scottsboro Nine, fascist violence in German-occupied Europe and Franco's Spain, and labor action at home in the form of strikes, brutal strikebreaking, and lockouts—was the hallmark of the leftist press. The *Daily Worker* was a frequent outlet for documentary photographers of the New York Photo League; more broadly, Wright's experience at the *Worker* put him in the mix of journalists, photojournalists, and state-sponsored writers that would crystallize in the founding in 1940 of the innovative, influential leftist daily, *PM*, premised on the use (and strikingly high-quality reproduction) of photographic images not as mere illustration but as "a *primary* means of conveying information."[11] From its inception, *PM* involved New Deal era players such as Margaret Bourke-White and Erskine Caldwell, various FSA staff photographers, the legendary photo-essayist Weegee—nicknamed "the urban reporter with a camera"—and Photo Leaguer Morris Engel, whose graphic *PM* images of New York City schools unfit for habitation were in part an extension of his work on "Harlem Document."[12]

Such exposure may not have originated, but it surely shaped, Wright's developing aesthetic. When he sought, in the landmark "Blueprint for Negro Writing" (1937), to distinguish himself from the vestigial influences of the Renaissance era and its leading figures, Wright did so by invoking notions of representational discipline, "autonomy," and unflinching realism for which the coalescing practices of Photo League documentary and New Deal–style photo-text were powerful, readily available models.[13]

By early 1938, the links were more direct and visible. Wright had become a member of a team of writers and photographers working under the auspices of the Federal Arts and Federal Writers' Projects to create two high-profile, commercially successful WPA guides to New York City. As editor for the "Negro Division," Wright was responsible for researching and writing the narrative on Harlem for *New York Panorama* (1938); to the far more substantial *WPA Guide to New York City* (1939), he contributed work, along with Claude McKay, on a "Negro Harlem" section. The two projects differed significantly in scope; they involved large numbers of agency contributors, which troubles any attempt to establish Wright's connections with specific photographers; and they segregated images from text in discrete portfolios, perhaps as a result of distinct production processes. Nonetheless, the guidebooks offer suggestive evidence not only of the porous boundaries between Harlem and downtown, or between state apparatuses and documentary projects, but also between the narrative work of representing modernity, with all its class and racial inequalities, and the genre of documentary photo-text.

In these guides, as a result of his status as Harlem "director," "chief," and representative, Wright's work appeared for the first time in conjunction with documentary images by the likes of the Man Ray–trained photographer Berenice Abbott (some of whose shots from the WPA-sponsored "Changing New York" project were used without her permission) and the Federal Arts Project photographers Arnold Eagle, Sid Grossman, and Sol Libsohn—who was at precisely this juncture also working with Aaron Siskind to produce "Harlem Document." However instrumentally their work was used to advertise the success of New Deal projects, or to affirm liberal uplift via the managerial ethos, they opened broader possibilities for camera work to which Wright was becoming attuned. Abbott's signature shot of the Murray Hill Hotel, reproduced in *New York Panorama*, exploits the surrealist effects of the camera's power to document the found juxtapositions that comprise the texture and temporal scale of urban modernity (figure 2.1).[14] Hal Morey's "Grand Central Light" explores the phenomenology of urban space even as it allegorizes the power

Figure 2.1. Berenice Abbott, Murray Hill Hotel from Park Avenue and 40th Street, Manhattan, 1935. From *Changing New York*. November 19, 1935. Photography Collection, Miriam and Ira D. Wallach Division of Art, Prints and Photographs, The New York Public Library, Lenox and Tilden Foundations.

Figure 2.2. Hal Morey, Grand Central Light, ca. 1935. Hulton Archive, Getty Images.

of photography—literally, light writing—as an agent of such experience (figure 2.2). A series of shots comprising the Harlem portfolio of the *WPA Guide*, which echo the logic of "Harlem Document" and the stylistics of Libsohn's and Grossman's work, offer up iconic spaces of the ghetto—the boarded-up tenement, the sidewalk—less for analysis or social redress than for open-ended interpretive engagement.[15] Although the New Deal guidebooks "sold [themselves] as factual and taxonomic," the images to which Wright's work was linked bespeak the multiple valences of documentary imagery, variously committed to fact-finding, allegory, lyricism, and formalist expression.[16]

It was, we can surmise, this variousness that increasingly attracted Wright to photography. By September 1938, he had made photographic documentation a generative part of his own creative process. On the research visit to Chicago he was conducting in order to complete the manuscript of *Native Son*, he toted a recently acquired camera to make snapshots of court facilities, holding cells, and even (by special permission) the electric chair in the Cook County jail.[17] Wright was presumably motivated by the same documentary presumptions that prompted him to study the well-known Cayton-Warner research file, a compilation of data based on ethnographic research at the Parkway Community Center on the South Side of Chicago, and to scrutinize press reports of the trial of Robert Nixon, on which Bigger Thomas's was partially based.[18] But Wright's activities as a photographer, seeking to reshape the materials of photojournalistic narrative to the requirements of the novel of black experience, already begin to exceed the accumulation of images as evidentiary raw material. The act of creating photographs seems to have afforded Wright both a distinctive purchase on the social data he was attempting to transform as fiction, and an equally productive purchase on his own authorial legitimacy.

In a gesture that attests to these aims, Wright impulsively bought a twin-lens reflex camera (perhaps the one featured in Ellison's talismanic image) from a "keen" semi-professional black photographer during his visit to Chicago. This was a not inconsiderable purchase, given the relative cost of such equipment and the stylistics with which it was then associated.[19] Constructed to make medium-format images of a clarity far exceeding that achievable (especially in larger print sizes) with the 35 mm instrument, the 6 × 6 twin-lens reflex camera challenged photographers to make use of its distinctive square format. That challenge was central to the early aesthetic of Lisette Model; it would later define the work of the storied postwar photographers Richard Avedon and Diane Arbus, who used it to transform the conventions of street documentary, reportage, and portraiture. But in the late 1930s the twin-lens reflex camera already enjoyed an iconic status: it was "every serious photographer's dream to own a Rolleiflex," whose precision Zeiss lens was known as "the Eagle's Eye of photography."[20] Whether Wright bought an actual Rolleiflex or a cheaper imitation, his acquisition attests to technical photographic ambitions and some interest in experimentation with portrait imaging, with which the medium format was strongly identified. Camera work, in other words, already suggests multiple possibilities to Wright under the rubric of documentation. Reportage and the use of images for narrative exactitude or socially conscious exposure jostle with an interest in the photograph as an expressive text, in photography itself as an expressive act.

Read in this context, Wright's developing commitments to photography, photo-text, and photographic culture seem far from uniformly negative, trained less on "the hegemony of photographic vision in modern racialism" than on the potential uses or counteruses of photography as a form of capital, at the moment of his own transformation from Chicago communist to Harlem intellectual and U.S. literary celebrity.[21] By the time *Native Son* had appeared in print, some six months after Wright's purchase, he had already become a seasoned darkroom technician capable of printing his own work.[22] He had also gotten himself hired as a collaborator with the *Life* photographer Hart Preston on a photo-essay on South Side Chicago, planned to mark the publication of *Native Son*. Although the essay was never published, the evidence suggests that, at least in subject matter—"dilapidated hovels, reefer dives, refuges where homeless boys slept on the floor, seedy pool- and dice-shooting rooms"[23]—its images yoked the iconography of urban poverty to sentimental conventions and sensationalism in characteristic documentary modes. Whatever the objections to the racialist gaze given shape in *Native Son*, Wright's activities in producing and promoting the novel suggest an ongoing interest in seizing on the various powers of the documentary camera: to body forth, for privileged onlookers and spectators, the other half, the twelve million, the one-third of the nation; to suture the experience of modernity to the recognition of social inequality; to probe regions of psychic uncertainty, negation, and longing; to document, by way of legitimating, his own authorial identity.

That Wright could both take up the twin-lens reflex camera, an instrument associated with modernist-inflected ideologies of depth and significant form, and serve, as he did in the spring of 1940, for the leftist journal *Friday* as sponsor of a national photojournalistic contest—"Youth in Focus": "[We want] pictures of youngsters on pogo sticks as well as parades, looking for trouble as well as for jobs, playing hookey as well as politics"—attests to these mixed motives.[24] So too does the very project, post–*Native Son*, that ostensibly attests to Wright's rejection of photography as a form of "framing" linked to "the juridical lie of the frame-up": his interest in pursuing a documentary photo-text on black youth—otherwise labeled delinquents—in Harlem.[25] The project never materialized. But Wright hoped to pursue it in collaboration with a photographer whose work he carefully followed: the one-time Federal

Figure 2.3. Helen Levitt, Untitled. New York, 1942. © Helen Levitt. Courtesy of Laurence Miller Gallery, New York.

Arts Project member and Photo Leaguer Helen Levitt, whose dynamic, lyrical images of children's street cultures and social networks in mid-1930s Harlem and East Harlem had a lasting effect on photographic practice (figures 2.3, 2.4).[26] Levitt's early career, including a 1943 exhibition at the Museum of Modern Art that Wright followed with avid interest, focused—without brief—on Harlem children's cultures: the improvisatory dynamism of their sidewalk play; the richness and resistance to sociological reading of their communicative codes. For the author of *Black Boy*, Levitt's images of play, and of the expressive power of black children's letters to the world in chalk drawings and graffiti, hardly suggested a managerial or scandalized response to the ghetto and its inhabitants (figure 2.5).[27] Rather, he views Levitt as an artist of the camera who uses her instrument as a poetic and subjective means of expression, creating images that have the capacity to evoke infinite wonder.[28] As Wright recognized, Levitt's Harlem work insistently evaded doctrinaire readings of poverty and delinquency, framing the ghetto street as a site of dynamic social interaction, agency, and expressive power. In so doing, it significantly altered the documentary contract between photographer and subjects, and consequently between the documentary image—uncontrived and subjective rather than instrumental and objective—and its viewer.

Figure 2.4. Helen Levitt, Untitled. New York, 1942. © Helen Levitt. Courtesy of Laurence Miller Gallery, New York.

Far from a concession to the criminalization of African Americans, then, Wright's interest in Levitt's work signals an interest in the camera's power to body forth a provocative vitality, mystery, and evanescence. However powerfully *Native Son* indicts the journalistic camera for its reckless eyeballing or its power to reify black manhood as other-than-human, Wright continued, restively but consequentially, to experiment with modes of documentary imaging. By June 1942, he had achieved enough recognition as a proponent of socially conscious and site-based image making to be invited to speak at a symposium at the downtown "people's gallery," ACA (American Contemporary Artists), held in conjunction with an exhibition that included the work of Lisette Model, Paul Strand, and Berenice Abbott. Wright shared the platform at this event not only with established painters such as Fernand Leger and Marc Chagall but also with Abbott, Strand, and the influential photography critic Elizabeth McCausland.[29]

These forays attest not to a dogmatic commitment on Wright's part to social realist codes but to the lability of photographic stylistics and practices in the transition from New Deal to postwar cultural imperatives. Tracing the arc of Wright's engagements with the camera, we give new life to his career after *Native Son*, in which photo-text becomes a powerful resource in his struggle "to free himself from the burden" of its success, and a key agency in his later

Figure 2.5. Helen Levitt, Untitled. New York, ca. 1939. © Helen Levitt. Courtesy of Laurence Miller Gallery, New York.

efforts to reconstruct himself as a transnational intellectual.[30] Conversely, Wright's engagement with documentary practice alerts us to its power as a model for a broad array of writers, particularly African American writers, at this critical juncture. Given distinctive shape by his exposure to photographic, photo-textual, and documentary projects in—or, perhaps more accurately, via—Harlem, Wright's career in photographic looking evidences the varied stakes and stances toward the documentary image that develop in service of the midcentury writer and the novel.

"An Honest and Frontal View": *Black Voices* and the Photo-Text Genre

In July 1940, mere weeks after *Native Son* had exploded into print, Wright began a collaboration with the FSA photographer and bureaucrat Edwin Rosskam that resulted in the publication of *Twelve Million Black Voices: A Folk History of the Negro in the United States*. Wright was, it might fairly be said, in recovery from his meteoric fame as the author whose book had (at least according to the cultural gatekeeper Irving Howe) changed American culture forever; by the time *Black Voices* was published, nineteen months after *Native Son*, that novel and its author were still dominating op-ed columns, sociological conferences, and the literary field.[31] In one important sense, *Black Voices* suggests a certain continuity with the "Harlem Document" project. Rosskam, like Siskind, was a Jewish American (born in Germany to American parents, and therefore classified as an enemy alien during the First World War); he started his life as a painter and writer in the ambit of Gauguin, Hemingway, and Greenwich Village bohemia, and came to practice photojournalism—a term he is sometimes credited with coining—as a way of experimenting with what he called "a new unit" of "workmanship": neither "the writer's paragraph nor the pictorialist's composed rectangle" but "the double-page spread."[32] Rosskam had begun his career at the Photo League, whose modes of documentary production continued to influence him as a practicing photographer-editor; the driving imperative he brought to bear on his collaboration with Wright—to "create a book that couldn't be read quickly standing in a bookstore"—chimes with Siskind's interest in social mystery, at odds with Luce and *Life*'s ethos of instant legibility.[33] Whatever Rosskam's credentials as an innovative editor and even artist, Wright's collaboration, like that of Milton Smith before him, was predicated at least in part on his shrewd awareness that "it did not hurt a Black man to have Jewish friends and to be a Communist."[34] *Black Voices* can also be seen to mark the apogee of state-sponsored New Deal photography, the moment when naming images as the product of the FSA "of course is the same thing as saying that they are excellent."[35]

Wright and Rosskam's volume was hardly the first instance of a text attempting to couple archival images with enhanced reportage or testimony. A notable trend in photo-text book publication had been established by Bourke-White and Caldwell's *You Have Seen Their Faces* (1937), whose fictively framed account of black and white tenant farmers in the rural South had a surprising commercial success, spawning volumes such as Archibald MacLeish's *Land of the Free* (1938), a long poem accompanied by FSA photographs, extolling the national virtues; Sherwood Anderson's *Home Town* (1940), a nostalgic homage to small-town America (by the author of *Winesburg, Ohio*, no less) in counterpoint with FSA photographs also chosen by Rosskam; and Dorothea Lange and Paul Taylor's *An American Exodus* (1939), deliberately fashioned using Lange's FSA work to rebut the contrived reportage of *Faces*. So great was the prestige and expressive power, as well as the commercial viability, of documentary images at this moment that any number of notable writers scrambled to make published use of them.[36] But few managed the impact achieved by Wright, as the case of John Steinbeck attests. Having been approached in 1937 by Horace Bristol, one of the founding documentary photographers at *Life*, to provide copy for a photo-text project on Dust Bowl migrants to California's Central Valley, Steinbeck was dissatisfied with the constraints of the format; the text was retooled for use in his acclaimed *The Grapes of Wrath*, and its photos ended up being used as casting aids for John Ford's monumental 1940 film version of the novel.[37]

This instability of boundaries between art and commerce, the media and the state, typifies the social context for photo-text production, as critics of the genre have insisted. More to the point, however, is the kind of success Wright's text, and Wright, enjoyed (and in part resisted). *Black Voices* was published within months of James Agee and Walker Evan's iconic *Let Us Now Praise Famous Men*, and the contrast in the projects' initial lives is striking. The latter, now celebrated as a masterwork not only of Evans's career but of visual and literary modernism and documentary, was "dismally unsuccessful" when it appeared; it sold fewer than a scant one thousand copies, in comparison with some three hundred thousand copies of *Black Voices*.[38] The implied contrast in reader response was underscored by critics, who accounted Wright's stirring first-person collective voice—his "undying words and burning feeling and acid satire," his "elegant and belligerent" turns of phrase—a triumph for the ages and, even more important, for the moment.[39] In tune with Bourke-White and Caldwell's hortatory strains but pitched in a "Negro" key, *Black Voices* could be advertised as heir apparent to *Faces*: it was a volume that "ought to be pondered by American citizens," not in spite but because of the fact that it will be "not pleasant for us white folks who have airy offices in which to work, well-equipped homes to go to at night and a fine board at which to dine."[40] Against the anxiously self-implicating cast of Agee's text, Wright's offered up a documentary rendering of unimpeachable—because racialized—authenticity. As one on-air radio interviewer in 1941 gushed, "I know of no other book that brings home as clearly to the white reader what it means to be a Negro."[41]

Black Voices has been canonized as a text that performed just this historical function—that is, extended or applied the FSA documentary project to black experience from an African American point of view, and thereby contributed to the project of managing racial difference in service of American modernity.[42] No wonder, then, that the project has often been treated as a footnote to Wright's career, or that the volume has featured more prominently on the Web pages of eBay and Amazon than in the annals of literary scholarship.[43] In the received reading of Wright and black cultural production, *Black Voices* remains an incidental project, an activity wedged between the Mercury Theater's staging of *Native Son* on Broadway in 1941 and Wright's public denunciation of the Communist Party in 1942. At most, it would seem, *Black Voices* suggests a last-gasp attempt on Wright's part to make the rhetoric of the Party serve his ongoing social-realist, sociological commitments.

It is possible, however, to read *Black Voices* not as a dead end, a final emblem of the Party line or the flattening trend of state-sponsored documentary, but in an altogether different way: as the inaugural text of a powerful, underrecognized vector of literary—even self-consciously modernist—experimentation. For just as a host of U.S. writers and intellectuals would struggle to respond to, negotiate, and push beyond the model of *Native Son*, so did *Twelve Million Black Voices* inspire a fervent series of attempts to exploit the prestige of the photo-text genre, even while wresting its signifying possibilities out from under the imperatives of didacticism, liberal management, and documentary exposé. In the two decades following the publication of *Black Voices*, during which resonant changes were being rung on race and public culture in the United States and documentary was increasingly discredited as a truth-telling enterprise, the photo-text genre continued to attract writers and photographers as a potentially powerful mode of cross-disciplinary expression. Many if not most of these projects failed critically or commercially or even more fundamentally, in the sense that they never achieved publication. But the continuing allure of photo-text as a mode of trial, negotiation, and proof for cultural critics and artists of every disposition, throughout the turbulent 1940s and sobering 1950s and even burning 1960s, is striking.

For the writers I consider in subsequent chapters, all responding in some fashion to his monolithic influence and the cultural imperatives that shaped it, Wright's work in *Black Voices* crystallized with both clarity and edge the competing possibilities of photo-text. Despite the gathering associations between Wright and Chicago, his work was a singular vehicle for centering photo-text as an experimental form in the unstable, freighted matrix of Harlem, during a period of self-conscious cross-racial exchange and heightened cultural bravado. After Wright, in response to Wright, photo-text becomes a Harlem project, a Harlem genre and possibility. This is not, however, to say that it becomes a resolutely black or Afro-centric form. Quite the contrary: photo-text after Wright offers an opportunity, within Harlem and in response to the complex entanglement of black, white, and other presences there, for meditation not only on histories of racial engagement and violence but on the history of their imaging and representation. This brief period of experimentation constitutes an obscured chapter in the history of modernism's afterlife. Working in and through photo-text, key writers remake modernist tropes for use in novels focused on African American experience, and they import photography's developing aesthetic stances and understandings of their social meaning onto the literary field.

Paradoxically, these effects of *Twelve Million Black Voices* become fully visible only when we return to the formal concerns of photo-textuality as explored in Rosskam's favored signifying unit, the photographic spread. With respect to its format, *Black Voices* both recalls and rejects key aspects of *You Have Seen Their Faces*. Subtitling the text *A Folk History of the Negro in the United States*, Wright divided it into four sections tracing the arc of black experience: abduction from Africa, the Middle Passage, and slavery in the early Republic; the hardening plantation system, westward expansion, war, and Reconstruction; the Great Migration and urbanization; and the industrial (soon to be postindustrial) present. Like Caldwell's, Wright's narrative is interspersed with captioned individual photos and small portfolios of images suggestive of critical arcs. Scholars often note the distinctive thrust generated by Wright's Marxist teleology, and by his magisterial use of the first person plural and the cadences of exhortation ("We millions of black folk who live in this land were born into Western civilization of a weird and paradoxical birth"; "Our humanity, however, did not save us").[44] But Wright and Rosskam's project distinguished itself in other, equally important ways from its predecessor, not least in its qualities as a physical object. Notably, it was not printed oversized, as were *Faces* and many of the photo-texts it inspired, but to standard dimensions. Its modest 6 3/4 × 10 inch trim size afforded tight layouts as well as opportunities for close cropping, dramatic alignment of photos and text, and effective use of borderless (full-page bleed) images.[45] The volume's specs may have been dictated in part by accounting concerns (in spite of a more costly photo-reproduction process, its size kept the volume's price down to a relatively affordable three dollars per copy, which helped boost sales), but they also dovetailed with Wright's aspirations.[46] The look and feel of the volume bespoke a certain intimacy of encounter, opposing a widening drift toward sensational imaging and the commercialization of trauma.

Even in its physical properties, then, *Black Voices* evidences the tensions inherent in photo-text conventions, and Wright's adherence to reigning documentary codes. Like *Native Son*, *Black Voices* is the product of practices rooted in leftist muckraking, ethnographic analysis, and documentary stylistics. Wright's insistence on sociological fact-finding; his investigation of black working-class life during a stint as a funeral insurer in Chicago, his extensive use of the Cayton-Warner research file, his diligent study of journalistic sources (collected in such numbers that newspaper clippings littered the floor of his Harlem bedroom), and his detailed interviews with representative laborers:

these procedures of documentation were so crucial to Wright's generation of literary narrative that fellow novelist Margaret Walker described his process as essentially a form of "reportage."[47] Responding purposively to *You Have Seen Their Faces*, and representing his work on the project as a WPA-style commission, Wright imagined himself trumping Caldwell and Bourke-White's documentary renderings of the black South with his own: he explicitly envisioned *Black Voices* as "such a book solely about black people."[48]

More to the point, Wright conceived of the photo-text enterprise in a recognizably instrumentalist way, as requiring certain visual elements to produce specific desired effects. When the body of FSA prints made available for his review at the Historical Section's Washington, DC, offices by Rosskam—more than nine thousand—failed to yield an image Wright anticipated for the volume's visual sequence, he took up his camera and produced it himself: a shot of a for-rent placard advertising rooms "Just Open to Colored" in a carefully chosen Brooklyn slum.[49] His production of the image attests to Wright's engagement with photographs as documentary evidence. But it also marks the extent to which Wright continued to work as a documentary outsider, even in the South Side Chicago with which he has become so closely identified. His status as such is sharply clarified in the record of his attempts to scout locations for images for *Black Voices*. When Wright, trailing the glory of his success with *Native Son*, asked his South Side friend John Gray to help him locate some "very poor black neighborhoods and places" to photograph for the project, Gray responded, "'Go home nigger, go home.'"[50] The dual interests Gray thereby dismisses, in photography as a kind of method and in the documentary stance, are themselves eloquently recorded in a photograph staged during a photo session Wright conducted on the South Side (figure 2.6). Making Wright's activities themselves a subject of documentary interest, the image indexes his concern with the authorial legitimacy afforded by his photo-text work.[51] In the end, however successful Wright's evocation of the folk history of black America, however convincing his adoption of a choric first-person plural voice, both were generated not (or not only) as the organic outgrowth of lived experience but via the mediating practices of documentary contact.

These links with documentary practice, and FSA image making in particular, make all the more notable Wright's departures from their logic. Meditating on the example of *You Have Seen Their Faces*, Wright exploits the occasion of photo-text production to develop an idiom of looking, observation, and witnessing that specifically addresses the history of black Americans. In so doing, he begins to undercut photo-text's conventional didacticism in favor of more nuanced meditation on the possibilities of the medium. From his prefatory

Figure 2.6. Photographer unknown, Untitled [Richard Wright on a Photo Shoot], Chicago, 1940. Yale Collection of American Literature, Beinecke Rare Book and Manuscript Library. © 1940 Richard Wright. Reprinted by permission of John Hawkin & Associates, Inc.

remarks in the volume through its historical arc and climactic moments, we can trace the uneven, suggestive uses Wright makes both of the photo-text enterprise, affording opportunities for productive friction between images and text, and of the rhetoric and realities of looking in the context of U.S. racial history.

Initially, at least, in his foreword to the volume, Wright offers a classic statement of documentary intention. Commenting on his provocative decision to suppress the experience of the Talented Tenth in favor of a history of "the humble folk," he asserts that "it is not . . . to celebrate or exalt [their] plight" but rather "to seize upon that which is qualitative and abiding in Negro experience, to place within full and constant view the collective humanity" (5–6). Camera and text in twain will serve, mutatis mutandis, as instruments of exposure, making steadily visible the lived truth of "the broad masses in their costly and tortuous upstream journey" (6). But Wright's interest in visibility as a form of racial history—a crucial trope for later entrants onto the field of photo-text—is also emphasized from his opening address to the reader. Chapter 1, titled "Our Strange Birth," begins with an implicit argument for the documentary gaze as a social remedy that will alleviate the harm of collective (white) blindness: "Each day when you see us black folks upon the dusty land of the farms or upon the hard pavement of the city streets, you usually take us for granted and think you know us, but our history is far stranger than you suspect, and we are not what we seem" (10). By contrast, the look of the documentary witness and photographic observer goes deep, all the way down, "beneath the garb" and the mask, probing the "uneasily tied knot of pain and hope" in which the nation's past and future alike are entangled (11).

The rhetoric of depth is virtually reflexive to photo-text narrative of the New Deal era; here, it acquires a Marxist spin as Wright's narrative unfolds. His rendering of the effects of class domination and false consciousness increasingly becomes a matter of impaired vision: "spli[t] . . . up into groups and classes," "whole segments of populations" are "so influenced by their material surroundings that they see but a little phase of the complex process of their lives and the whole is obscured from them"(24). Yet the DuBoisian linkage of second sight and double consciousness is always within view. Consciousness, false or otherwise, is also colored by racial history, and Wright's black folk have the dubious advantage over their white counterparts and antagonists of a certain insight, since no gesture, not even the slightest or most private, is ultimately free: "Before we black folk can move, we must first look into the white man's mind to see what is there, to see what he is thinking" (35). From plantation to factory, under the "Bosses of the Buildings" as under the "Lords of the Land," both group history and survival are contingent on the exercise of "our observing Negro eyes" (102).

This reprisal of familiar DuBoisian themes in a Marxist key becomes a running commentary on the procedures of photo-text, at least as practiced by Bourke-White and Caldwell. Allegorizing the relation between black and white sharecroppers kept fatally divided by the Lords of the Land as an exchange of hostile gazes, Wright makes the play between white "faces" and black looking emblematic:

> Sometimes, fleetingly, like a rainbow that comes and vanishes in its coming, the wan faces of the poor whites make us think that perhaps we can join our hands with them and lift the weight of the Lords of the Land off our backs. But, before new meanings can bridge the chasm that has been long created between us, the poor whites are warned by the Lords of the Land that they must cast their destiny with their own color, that to make common cause with us is to threaten the foundations of civilization. Fear breeds in our hearts until each poor white face begins to look like the face of an enemy soldier. We learn that almost all white men feel it is their duty to see that we do not go beyond the prescribed boundaries. And so both of us, the poor black and the poor white, are kept poor, and only the Lords of the Land grow rich. (46)

We have seen *their* faces, Wright wryly suggests, and the effect is catastrophic. There is no covenant here, under the sign of the rainbow, with the Lords of the Land. Rather, segregation itself functions to bind black and white workers in an unholy fashion: at the crossroads of industrialization, both "stay fixed in attitudes of opposition, as though" the code of the South "had waved a magic wand and cast a spell upon us, a spell from which we cannot awaken" (47). (It is "only through a heroic effort of will," presumably known as revolutionary socialism, that "either of us can cast off this spell" [122].) The living subjects of "Queen Cotton" have been reified, figuratively and literally, as photographic subjects. Trapped—much like the sharecroppers of Bourke-White's *Faces*—in postures of terror, submission, and brutality, they are frozen in atavistic tableaux from which no yearning for modernity can lend them means to escape.

Wright's use of the collective voice, the eponymous subject of the text, extends and explores this local insight. He fashions a subject that simultaneously observes, bears witness, and remarks its own condition as an object of the documentary gaze. This rendering of the black underclass comports respectfully with the then-going Party line, gesturing as it does toward the ripeness of workers for political awakening and the status of black Americans as a nation within the nation.[52] But Wright's collective voice also registers the problematic history of photo-text as an instrument of racial representation and feeling, and probes the possibilities of the genre for reversing its own effects— that is, for generating depth, forestalling managerial imperatives, and deepening the mystery of encounter with the very "folk" it tended to patronize.

Nowhere does *Black Voices* make Wright's self-consciousness about this possibility clearer than in the use of key image-text pairings. Admittedly, a certain number of the volume's photographs (at least as viewed in retrospect) serve the function of documentary illustration. Shots depicting "the black maid," "the black industrial worker," and folk spiritual practices essentially confirm Wright's narrative story line, providing visual evidence of the effects of systematic oppression under Queen Cotton and beyond. Even some of the text's more self-conscious images ultimately function to confirm the status of black workers, in a favored phrase of Wright's, as modernity's "tools"—for example, Jack Delano's shot of a white-jacketed waiter, calibrated to emphasize his gesture of obeisance to a white patron (22), or Marion Post Wolcott's image of workers stooping in a cabbage field, neither fully individuated nor framed so as to convey fully the reality of their labor as such (82). White cotton traders, straw bosses, and cops; endless fields of cotton in all their terrible beauty; decrepit tenements; dignified black labor and life-affirming black folk cultures: throughout, the reader encounters images that function as illustrations (no more, no less) of key tropes and highlighted practices.

But we also encounter marriages of text and image that are artfully orchestrated, freed from the imperatives of illustration to do more complex work. On the introductory page of section 2, titled "Inheritors of Slavery" (29), appears a shot by Delano of a preacher and his wife at their home in Heard County, Georgia, seated beneath photographic portraits of themselves made twenty years previously (figure 2.7). Within *Black Voices* and the FSA archive, the image is remarkable in several ways. Unlike the vast majority of portraits of sharecroppers, migrant workers, rehabilitation clients, and the rural dispossessed (particularly African Americans), this one features subjects fully inhabiting a space that evades the FSA iconography of the shack, cabin, or hovel. In distinct contrast to the domiciles of Wolcott's North Carolina farmers, Russell Lee's Missouri sharecroppers, and Dorothea Lange's Mississippi Delta subjects (figure 2.8), this space is offered up by the camera as a home, impressed by the specific histories of its occupants; its plank walls are tight, neatly trimmed, and adorned with aesthetic objects. Although the original negative shows that both subjects wear boots that are frayed, split, and heavily patched, the image has been cropped to suppress this detail. Their clothing is utilitarian but also whole; the woman's dress sports decorative stitching and cutwork, and the man's overalls appear

Figure 2.7. Jack Delano, Negro Preacher and His Wife Sitting under Photos of Them Taken Twenty Years Ago, Heard County, Georgia, 1941. Farm Security Administration/Office of War Information Collection, Library of Congress.

Figure 2.8. Dorothea Lange, Sharecropper's Cabin and Sharecropper's Wife, Ten Miles South of Jackson, Mississippi, 1937. Farm Security Administration/Office of War Information Collection, Library of Congress.

relatively new. The pair of keys the woman wears on a string around her neck, which initially appears to be a necklace, suggests ownership, responsibility, some relationship to bourgeois property. As used in the sequence of *Black Voices*, the image engages with—enhances—the dignity of its subjects by proposing not their difference from but their likeness to the viewer, presumably examining this very work of photo-text in the comfort of a bourgeois home.

Not until the viewer looks more closely does he or she observe the distinctive shape—and perhaps disfigurement—of the man's left hand, whose index finger appears to be missing or folded in painfully arthritic fashion onto his palm. Like other images marking the impress of labor or violence on human bodies—Evans's luminescent portraits of furrowed faces and Delano's and Lange's close-ups of workers' hands come readily to mind (figure 2.9)—this one creates a delicate balance between the vulnerability and the earned gravitas of its subjects. But it does so in large part by posing those subjects, or allowing them to pose themselves, in dialogue with their own images. Most striking is the visible gap in presentation between the couple in the foreground and their earlier photographs above: in the latter, the woman's lace collar, the man's

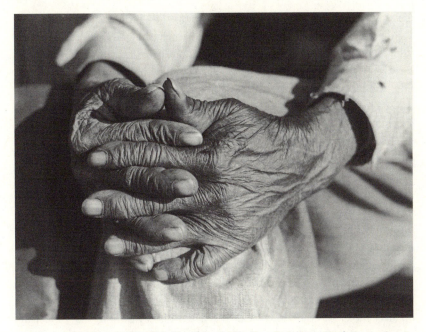

Figure 2.9. Jack Delano, Hands of Mr. Henry Brooks, Ex-Slave, Parks Ferry Road, Greene County, Georgia, 1941. Farm Security Administration/Office of War Information Collection, Library of Congress.

neat suit and tie, bespeak better times, at what would historically have been the epoch of the Great Migration and the New Negro Renaissance. Could they have been beneficiaries of the tenet of uplift, only to find themselves betrayed or deserted by it? What place might New Negroes as such have had in the Old South? At the very least, the framed portraits suggest, this couple had the economic wherewithal to command satisfying self-representations, under conditions presumably quite different from those obtaining here.

In the context of the FSA project, the disparity between the sets of portraits might well read as an object lesson in the common fate of all Americans, or at least the vast numbers of forgotten men in the grip of the Depression. Within *Black Voices*, however, the image is overstruck with the caption "Inheritors of Slavery," and so the represented gap between past and present resonates more roundly. Unlike the majority of iconic FSA images of suffering, heroic, and devastated black folk, this combination of image and text gives back to the represented subjects their own experience of temporal duration; it restores them to the ebb and flow of felt, rather than merely quantifiable, loss and change. Thus rendered, the subjects of the image can function as something other than illustrative figures. Their presence here, as framed by Wright, counters precisely the documentary tendency he has already named, the one that "fixe[s]" black subjects within an atavistic, irremediably distant past (47). Situated within history, yet beyond the reach of any obvious narrative about trauma or rehabilitation, the black preacher and his wife join Wright in posing the question addressed by *Black Voices* itself: how might black Americans, inheritors of slavery and inhabitants of the now, undertake the creation of a usable past?

The use of the double portrait, as here captioned, thus turns the power of photo-text back onto itself. If *Black Voices* achieves this gesture only fitfully, it nonetheless opens possibilities that later practitioners of photo-text would develop more fully. Its success on this score here must be credited largely to the way Delano predicates his image on frontality, as emphasized by the two uncannily linked pairs of gazes trained directly on the viewer. Even within the increasingly varied FSA canon, the choice of frontality often bore the baggage of didacticism, framing the returned gaze of the subject as an admission of abjection, or a performance for the presumed viewer of the racial and regional picturesque. In negotiating the relations of images to the text, with its emphasis on black looking as the source of an alternative history of American modernity and of its coming-into-being, Wright and Rosskam make careful use of images featuring frontal gazes. At their most suggestive, these choices foreground—if not create—a dialectical play between black subjects and white photographers, between instrumental contexts and radical or experimental aims.

A powerful example is the use made in *Black Voices* of an image by Ben Shahn featuring cotton pickers on the Alexander Plantation in Pulaski County, Arkansas (figure 2.10). Like Aaron Siskind, Shahn was a product of the Jewish Lower East Side and a latecomer to photography; his images in the FSA canon are often read as resistant to easy assimilation in progressive or radical projects. This may be so because, as Nicholas Natanson has argued, Shahn's FSA work often emphasizes the mystery of human being in labor regimes. Eschewing "such obvious marks of injustice as gnarled hands, worn kneepads, battered shoes, and desperate faces," Shahn focuses instead on individualizing distinctions in mood, attire, and stance, made manifest in the landscapes and moments anterior to or separate from the act of labor itself.[53] Deliberately shot in settings that speak obliquely to the FSA's list of "Recommended Shooting Subjects" (which included abandoned farms, rehabilitation camps, steel mills, and company towns), Shahn's images evade both instrumental and sentimental readings.[54] Against the grain of liberal exposés that urge viewers to pious sympathy or the tacit acceptance of managerial aims, Shahn insists on the

Figure 2.10. Ben Shahn, Cotton Pickers, Pulaski County Arkansas, as published in *Twelve Million Black Voices*, 34.

multiple, nuanced, profoundly intimate responses of his subjects, both to the circumstances of their labor and to the presence of the camera.

This trademark rendering of subjects neither as undifferentiated masses nor as a unified collective but as "*alone* together" owes much to Shahn's use of the famously unobtrusive Leica, further equipped by him with an angle finder, a device that allowed him to shoot subjects frontally without direct contact.[55] Shahn himself remarked that this practice suited him because it "t[ook] away any self-consciousness" his subjects might have felt.[56] But the visible effects of Shahn's working mode seem more mixed than he allows. If some of his subjects seem unaware of the camera's presence, others appear to note it keenly, and with striking results. In "Cotton Pickers," the three subjects caught at the middle distance in the foreground all confront the camera directly, with attitudes ranging from wary to hostile. The man on the left, his parted fingers lifted to his mouth for a drag on his cigarette, appears to study Shahn's camera (if not its user) with cool deliberation; the woman, poised as if in the act of shouldering her picker's bag, looks back with the heightened self-protective gaze Walter Benjamin identifies as a hallmark of modern, traumatophilic subjectivity. "Self-consciousness" is hardly an issue for these subjects—indeed, quite the reverse. Indeed, the meaning of the image resides in the fact that they are unified not by their status as laborers or victims of the cotton system, but by their steady refusal either to compose themselves for Shahn's camera or to look away. Shahn's mode of documentation generates a response to the protocol of photographic stealth; to his credit, he makes that response inseparable from the specific social circumstances—plantation system, white control of black labor power, freighted modes of documentary looking—in which the image was obtained.

Wright and Rosskam employ a certain stealth of their own, importing Shahn's image into a textual context that heightens the power of the subjects' looks back. To begin with, the shot is decisively cropped; the version published in *Black Voices* excludes the woman standing in the right foreground and the woman seated at a distance behind her, gazing out of the frame (compare the uncropped version in figure 2.11). Focusing more tightly on the three figures who remain—the man and woman, foreground, and the figure seated in the background against the barn wall, his face shadowed by a dark cap—the cropped image intensifies the effect of their response. Paradoxically, the reduction in its number of subjects heightens the image's power of suggestion. The presence of the seated man disrupts a reading of the figures in the foreground as a couple, while the relative positions and stances of the three make it difficult for the viewer to assimilate them as interchangeable hands or "tools."

With respect to Wright's text, this effect seems quite intentional. The image is placed in the midst of one of the most often-cited passages of *Black Voices*—and one over which, manuscript evidence suggests, its author labored strenuously: a paean to the landscape of the South.[57] In an extended lyrical turn, Wright limns the beauty of "our southern springs," when "apple buds laugh into blossom" and "sunflowers nod in the hot fields"; the heady summers when "magnolia trees fill the countryside with sweet scent for long miles"; the autumn land "afire with color," with the sky "full of wild geese winging ever southward" and night winds that "blow free"; and even winter, with its "leaden

Figure 2.11. Ben Shahn, Cotton Pickers, Pulaski County, Arkansas, 1935 (uncropped). Farm Security Administration/Office of War Information Collection, Library of Congress.

days of cold" and the "snap and crack"—still, surely, monitory for black South-erners—of "the guns of hunters" (32):

> Long days of rain come, and our swollen creeks rush to join a hundred rivers that wash across the land and make great harbors where they feed the gulf or the sea. Occasionally the rivers leap their banks and leave new thick layers of silt to enrich the earth, and then the look of the land is garish, bleak, suffused with a first-day stillness, strangeness, and awe. (33–34)

It is at this juncture that the reader encounters the cropped image of the cotton-pickers. What is at stake is surely not "the look of the land" as a poetic object but the returned gaze of those who work it. Just beneath the image, functioning in effect as its caption, appears the ostensible conclusion to Wright's homage to Southern nature: "But whether in spring or summer or autumn or winter, time slips past us remorselessly, and it is hard to tell of the iron that lies beneath the surface of our quiet, dull days" (34). The combination of text and image produces a resounding reversal of effect. Far from oppressed, noble, even dig-nified "tillers of the soil" (31), the subjects of Wright and Rosskam's photo-text embody "the iron that lies beneath the surface"; if not menacing, they bespeak an incipient will to modernity and to power. Thus inserted into the narrative, the subjects of the image gesture ahead to a stark pronouncement,

Figure 2.12. Edwin Rosskam, Children in Front of "Kitchenette" Apartment, Black Belt, Chicago, 1941. Farm Security Administration/Office of War Information Collection, Library of Congress.

writ via a sudden shift into the ambiguous second-person: "If [black Americans] act at all, it is either to flee or to kill; you are either a victim or a rebel" (57). *Awe* might well name the cumulative effect on the reader, who recognizes that, existentially speaking, there are no victims here.

In such canny uses of photo-text, Wright and Rosskam inaugurate a crucial transformation from the effects of FSA frontal camera work to conveyance of what Wright calls "the honest and frontal vision" of black subjects themselves (130). Paradoxically, this shift is achieved in part through the use of the very methods—selective attention, tendentious framing—that make FSA images so susceptible to hermeneutic suspicion throughout their afterlife. A key example is *Black Voices'* use of an image made by Rosskam himself (137), featuring a young boy in a group of children outside an apartment house in a notorious section of Chicago's Black Belt—the kind for which Wright had been actively searching (figure 2.12). Shot in a sequence of portraits of children on the street, framed in postures of boredom, physical privation, or constraint, Rosskam's photo was originally intended for inclusion in a series on the stunting effects of the kitchenette, the quintessential slum space created through aggressive subdivision of existing housing stock, rented by white owners at highly inflated rates and often devoid of even the meanest amenities.[58]

In a passage that became a kind of mantra in sociological as well as literary circles, one that flaunts its ancestry in the progressivist screeds of Jacob Riis, Wright waxes thunderous on the lived reality of the kitchenette: it is "our prison, our death sentence without a trial, the new form of mob violence that assaults not only the lone individual, but all of us, in its ceaseless attacks" (106). "With its filth and foul air, with its one toilet for thirty or more tenants," life there "kills our black babies so fast that in many cities twice as many of them die as white babies" (106): the kitchenette is "the funnel through which our pulverized bodies flow to ruin and death on the city pavements, at a profit" (111). Interspersed with this jeremiad is a series of images: a filthy shared toilet; decrepit interiors in which sleeping bodies lie inert like so much discarded rubbish; families posed, child after child, around battered tables empty of food, or in rooms crowded with worn and dirty objects. What, we might ask, does Rosskam's portrait of the young boy have to do with the hortatory intention of this sequence? Posed or caught leaning against an iron post, whose decorative motif gestures toward formalist ordering and the power of craft, the boy's arm is angularly crooked, his fist athwart his hip; he has adopted what Alan Trachtenberg identifies as the classic "distant gaze" of ennobling portraiture.[59] Thus composed, the subject embodies an agency and a resistance to type that ill suit the tenor of the accompanying narrative.

No wonder that Wright and Rosskam choose to insert this image in the closing section of the chapter, gesturing toward an unseen future from which "no voice of ours can call" the children of the city "back," and in which "our time"—that of the subjects of the Great Migration—"is nearing its end" (136). So placed, Rosskam's image functions as testimony to the power with which black youth (particularly black manhood), poised on the threshold of adulthood and modernity alike, constitutes a defining challenge for the nation. Underneath the image, Wright's caption proclaims: "Strange moods fill our children" (137). Both the strangeness and the moodiness suggest that the offspring of black "folk" have become exemplary city dwellers: mobile, restive, searching figures of lyrical desire, instinctively responsive to the streets "with their noise and flaring lights" (136). From their parents, whose "tired eyes turn away" from "the tumult," these new urban subjects are distinguishable by the practiced use of their very different, "impatient eyes" (137). Such strangeness and impatience have additional resonances, however, as the text set on the facing page suggests:

As our jobs begin to fail in another depression, our lives and the lives of our children grow so frightful that even some of our educated black leaders are afraid to make known to the nation how we exist. They bec[o]me ashamed of us and tell us to hide our wounds. And many white people who know how we live are afraid of us, fearing that we may rise up against them. (136)

Not yet adolescent—that is to say, not yet readable as an incipient Bigger Thomas—the child in Rosskam's photo is made by its context to occupy a curious space between victimage and threat. His deliberative stance, strikingly conjoined with the meditative quality of his gaze, places him beyond the reach of patronage, rehabilitation, and uplift alike. The burden of the image as invoked in context is the boy's existential self-consciousness, the somehow distinctive yet exemplary quality of his aloneness.

Wright here exploits the instability of photo-text to catalyze the transformation of black subjects of FSA work as subjects of modernity, seeking not state-sponsored "relief" so much as release from the conditions of their estrangement. In so doing, he also poses a particular interpretive problem for the reader. The tension created by the interplay of image and narrative—implying, on the one hand, noble black sufferance and, on the other, militant embrace of "battle" (136)—can only be resolved through the reader's identification with the child, as he is made to embody a singularly modern longing for individuation and meaningful social recognition. Poised between childhood and adolescence, framed as a black boy rather than a native son, the subject of Rosskam's portrait embodies not the fact of blighted innocence, or even the inevitability of his own future desolation, but a reflexive, affective capacity whose denial or waste bodes ill for the modern nation.

Wright's use of Rosskam's image is ultimately designed to prepare the reader for the predictive rhetoric of the text's concluding section, titled "Men in the Making." There, Wright proclaims that, at "the very center of the most complex and highly industrialized civilization the world has ever known, [black Americans] stand today with a consciousness and memory such as few people possess" (146). The recognition of these faculties is vital to the nation's destiny in the American century: "If we had been allowed to participate in the vital processes of America's national growth, what would have been the texture of our lives, the pattern of our traditions, the routine of our customs, the state of our arts, the code of our laws, the function of our government!" (145). Somewhere in the midst of this list—which notably recalls Henry James's account, in his 1879 study of Nathaniel Hawthorne, of the failings of nineteenth-century America—the first-person plural pronoun ceases to refer to the "inheritors of slavery" and firmly implicates all Americans. The reader, Wright suggests, ignores the crisis of such a subject as Rosskam's at the nation's peril.

Workers' revolution, racial uprising, the failure of industrial progress in its own terms: whatever the specific disaster, it will be averted only by an honest and frontal "look into the mirror of our consciousness," where America "will see" not the faces of its others but itself, "the *living* past" with which it must inevitably reckon (146, italics original).

The exhortatory quality, even threat, conveyed by the closing sequence of images and text was hardly lost on the volume's readers. The FBI began investigating Wright in early 1943, based on the assessment that *Black Voices* was "responsible for serious violations of law and order in all parts of the country," that it linked up "with one of the most dangerous appeals to racial dissension of alien origin" (i.e., radical socialism) and was thereby "treasonable."[60] What the Feds' risibly narrow reading missed, among other things, was the text's uneasy oscillation between revolutionary fervor and plangent cross-racial appeal. Like the Communist Party line he would soon disavow, Wright's narrative conspicuously defers on the issue of race to continuities and analogies rather than radical ruptures. In the context of post-Depression, and then wartime, exigencies, "the differences between black folk and white folk are not blood or color, and the ties that bind us are deeper than those that separate us. The common road of hope which we all have traveled has brought us into a stronger kinship" (146). At the text's conclusion, the idiom of communism may be vitiated, but it serves as a vehicle for Wright's continuing investments in shared endeavors across color lines. If the platform of the left had already revealed itself to Wright to be irremediably flawed on this score, the procedures and techniques of photo-text were nonetheless available to experiment with new modes of collaboration and address. It is the genre itself, rather than Party rhetoric, that bears the weight of Wright's effort to sustain confidence in the possibility of cross-racial enterprise. To that enterprise, neither workers' consciousness in the industrial North, nor recent labor and activist history, but rather *Black Voices* itself stands as the most plausible and eloquent testimony. Photo-text, in Wright's hands, thus becomes—after the New Deal, after the Popular Front, in the teeth of war abroad and rising racial violence at home— both an aesthetic model and a mode of social practice.

This dual investment is what *Black Voices* bequeaths to writers in its wake. Wright's photo-text work set two linked precedents. It offered key images, hijacked from the notoriously instrumental context of state rehabilitation, of black subjects such as Rosskam's young boy in existential guise. If they remain irreparably marginal figures, their condition of dispossession implicates more than disciplinary sociological debate. Exemplars of modernity, they become embodiments of a crisis of recognition—outsiders whose race or color is at once definitive and ancillary to their predicament, less than fully causal yet singularly revealing.[61] Along the way, *Black Voices* highlighted tropes of visuality that would lend themselves, in developing literary contexts, to more-pointed explorations of social and existential visibility. Without Wright's photo-text example, neither Ellison's *Invisible Man* nor Baldwin's lacerating explorations of color as psyche would have been possible in their achieved forms. It is not only, in other words, the "Negro migrant" at the center of *Black Voices* but Wright himself who is "a man on the frontier of contact."[62] Both his investments in photo-text and the modes of his engagement with its practices would be critical precedents for at least two decades to come. But they would first serve as precedents for Wright himself, in his own on-going struggle for a writing life and a cultural afterlife. In his post-1940s self-fashioning as a globalist, an uneasy pan-Africanist, and a transnational intellectual, photography would continue to play a critical role.

"A Howl of Black Laughter": *Black Power* and the Ends of Documentary

In March 1956, Ben Burns—former executive editor of *Ebony* magazine, editor of the *Chicago Defender*, and the only white journalist of the postwar moment to devote his career to work in black-owned media—launched an attack on Richard Wright as the doyen of expatriate African American writers. Wright had produced an article for *Ebony* (which it rejected) titled "I Choose Exile," which reaffirmed his commitment to representation of "the facts of Negro life in America"—themselves, he noted dryly, "a kind of anti-American propaganda" in the context of the intensifying cold war.[63] Inflamed by this commitment, Burns singles out "I Choose Exile" as exemplary of a "hate school of literature" propounded by self-important "expatriates at sidewalk cafés." For Burns, Wright's "venom" is particularly infectious because it has so thoroughly "poison[ed] European thinking about racial problems in America."[64]

Such screeds, even by former friends, were hardly unfamiliar to Wright, who had refashioned himself as an African American outsider in exile from Harlem and the cold war era United States. What makes Burns's denunciation singular is its linking of Wright's defection as literary figure and black intellectual with the work of Langston Hughes's onetime fellow traveler, Henri Cartier-Bresson. During his stint at *Ebony* in Chicago, Burns recounts, he accompanied the roving photographer, with his "caseful of Leicas," on a postwar photographic tour of the South Side; eager to show off the "wonderful new housing projects"

Figure 2.13. Henri Cartier-Bresson, Harlem, 1947. Magnum Photos.

and "remarkable Negro business establishments," Burns is distinctly miffed when Cartier-Bresson inquires, "Where are the slums?"[65] Cartier-Bresson errs, in Burns's view, in stressing the familiar iconography of racial poverty and segregation rather than the march of liberal progress: the photographer "went wild with elation . . . in alleys and streets shooting at patched-up back porches, a black lad climbing over a back fence, a dog foraging in a pile of garbage"; at a funeral, "his camera focused on weeping women rather than on the plush buildings of a million-dollar Negro business."[66] This putatively blinkered realism—which produces "not a fair picture"—frames Burns's claims for Wright's promotion of "warped and prejudiced views about American Negroes."[67]

Presumptions about petit bourgeois success aside, there is something decisively wrong with this picture. The images Cartier-Bresson made on the South Side, and for that matter during a similar foray into Harlem in the same year, are hardly the "hackneyed portrait of tenement idlers" that Burns describes.[68] Among them, a characteristic shot of three men on a Harlem street (figure 2.13) exploits the physical architecture of the ghetto setting—note the strong horizontals created by the building's facade, the window frame, and the chain-link fence—to explore the shared solitude with which its subjects inhabit their life-world; the very proximity of the elderly man in the window to the pair of younger men seated beneath it only serves to emphasize the psychic distance

Figure 2.14. Henri Cartier-Bresson, Chicago, 1947. Magnum Photos.

between generations, forms of migration or mobility, and histories of labor. By contrast, the image of a man reading job postings in an unemployment office achieves its effect not through predictable framing or even compositional excess of the kind Burns implies, but through austerity (figure 2.14). Marshaling stark background, uneven figure placement, and evocative lighting, it transforms the raw materials of "hackneyed" photojournalism—unemployed African American man, desperate to maintain his status as provider for a vulnerable daughter—into a contemplative tableau, a meditation on the complex fashion in which hard social facts mediate intimate relations. In their evasion of predictable iconicity and didacticism, Cartier-Bresson's "slum" images typify his work and its underlying premise, summed up in the title of his widely celebrated 1952 volume, *The Decisive Moment*. Embracing the camera as an instrument of epiphanic "recognition," Cartier-Bresson argued that its images can be made to articulate "the significance of an event" precisely as they achieve a "precise organization of forms which give that event its proper expression."[69]

In linking Wright with Cartier-Bresson, Burns unintentionally provides a frame for reading Wright's ongoing interests in documentary photography— and in particular, Wright's return to the camera, as a producer of images, in the culminating project of his career. *The Decisive Moment* implicitly argues for the documentary street photograph as a mode of representation that braids modernist significant form with concern for social practices and "significance." Fifteen years after the publication of *Black Voices*, Wright continues to struggle with his own version of these twinned preoccupations; he does so in the context of what has been widely described as a postcolonial or transnational turn in his subject matter and cultural stance. Just as his engagements with documentary photography stake Wright's attempt to create a collective African American voice, they vigorously shape his self-representation as African American writer and intellectual in an emergently postcolonial context. Paradoxically, Wright's very inability fully to reject the presumptions and stances of FSA-rooted documentary enables him to achieve the most complex dialectical expression of his aesthetic and social commitments. After his painful trials of novelistic existentialism during the 1950s (which were roundly criticized by other black writers, politely evaded by the critical establishment, and almost wholly shunned by readers), Wright's heightened self-consciousness about his own relations to camera work became structural to his project. The expression of that self-consciousness, which marks his attempt to achieve a Bressonesque resolution of expressive and social aims, is what powers *Black Power*.

In the summer of 1953, Wright undertook a ten-week visit to the Gold Coast to witness firsthand the activities of Kwame Nkrumah's Convention People's Party, then campaigning for independence from British rule (achieved in 1957, when Ghana became the first postcolonial African state). The resulting text, *Black Power: A Record of Reactions in a Land of Pathos* (1954), was the first in a series of nonfiction accounts—at once travelogues, ethnographies, and political commentaries—that comprised the final turn in Wright's career.[70] In its avowed interest in probing Wright's own stance as witness and observer, *Black Power* was hardly uncontroversial; it may even be safe to call it the most roundly reviled of all his texts.[71] The controversy turns on Wright's sustained strategy of self-differentiation from the Africans he observes. Choosing as his initial epigraph Countee Cullen's ambivalent query, "*What is Africa to me?*" and opening the text with a profession of his own radical skepticism about any knowledge of Africa "on the basis of a common 'racial' heritage" (4), Wright insists on his overdetermined status as what he would elsewhere famously call "the lonely outside[r]"—to Africa as a Western intellectual; to America and the West as a black man; to "racial" logic as a writer embarking on a quest not for identity but for self-knowledge.[72] Far from the empowering heritage tours enacted by latter-day black intellectuals such as Maya Angelou and Henry Louis Gates, Wright's journey is explicitly framed as a mode of testing his own authorial procedures and aims. The naturalist inflections and positivist methodology of *Native Son*, as well as the more lyrical or existential gestures of *Black Voices* and later novels such as *The Outsider*, will be turned to account not only (or even primarily) for Gold Coast Africans in their social context but for Wright himself in the stance of documentary observer. Testing the power of his favored modes of observation, which were forged in the press of New Deal and postwar concerns, *Black Power* may profitably be read not as an outbreak of new designs on Wright's part but as an attempt to make the constellation of his documentary interests serve changing contexts for the work and cultural authority of black intellectuals.

Numerous readers have noted the insistence with which Wright declares his status as outsider to Africa, confronting cultures, people, and landscapes that remain utterly "foreign," "bewildering," resistant to his circuitous attempts "to look, to know, to be shown everything" (68).[73] More to the point, Wright persists in embracing his status as "a stranger, a foreigner," someone who "must be spoken to cautiously, with weighed words" (112). In spite of the confident prediction of a prominent African intellectual and colleague that he will "*feel* his race," Wright remains firmly committed to representing and assessing the absence of such feeling (241). In its place he sustains "a mild sense of panic, an oppressive"—and productive—"burden of alertness" (44). In fact, the narrative of *Black Power* is calculated to reiterate how frequently racial "feeling" is beside the point. In an often-cited moment of early encounter, Wright observes members of an extended family dancing at a funeral. His readers generally emphasize the initial moment of his narrative, in which he recognizes—with nicely staged shock, and a certain anthropological interest—the similarity of the dance rhythms and bodily motions he observes to certain cultural survivals, the "snakelike, veering dances" of African American religious worship (62). But the sharpest thrust of the narrative is to underscore Wright's own distance from both expressive forms, which are equally "dumbfounding" to him: "Never in my life had I been able to dance more than a few elementary steps, and the carrying of even the simplest tune had always been beyond me" (62). At this historical and authorial remove from the work of *Black Voices*, the possibility of a unitary first-person plural voice, or of any experiential collective, decisively disappears from view. Of the relevant phenomenon writ large, Gold Coast Africa on the brink of decolonization, Wright raises a benchmark question for himself as witness, observer, black American, and writer: "Why could I not feel [racial belonging]?" (63).[74]

Wright's insistence on difference and on an analytic mode—documentation, recourse to textual evidence, fact-finding—for confronting the challenge of Africa has been variously read as the reflex gesture of Eurocentric anxiety or as an extension of his existentialist concerns onto the field of world historical action. But that insistence also marks the culmination of Wright's engagement with photography, and in particular with the camera as an instrument for documentary practice. Throughout *Black Power*, Wright's "bewilderment" links closely with his activities as a maker of photographic images, and with the camera he wields as a symbolic object, an occasion for encounter, and an object of potential exchange. Indeed, the camera never disappears from Wright's narrative, even when it remains unnamed. His archive includes a significant number of the 1,500 images he methodically produced, carefully printed, cropped, and captioned, during his travels in the Gold Coast, often under highly demanding conditions.[75] Read as a body of response to the challenges of alterity, these images ground two crucial arguments. First, *Black Power* is in its production and internal dynamic a photo-text; its narrative structure and gestures are dependent on Wright's images (which may originally have been intended for publication on the model of *Black Voices*). Second, with *Black Power*, and the emergently postcolonial travelogues that succeeded it, Wright was revisiting his own engagements with photography and the conventions of documentary in order to extend their possible uses and meanings.[76] Like all of Wright's later texts, *Black Power* is ultimately limited by its commitment to some version of documentary epistemology. But it nonetheless attests to the sustained centrality of documentary visual codes and of photographic practice to Wright's self-conception. It thus traces alternative vectors of influence, aspiration, and exchange between midcentury novelists, relevant not only to their texts but to their cultural offices as representative, exemplary, and legitimating figures.

In *Black Power*, Wright foregrounds his self-understanding as a documentary witness from the very moment of his arrival. At the port city of Takoradi, as he emerges from the interior spaces of state control into a bustling cityscape, he claims, "I saw Africa for the first time with frontal vision" (38). At once "riveted" and "startled," Wright in the ur-moment of encounter aspires to something like the "honest and frontal view" that the black Americans of *Black Voices* model, by way of conscious confrontation with the raw turbulence of history in the making. Yet here on the shores of a motherland refused as such, Wright's documentary stance serves primarily to underscore its own fragility, inevitability, and limitation. From the moment he "t[akes] out my camera to photograph," his encounter with Africa and Africans becomes subject to the aspirations, fantasies, and demands of his subjects, looking awry, looking away, or looking confrontationally back. Just as Wright resists artificial kinship with his encountered African subjects and informants on the grounds of racial sameness, they resist their inevitable representation as picturesque relics, ethnographic specimens, or documentary objects—"girl . . . pounding *fufu*"; "girl . . . squatting"; "girls . . . playing *ampe*" (74, 75).[77] Notably, Wright's initial foray through the streets of Accra—whose documentary aim is "just to look at Africa" (74)—devolves into a comic reversal. The women he encounters respond to the sight of his camera by covering their breasts (objects of no little interest to Wright) and scattering; Wright ends up running through the streets to evade a swarm of children—"they came on and on, their ranks swelling as they ran"—who demand "Take me! Take me!" (75). His recorded response—"Didn't their mothers miss them? Wasn't there anyone to look after them?" (75)—calls attention to itself as a classic gesture of displacement. Bourgeois codes of maternity miss the point; the key fact of encounter is Wright's reluctant admission that "chances of a natural photograph"—*natural* here signifying some objective documentation of unmediated Africa—"were impossible" (75).

The copious images Wright produced in the Gold Coast, thirty-four of which were included in the 1956 British edition of *Black Power*, suggest both his inability to abandon altogether the presumptions of FSA-style documentary, with its inflection on the "natural," and his restive attempts to make narrative use of his own photographic standoffs within the play of the larger text.[78] Ngwarsungu Chiwengo has catalogued Wright's professions of distaste for the "bestial and barbaric" in Africa, noting with a certain acerbity that this register is "not reflected in Wright's pictures"—indeed, she points out, "Most of the Africans are dressed and beautiful . . . and even seem to be civilized."[79] Yet what Chiwengo reads as contradiction, the unwitting betrayal of a Eurocentric "indoctrination" on Wright's part, can more profitably be read as an attempt to create productive multiplicity, even tension, juxtaposing narrative and images in a fashion that replicates Wright's insistently named experience of fraught encounter and failed resolution.[80]

Many of the images chosen for publication suggest the overdetermined evidentiary status of the FSA project; in this they resemble the often predictable uses of the image found in *Black Voices*.[81] But Wright's photographic record includes shots that suggest a more complex, dialectical relationship with the narrative. Again and again, Wright explores his labile status as self-conscious artist, member of the tribe, and outsider, oscillating among socially conscious, formalist, and nonobjective modes. Visual formalism, recalling the images of

Figure 2.15. Richard Wright, Ghana, 1953. Richard Wright Papers, Yale Collection of American Literature, Beinecke Rare Book and Manuscript Library. © 1953 Richard Wright. Reprinted by permission of John Hawkins & Associates, Inc.

Berenice Abbott and Paul Strand, becomes a mode for managing overwhelming alterity, as in Wright's image of fishing boats in the port of Takoradi (figure 2.15), or his shot of a tribal chief, with its tight focus and emphasis on texture and pattern formed by the objects of Ashanti power (figure 2.16). At the same time, the protocols of documentary portraiture allow Wright to image himself as an outsider troubled by—and troubling—presumptions of racial solidarity. In one shot of a woman and her child in Accra's market, the same "frontal gaze" Wright initially embraces as a documentary observer is leveled coolly back at him (figure 2.17). Both mother and child clasp their hands; the mother, comb lying in her lap, has apparently ceased to braid her hair in response to

Figure 2.16. Richard Wright, Ghana, 1953. Richard Wright Papers, Yale Collection of American Literature, Beinecke Rare Book and Manuscript Library. © 1953 Richard Wright. Reprinted by permission of John Hawkins & Associates, Inc.

the intrusion of the camera. Guarded, dignified, fully present, these subjects defy inclusion in the framework of encounter Wright has offered. Neither "half-nude" nor intent on covering themselves (43), apparently demanding neither face time nor payment, they simultaneously contest Wright's documentary logic and stake a certain claim to participation in the process.

By contrast, in an image Wright shot in a village outside Accra, three men—two in traditional tribal dress, flanking a third in Western clothes holding a ceremonial instrument to his lips—pose self-consciously, apparently wary, anxious, and indifferent by turns. Yet these subjects also evade the narratives Wright has told about Accra's aspiring "lad[s]" and Fanti and Ashanti village

Figure 2.17. Richard Wright, Ghana, 1953. Richard Wright Papers, Yale Collection of American Literature, Beinecke Rare Book and Manuscript Library. © 1953 Richard Wright. Reprinted by permission of John Hawkins & Associates, Inc.

youths, which tend to emphasize the "pathos" of their embeddedness in tribal practices and colonial institutions (109). (An exemplary anecdote from this section of the narrative features a James Town youth who asks that Wright make a gift of his precious camera, promising, "I'd pay you back; I'd send the picture to you; I swear, sar" [110].) Put in dialogue with the narratives they are apparently made to illustrate, Wright's images not only accentuate the self-reflexive character of the text as such, its straining against the limits of documentary analysis, they also suggest Wright's awareness of the possibility for productive tension and disjunction as defining facts of a text that seeks to explore both the historical grounds and the affective dialectic of cultural sameness and difference.

It would be a stretch to claim that any of Wright's images, even the most self-conscious, were composed as allegories of the failures of documentary practice. But their notable divergences from his narrative—the alternative stories they imply—do suggest deliberate exploration of such failures. For every shot featuring subjects caught at the long or middle distance, apparently unaware of the camera, Wright made another taken at close or middle range, in which the tensions of transaction—Western black man highly resistant to the call of the ancestral making images of colonized Africans struggling to create conditions for decolonization and productive forms of modernity—leave various traces (figure 2.18). Collectively, these images form a running commentary on *Black Power*'s uses of the camera as a narrative trope, an object symbolic of Wright's authorial status and determined outsidership. In incident after incident, Wright emphasizes his frustrated attempts to get the shot he seeks, the insufficiency of photography as a point of entry, the liability (and even danger) resulting from his attempts to make images and to achieve a self-consciously critical mode of knowing.

In one key scene, whose recounting inaugurates an ongoing meditation on Akan spirituality as both a mass political force and an impediment to industrialization, Wright is called by a fellow hotel resident to "get your camera" to make images of a passing funeral procession for a deceased chief (142). To his surprise, the rite features not only exuberant forms of dance, chanting, and the random firing of muskets—a fairly dramatic gesture, given that the number of marchers reaches about five thousand—but the spectacle of a heavy brass coffin borne aloft by marchers and "twirled" vertiginously through the air. The challenge to Wright's documentary aims is irresistible: "Some ritual whose significance I could not understand was taking place," and he accordingly moves to street level to "get the photograph I wanted" (143). But when he does organize his equipment, all his viewfinder arrests is "a forest of naked

Figure 2.18. Richard Wright, Ghana, 1953. Richard Wright Papers, Yale Collection of American Literature, Beinecke Rare Book and Manuscript Library. © 1953 Richard Wright. Reprinted by permission of John Hawkins & Associates, Inc.

black" and "elongated breasts," as a small army of women pass by, knocking short wooden sticks to thunderous effect (143). "Too astonished to act," Wright is left gaping at the parade. The serendipitous moment results not in dramatic images or materials for sober analysis, only the painful conviction that "I had understood nothing, nothing" (144).

Yet Wright's archive shows that he actually did produce numerous images of this event. All the more telling, then, that the narrative goes on to make rich capital of Wright's self-representation as failed photographer and documentary analyst. In an ensuing exchange with a male bystander, an African in Western dress, Wright's bewilderment becomes the stuff of comic dialogue. In vaudevillian (if not minstrel) fashion, Wright plays the part of interlocutor to the bystander who explicates the practices of their shared "ancestors" (144):

"Why do they fire those muskets?"

"Who knows? Some say that they got that . . . from the Europeans during the fifteenth century. . . ."

"But the dead man, won't he fall out of the coffin?"

"There's no dead man in the coffin."

"What? It's *empty*?" I asked. "Then why are they rushing about with it like that?"

"The coffin has the dead man's hair and fingernails in it. . . . The body is buried somewhere in secret, after the brain is taken out."

"Why bury it in secret?"

"So no one will find it."

"But why would anyone want to find it?"

"Well, there are several reasons. . . . You see, a chief's body is sacred. . . . If somebody finds it, they can use it. . . ."

"Then why don't they stand guard over the body?"

"They've *got* to hide the body; they're hiding it from the man's spirit—"

"But the man's *dead*," I protested. (145)

The exchange dramatizes the (at least momentary) irrelevance of Wright's analytic framework and the search for "natural pictures" intended to support it; no kind of documentary image making or objectivist stance, the text implies, could be adequate to this encounter. Yet as Wright's photographic aims (at least as he represents them) become increasingly frustrated and inadequate in his intensifying contact with "ancestral" practices, his camera occasions ever more complex exchanges. In their recounting, Wright's self-consciousness as a would-be participant-observer is heightened as a challenge for the reader.

An exemplary instance of this effect occurs during Wright's first attempt at "seeing Africa by taxicab" (156), when he hires a private car to bring him outside Accra, beyond British colonial sponsorship and control. In the fishing village of Labadi, a "mixture of the primitive and the modern" (157), Wright befriends a young electrician and proceeds to inquire about malaria, infant mortality, missionary schooling, and other material "conditions" dear to classic documentary inquiry (163). The conversation breaks off when Wright observes "a magnificent woman who sat nursing a fat black baby," the "long red rays of the setting sun l[ighting] her ebony torso to a soft distinctness" (162). The picturesque subject—motherland? African Madonna? the twilight of ancestral tradition?—proves irresistible, and Wright asks the boy to ask the woman to let him take a picture.

> He spoke to her and she nodded her head.
> "Penny, Massa," she said, extending her hand.
> I fished a shilling out of my pocket and gave it to her. She rose, laughed. I tried to focus my camera and she lunged past me, holding the baby with one hand under its belly, and made a beeline for the mud hut; she was out of sight before I could utter a word. A howl of black laughter echoed through the compound. I stood looking like a blundering fool. She had outwitted me. I laughed too. She had won. (163)

This moment in which Wright decisively fails to get the picture is the first, and one of the few, in which he shares an affective stance with his African subjects. The failed exchange highlights the fundamental contradictions within the documentary enterprise as Wright has adapted it, as an instrument for analytic knowledge and ultimately for redress of social inequalities in the colonial context. But it also eventuates in a bracing meditation on the meaning of documentary process as a form of self-knowledge: "suddenly . . . self-conscious," Wright begins to "question myself, *my* assumptions" about the value in this context of industrialization, literacy, Western institutions—and of his own practice of "disinherit[ance]" as a cultural stance (163). Bested in a specific form of exchange—Western money for the power to represent—on which his status as multiple outsider is predicated, Wright purposively undermines the agency of documentary observation to render instrumental judgments ("if not [embrace of Western modernity], then what? I didn't know" [163]).

The "howl of black laughter" that thus schools Wright is a far cry from the unitary chorus of *Black Voices*, and its effect is structural to *Black Power*, despite Wright's attempts to contain or redirect it. During his final travels in the Gold Coast, into the interior mining and timber enterprises of Kumasi, Wright visits the company town of Bibiana, home to a gold mine in which labor some four thousand African workers from all over British and French West Africa. His narrative—here echoing the strains of *You Have Seen Their Faces* and classic FSA-era projects—aims to document the "disorder[ed]," squalid life of the workers' camp, lived "by the imperious rule of instinct" made necessary under "the tight corporate unity" of rapacious colonial rule (348, 347). In the midst of this narrative, Wright recounts a curious incident: "I passed a tall, naked black boy; he stared at me, at my camera, my sun helmet; then, seemingly unaware of what he was doing, he squatted and evacuated his bowels upon the porch of his hut, still staring at me . . ." (348; ellipses original). Wright's narrative immediately veers into an observation about the "curbing and disciplining of instincts," the "control of the reflexes of the body" necessary for "industrial activity": "Again," he writes, "I felt that pathos of distance" (348).

This reflex move to order fails to "evacuate" another possibility: that the "black boy" in question is only "seemingly unaware"; that he responds to Wright's documentary presence, and camera, precisely by shitting on the job. (At the very least, he thereby definitively refuses to comport with the conventions of documentary exchange.) Yet Wright's narrative exposes this possibility in spite of itself. The "pathos of distance" to which he resorts—presumably of the Africans from modernity; of bodily instinct from rational order; of "unaware" documentary subject from self-conscious observer—reminds us of the source for this phrase, one Wright explicitly names earlier in the text: Nietzsche's *On the Genealogy of Morals*. There, the "pathos of distance" defines Nietzsche's understanding of morality (at least Western Christian morality) as an expression and instrument of power.[82] If Wright's move to cordon off the worker's response to his camera is itself an invocation of pathos in the mode of Nietzsche's master, it also reminds us that the "pathetic" of slave morality functions as an extraordinary will to power, an aggression by which the disempowered comes to install his own oppression as a dominant cultural force.

Wright comes short of identifying this dynamic as a possible meaning for the worker's response to the presence of the camera. But his narrative retrospectively opens that possibility in the course of reporting on the conditions of being in the colonial work camps, in which African workers perform backbreaking labor for as little as four shillings a day. The press of events as Wright recounts them suggests an alternate meaning for the failed photographic encounter. As he observes "the elaborate mechanical and chemical processes by which gold was extracted from rock" (348), he questions his guide about problems with theft: "'if I were that boy, I'd swallow that gold if I had a chance,' I told him" (349). That tacit connection between this apparently random response and the squatting boy is made explicit in the guard's reluctant admission that workers do attempt to "swallo[w] a bit each day and recove[r] it"; "It's smelly but highly profitable" (349). Caught in the grip of necessity, ressentiment, and dependence, the African worker stoops to shit and thus to conquer—or at least to reclaim some tiny portion of the resources being so brutally "extracted" and "evacuated" from his ancestral lands. But this, the text implies, is a reality neither Wright nor the camera, however freed from bourgeois constraint, could manage to record.

This suggestion affirms the real pathos of the text—not a pathos of distance, but that of lived experience in colonial history, and of Wright's attempts to observe, analyze, and document it as a remediable social problem, in his own person as Western, exilic intellectual, himself an emblem of a cultural era in passing. By way of narrative climax, this pathos is brought roundly home to Wright. In the final encounter of his journey into Kumasi, as a guest of the manager of the world's largest plywood and timber mill at Samreboi, Wright is forced to endure the kind of "hilari[ous]" anecdotes about Africans that pass for colonial socializing (360). Predictably, these narratives turn on primitive bodily hexis and linguistic misrecognition (as in a story about an African woman who is made by a local leader to run, nude and holding one breast, through a crowd gathered for a speech by Winston Churchill; she has been instructed to do so in response to press reports of earlier speeches in which "*a titter ran through the crowd*" [362]). The key moment, however, is pointed with respect to Wright's self-representation. As the guests fall silent, the "coughing, sucking sound" of plumbing newly installed in the manager's home becomes unavoidable: "One of the young men lifted his eyes cynically toward the ceiling and announced in stern tones, struggling against the laughter that tried to break through his lips: 'SOMEBODY IS BEING DESTOOLED!' " (362). This scatological thrust puns on the disempowerment, both under colonial occupation and under Nkrumah's emerging rule, of Ashanti tribal chiefs, whose symbolic power is vested in their ornate wooden stools—but it also implicates Wright, who has closely identified throughout the text with the stool as a poetic emblem and a narrative device.[83]

The ensuing "explo[sion]" of white laughter at this thrust resonates against the earlier "howl" of black laughter; together, they collapse whatever pathos of documentary distance Wright has inhabited (362). In recognition of this fact, Wright ends the story by recounting his return to the modern bungalow in which he is housed. From its window, he stares "into the blackness" of the "jungle out there," startled by "a dreadful kind of moaning":

It began like a baby crying, then it ascended to a sort of haunting scream, followed by a weird kind of hooting that was the essence of despair. The sound kept on and on, sobbing, seemingly out of breath, as if the heart was so choked with sorrow that another breath could not be drawn. Finally, a moan came at long intervals, as though issuing from a body in the last extremities of physical suffering. And when I could no longer hear it, I still felt that it was sounding in my mind . . . (363; ellipsis original)

If the jungle reads here like a trope from *Heart of Darkness*, that fact only emphasizes the urgency of Wright's move to personification. At the climax of this extended sequence of encounter, the documentary image has been displaced by sound, prelinguistic and untranslatable; even the narrative of failed photographic encounter is insufficient to Wright's implication in the "destooling" exchange. But Wright seizes on the pathetic fallacy not to create magisterial distance so much as to emphasize his continuing commitment to the stance of detachment. The "despair" and "suffering" to which the landscape gives voice are the cost of Wright's attempts to remain "devoid of illusions" about intimacy with his subjects (230), in the face of his bedrock belief that "If one allowed one's feelings to become identified, here, one could no longer see anything" (171). In this climactic moment, the irrelevance of the camera as fact-finding instrument paradoxically heightens its power as a symbolic object, an objective correlative for Wright himself. The practice of documentary generates and structures Wright's encounters: not in spite but because of its failures, it allows for more mobile forms of self-recognition and cultural consciousness—and for more fluid forms of narrative about them.

Arguably, the impasse Wright reaches here, with the camera and documentary knowing, constitutes the climax of his narrative. The concluding sections—which describe his visits to Christianborg, Cape Coast, and Elmina castles, the "great slave headquarters" in which traders imprisoned and sold their captives for embarkation on the Middle Passage, and which offer his infamous open letter to Nkrumah about Africa's future (383)—are, as many readers have suggested, curiously lifeless and anticlimactic.[84] To make such a claim is not only to argue that *Black Power* fundamentally undertakes a version of documentary analysis and knowing—one extended from *Black Voices*—in which the observer's engagements, their conditions and contexts, are central to the narrative of encounter as such. It is also to argue that *Black Power* is continuous with—in some sense climactic of—Wright's earlier work, with its gathering interests in photography, visual evidence, and the documentary mode. In its creation of complex tensions, its resistance to easy "empathy"

(237), its unevenly intentioned uses of photography as a structural and symbolic object, *Black Power* continues to work at the limits of documentary as a cultural form. In this way, it resembles Siskind's late work in Harlem and partakes of the structural logic of Harlem's afterlife. It also crystallizes an alternative genealogy of postwar writing and cultural response, in which Wright's experiments with photography—however limited, however unstable in effect—generate their own afterlife, in a body of work to which I now turn.

Chapter Three

Ralph Ellison, Photographer

Among the copious materials housed in Ralph Ellison's archives at the Library of Congress is an inconspicuous manila folder. Labeled "from wallet 1930s," it contains three apparently unremarkable photographs. Two, a portrait of the author's mother and a group shot of his classmates from Tuskegee, are predictable appurtenances for a young man from the provinces, or at least the former territories, struggling for traction in the big city (as Ellison then was). The third photograph, however, bears closer inspection. Worn and creased, some 3 × 4 inches, the image was obviously much handled in its time; it appears to have been cropped or torn from a larger print so as to fit into the wallet.[1] Its subject, obviously slightly older than the then twenty-something Ellison, is an African American man whose hands cradle what appears to be a professional-grade twin-lens reflex camera. Without a very close look, given the well-worn quality of the print, a casual observer might fail to note that the subject of the image is Richard Wright.

This archival object powerfully confirms Wright's commitment to photography that the previous chapter details. But it also opens a new view of Ellison as his literary successor, counterpart, and rival. That the aspiring, restive Ellison would keep an image of Wright ready to hand, part of his protective arsenal, is in itself unsurprising. Wright remained by all accounts a significant if problematic colleague, editor, and friend throughout the decade: he was the man to whom Langston Hughes introduced Ellison to launch the latter as a writer, the figure at whose feet Ellison more or less literally sat, observing the storied, commanding author of *Uncle Tom's Children* and *Black Boy* as he conducted his political, editorial, and literary lives.[2] What is revelatory is the insistence on Wright as an iconic figure not for the camera but in command of it. If the Ellison of the late 1930s, poised on the threshold of his literary career, was constructing a usable past—a kind of genealogical work hinted at in the archival trio of photos—the presence of the camera in the hands of his most significant and formidable predecessor bears remarking. Memento, talisman, goad, Ellison's image of Wright bespeaks what we might call an invisible genealogy linking African American writers at midcentury: the unacknowledged role played by photography in their self-imagination, cultural politics, and literary work.

If the assertion of such a claim flies in the face of received wisdom, the flight is particularly bold with respect to the onetime musician Ellison. The well-known essays of *Shadow and Act* (1964) and *Going to the Territory* (1986), which have both supplemented and come to stand in for his work as a novelist, direct us to read Ellison as an "ambidextrous" figure riffing on literary and musical histories, someone whose "basic form of artistic sense is musical."[3] And critics, from contemporaries such as Albert Murray to scholars such as Houston Baker, Robert O'Mealley, Horace Porter, and John Callahan, have taken this direction.[4] Among admirers and detractors alike, Ellison's work is taken to exemplify the aperçu that, throughout their history and in response to the social conditions of their emergence, all black arts aspire to the condition of music—most particularly, the high-flying, self-styled, magisterial flights of improvisatory jazz.[5]

But Ellison's self-constitution as writer and his novels themselves owe an unacknowledged debt to another cultural form with which he purposively experimented, and not merely the visual arts broadly writ. Well beyond mere wallet snapshots, his archive includes a significant body of materials that document Ellison's lifelong, ongoing interests in photographic images, practitioners, and ways of making meaning. As the introduction to *Invisible Man* notes, Ellison supported himself during its writing (a not inconsiderable interval) through his work as a photographer, producing a respectable body of commissioned portraits, images made on journalistic assignment, and shots of art objects for use in exhibition catalogues.[6] During the late 1940s, he worked closely with the photographer, soon to be filmmaker, and sometime hustler Gordon Parks, collaborating on a photojournalistic essay on Harlem and the psychic conditions of life in America's most storied black ghetto.[7] His communications from the mid-1940s through early 1950s—the period when Ellison most intensively rewrote *Invisible Man* and shepherded it into publication—are jotted on his professional letterhead, memoranda sheets that bear the inscription "Ralph Ellison, Photographer." As the latter-day reader sorts through the boxes and folders in which have been preserved Ellison's own photographs, negatives, and prints, his clippings on photography exhibitions and series, notations on shooting style, working instructions to himself on the niceties of light-metering, film speeds, and image composition, it becomes clear that photography was far more to Ellison than a day job, pastime, or mode for memorializing private events. For Ellison, photography was no less than an interpretive instrument, a resource for critical reflection on American cultural practices and norms.

As both the wallet snapshot of Wright and the preceding chapters of this book suggest, Ellison's well-developed interest in photographic images was to some extent representative. He was, in other words, an intellectual who came of critical age in the years spanning the New Deal and a postwar aesthetic, both deeply indebted to photographic canons and examples. As I have argued in preceding chapters, the legacy of New Deal and commercial documentation, with its iconic images of black poverty, disenfranchisement, and despair, had distinctive resonances for African Americans; even as it heightened black skepticism about visuality and cultural visibility, it also made the will to power through the image all the greater. In spite—and because—of its instrumentality in "exposing" the racial and class conditions it inadvertently naturalized, documentary photography invited black writers to counter its dehumanizing trends, to use images to wrest the fullness of experience out from under the rubrics of poverty, delinquency, and oppression. But while this desire impelled any number of writers of Ellison's generation, it had a singular power and distinctly productive uses for him.[8]

To make such an argument is, of course, to run counter to the received wisdom not only on Ellison's relations with jazz and vernacular music but on vision and invisibility, the core issues of *Invisible Man*. Embedded in his landmark novel are a myriad of symbolic figures and objects that challenge longstanding associations between vision, knowledge or self-knowledge, and social progress—and further, implicate photography, the work of the third eye, in the failure of these linked projects. The narrator's achingly durable hope as he is led, blindfolded, to the Battle Royal; the sense of "the veil" being "lowered," rather than lifted, in images of the hallowed Founder of the college;[9] the sightless eyes of the Reverend Homer Barbee; the summons of the veteran at the Golden Day to "look beneath the surface" and "come out of the fog" (151); Emerson junior's anxious advice about "what lies behind the face of things" (185); the lobotomy technician in the Liberty Paints plant hospital, who examines the narrator through the lens of "a bright third eye" (226); the "Cyclopean" glass eye of Brother Jack, bespeaking all he and the Brotherhood choose not to recognize (463): with these and other resonant episodes, *Invisible Man* serves as something of a primer on how modern apparatuses of vision and insight, real and figurative, function to occlude and deceive, to squander hard-fought humanity in the service of specious and racially punitive ideals. No wonder, then, that photography has been written off by Ellison's readers as an instrument of the very logic of invisibility his novel seeks to probe.[10]

But this reductive synecdoche, by which the camera's eye comes to stand for photographic practice, with all its aesthetic and social complications, has itself occluded Ellison's various, long-standing investments in photography. Close examination of his archival materials, specifically of Ellison's relationship to the developing history of documentary and street photography in New Deal and postwar New York, suggests quite the opposite of what his landmark fiction encourages us to assume. It suggests, that is, that photography serves Ellison as a powerful resource for imagining the transformation of lived experience into narrative, of social fact into aesthetic possibility, and vice versa. Taking Ellison's photographic work and interests into account, in the context of their emergence and pursuit, allows us a new purchase on the logic of invisibility—not only as a thematic in his only completed novel, but as an informing trope for the complex cultural politics in which he engaged. Kenneth Warren has argued that *Invisible Man* is best read as an "occasional piece," struggling (with less than full success) to speak for possibilities beyond the conditions that shaped it.[11] If this is so, then a productive way to understand the novel's occasion—the possibilities that occasion opened, the constraints it imposed— is by recovering photographic practice as an informing context.[12] In what follows, I reconstruct the meaning of Ellison's self-invention under the sign (and eye) of the camera so as to provide an alternative, or at least supplementary, account of how invisibility was born; and how it made new, even perdurable, sense of the novel as an American form.[13]

In the autobiographical essay "Hidden Name and Complex Fate," published in the collection *Shadow and Act*, Ellison offers an allegory for his coming-into-being as a son, a writer, and a citizen of these United States. While "seeking adventure in back alleys" in his hometown of Oklahoma City, the young Ellison serendipitously finds "a large photographic lens":

> I remember nothing of its optical qualities, of its speed or color correction, but it gleamed with crystal mystery and it was beautiful. Mounted handsomely in a tube of shiny brass, it spoke to me of distant worlds of possibility. I played with

it, looking through it with squinted eyes, holding it in shafts of sunlight, and tried to use it for a magic lantern. But most of this was as unrewarding as my attempts to make the music come from a phonograph record by holding the needle in my fingers. I could burn holes through newspapers with it, or I could pretend that it was a telescope, the barrel of a cannon, or the third eye of a monster—*I* being the monster—but I could do nothing at all about its proper function of making images; nothing to make it yield its secret. Still, I could not discard it. Older boys sought to get it away from me by offering knives or tops, agate marbles or whole zoos of grass snakes and horned toads in trade, but I held on to it. No one, not even the white boys I knew, had such a lens, and it was my own good luck to have found it (CE, 196–97).

The young boy's initial inability to "find a creative use for my lens" is part of an overdetermined process; it both exemplifies and inaugurates Ellison's attempts to "master" his overdetermined name. Not by accident, one assumes, this portrait of the artist as a young man recalls Ellison's namesake, that other Ralph Waldo—or at least Emerson's description of the observing writer in *Representative Men*: "Whatever he beholds or experiences, comes to him as a model, and sits for its picture. . . . In his eyes, a man is the faculty of reporting, and the universe is the possibility of being reported."[14] And Ellison's gesture toward the optical instrument can be seen to position him not only as revisionary heir to America's first philosopher but as the contestatory successor of a nearer heir to Emerson, W.E.B. DuBois. In *The Souls of Black Folk* (1903), the latter's famous pronouncement on the Negro American's double consciousness comes in response to the account of a failed exchange of card photographs, a ritual of recognition or hailing that had come to define bourgeois American social life: it is only as a white schoolgirl, after a cutting "glance" at the gift of an image the young DuBois has proffered, refuses it, that he experiences for the first time the wounding "gif[t]" of his own "second sight."[15] The young Ellison, however, is spared such a scene of misrecognition. In his self-representation, he is never the victim of a framing gaze, and his potential as a maker of images remains uncontested. While it may be canonical poetry that occasions the signal "act of will" by which Ralph Waldo Ellison recreates himself, or the lure of music that comes to "fascinat[e]" the writer-to-be, the camera as instrument and symbol has become part of his arsenal and his self-representation, a complex fact of the aspiring intellectual's "own hard-earned sense of reality" (CE, 166).

However fleetingly, Ellison's autobiographical account proposes a nexus between his identity as a nascent writer, struggling to make a place for himself in an American cultural genealogy, and the instruments of photographic looking.[16]

In so doing, it undercuts critical assumptions about Ellison's gestures toward camera work as a categorical rejection of its sociological designs. Duly aware of its power in codifying ethnographic and popular assumptions about the Negro, Ellison—like his onetime mentor Wright in the wallet portrait—represents himself as an active agent, the man behind the lens rather than an ethnographic or sociological subject. Throughout his developing career, this posture allows him to evade the reductive typology of documentary and sociological gazes, with all they imply about racial subjectivity, and to harness the growing power of midcentury camera work to produce allegorical, symbolic, and otherwise allusive effects. Like the "treasure" and "defect" of his given name, the photographic lens represents both an inheritance against which the writer struggles and a tool of self-creation. An alternative way of negotiating the imperatives of name and fate, photography serves Ellison as a language for the simultaneous no and yes, the affirmation that is also a form of critical challenge.

That Ellison's interest in the camera is indeed an aspect of his creative life, however obscured by his published writings, is made abundantly evident by materials in his archive. In letters, notes, and other private writings, he details his ongoing acquisition of cameras and photographic equipment from at least the mid-1940s. Not only did Ellison purchase an impressive array of cameras, lenses, and other technical apparatuses (itself telling, given the relative stresses on his income during the first part of his career); his collection of photographic equipment reflects the changing styles and imperatives of documentary and street photography.[17] From a classic Leica (the model of choice for photographic practitioners in the wake of Henri Cartier-Bresson) to a state-of-the-art 35 mm Pentax (increasingly favored by street shooters for its mobility and ease of loading) to the view camera (a format linked with the austerely formalist work of practitioners such as Edward Weston and Paul Strand, as well as the self-conscious documentation of Walker Evans and Aaron Siskind) to the late-model Polaroid, Ellison seems to have experimented with their varying properties of speed, deliberation, monumentality, and spontaneity.[18] Over some four decades of photographic observation, snapshooting, printing, and portrait work, he produced a notable variety of images, bespeaking wide interests in photographic realism, the conventions of the fashion and glamour shot, experimental art photography, and documentary.

Telling as Ellison's own images are—and I will turn to them later—the reader of his archive is first struck by the self-consciousness with which he employed the camera as a tool for self-creation. Each of these different camera models, with its own attendant mythology and history of uses, allowed Ellison to create a different role for himself, to put himself in a distinctive relationship to the photographic subject: that of studio professional, producing artistic renderings of fellow (and in some cases competing) authors; of participant-observer and photographic witness, recording the daily facts of Harlem life; of avant-garde, testing the expressive possibilities of the medium; of sympathetic outsider, documenting the lives of the marginalized. At the apex of photography's power as a symbol of modernity and of its authority as social critique, Ellison was as interested in the purchases on contemporary urban culture and identity afforded the self-styling photographer as in the production of specific images. That interest was persistent enough to find expression in the opening essay of *Going to the Territory*. "The Little Man at Chehaw Station" (1977–78) offers a key figure for the uniquely American vernacular stoutly championed by Ellison: an aggressively miscegenated man cruising on Riverside Drive in a Volkswagen Beetle with a Rolls Royce engine, clad in English riding breeches, dashiki, and Afro, who turns out to sport "an expensive Japanese single-lens reflex camera" (CE, 506). Brandishing his instrument, the young man proceeds, in "a scene to haunt one's midnight dreams and one's noon repose," to make show- (and traffic-) stopping self-portraits that, in the very process of their production, "projec[t] and recor[d] . . . something of his complex sense of cultural identity" (CE, 506).

Whether observed or fictive, this "apparition" (CE, 506) has an analogue in the self-presentation of the novelist in the making. Again and again throughout the 1940s and 1950s, Ellison—always a guarded subject—posed for photographs and self-portraits with camera in hand. An image by his second wife, Fanny Ellison, which appears to have been taken not long before the publication of *Invisible Man*, shows a reflective Ellison in Central Park. Turned away from her camera, grasping his own—apparently a small-format view model—as if in preparation for a shot, Ellison evades the camera's intimate gaze by enacting the role of meditative witness or seer.[19] Other series of portraits show Ellison at work with camera and tripod, preparing to shoot Fanny as she shoots him; still others are double portraits of Ellison and other writers—Langston Hughes, Chester Himes—in which Ellison's camera again prominently figures.[20] This penchant for self-presentation as a photographer hardly went unnoticed within Ellison's circle. By way of a Christmas card apparently made in the 1950s, a journalist acquaintance offers a triple portrait: Fanny Ellison is shot from the rear, holding aloft a camera to take her own shot of Hughes and Ellison, who in turns poses in the act of fingering the camera around his neck, prepared to make a photograph of Fanny.[21]

By turns reflective, authoritative, and absorbed in the delicate intricacies of recording the lived moment, the Ellison who appears in this archive of images wills himself into being as artist and seer even as he deflects the camera's scrutiny. Of a piece with his lifelong self-representations as urbane intellectual and dandy, the image of Ellison as image maker or auteur—"Ralph Ellison, Photographer"—affords him a certain cultural authority, and what we might well call invisibility: a mode of open self-concealment. That this strategy was both intentioned and foundational to Ellison's writing life is evidenced in an admission he later made to fellow writer Albert Murray, in a letter requesting the latter's help in purchasing new equipment for Ellison's beloved Leica: "You know me, I have to have something between me and reality when I'm dealing with it most intensely."[22] That "something," often, was the camera, which in this archive of portraits and self-portraits becomes a version of the mask as Ellison famously describes it in "Change the Joke and Slip the Yoke" (1958): an object for "purposes of aggression as well as for defense," for "projecting the future and preserving the past" (CE, 109). In the context of photography's changing practices and its cultural power, the camera becomes an overdetermined resource for Ellison's project: a prop for self-staging, an instrument for screening contemporary realities, a mode for navigating the turbulent politics of New York's postwar left.[23]

Ellison partially acknowledges this multiple instrumentality in his preface to *Invisible Man*, when he describes the genesis of the novel. There, he figures himself akin to his own character, Mary Rambo, who admonishes the narrator, "Don't let this Harlem git you. I'm in New York but New York ain't in me" (255).[24] Of "indefinite status"—the writer making his career is "neither a thug, numbers-runner, nor pusher, postal worker, doctor, dentist, lawyer, tailor, undertaker, barber, bartender nor preacher," and thus essentially outside the complex but legible economies of life on the Harlem street—Ellison is accused by the corner "wino lady" of being "some kinda sweetback," a pimp.[25] His unreadability as writer and intellectual is not only linked with, but given form by, his activities as a photographer, as his "woozy" critic suggests: "'all I ever see *him* do is walk them damn dogs and shoot some damn pictures!'" (ix). It is, Ellison notes, the presence of the camera and the pursuit of its possibilities that ensures this cherished alterity: "since I was returning home with fifty legally earned dollars from a photographic assignment I could well afford to smile while remaining silently concealed in my mystery" (x). Hiding in plain view behind the lens, Ellison appears to brandish the camera and photography itself as a version of Rinehart's shades; they afford the ultimate freedom of expression. Like the invisible man's adoption of the signature icon of the hipster, this manipulation of the camera as a cultural accoutrement is "flooded with personal significance" (482). Behind its lens, Ellison experiences himself both as "concealed" and self-inventing, occupying a found space of both "isolation" (13) and revealing "contact" (3).

Of course, Ellison not only employed his camera as prop, screen, and emblem of postwar cultural "fraternity" with a labile cultural left (485), he also made photographs: by choice and by commission, for "taking notes" and for sale.[26] His archived images are remarkable less for their quality (notably uneven) than for their implied interest in the available range of visual modes defining postwar photographic practice. Even the somewhat random photographs housed with Ellison's papers suggest a certain rehearsal of the menu of representational possibilities: formalist, socially conscious, reportorial, detached, nonobjective, intimate. One dramatic shot, which appears to have been made and printed by Ellison in the 1940s, shows a steel structure with a mechanical pinwheel affixed to its apex, surrounded by parachutes gracefully wafting toward earth. For the viewer attuned to photographic history, this image rhymes with the celebratory large-format photographs of the Fort Peck Dam, George Washington Bridge, and other emblems of industrial modernity shot by the most widely recognized U.S. photographer of that decade, Margaret Bourke-White. Featured prominently on the covers of *Life* and *Fortune*, ruthlessly promoted by Henry Luce as emblematic of the power of the picture magazine, Bourke-White's work made her the highest-paid photographic professional in the United States and a household name.[27] As I will argue, it also made her something of a touchstone for Ellison's experiments with the novel as a form of response to modernity and its racializing guises.

Alternatively, among Ellison's images are various spontaneous portraits made on the streets of Harlem and downtown New York, themselves (as previous chapters attest) linked sites of longstanding interest for documentary photographers.[28] A significant number of his printed images take children as subjects, probably an outgrowth of Ellison's work collecting their oral narratives, riddles, and jump-rope rhymes in Harlem in 1940–41, during his stint on the payroll of the Federal Writers' Project. It was these vernacular narratives—perhaps Ellison's earliest experiments with a narrative, dialogical rendition of African American speech—that were chosen to accompany Aaron Siskind's photographs of children's cultures in the published version of *Harlem Document*. Thus linked, however belatedly or serendipitously, to Siskind's attempts to generate photographic practices responsive to the challenges of Harlem, Ellison's images can be seen to explore similar issues. In his spontaneous shots of Harlem children and passersby, Ellison tenders subjects who return his gaze confidently or meditatively (a young girl caught in the midst of a sidewalk game; a group of boys resplendent in adult suits and hats striking up their best manly manner) as well as those unable to return it at all (an adolescent girl enfolded in her own cares; a young man lingering, rapt, in front of a shop window, inhabiting a distant dream world). Collectively, Ellison's Harlem street photographs limn the essential problem of postwar street work: negotiating documentary photography's own tendency to rob its subjects of the power, the right, or the psychic means to look back.

Brought to bear on these images, the context of *Harlem Document* suggests Ellison's interest in the self-conscious camera as an analogue for the problem of the self-conscious writer at midcentury, struggling with the imperatives of speaking as and speaking for. But it also suggests the limits of such an analogy—or, more precisely, the degree to which Ellison invokes photography to sustain a particular vision for the novel and its social import. If Wright's initial photographic engagements turned primarily on the truth claims of documentary, Ellison's appear to have been more searching and mixed, attuned to changing and competing photographic practices and ontologies. During the 1940s, the genre of documentary was undergoing strenuous revision, as the tenets of New Deal era image making—rooted in direct observation, an affinity for socially marginal subjects, and a commitment to social change through the impact of photographic narrative—were redirected, under pressure of red-baiting and experimentalism alike, toward a more allusive aesthetic. By the time of the publication of *Invisible Man*, an influential and highly visible group of photographers, including Weegee, Levitt, Louis Faurer, Ted Croner, Sid Grossman, Richard Avedon, and Lisette Model, were coalescing into something aptly (if retrospectively) called the New York School. Highly individualist, privileging images of marginality and solitude, they cohered in focusing on the city street as an interpretive site, on urban perception as a unifying subject, and on the visual experience of modernity.[29]

Whether themselves immigrants (Model, Weegee), the children of immigrants (Levitt, Faurer, Croner, Grossman), or thoroughly assimilated ethnic Americans (Avedon), this generation of photographers descended in a specific sense from the photographic ferment of the Jewish Lower East Side. In a reenactment of the trajectory that had launched not only Aaron Siskind but numerous other image makers of the socially conscious era—including Ben Shahn, Morris Engel, Walter Rosenblum, Jack Manning, Rebecca Lepkoff, Arnold Eagle, Sol Libsohn, and Leon Levinstein—the majority of New York School photographers began their careers working in and with Yiddish-speaking, African American, working-class, gay and drag, and other marginalized communities, from the Lower East Side and Harlem to Hell's Kitchen, from Coney Island to upper Broadway and beyond.[30] That shared experience contributed

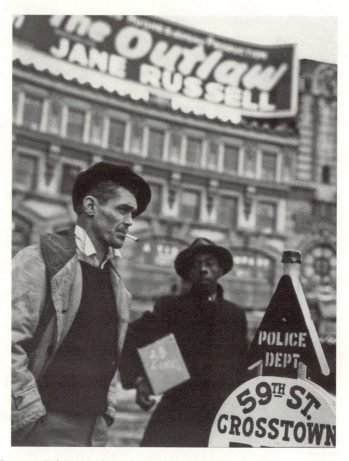

Figure 3.1. Ted Croner, The Outlaw, ca. 1945. © Ted Croner Estate. Courtesy Howard Greenberg Gallery, New York.

to dramatically new photographic styles and ways of apprehending the postwar city, founded in contingency and expressive complexity. In a specific sense, their work took up where Siskind's left off; it made striking uses of social and experiential distance as a framing convention and social fact. Collectively, their photographs emphasized the tension between the physical proximity, even intimacy, of city dwellers and their mutual impenetrability and psychic distance. Weegee's Bowery alcoholics, Croner's Times Square drifters (figure 3.1), Faurer's shadow dwellers (figure 3.2), Model's solitary figures of the urban street and coffee shop: such figures collectively depict America's modernity as an existential struggle—not with hard luck or poverty, but with alienation from

Figure 3.2. Louis Faurer, Self-Portrait, 42nd Street El Station, 1946. By permission. Courtesy Howard Greenberg Gallery, New York.

the march of postwar progress and from the increasingly monolithic cityscape that was its emblem. New York School photographs, in other words, take a certain invisibility as their subject; they wield the camera not as a tool for New Deal era "exposure" or "enlightenment" of the conditions that produce it, but as an instrument for heightening the viewer's experience of its psychic depths and social meanings.

No wonder, then, that Ellison was fascinated by the evolving history and artifacts of documentary photography as it roamed the streets and covered the lonely crowd. Among black writers and intellectuals on the cultural field at midcentury, he was pivotally positioned with respect to the state of the novel between the New Deal and civil rights. Born in 1913 (against Wright in 1908 and James Baldwin in 1924), committing belatedly to the self-imagination and work of the novelist, Ellison strategically defined himself as a writer—*the* writer—charged with creating a novelistic form that would move decisively beyond the logic of protest and its forcible alignment with sociological methods for studying "the Negro" and the conditions of "inferiority."[31] In the evolving canons of documentary photography he found a resource for that movement. But his move via photography to allusiveness, mystery, and psychic depth was inextricable from an abiding interest in the camera's categorical power to bestow social value on its subjects. At a moment when the project of black self-affirmation had become both more urgent and newly possible, this facet of documentary tradition continued to assert itself as a cultural resource. Well into the civil rights years, neither Ellison as a novelist nor black America as a citizenry was ready to abandon the project of rendering visible its repressed or forgotten histories, the perdurable facts of white violence and appropriation.[32] The project of documentary photography offered itself as a way to make claims for experience rendered forcibly invisible, to relocate the meaning of social experience within everyday spaces—the tenements and alleys and basements; "the gin mills and the barber shops and the juke joints and the churches" where, as Ellison's narrator argues, a "whole unrecorded history is spoken" (460).

This double valance of documentary as an evolving practice—a source for devastating misrepresentation of African Americans and a resource for combating the same; a tool for social redress, analysis, and racial management being refitted as a rejection of the managerial imagination itself—helps explain how the visual genre that Ellison at times so powerfully critiques remains central to his self-imagination as a writer, how it both serves and limits him. His own street photographs hardly achieve the taut complexity or technical virtuosity of the iconic images of the New York School. But they suggest that Ellison understood the evolving canons of street photography as a resource for transforming the essentially didactic logic of documentary into a more richly ambiguous critical mode. In aiming for such transformation, Ellison echoes the project of postwar street photography as influentially described by Lisette Model: the search not for fidelity to social fact or for the truth value of indexical meaning, but for the mode of "*analogy*" with a social landscape that images both frame and contest.[33]

Nowhere is this process of transformation more graphically attested to than in a binder among Ellison's papers, undated but apparently part of his collection of working materials prior to 1944, and marked "Photographs Miscellaneous Invisible Man" (figure 3.3).[34] At one point, the binder apparently included a stack of images; it now houses a single print: the photograph of an unidentified woman, race unknown, shot at relatively close range, lying on a city

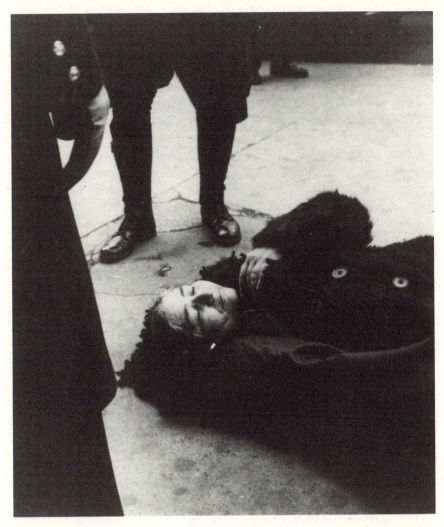

Figure 3.3. Ralph Ellison, Untitled, ca. 1937. Ralph Ellison Papers, Prints and Photographs Division, Library of Congress. By permission.

Ralph Ellison, Photographer   125

sidewalk as passersby ignore her or look on. From the position of the subject's body, it is impossible to determine whether she is dead or merely unconscious; she might be a crime victim or drug user or an unfortunate fallen literally by the wayside. What rescues the image from a kind of documentary banality—and makes such banality, the ease with which the camera affords a voyeuristic view of failure and pain and want, part of what we confront—is a series of telling details, luminous in their particularity. The woman's hand is placed precisely, beneath her chin, as if she were arrested in deep thought; the buttons on her dark sweater are absurdly oversized, as if, transported beyond the realm of fashion, they had become amulets donned to ward off this very disaster. The implied presence of authority, in the shape of two male police officers visible only as a massive torso and legs ending in thick work boots, is likewise (to use the obvious phrase) arresting. Their postures indicate neither succor nor confrontation but an indifference that makes the subject's fate all the more mysterious.

Borrowing from the visual appeal of the crime scene shots of Weegee, this one indeed gives us a window onto an otherwise invisible world. But unlike infamous Weegee photographs such as "Gunman Killed by Off-Duty Cop" (figure 3.4), "Joy of Life," and "Bodies Taken from Burning Building," Ellison's image locates itself in an American social space illegible in terms of murderous violence or sensational catastrophe; the logic of the woman's misfortune is unavailable to us. Nor does the image bear content or a title that would locate (and thus cordon off) the experience it registers within such "underworld" spaces as Harlem, the Bowery, Hell's Kitchen, or the Lower East Side—sites metonymic for midcentury Americans with criminality, chronic poverty, ethnic or racial alterity, and low life. Indeed, none of the usual narratives—fallen woman, city-dweller down on her luck, class or ethnic specimen, urban victim—helps the viewer make sense of the subject. In lieu of exposing an underworld for the purposes of shock or rehabilitation, the camera portrays a more nuanced social condition, an unreadability that troubles the very categories evoked to resolve it.

Archival evidence shows that Ellison shot this image as part of a series of street photographs exploring the same dissonance and mystery courted by the New york school. He apparently saved it, absent a caption or identifying narrative, in the work folder for his novel-in-progress because it records and enables a crucial transition: from the "Forgotten Man" of New Deal nation building to the "Invisible Man" of his writerly imagination. A decade after Franklin Delano Roosevelt's famed campaign address of April 7, 1932, which

Figure 3.4. Weegee (Arthur Fellig), Gunman Killed by Off-Duty Cop, 1942. Collection of
the International Center of Photography. © Weegee/International Center of Photography/
Getty Images.

inaugurated the New Deal by calling for economic programs "that put their faith once more in the forgotten man at the bottom of the economic pyramid," Ellison's shift in notation suggests a decisive rejection of rhetorics of uplift— New Deal, communist, and black bourgeois alike—and an interest in forms of invisibility, marginality, and social experience resistant to conventional political redress.[35]

At least two points need emphasizing. First, it is the camera that provides the suggestion or inspiration—the agency—for the kind of invisibility in which Ellison is interested; it is the camera, this photograph attests, that serves as both an instrument and an emblem of transition from the didacticism of protest to the possibilities of expressivity; from uplift to an aesthetic fashioned as critique; from redress for the "forgotten" to imaginative engagement with the worlds of the "invisible." Second, however serendipitous this particular image, its placement in Ellison's personal archive indicates that the body of a woman, and its self-conscious representation, serve him as some kind of allegory for the conditions of invisibility. Against the cropping and tearing of the female body from his wallet image of Wright, in the service of a closer fit with Ellison's authorial self-imagination, the careful preservation of this figure marks a striking difference.[36]

I will return to images of the female body—dismembered, remembered— and their role in the argument of and with *Invisible Man*. Here, it will suffice to remark that what I read as a founding image for the novel begs us to revisit several kinds of questions about Ellison's aims, and to understand them as irrevocably linked. Whether we follow Claudia Tate's influential argument emphasizing the role of women as latter-day "stationmasters" who "assist the Invisible Man along his course to freedom," or myriad other critics who insist that Ellison trades on troubling typologies of femininity and sexuality; whether we construct the relationship between *Invisible Man* and Ellison's body of critical work on the postwar novel and its cultural surround as symbiotic, illustrative, defensive, or misleading; in whatever fashion we trace the fate of Ellison's commitments and indebtedness to his experiences of communism, socialist intellectual formations, and the infrastructure and players of the political left in Harlem: in the case of each of these ongoing debates, our picture of Ellison will be altered as his stakes in postwar images, and in the shifting radicalism and modes of photographic critique, are accounted for.[37] Like much of the scholarship following on the publication of previously unavailable materials, a reading that foregrounds Ellison's interests in image making may well undermine the longstanding reception of *Invisible Man* as sui generis, and of its author as the startlingly emergent figure of a "precocious black modernism" animating "the wasteland of depression-era naturalism."[38] But it will nonetheless heighten our awareness of the suppleness and probity with which Ellison exploits available resources for rethinking the novel as an American cultural form. If the extensive body of his critical essays suppresses that work, the pages of *Invisible Man* bear the imprint of his forays into photography, that mode of apprehension defined by its power to retain traces of the real even as it irrevocably transforms them. To those pages, with an eye for the uses Ellison makes of photography as an analogue for the novel and of its newly analogical mode, I now turn.

Photographic Practice and the Matter of *Invisible Man*

One useful, because counterintuitive, place to begin reconstructing Ellison's uses of photography is in response to the second chapter of *Invisible Man*. At its center, as most readers will readily remember, lies the shocking Trueblood incident, one of the most often cited episodes of the novel and the occasion for a formidable body of criticism that might be described as incidentally antivisual. To a large degree, Ellison's readers have focused on the ways in which Trueblood's narrative confirms or undercuts claims for Ellison's commitments to blackness or the laboring classes, the degree to which it aligns Ellison with or against sociology as a disciplinary form.[39] Given these interests, such readings understandably emphasize the monocular, self-serving effects of the ethnographic "vision" that occasions Trueblood's narrative. But the invisible man's presence in this episode is itself framed by a meditation on vision, as an act linked and opposed to photographic seeing, that requires further accounting. At the very least, I want to show, Ellison's maneuverings with respect to the models and legacy of sociological inquiry turn on his interest in photography as a power to be harnessed as well as resisted.

The incident proper begins with the narrator's account of driving for Norton, that trustee of consciousness, Brahmin Bostonian, teller of "polite Negro stories," and bearer of the white man's burden (37). Placed (or rather misplaced) in the driver's seat, the invisible man can only view Norton "through the rear-view mirror" (38). In this initiatory context, the optical device takes on something of the resonance of the disembodied lens Ellison describes in "Hidden Name and Complex Fate." Used with directed intention, such an implement—which reveals, in the form of optical reversal, objects that would otherwise remain out of view—might yield an important truth or secret, awareness of what Bledsoe later calls "the difference between the way things are and the way they're supposed to be" (142). That the narrator has here failed woefully to make use of his implement, to see that he doesn't see, is emphasized by his own account of the effect of his encounter with Norton as "Founder" (39):

> As I drove, faded and yellowed pictures of the school's early days displayed in the library flashed across the screen of my mind, coming fitfully and fragmentarily to life—photographs of men and women in wagons drawn by mule teams and oxen, dressed in black, dusty clothing, people who seemed almost without individuality, a black mob that seemed to be waiting, looking with blank faces, and among them the inevitable collection of white men and women in smiles, clear of features, striking, elegant and confident.

In effect, the invisible man dismisses these photographic documents (and, more to the point, the lived history that produces them) as "blank" and inert, capable of animation only on "the screen of my mind." He thus simultaneously experiences himself as a witnessing writerly consciousness—"You must write me and tell me the outcome," Norton demands (44)—and as a self-willed outsider to what Norton describes as "your whole race" (45). Indeed, the passage suggests, the invisible man's experience of himself as protowriter depends crucially on this careful distancing. In a parodically literal paraphrase of the motto Trueblood will soon elaborate with such splendid folk wit, the narrator moves ("As I drove") without being moved by the specter of black folk or mass experience (the "blank faces," the figures "almost without individuality"). *His* imaginative engagement with Norton is the agency that transforms the dead letter of black history, all that "had never seemed actually to have been alive," into a moving picture; *his* epiphanic response accords the images "more meaning than I could fathom," imbuing what had previously seemed the kinds of instrumental "signs or symbols one found on the last pages of the dictionary" into expressive figures for the young man's self-determination (39).

But the still photograph as an expressive possibility has not yet been exhausted. If the documentary image of the black folk becomes an instrument for the invisible man's self-invention, the "identifi[cation]" with Norton the image occasions takes shape in another photographic exchange. As the narrator observes Norton "through the glass" of the rearview mirror, "gazing at the long ash of his cigar," the latter embarks on the eerily revealing account of his lost daughter, that being "more rare, more beautiful, purer, more perfect and more delicate than the wildest dream of a poet" (41, 42). "Fumbl[ing] in his vest pocket," Norton thrusts at the startled narrator a portrait of the lady, a "tinted miniature framed in engraved platinum" (42). This object—represent-

ing "[a] young woman of delicate, dreamy features"—is pointedly anachronistic. With her "flowing costume of soft, flimsy material" in lieu of the "smart,
well-tailored, angular, sterile, streamlined, engine-turned, air-conditioned
modern outfits you see in the women's magazines," the photograph's subject
achieves an uncanny presence: the effect of her direct gaze—a gaze denied the
black folk of the archival documentary image—is so startling that the narrator
"almost drop[s]" the miniature, even as he "seem[s] to remember her, or
someone like her, in the past" (42, 43).

Norton's image itself thus recalls a long outmoded but resonant photographic object, one closely linked, as Alan Trachtenberg has argued, with the
project of the democratic republic: the daguerreotype, at once an uncannily
animate representation of the human subject and a kind of looking glass in
which viewers behold their own reflections.[40] Ellison would likely have known
daguerreotype and other nineteenth-century portraits from his early days, as
part of the archive of the move up from slavery prominently on display at
Tuskegee—what the invisible man calls "the relics . . . from the times of the
Founder" (137).[41] Although the daguerreotype itself was historically short-lived
as a mode of portraiture, the questions it occasioned about aura, presence,
and the recognition and possession of human being influenced photography's
changing self-representations well into the twentieth century. The definitive
uncanniness of the daguerreotype, and more broadly of the photographic
miniature, closely suits Ellison's purposes: it mirrors a past that remains unavailable to the narrator even as it reveals him to be the secret sharer, the ghostly
double, of the daughter embalmed in her status as racial icon.[42] More to the
point, this kinship in iconicity emphasizes the iconic quality of the landscape—
that is, both the literal and symbolic grounds—on which the invisible man
encounters Trueblood.

Like Norton's miniature, the sharecropper's landscape smacks of archaic
significance ("Is that a *log* cabin?" Norton demands), and it too is charged
with uncanniness: "as we took a hill we were swept by a wave of scorching air
and it was as though we were approaching a desert. It almost took my breath
away" (46). This "countryside," with its "collection of shacks and log cabins,"
is reminiscent not only of historical "slavery time" and the mythic bondage in
Egypt but of the lived experience of that quintessential photographic phenomenon, the Dust Bowl. It was, in fact, Ellison's home place of Oklahoma—
indeed, the very word *Okie*—that served as a "national symbo[l] for destitu-
tion" throughout the 1930s and well into the Second World War.[43] More to
the point, it was the rhetorical possibilities of the Dust Bowl and its effects, in
conjunction with the conditions of peonage in the sharecropping South, that

Figure 3.5. Russell Lee, Cabin in the Cotton, Muskogee County, Oklahoma. Abandoned Farmhouse, 1939. Farm Security Administration/Office of War Information Collection, Library of Congress.

came to define the aims and the look of New Deal era documentary. The FSA portfolio amassed by Russell Lee, Dorothea Lange, and Arthur Rothstein, alongside Bourke-White's influential work in *You Have Seen Their Faces*, made icons of a rural landscape laid waste, buried under the weight of its own history (figures 3.5, 3.6). Read against an archive that superimposed the rural, the ravaged, and the regional, the landscape through which Ellison's narrator moves—its ramshackle cabins "bleached white and warped by the weather," its children in "stiff new overalls," its women in gingham "washing clothes in an iron pot" (46, 47)—can be seen to graft the territorial West onto the plantation South, mapping a palimpsestic site of photographic agency with which Ellison's narrator and his novel must contest.

If the resulting landscape draws on Ellison's own experience, it is "new territory" for the incredulous Norton, who notes, "I've never seen this section before" (46).[44] Invoking the frontiersman's aim of conquest, the ethnographer's alertness to fresh native informants, and the social scientist's imperative

Figure 3.6. Arthur Rothstein, Abandoned Farm in the Dust Bowl Area, Oklahoma, 1936. Farm Security Administration/Office of War Information Collection, Library of Congress.

to parcel and taxonomize all in one, Norton indeed embodies what Warren has called "an anthology" of managerial stances.[45] But Norton's shock and desire, not to mention the rhetoric in which he couches them, strike a note quite other than that of the Chicago School and its measured pronouncements on the social structures of poverty and race.[46] By contrast, Norton's effusions are thunderous, far more reminiscent of the rhetorical strategies employed in *You Have Seen Their Faces*, whose influence long past its publication remained profound.[47] The comic distance between Norton's moral rhetoric—"You feel no inner turmoil, no need to cast out the offending eye?" (51)—and Trueblood's folkish literalism—"My eyes is all right too. And when I feels po'ly in my gut I takes a little soda and it goes away" (51)—echoes a similar dissonance structuring Bourke-White and Caldwell's text. Throughout, Caldwell engages in a kind of homiletics, depicting the Negro tenant farmer as a Job-like "descendant of the slave," who "for generations . . . has lived in mortal fear" and "seen his women violated and his children humiliated. Every white face he sees is a reminder of his brother's mutilation, burning, and death at the stake."[48] Against Caldwell's biblically inflected language of injured human-ity and depraved indifference, the reader encounters captions—entirely in-vented by Bourke-White—like that attached to the first image of the text: "Blackie ain't good for nothing, he's just an old hound dog." Attached to the image of a young boy and his dog poised in the rude doorway of a battered cabin (figure 3.7), the caption exemplifies her belief that "most of the people we photographed were way too ignorant to know what it was all about"; fur-ther, it bespeaks a celebration of the power of the camera to construct its own symbolic field—in this case, "the South that you bring back on sheets of Panchromatic film."[49]

The rank invention of voices for the dispossessed in a seminal documentary photo-text highlights the challenge of Trueblood as a figure for both the narra-tor and Ellison. Disdaining any physical likeness or contiguity with a man who appears to be the creation of ethnographic discourses and the psychosexual fantasies of white America, the invisible man desperately "sh[akes] off" the touch of Trueblood's hand on his shoulder, all the while knowing that he can "explain nothing" of his own predicament (52). Inexorably drawn into the threesome, the narrator becomes, against his will, a figure of mediation: "We sat on the porch in a semi-circle in camp chairs, me between the sharecropper and the millionaire" (52). Thus hemmed in, seething with shame, rage, and ressentiment, the invisible man obviously reckons with his status as excluded middle in a sociological framework that recognizes only Negro primitive against enlightened modern.[50] But he also embodies the dual challenge of the look back: the writerly return to a haunted past that must be made usable; the problem of the returned mutual gaze of the documentary subject. In the only chapter in the body of the novel to be formulated in the retrospective mode, Ellison's gestures toward photographic history not only frame the narrator's vision problems. They also suggest that the project of making use or sense of the past is conjoined with the problem of the novel's relation to the photo-graphic archive.[51]

Not surprisingly, then, for all the power with which photographic prece-dents figure racial nostalgia, dispossession, and false consciousness in the Trueblood episode, the image—or more precisely, the possibilities opened by the conjunction of image and word—continues to be pressed into service.

Figure 3.7. Margaret Bourke-White, East Feliciana Parish, Louisiana, 1936. By permission. Margaret Bourke-White Collection, Special Collections Research Center, Syracuse University Library.

Some two years after the publication of *Invisible Man*, Ellison continued to produce what we might call photographic referents for it, as if to contest the iconography of the South and its black and folk cultures installed by documentary work like Bourke-White's. In a series of images Ellison made in Alabama during a visit in 1953, he takes for his subject what appears to be an abandoned brick building, arresting in its combination of architectural rhythm and decay. Shot at the middle distance with a resolute frontality and an obvious aspiration for clarity, the image self-consciously recalls the work of Walker Evans—which Ellison knew, likely through Evans's groundbreaking *American Photographs* exhibition at the Museum of Modern Art in 1938, and through social encounters with Evans himself.[52] It's tempting, with respect to this context, to read Ellison's series as a straightforward gesture of photographic mimicry, his attempt to achieve something like the complexly "anti-graphic" effects that characterize Evans's work.[53] But Ellison's notation on the back of these prints suggests another aim; it reads: "Golden Day ? Alabama 1953."[54] What his images document is not the "real" landscape of the rural South but Ellison's quest to find, after the fact, a photographic correlative for his own novelistic inventions. The aim is neither illustration (showing what the Golden Day was supposed, in the pages of *Invisible Man*, to look like) nor straightforward documentation (what Barthes calls the deictic urge to proclaim, "'Look,' 'See,' 'Here it is'") but rather "analogy" in Model's quite specific sense: a negotiation of the documentary, the fictive, and the experiential as mutually mediating registers.[55] Beyond *Invisible Man*, as part of an afterlife for the novel with which its writer must contend, the camera continues to serve Ellison as an agency for exploring—and producing—such mediation, in the face of its own history of more narrowly instrumental effects.

In *Invisible Man*, Ellison hazards a version of this transformation from documentary to analogy—a project sketched more than a decade earlier, in the Invisible Woman photograph—in a scene that takes up where the Trueblood incident has left off: at the point where photo-text has become a signal form for registering the felt effects and conditions of American modernity. The scene in question occurs in chapter 13, when Ellison's protagonist (who has just been released from the Liberty Paints factory hospital and ejected from the genteel sanctuary of the Men's House) takes to the streets of Harlem. In response to a surge of nostalgia, the narrator pauses to buy a "hot, baked Car'lina yam" from a street vendor (263), savoring the "intense feeling of freedom" afforded by his appetite for such a down-home, folk-tainted, "*Field-Nigger-is[h]*" object (264, 265). But the "freedom to eat yams on the street" turns out to be "far less"—far less consequential, that is—"than I had expected" (267).

Unlike the madeleine of Proust's Marcel, which opens access to a yearned-for past, the yams leave "an unpleasant taste bloom[ing] in my mouth" (267). They bring the narrator the discomfiting recognition that an identity forged in diametric opposition to "what was expected" is no less conventional, no less forcibly bound by the dehumanizing realities it strains to escape (266). Literally central to the novel, then, is a moment of existential and historical crisis: how to generate modes of subjectivity and cultural expression embedded in experiential history, from the geography of slavery to the Great Migration, yet free of the deterministic clutch of the past?

Whatever the effects of the narrator's experience of himself as subject to documentary looking in the Trueblood incident, the experience of documentary imaging plays a crucial part in Ellison's response to the question. Having discarded his frostbitten yam, the invisible man continues walking the streets, only to come upon that staple of Harlem life throughout the Depression and postwar years, an eviction. As he attempts to make sense of the event, a new language of visuality becomes insistent: "Just look what they doing to us. Just look," the elderly female evictee urges him; "Just look at what they're doing" (268). Of the "paddies" removing furniture, an outraged bystander yells, "Look at that" (268); "Look, lady," one of the dispossessors urges in turn (270). "Feeling my eyes burn," resisting his own transformation into a "witnes[s] of what [he] did not wish to see" (270), the narrator "turn[s] aside and look[s]" instead at the household objects thrown pell-mell into the street: the knocking bones of a minstrel; a hair-straightening comb and curling iron; an Ethiopian flag and a cracked plate commemorating the St. Louis World's Fair; a set of tarnished cuff links, a yellowed breast pump. Powerfully auratic in their specificity, these bent and faded objects comprise a material history, a kind of museum, of black life in America, in all its richness and its impoverishment of opportunity. Thus arrayed, they indeed mime the effects of Walker Evans's storied images of the inventories of country stores, the contents of rural homesteads (figure 3.8). But while Evans's catalogue is, as Sontag has noted, "decidedly random" and all the more nostalgic for being so, Ellison's is anything but.[56] The first thing the invisible man "look[s] down to see" is a nineteenth-century portrait of the couple being dispossessed. Quite unlike Norton's daughter, these home people "loo[k] out of an oval frame" with a gaze that calls to the invisible man as both "a reproach and a warning," and their hortatory message is clarified only when the narrator completes his act of witnessing (271). Last of all, half-buried in the snow, as the narrator searches for "anything missed by my eyes," he finds "a fragile paper, coming apart with age":

Figure 3.8. Walker Evans, Interior of a Farmhouse Near Ridgeley, Tennessee, 1937. Farm Security Administration/Office of War Information Collection, Library of Congress.

the free papers of the woman's husband—"*my Negro, Primus Provo,*" "*freed by me this sixth day of August, 1859. Signed: John Samuels. Macon*" (272).

Photograph and text; image and testifying narrative: the objects of the narrator's encounter frame him as viewer and witness to a vast photo-text assemblage, randomly arrayed and brutally shorn of the confident (and misleading) assumption of equivalence between visual and verbal signs.[57] Nothing could be farther from the implied precedent of Bourke-White and Caldwell's work, yet the framing power of photo and text is made central to the mysteries the narrator confronts: Who bestows freedom on whom? How is autonomous identity earned, expressed, given shape? The narrator is shocked by the raw intimacy of these objects—so much so that the "unpleasant taste" left by the yams becomes "a bitter spurt of gall" (273); he finds himself in thrall not to the objects themselves, but to the animating force of the photo-text frame; to its power to implicate him metonymically in the "linked verbal echoes, images," of a collective "home" (273). Unlike his earlier metonymic stance of imprisonment "between the sharecropper and the millionaire," this photo-text experience alters the terms of the narrator's engagement with the documentary image world, even as it hews to progressive ideals for that engagement: it prompts a revelatory recognition that spurs social action, a spontaneous oration on behalf of the evictees that paves the narrator's way to the Brotherhood and a higher education in the realities of power. Whatever its limits or false premises, the invisible man's public voice—the one that will lead to his eventual self-understanding as a writer—begins here, in his stance as a viewer of photo-text. In one of its many arcs, the narrative has taken him from the falsely animated pictures generated by his stance at the wheel of Norton's vehicle to these very differently moving pictures. This is the moment, as Brother Jack suggests, when "*History* has been born in your brain" (291).

At this juncture, documentary is transformed from a method of exposure—a technique applied to the hapless, the forgotten, the unself-conscious—into a powerful exercise, at once aesthetic and political, of self-knowledge. In place of the hortatory rhetoric of *You Have Seen Their Faces*—and, for that matter, of Wright's *Twelve Million Black Voices*—Ellison offers the narrator's intensely felt account of his own witnessing, the narrative of an existential nausea born of terrible beauty, of "beautiful absurdity" (559). To put it another way, the self-understanding categorically denied Bigger Thomas, by virtue of Wright's commitment to exposing intractable social realities, is opened as a possibility in Ellison's text through the narrator's encounter with the objects of documentary. But here the logic of photo-text amplifies (rather than "explicates" or "exposes") the mysteries of that encounter. Like the anti-instrumental images of the New York School, Ellison's text emphasizes the power of the documentary stance to evoke powerful yet ambiguous responses, states of being that move the subject "*far beyond*" the witnessed artifacts' "*intrinsic meaning as objects*" (273; italics original).

Confronting this excess or surfeit of signification, the invisible man has not only moved decisively beyond the place (phenomenological or imaginative as well as social) of his encounter with Norton, where the archaic portrait of the daughter presents him with "more meaning than I could fathom." He has entered into the project of postwar photography as shaped by an immigrant, exilic sensibility and made to comment on the brokenness of post-Holocaust Europe. When the Hungarian-born and Jewish André Kertész, a veteran photographer of the intimacies and horrors of everyday life during the interwar period, fled Paris for New York in 1937, Luce's editors at *Life* rejected his work because they claimed that his images "spoke too much" of "a meaning different from the literal one"; inducing the viewer "to think," they resisted incorporation into the progress narratives and brisk visual rhythms of *Life*'s photostories.[58] The archive of objects the invisible man confronts invites precisely such a pensive stance; for the first time, he meets the challenge they pose. The items spilled heedlessly onto the snow—the "useless inhalant" and "tarnished" beads, the "worn baby shoe and dusty lock of infant hair" (272)—evoke such powerful mixed response (the narrator is "both repelled and fascinated" [275]) because they testify not to social fact but to the mysterious alchemy by which lived experience, including his own, becomes the stuff—traumatic, unspeakable, irresistible—of history. Like the storied images of the New York School, what Ellison's scene of photo-text encounter foregrounds is the perhaps irreparable loss sustained by social beings whose work on the world produces nothing more or less than their own alienation. No wonder, then, that the narrator's spontaneous question to the assembled crowd about the former slave, now dispossessed tenement-dweller, Provo, is so resounding: "Then where did his labor go?" (278).

Just as the photo-text impels Ellison's narrator to speak in his first spontaneous oration, photography as a context and model enables Ellison to make trial of a narrative voice that rejects the instrumentality of protest, as it demands that the conventions of novelistic identity making answer to the realities of contemporary social experience. Famously, the conclusion to *Invisible Man* offers a challenge (or a rhetorical question, depending on one's view) cast in the modality of jazz: "Who knows but that, on the lower frequencies, I speak for you?" (581). But the final arc of the novel speaks eloquently to the context of postwar photography, with its dual emphasis on social critique and affirmation. This arc suggests that the author of *Invisible Man* is inseparable from Ralph Ellison, Photographer; it demonstrates how richly the experience of Ellison as an image maker helps account for the novel's play with invisibility as a historical condition, a mode of urban perception, and a symbolic language.

For evidence of Ellison's attempt to make his own novel function in something like the way the serendipitous photo-text of eviction does, I turn to its extraordinary final chapter. Here, the narrator has returned from an ill-fated attempt to seduce Sybil, the wife of a prominent Brotherhood leader, to a Harlem ablaze; in response to the death of Tod Clifton, what one participant calls a "sho 'nough race riot" has begun to break out (553). Steeped in perceptual and moral confusion, the narrator has a shocking (to him, anyway) insight: "Could this be the answer, could this be what the [Brotherhood] committee had planned . . . ? . . . It was not suicide, but murder. The committee had planned it. And I had helped, had been a tool" (553). Outraged, he runs aimlessly from one scene of violent encounter to another; the streets on which he flees have become an alien landscape, where shattered glass glitters "like the water of a flooded river" on which "distorted objects," snatched and abandoned by looters, appear "washed away by the flood" (556). In this moment—both a baptism and a drowning—the narrator is stopped short by a ghostly and ghastly vision:

> Ahead of me the body hung, white, naked, and horribly feminine from a lamppost. I felt myself spin around with horror and it was as though I had turned some nightmarish somersault. I whirled, still moving by reflex, back-tracking and stopped and now there was another and another, seven—all hanging before a gutted storefront. I stumbled, hearing the cracking of bones underfoot and saw a physician's skeleton shattered on the street, the skull rolling away from the backbone, as I steadied long enough to notice the unnatural stiffness of those hanging above me. They were mannequins—"Dummies!" I said aloud. Hairless, bald and sterilely feminine. And I recalled the boys in the blonde wigs, expecting the relief of laughter, but suddenly was more devastated by the humor than by the horror. But are they unreal, I thought; *are* they? What if one, even *one* is real—is . . . Sybil? I hugged my brief case, backing away, and ran . . . [.] (556; ellipses original)

Numerous readers of *Invisible Man* have singled out this passage for commentary, but none have noted that it reiterates the transformation recorded in chapter 13, from the fact of documentary eyewitnessing to a more complex form of self-expression. Ellison was himself an observer of the 1943 Harlem outbreak; he published a less than sympathetic on-the-scene account in the mainstream white press, and later testified before a commission assembled by then-mayor LaGuardia on the causes and meaning of the event.[59] But this novelistic version rings serious changes on the work of documentary observation, not least by framing the event of the riot as a decisive moment in the evolution of an artist's self-understanding. In confronting the spectacle of the skeleton and mannequins, Ellison's narrator enters a zone of liminality, a state of being in which the "real" and the "unreal," "humor" and "horror," are continuous if not indistinguishable, and their intersection is the individual's rebirth within the devastation of "History" (556).

The full force of this liminal moment, and of Ellison's appropriation of Harlem iconography, becomes available only when we read them in the context of a widely disseminated body of photographs meditating on just that intersection. Ranging from early twentieth-century shots by Eugène Atget of the storefronts and small shops on the outskirts of a rapidly industrializing Paris through art world appropriations by Dadaists and Surrealists of the possibilities of the mechanical human form, these images offer up the mannequin as a symbol or allegory of urban modernity and as an object of apprehension—in both senses—that deeply troubles liberal or progressive management of social difference and change. A prop for burgeoning consumer culture; a cause and effect of the cultivation of personal image; a figure for the radical alienation of human labor and consciousness under advanced capitalism: the mannequin as found object had already become, by the late 1940s, a powerful tool for photographers seeking the effect of estrangement from routine habits of perception and self-understanding. Wrenched out of its usual instrumental contexts, the mannequin offered itself as an overdetermined object of fantasy and meditation, richly available for what Ellison calls "dramatic study in comparative humanity" (xviii).

This is, at least, the logic of the mannequin in the photographic images of that key practitioner and influence on the New York School photographers: Henri Cartier-Bresson. In following Cartier-Bresson's work Ellison also followed in the wake of his onetime mentors Langston Hughes and Richard Wright, but traveled farther than both.[60] Although he may or may not have met the most storied photojournalist of the postwar era, Ellison's archive provides ample evidence—clipped articles, reviews of shows, announcements of relevant exhibitions and publications—of his engagement.[61] And no wonder: having begun as a painter in the ambit of interwar surrealism, Cartier-Bresson took up the camera as a more powerful instrument for probing realities hidden beneath the banal, slick, even repellant surfaces of everyday life. Certain critics derided Cartier-Bresson for being infatuated with slums and low life throughout his travels in Mexico, Spain, Italy, France, and Eastern Europe, but what he sought to convey was not social fact, remediable or otherwise, so much as the irrepressible energies of differently threatened life-worlds—brothels, back alleys, flea markets, Jewish ghettos—in all their intimate social realities.[62] Imbued with a certain phantasmatic quality, insisting on these venues as sites of drama and adventure, his images consistently evade the closure of conventional documentary. In Cartier-Bresson's early body of work, some of his most powerful photographs are shots of storefront mannequins in modernity's outlying districts. One such image ("Untitled," 1929; figure 3.9) focuses tightly on a jumbled pile of molds for producing artificial hands and feet, the edges of each appendage roughly severed. Even before the Holocaust, the sense of human labor being obscenely misdirected toward the production of its own specious emblem and replacement is palpable. In another shot, the head of a male mannequin presses up against the front of a shuttered shop, its unblinking gaze and the tattered window dressings around it belying an adjacent poster, which touts an outmoded vision of the city as source of the bourgeois good life ("Budapest," 1931).[63]

Such images create a far more complex effect than that of obvious irony, which helps explain the power of Cartier-Bresson's work as a significant resource for Ellison. In the enigmatic "Rouen, 1929" (figure 3.10), the camera focuses on a trio of mannequins sporting menswear, placed outside a shop in the downscale market district of that provincial city. Two feature spindles instead of heads; the third has a full complement of appendages—including "African" features and a black face. Carefully calculated to take full advantage of its subject, the image makes the experiences of commerce, looking, serendipity itself, inseparable from racial feeling, as it raises persistent questions about the presence of the African in this apparently unlikely place. Indeed, the image insists on a rhythmic progression: the two model forms on the left appear almost to give birth to the erect figure on the right, fully clothed down to its three-piece suit and neatly seamed gloves.

If this sequence ends in a figure of assimilation, whereby the African is resplendently transformed in the image of a still-coalescing bourgeois modernity, Cartier-Bresson's record of that transformation is far from celebratory. At the still center of the photograph runs the diagonal shutterpole of the shop front; from the viewer's perspective, it appears to intersect the gleaming metal hoop that holds the mannequin in place, a fettering that bespeaks the long history of commodification of black bodies in the service of Western fantasies. Like vast numbers of his cultural cohort during the 1920s, Cartier-Bresson indulged in the liberating effects of veneration of the primitive.[64] Yet this image, produced in the very moment of the demise of that vogue for the Negro formalized as the Harlem Renaissance, seems to leave such facile identification behind. Accessorized yet inert, inviting desires it variously troubles, the black mannequin is made the object of social exploration and the viewer's self-understanding alike. Oscillating between literal and symbolic resonances, Cartier-Bresson's

Figure 3.9. Henri Cartier-Bresson, Untitled, ca. 1939. Magnum Photos.

photograph emphasizes the centrality of the figure of the African to the business of modernity, probing the entangled facts of visibility, race, longing, and belonging.

Just as Ellison followed Cartier-Bresson's body of work, he was also attentive to the work of Lisette Model, who came to New York (shortly after Ellison) in 1937.[65] Having (like Ellison) begun her life in art as a musician, a student of the composer Arnold Schoenberg, Model inaugurated her photographic career with a series of portraits of bourgeois vacationers on the French Riviera, published in January 1940 under the title "Why France Fell" in *PM*—a journal Ellison knew well, both through its wide circulation in Harlem's cultures of the left and via Richard Wright's close connections there.[66] It was, perhaps, not a far step from Model's unsparing, monumental images of the pampered bourgeoisie, rendered absurd and even surreal in the artificiality of their self-presentation, to her first American body of work. Titled "Reflections, New York," the series comprised images of mannequins, passersby, and their multiple refractions in plate-glass shop windows in the glittering precincts of Fifth Avenue.[67]

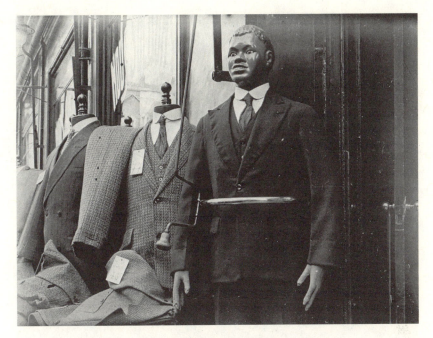

Figure 3.10. Henri Cartier-Bresson, Untitled, Rouen, 1929. Magnum Photos.

Like Cartier-Bresson's, Model's early work can be read as an analogue if not a direct source for Ellison's own. Confrontational yet nuanced, linking the spaces of postwar privilege with the realities of life on the other side of the tracks and the color line, her "Reflections" images bespeak the perceptual challenge of urban experience, the uncanny fixity of American cultural identity, and the unacknowledged links between the two. In one exemplary "Reflections" shot (figure 3.11), Model exploits the found landscape of the city street to produce an image both literally illegible and profoundly revealing. With considerable virtuosity, she frames the angled panes of a plate-glass window display so as to locate the mannequins within it, the reflections of facades across the street, and the movements of passersby (as well as her own hand) in what appears to be a unified plane. Deprived of a stable vantage point or obvious perspectival logic, the viewer confronts the problem of reading the relationships among its subjects. Model's signature play between transparency and opacity—what we see and what we see through—makes it impossible to understand the mannequins as a straightforward metaphor for their human counterparts, drifting yet unmoved. Rather, the photograph asks us to take our affective bearings from its artificial figures. If the stiffly posed torsos

Figure 3.11. Lisette Model, Untitled, from "Reflections, New York," ca. 1939–45. By permission of The Lisette Model Foundation, NY. The National Gallery of Canada, Ottawa.

framed in Van Raalte's exhibition windows signify commerce and the manufacture of desire, the ghostly reflections dominating the image—the partially visible mannequin and the monumental hand, curved in a receptive gesture that appears to emanate from the distant body—have a different effect. That its auratic quality is lost on the human passersby below, their faces unfocused, their gazes turned purposelessly elsewhere, is the point of the image. Playing with the uncanniness of the mannequin, Model uses the camera as an agency to highlight the complexities and contradictions most fundamental to American social life: what is readily on display offers up deeper truths of our social being and its limits, which yet remain, by virtue of our habits of perception, all but invisible.

Model's larger body of images gestures toward a racialized understanding of this problem of visibility; she wrote, for example, of her freelance work for the Hearst empire, which included significant photographic outlets such as *Harper's*, that vast amounts of it never saw the light of day because founder and owner William Randolph Hearst "did not like pictures of Black people."[68] Other bodies of photographs explicitly link the mannequin as a device with Ellison's purchase on black experience. In the photojournalistic response to the 1943 Harlem riots, the mannequin was ready to hand as a densely symbolic object of response. Innumerable photographs focus on the very scene Ellison invokes both as eyewitness and as novelist after the fact: broken shop fronts, the streets littered with debris from looting, particularly the remains of display mannequins decapitated or disassembled in the process. These images circulated widely in mainstream newspapers such as the *New York Times*, the *New York Herald Tribune*, and the *Daily News*.[69] Their subjects, composition, and dynamics generally suggest outrage about the destruction of white-owned property and loss of revenues, even as they stoke white readers' anxiety about the implied (or real) threats to (real) white bodies downtown. But some few of these shots do more complex work, analogous to Ellison's novelistic aims.

Among the riot mannequin images is a widely reproduced UPI wire service photo that featured prominently in a photo-essay in the *New York Amsterdam News*, among other newspapers (figure 3.12).[70] In it, the pavement in front of a department store has taken on the look of a battlefield; only human violence could have created such programmatic devastation. The store's display mannequins have been stripped of clothing, disassembled, and strewn about. Their inert nudity reinforces the uncanny charge of their likeness to scenes of patriotic gore, the nation's fallen dead. Cropped to produce a tighter focus on the one mannequin with a head that remains upright, the image offers that figure as both a watchful survivor and a haunting testament to the logic that produced

Figure 3.12. UPI, Harlem after the Riot, View of Looted Street, August 2, 1943. Corbis.

this landscape: economic opportunism, unacknowledged labor, a consumer logic predicated on white-owned institutions and Anglocentric artifacts. With its rouged and hollowed cheekbones, its marcelled hair, its sultry survey of the devastation, the mannequin becomes obscene and foreboding, its knowing glance that of the Sybil whose hypnotic vision foretells disaster. Like the invisible man's Sybil, who drunkenly beseeches him to perform as her own "domesticated rapist" (510), the mannequin seems here to invite a violent response that can only confirm the dehumanizing power of the racial fantasies it embodies.[71]

All the more telling, then, that Ellison invokes the figure of the mannequin, and this body of photographic meditation on it, to articulate the narrator's sense of agency. In witnessing those uncanny objects, bespeaking a humanity they mimic yet lack, the invisible man comes fully to recognize both the lacerating fact of his structural invisibility as a black American, and the liberating possibilities for self-creation in his embrace of that condition. Forced to confront the paradoxes of visibility and identity embodied by the mannequins, the narrator ceases to be a mannequin himself: a "zombie" or "automaton," "a walking personification of the Negative" (94). Raising the existential question "What if one, even *one*, is real—?" (556), the invisible man acknowledges the effects of his own attempts to play at invisibility: "By pretending to agree I *had* indeed agreed, had made myself responsible for that huddled form lighted by flame and gunfire in the street" (553).

This mode of responsibility differs markedly from other invocations of the word throughout the text: the narrator's desperate parroting, in his speech after the Battle Royal, of the mantras of "social responsibility" and social "equality" (30–31); Norton's "kindly" denial to Bledsoe of the narrator's responsibility for his injury (103); the narrator's response to the zoot-suiters he observes after Clifton's death, who make him feel "responsible" for his political failures (444); the Brotherhood's disciplinary response to the invisible man's "personal re-spon-si-bility" (464). For the first time, "responsibility"—the notion that "even an invisible man has a socially responsible role to play" (581)—gestures toward a mode of affirmation that implicates both the narrator's acts in the world of social experience and his narrative about them, both the realities of political struggle and the expressive energies that name and transmit it. Here, in view of these figures of devastation, politics and aesthetics—or politics and "love" (to use Ellison's phrase)—are at last, however tentatively, however ephemerally, comprehended in one. And photography, as archive and practice, is the means through which the novel achieves that comprehension. Appropriating and suppressing the image as referent, *Invisible Man* becomes at its climax a photo-text without photographs, a text both indebted to and exceeding the cultural genres shaping the era of its emergence.

Photographic Rereading: Beyond *Invisible Man*

If *Invisible Man*'s uses of the photograph help us chart its aspirations for the novel as a midcentury genre, they also help us consider its limits. In many quarters, the "comprehe[nsion]" the narrator achieves has been judged inadequate to what emerges as *Invisible Man*, and its pre–civil rights context of production, draw to a close: rising nationalism, opportunistic race-baiters, the violent paradox of "their American identity and mine" (559). Indeed, the mannequins the narrator confronts might stand for what has often been judged the stasis of the novel's ending (particularly in the epilogue): its perceived lack of narrative and broadly social resolution, read through Ellison's refusal to commit to a black aesthetic or through his sustained investment in the novel as a mode of response to urgencies of the civil rights era. But that effect of stasis reads somewhat differently in the context of the photographic archive with which Ellison was in dialogue. The suspension of narrative and affective movement in *Invisible Man*'s final sequences bespeaks the dilemma of the novel's midcentury project as Ellison envisaged it. Whatever Ellison's real or perceived failures as spokesman for black liberation, or for cultural expression in the idiom of civil rights and beyond, he sought to achieve a novelistic mode analogous to the photographic practice he pursued: at once responsive to social contestations and capable of exploiting them as resources for imaginative engagement with historical process and change.

This dual aspiration shows itself as such as the invisible man encounters the hanging mannequins. What makes the questions that punctuate this sequence of the narrative—"But are they unreal, I thought, *are* they?" (556)—readable as rhetorical, closed off to self-evidently social action, is the indeterminate status as signifying objects of the mannequins themselves. They are, of course, offered up as metaphors, objects whose likeness to human bodies throws into sharp relief the devastating violence of refused or withheld recognition of irreducible human being. But this metaphoric—that is, universalizing—thrust is in a powerful way at odds with the mannequins' tendency to resonate materially. However figurative, they are most starkly the effects of a proximate but absent social cause; objects "directly connected to reality," like the smoke from the "licking" fires set by Dupre, Scofield, and company; indexical traces, along with the shattered glass and "fumes of alcohol and burning tar" (554), of the rioters' parody of lynching and thus of lynching's history.[72] Ellison uses the mannequins, in other words, to embody a standoff between kinds of meaning his own narrative might seek to produce. On the one hand are (metonymic) meditations on causality; the lingering, haunting effects over time of the human act or gesture; the displacement via which we produce narrative, and simultaneously veil desire and agency. On the other are (metaphoric) explorations of sameness and difference, the creation—or failed creation—of iconicity, the felt experience of likeness in categorically different objects. Like the narrator "plunging" from one riot scenario to the next, careening between "fierce excitement" and horror (549), the narrative itself alternates between, but does not resolve, these signifying imperatives.

The mannequin episode is thus profoundly suggestive with respect to Ellison's ongoing interests in postwar photography, as it seeks simultaneously to heighten a sense of social crisis and to resist instrumental responses to that crisis. The flattening effects of *Invisible Man*, so often ascribed to Ellison's obsession with generating symbolic or Freudian (or merely Eurocentric) flourishes, can more productively be attributed to the consistency with which the novel checks the production of metaphor, insisting on the bracing contiguity, the hidden causal or temporal relations, embodied by its key symbolic objects.[73] This tendency to frustrate symbolic resonance via the redirection into social reality is a mirror image of postwar photography's aspirations to undercut its documentary status as record and evidence, to trouble its indexicality by insisting on diffusely symbolic and analogical effects. With respect to *Invisible Man*, the aim of arresting meaning (in particular the production of metaphor) can be seen as an operative principle of the novel as such, a narrative strategy that both hazards and limits its agency as a social act.[74] Gesturing toward photographic representation so as to harness its power to dislocate, to arrest historical experience, the mannequin sequence hovers between metaphor and metonymy, between sameness-in-difference and difference-in-contiguity, between the violence of revolution and the stasis of art. In the persistence and irreconcilability of these possibilities Ellison locates the power of fiction, shapeshifting to accommodate not only a historical present shot through with conflict and threat but a historical past remade in the present's image.[75]

That this rhythm of displacement, or oscillation between mythic and social registers, is both deliberate and productive becomes more evident when we consider the relation to *Invisible Man* of Ellison's extensive body of nonfiction writing—and of his famously uncompleted, posthumously published novel *Juneteenth*. Taking a cue from the mannequin episode, we might well ask why Ellison so strategically suppresses the visual referents or resources of *Invisible Man* in its climactic episodes: with all its shrewd invocations of oral and mass expressive forms in postwar Harlem, visual culture remains conspicuously, even puzzlingly, absent. At first glance, this absence would also seem to characterize Ellison's essays, from his early critical work of the 1940s in *New Masses*, *Negro Quarterly*, and the *New Republic*, through his *Saturday Review* essays on music beginning in 1954, right down to the canonical anthologies of *Shadow and Act* and *Going to the Territory*. There are, of course, obvious occasional pieces: Ellison's 1942 review in *New Masses* of the leftist photodocumentary *Native Land*, with its praise for the documentary "vision of [Paul] Strand and [Leo] Hurwitz"; or "Harlem Is Nowhere," his 1948 shooting-script-cum-essay for the planned photo-text collaboration with Gordon Parks, characterized by its visually directive renderings ("One must descend to the basement and move along a confusing mazelike hall to reach it. Twice the passage seems to lead against a blank wall; then at last one enters the brightly lighted auditorium. . . . One has entered the Lafargue Psychiatric Clinic"); or his 1968 essay for an exhibition catalogue of Romare Bearden's experiments with collage and photo-projection, which comments in detail on Bearden's uses of (among other materials) found photojournalistic and documentary photographs by way of "destroying moribund images of reality and creating the new."[76] But where, the skeptical reader might ask, is foundational evidence in what turns out to be Ellison's weightiest body of work for his visual engagements? And how might the presence or absence of the latter in Ellison's essays help explain the return with a vengeance of visual practices and objects as structural elements of *Juneteenth*?

On closer inspection, the essays are far from unmarked by the experiences of Ralph Ellison, Photographer; indeed, to invoke a favored epithet of Ralph Ellison, essayist, we might more accurately understand them as innocent of sustained references to that experience. The very title of Ellison's storied first anthology—the text Paule Marshall has identified as in effect his second novel—is drawn from an incidental film review that critiques postwar Hollywood films (unsurprisingly) as racial "illusion," purveyors of "negative images" that "constitute justifications for all those acts . . . which we label Jim Crow" (CE, 305).[77] But Ellison's act of naming and entitlement—always a productively fraught experience throughout his nonfiction work—suggests a central, even definitive, struggle with the image-world writ large. In an inverse of mass film's flickering images of servile, bumbling, and subhuman Negroes, which Ellison calls the "shadow" to the practice of Jim Crow as social "act," *Shadow and Act* limns the postwar landscape as a Plato's cave of shadows to which the entirety of Ellison's practice—his own social action—as a writer responds. The very structuring of the anthology in three sections—"The Seer and the Seen," "Sound and the Mainstream," "The Shadow and the Act"— segregates visual tropes and contexts from the more affirmative contexts of music only to suggest the framing power of the former—as well, one might argue, as the insufficiency of that conceptual barrier against the subtle promiscuity of Ellison's own visual tropes.

Perhaps no single essay exemplifies this condition better than Ellison's early essay, "Richard Wright's Blues." First published in *Antioch Review* in the summer of 1945 (that is, around the moment when *Invisible Man* was beginning to take shape), the piece has been canonized as "a seminal statement of Ellison's philosophy of the [blues]"; it appears, however, in "The Seer and the Seen" section of *Shadow and Act*, rather than in the section on sound.[78] In a bold account (bold, that is, for a writer who had yet to publish or even complete a novel of his own), Ellison defines "the Negro blues" as the shaping context for Wright's "attitude toward his life": as "an impulse to keep the painful details and episodes of a brutal experience alive in one's aching consciousness, to finger its jagged grain, and to transcend it . . . by squeezing from it a near-tragic, near-comic lyricism" (CE, 129). Part of the point of this definition is to note that, while *Black Boy* "presents an almost unrelieved picture of a personality corrupted by brutal environment" (CE, 131), it "also presents those fresh, human responses brought to its world by the sensitive child" (CE, 132). At this juncture, Ellison cites from Wright's work at some length, and with an emphasis worth noting:

> There was the *wonder* I felt when I first saw a brace of mountainlike, spotted, black-and-white horses clopping down a dusty road . . . the *delight* I caught in seeing long straight rows of red and green vegetables stretching away in the sun . . . [. . .] the vague *sense of the infinite* as I looked down upon the yellow, dreaming waters of the Mississippi . . . [. . .] the *love* I had for the mute regality of tall, moss-clad oaks . . . the hint of *cosmic cruelty* that I *felt* when I saw the curved timbers of a wooden shack that had been warped in the summer sun . . . and there was the *quiet terror* that suffused my senses when vast hazes of gold washed earthward from star-heavy skies on silent nights . . . [.] (CE, 132; italics Ellison's)

Ostensibly marking the "human" capacities of the "sensitive" black boy, Ellison's inflections are curiously ungainly—and, we might note, considerably at odds with the lyrical rhythms of Wright's prose; indeed, one has only to compare Ellison's rendering of Wright here with the structurally analogous passage from *Twelve Million Black Voices* on the rhythms of nature in the Southland to sense how studied the ungainliness of these inflections is.[79] What we might call Ellison's scoring of the text of *Black Boy* serves to obscure Wright's marked designs on his writerly status as "seer," a subject of visual experience and an agent of visual power: "when I first saw"; "the delight I caught in seeing"; "the vague sense of the infinite as I looked"; "the hint of cosmic cruelty that I felt when I saw." The dislocation thus effected suggests that, while Wright's text indeed offers Ellison a choice opportunity to riff on blues humanity and expressive codes, it also allows him to stake other fundamental claims. Deflecting Wright's investments in the seeing self and in visual framing as a resource for aesthetic consciousness and self-representation, Ellison at a critical juncture reserves the power of metaphoric and metonymic play on visuality for his own literary work. The conclusion to his reading of Wright makes clear that these stakes are quite high: if Wright's "most important achievement" is to have "converted the American Negro impulse toward self-annihilation and 'going-under-ground' into a will to confront the world," he has already anticipated in autobiographical form the thrust of the novel Ellison himself is undertaking (CE, 144). Thus the wallet image of Wright as image maker might be said to haunt "Richard Wright's Blues," whose authorial self-fashioning is conducted not (or not only) on the grounds of psychology or sociology or folk culture, but on the charged territories of visuality and image making.

Ellison's essay on *Black Boy* and its maker is not the only instance of his investments in visuality and the photograph as marked properties and resources, but it is an exemplary one. Borrowing its tropes, I would suggest that for Ellison the invocation of visual objects and powers is to his own critical practice what the experience of "severe beating" within the "Southern Negro famil[y]" was for Wright: a "homeopathic" strategy intended to curtail, to redirect, an oppressive force—in Ellison's case, that of the mass image archive (CE, 136). Like violence in the black home (or at least Wright's home) in the rural South, visuality is an "administered" strategy (CE, 136); on the field of critical engagement, its selective use enables an authoritative purchase on the image repertoire, on the creation of the Negro as an icon, and on the Negro writer on the literary field. With respect to the latter concern, a survey of Ellison's nonfiction writing foregrounds the deliberateness with which he reserves invocations of the photographic for accounts of his writerly practice, and of the genesis of *Invisible Man* in particular. The trope of the photographic, as Ellison deploys it, helps shape and sustain the myth of his singular novel as born organically from the writer's imagination.

Thus in his introduction to *Shadow and Act*, Ellison describes his earliest essays as a kind of light writing. "None," he informs us, "has been retouched" and all are "the products of an activity, dreamlike yet intense, which was waxing on the dark side of my mind" (CE, 49). In a "special message to subscribers" for the 1979 Franklin Library edition of *Invisible Man*, Ellison offers a more explicitly photographic figure for the novel's origins:

> But then, one afternoon, when my mind was still bent on its nutty wanderings, my fingers took over and typed what was to become the very first sentence of the present novel, 'I am an invisible man'—an assertion so outrageous and unrelated to anything I was trying to write that I snatched it from the machine and was about to destroy it. But then, rereading it, I became intrigued. . . . Slowly, like an image surfacing from the layers of an exposed Polaroid exposure, a shadow of the speaker arose in my mind and I grasped at his range of implication.[80]

In a 1974 address to Harvard alumni, Ellison similarly frames a response to his receipt of a letter from Harvard addressed to "Ralph Waldo Emerson": in light of "the incongruities abounding in a man-and-mammy-made society," "the image of a Negro American novelist" is "made to show forth through the ghostly . . . lineaments of a white philosopher and poet." Precisely through this daguerrean doubling or spectral overprinting, the latter-day Ralph Waldo—much like the young boy of "Hidden Name and Complex Fate" musing on his optical lens—stakes his claim to the social meaning of "conscience and consciousness."[81] Again and again, Ellison's writing attests to the power for his imagination of a mythic process: from the shadow of the image archive, with all its justificatory, mystifying, powerfully real effects, is born the act of consciousness, the willed agency of the writer to confront the world as found and to remake it in his image.

If anything, Ellison's homeopathic investment in photographic tropes and idioms becomes clearer, more exposed, over the course of his career. In particular, certain essays after *Invisible Man* begin to stake suggestive differences between the still image and the moving picture, coded as opposed modes of stasis and dislocation, disjuncture and continuity, sameness and difference. In "Tell It Like It Is, Baby," begun in 1956 but unfinished until 1965, Ellison sums up the weighty burden of the "Negro American novelist" who must of necessity confront a mobile archive of "conflicting images."[82] Within the essay, his response to this writerly challenge is the narration of a nightmare in which he finds himself in attendance, in the costume and person of a young slave, at the hideously carnivalesque event—virtually a lynch mob—of Abraham Lincoln's funeral. Ellison's presence here, on the scene of living history, is predicated on a specific turning point: "as I emerged into a crowded thoroughfare it was as though a book of nineteenth-century photographs had erupted into vivid life" (CE, 34). As the dreamscape becomes increasingly violent (eventually even cannibalistic), the narrator-dreamer attempts unsuccessfully to evade the action, now a full-fledged "scene on a movie screen," by "watching from a distance" with a magisterial "clarity": he tries, in other words, to reconvert the montage effect of film spectatorship back into the disjunctural logic of photographic viewing (CE, 44).

Recent readings have stressed the weakness of the essay's resolution, in which Ellison recounts his recitation, on waking, of the Gettysburg Address as an act that dispels the "nightmare images" via "remembered art, the words and images of hope and reconciliation" (CE, 45).[83] But more to the point for my purposes is Ellison's tentative marking of a usable difference between photographic and film temporalities (a difference that would be memorably theorized, two decades later, by Roland Barthes). Here, as elsewhere in Ellison's essays, that difference comes to underwrite what we might call his distinctive time signatures: the characteristic shifts in perspective, autobiographical moment, and social location that stake his claims for the yet-to-be-realized effects of the past, for the power of art as "the mystery which gets left out of history."[84] If the formal rhythm of *Invisible Man* is dictated by the oscillation between metaphoric and metonymic modes, the figures of "Tell It Like It Is, Baby" evidence Ellison's evolving interest in photography—in marked distinction to film—as a referent that might underwrite his use of disjunctive, competing temporalities, and thus his exploration of the recurrence, erasure, and long reach of the collective past.

All of which brings us to *Juneteenth*, that long-belated novel concerned with the as yet to be realized cultural fulfillment of the nation's founding ideal, figured by the announcement in Galveston, Texas, on June 19, 1865—more than two years after Lincoln's delivery of the Emancipation Proclamation—of the legal emancipation of U.S. slaves. To the multiple temporalities thus instanced, visual objects and experience, in particular photographic experience, turn out to be crucial. Indeed, the visuality that has been accessed, appropriated, and systematically recoded in *Invisible Man* returns with a vengeance in the pages of *Juneteenth*. There, the exploits of the itinerant Mr. Movie Man—en route to becoming the Reverend Adam Sunraider, and having once been the boy preacher Bliss—burst into Sunraider's semiconsciousness, after an assassination attempt, with the force of images wrenched from involuntary memory. In direct opposition to the Reverend Hickman's flow of words—the soulful, jazz-inspired signifying that carries him from his life before redemption "into the pulpit at last"—the youth in flight from the predicament of his racial and existential uncertainty chooses the image as his medium: the profane to Hickman's sacred, the power of "blasting" to that of Hickman's blessing.[85] This contestatory possibility is opened by Hickman himself when he takes the very young boy to see, for the first and (ostensibly) last time, a moving picture, whose images—like Bliss himself in Hickman's religious scam-cum-redemption—"come out of [a] box," and require one to "be in the dark to see" them (230, 226).

The moving pictures Bliss watches exemplify everything dangerous and illusory about the image-world, and not only from the perspective of a canny preacher guarding against worldly temptations and their "crop of confusion" (222). (So an old-timer in the colored gallery of the theater dryly remarks of the featured "shoot-'em-up"—an amalgam of horse opera, plantation romance, and Civil War reenactment—that such revisions of history "don't have no end or beginning but go on playing all the time. They keep on running even when the lights is on . . . just like the moon in the daytime" [237].) But the real danger, for the boy of uncertain parentage, is the confluence of this "marvelous" and "terrible" shadow world with fantasies of origin (243). As the richer idiom of the ravaged Sunraider tells it, the boy primally fears the temple of the image: he "wanted to leave the place unentered, even if it had a steeple higher than any church in the world, leave it, pass it ever by, rather than see it once, never to enter it again—with all the countless unseen episodes to remain a mystery and like my mother flown forever" (235). In the moment, the boy is terrified by an actress on screen, whom he mistakes for the red-headed white woman who had recently disrupted his performance in a June-teenth revival, claiming Bliss as her son. But from within Sunraider's fugal state, we see that the real terror of the cinematic moment is the inseparability of the mystery of the image (dead letter, "*gaudy illusion*," and willfully made reality in one) from the mystery of that other dark place of coming into being: "*No*, I thought, *it's her. [Daddy Hickman] doesn't want me to know, but just the same, it's her.* . . . And I tried to understand the play of light upon the dark whiteness, the rectangle of cloth that would round out the mystery of my mother's going and her coming" (244; italics original).

That the unspeakable power of the moving image is conflated with the un-speakable power of woman's body (and in particular the white female body) is a fact to which I will shortly return. My concern here is the way in which the narrative as such counters that power precisely by checking the movement of images as such—precisely what the dreamer/narrator of "Tell It Like It Is, Baby" cannot do. Here, the all-pervasive, "terrible" force of filmic montage—the irrevocable sense of reality, the oppressive filial connection, created by the magic of sutured images—is disrupted by temporal instability, as the narrative hovers between the present and multiple pasts, between the consciousness of Sunraider, that of the vanished Mr. Movie Man, and that of the long-forgotten Bliss. In other words, the radical fragmentation in *Juneteenth* that one critic has identified as cubist can be richly understood as Ellison's attempt to emulate the essentially photographic strategy of the Movie Man, who locates himself in the elided and shaping space between shots, in "the darkness between the frames" (86).[86] Like that figure, Ellison seeks to transform the flow of repre-sented experience back into still, even static, images, whose reassemblage be-comes a matter not just of the kind of interpretive puzzling familiar to readers of modernism but one of dialectical engagement with the historical complexi-ties that generated them.

Throughout *Juneteenth*, Ellison makes the familiar argument against mass visuality—its too-easy pleasures, its leaching and flattening of history, its framing of all things American in black and white—central to his exploration of Sunraider's metamorphosis. But he also stakes the power of narrative, partially modeled on a salient form of photographic response, to counter that force. Like the practice of analogy embraced by Lisette Model, the narrative mode of *Juneteenth* troubles the assignment of symbolic or universalizing meaning to its key objects and keywords, even as it presses for more dynamic constructions of historical (and racial) cause and effect, in the strenuous work of "fit[ting] the links into a chain" (296). The "uncomplete" quality (or fragmentation or "lag") of Ellison's posthumous novel, in other words, is hardly symptomatic of a failure of political will. Rather, it is powerfully indicative of his bracing ambitions for the novel form, a bid for art as the rigorous practice of engagement with icons and myths, half-buried yet undead, in whose image a new kind of battle for the life of the desegregating nation has begun to be waged.

Finally, the photograph as object and photography as a cultural stance and power allow the reader of Ellison's work to fit its links into a different kind of chain, one that makes for some surprising literary contiguities. From his earliest gestures through the pages of *Juneteenth*, we can trace a certain set of connections in Ellison's career. In the talismanic wallet photograph of Richard Wright (no less a luck piece and legacy than that signal metonymic object, Brother Tarp's leg chain), the figure of the woman has literally been torn away, framing the relation between men—African American men, writers, writers at the apex of the New Deal and of the regime of Jim Crow—as the generative context of Ellison's creative coming into being. Yet that dismembered figure gives way, in Ellison's elaborate drafting of *Invisible Man*, to the figure of the unidentified fallen woman, the ur-image of invisibility, she who embodies the transformation of protest and documentary conventions as a newly dialectical engagement. In turn, that invisible woman is resurrected in the published pages of *Invisible Man* as the mannequins who are not—but might be—the Sybil who has become the narrator's responsibility (as Bliss's mother becomes, in a violently redemptive moment, Hickman's own). And at the far end of this less-than-intended but more-than-accidental metonymy stands the primal image of the preacher boy's mother, shadowy, ghostlike, insubstantial, forever lost and never to be known. These figures are quite obviously versions of that most dreadful icon of American racial history, the white female body, from which the myth of purity and the terrifying logic of racial violence are born. But this linked set of figurations also returns us to the unregenerate cave of Plato, the place in which the power of human and social origins as images—illusory, prophetic—

is perforce encountered; the place where that power might be meditated on and resisted. In the same end-of-century decade as the belated *Juneteenth*, Toni Morrison would publish a novel that similarly explores the primal, engendered mystery of origins and images, similarly takes photography as both a goad and a generative resource, dwelling in the space of Plato's cave so as to confront and to harness, for her own recounting of black and white history, the power of iconicity and illusion. Linked with this latter-day work, Ellison's engagement with photography's powers looks less dated than prescient, anticipatory of the concerns of the novel in a cultural context being shaped by new urgencies of identity and cultural representation. At the very least, the shadow images of Ellison's career suggest that his belatedness is that of the photograph itself, not a dead letter but a bearer of multiple temporalities: what has been, what might have been, what may one day be brought again into being.

Chapter Four

Photo-Text Capital:
James Baldwin, Richard Avedon,
and the Uses of Harlem

In the opening scenes of James Baldwin's belatedly completed first novel, *Go Tell It on the Mountain* (1953), the protagonist John Grimes spends the morning of his fourteenth birthday doing housework in the cramped, grimy Harlem apartment occupied by his restive family. His labor strikes John as positively Sisyphean: to sweep "the heavy red and green and purple Oriental-style carpet that had once been [the front room's] glory" is "his impossible, lifelong task, his hard trial"; as storms of dust rise, "clogging his nose and sticking to his sweaty skin," he becomes convinced that, "should he sweep it forever, the clouds of dust would not diminish, the rug would not be clean."[1] However painful that "so much labor brought so little reward" (24), the worst of John's ordeal is his charge "to excavate, . . . from the dust that threatened to bury them, his family's goods"—most important, the "procession" of photographs arranged against a mirror on the mantel, photographs that constitute "the true antiques" of the Grimes family (25, 26).

John's encounter with these images yields the self-negation habitually attached, as Michele Wallace has noted, to African American visual experience.[2] Most immediately, John's own image, a "cunning" shot "taken in infancy" as he "lay naked on a white counterpane," provokes "shame and anger," the opposite of recognition (26). Like the worn, streaked mirror against which the photos are propped, the camera can only image back "the face of a stranger," another self that withholds the truth "he most passionately desired to know: whether his face was ugly" or capable of inspiring love (25). For an adolescent on the brink of rejecting the sanctified life and of recognizing his own homoerotic feelings as such, to look on this degraded image is indistinguishable from being looked at by the sinners along the avenue who watch, "muddy-eyed and muddy-faced," as the Grimes family makes its way to church (10), and from the memory of his own acts of voyeurism—as when he and his brother Roy "had watched a man and woman in the basement of a condemned house" who "did it standing up. The woman had wanted fifty cents, and the man had flashed a razor" (10). Likewise, the photographs of John's elders, "bur[ied]" in dust—his aunt, with her hair "in the old-fashioned way," once (but no longer) beautiful (26); his father, shot in a hard sun that "brutally exaggerated the planes of his . . . face" (27)—embody and magnify John's profound disconnection from the past, from the hard-fought experience (racial, cultural, and psychic) that has shaped the harshly mysterious conduct of his parents and the realities of his own "bewilderment" (30). Unwanted legacy, agency of misrecognition, object of fruitless labor, the photograph bears witness not to lost truths or ways of being so much as to an irremediable state of what the sanctified imagination calls damnation, and what the reader understands as radical estrangement.

But the photograph, in the form of an imagined possibility rather than a material relic, also offers a source of connection to the hidden logic of that past, the intuition (rather than discovery) of which holds open the promise for John of another redemption—not via the awesome rituals of the saints, but in the embrace of a writing life. In his encounter with the photographs, and in Baldwin's depiction of that encounter, visuality begins to suggest a new kind of agency, one that takes shape for John as an authorial self-understanding. The seeds of this understanding have long since been planted, as Baldwin's careful plotting of the narrative makes clear. In a striking reversal of the negative scene of instruction foundational to black autobiography—typified by the unnamed narrator of James Weldon Johnson's *Autobiography of an Ex-Coloured Man*, who to his consternation is asked by a school principal to remain seated while white scholars are invited to stand—a very young John is singled out at school by his white principal, "of whom everyone was terrified," for the perfection of the letters he has written on the blackboard (18).[3] Being thus "distinguished" by her notice, John enters not into the racial law on which his father insists ("all white people were wicked . . . not one of them had ever loved a nigger. He, John, was a nigger, and he would find out, as soon as he got a little older, how evil white people could be" [34]), but into a fledgling self-consciousness as a writer, someone with "a power that other people lacked"—a power "that he could use . . . to save himself, to raise himself," with the possibility of winning love (18).

Paradoxically, the possibility of such redemption suggests itself just as John looks on the face of his father's monitory, "brutally exaggerated" image, which recalls in a haunting fashion the "shadowy woman, dead so many years," to whom the younger Gabriel had once been married, and to whose story the reader (unlike John) will become privy in the second part of the novel (27). Remaining for him an image behind the image, the shadow woman holds "the key to all those mysteries he so longed to unlock," "because she had looked into those eyes before they had looked on John" and "knew what John would never know—the purity of his father's eyes when John was not reflected in their depths" (27). Thus meditating, John shares with Roland Barthes a form of intuition and an understanding of the photograph as an object and a challenge to the viewer's subjectivity (Barthes: "I realized . . . with an amazement I have not been able to lessen since: 'I am looking at eyes that looked at the Emperor'").[4] Witness to mysteries of origin it cannot fully index, but which it nonetheless makes felt, the image compels John to embark on a writerly quest for experience via a "refus[al] to inherit anything from another eye than my own."[5]

All the more powerful, then, is the determinative encounter that follows between John and Gabriel over the body of John's brother Roy, wounded in a knife-fight, as it plays out this logic. Characteristically, Gabriel's wrath finds vent in a sanctified language in which the call to witness serves as a form of discipline and punishment; thus he intones over Roy, "It's just the mercy of God . . . that this boy didn't lose his eye," by way of admonishing John: "Look here. . . . You come here, boy, and see what them white folks done done to your brother. . . . Look here, . . . look at your brother" (42, 43). Baldwin goes so far as to mark the violence of Oedipal feeling—which "hung in the room like the infinitesimal moment of hanging, jagged light that precedes an explosion"—as another form of light writing (46). While the climax of this antagonism is deferred in terms of the novel's plot, Baldwin enacts its expression and resolution at the level of signification. As father and son stand "staring into each other's eyes," "John saw that his father was not seeing him, was not seeing anything unless it were a vision. John wanted to turn and flee, as though he had encountered in the jungle some evil beast, crouching and ravenous, with eyes like Hell unclosed" (46).

Just as characteristically, Baldwin's protagonist remains immobilized, even in the face of his own "certain destruction" (46). But Baldwin has clearly conjured the spirit of another (this time chosen) ancestor, Henry James, from whose writing the self-implicating figure of the beast in the jungle is borrowed. James's presence here as a source of literary self-imagination gives warrant for John's alternative mode of witnessing—and for Baldwin's reclamation of his own experience as a resource for narrative art.[6] The play of gazes, with its photographic intensity and its interest in an achieved insight that counters the threatening look, prepares John for a journey that will commence not on the threshing-floor of the church but on the threshold of his Harlem tenement, where the brooding youth will stand "ready," "coming," and "on my way" to revisit the "long shadows" of the life within, via the high road of art (215).[7]

The opening book of *Go Tell It on the Mountain* can thus profitably be read not only as the inaugural fiction of Baldwin's career but also as something of an allegory for his complex, ongoing relations with visuality, and more specifically with the photograph as a witnessing document, a call to which the work of the writer as witness responds. Readers of Baldwin (especially his detractors) often note how much of his writing life constituted a dance of embrace and evasion of the subjectivity afforded him as a Negro spokesman, public intellectual, and exemplary figure of exposé, reportage, or photojournalism—a dance that ultimately produced the kind of self-negation his own protagonist bids to escape. Scholars have explored Baldwin's work as a response to his public status, and his lifelong interest in the movies as an expressive form and cultural phenomenon. But his shifting designs on the stylistics and evolving history of documentary and photo-textuality have remained obscured.[8] Given Baldwin's penchant for the autobiographical mode, and for the deflection of literary or textual production into a broad range of authorial performances—particularly those in which his work as witness is aligned with documentary stances—a substantive account of Baldwin's engagements with photography is called for.

In a small but resonant gesture of reinvention, *Go Tell It on the Mountain* offers a clue to the moment (in both senses) of these engagements. The birthday John Grimes celebrates occurs—unlike Baldwin's, which fell in August— "on a Saturday in March, in 1935" (15). This temporal shift in the transfiguration of life as art not only allows Baldwin to avail himself of the imagery and resonances of winter's end, and the as yet unaccomplished awakening of spring. It also locates the fateful day in question at the moment of the first Harlem riot, whose representation in journalistic and documentary images inaugurated a new life in iconicity for Harlem and black America. Linking the "something irrevocable" that is transfiguring John, newly alive to "the menace in the air around him," with the uprising to come, Baldwin implicitly suggests an emerging documentary/representational context as the critical field of action for the emerging writer (15). (This gesture, we might note, is mirrored in the often-cited essay "Notes of a Native Son" [1955], which opens with the convergence of his father's death and funeral, Baldwin's own coming of age, and the 1943 Harlem outbreak; the simultaneity of these events shapes the essay's famous conclusion: "It began to seem that one would have to hold in the mind forever two ideas which seemed to be in opposition.")[9] In what follows, I aim to excavate Baldwin's forays onto that field of action, and his investments as a writer in the forms and histories of documentary imaging. Focusing on his episodic collaborations with the photographer Richard Avedon, from the moment of his entry onto the literary field through their jointly authored photo-text *Nothing Personal*, not only yields a clearer sense of Baldwin's own struggles with the logic of self-negation, it affords a fuller understanding of the possibilities of photo-text as an experimental form, a last, late repository of modernist ambition for the styles of radical will.

From "Harlem Doorways" to "The Harlem Ghetto": Baldwin, Avedon, and Modernist Self-Fashioning

Paradoxically, no view of Baldwin's interest in photographic models (or obstacles) is possible without an acknowledgment of the power as precursor of Richard Wright—the same Wright whose *Native Son* Baldwin so blisteringly rejected in his authorial coming-out pronouncement, "Many Thousands Gone" (1951), as "one of the most desperate performances in American fiction."[10] But Wright's offices as an author of photo-text, and the force of his collaboration on *Twelve Million Black Voices* with Edwin Rosskam, were exemplary of a genealogy of photo-text production in which Baldwin would seek, from the very start of his writing life, to feature. Mapped onto the cultural dynamics of mid-twentieth-century New York, that genealogy traces a direct and heavily trafficked link between the precincts of Jewish and African American striving. As I have suggested, "Harlem Document" writer Milton Smith operated in Harlem under the nom de guerre Michael Carter, wrapping his journalistic projects in the mantle of disinterested sociology as an inducement to secure the participation of Jewish leftists-cum-photographers from the East Side and downtown.[11] Likewise, on his arrival in Harlem, Wright had quickly ascertained the value in leftist circles of "Jewish friends"; he identified Rosskam in his letters to fellow writers not as an FSA official or fellow traveler in New Deal circles but as "a young Jewish photographer," perhaps to embellish his own credentials in the wider networks of the Communist Party and the WPA.[12] Both writers responded to the realities of a specific cultural field—the forms of representation, reportage, and aesthetic trial known collectively as documentary—traversed by the traffic between the Lower East Side and Harlem, between immigrant Jewish American and migrant African American histories. By dint of accident, historical circumstance, and occasional design, the vector of cultural enterprising traced by Siskind and the Photo League—from the Bowery and the ghetto tenements of the East Side to those of 145th Street—continued to shape photo-text production after the documentary moment, in a broad range of experimental and radical contexts.

Case in point for this generative fact of postwar photographic engagement was the fitful yet ongoing collaboration between James Baldwin and Richard Avedon. Hailed in the early part of his career as the most inventive fashion photographer of the postwar era, later the object of notoriety for his startlingly original and unsparing portraiture, later still installed as the first staff photographer at the *New Yorker*, for which he created an unprecedented visual archive of America's most influential culture makers, Avedon seems an unlikely partner for Baldwin in his heyday, touring the precincts of civil rights organizing, delivering in person and in print the thunderous irony that made him, by the early 1960s, a household name. But Avedon and Baldwin shared a long if uneven history, and it culminated in the publication in 1964 of perhaps the most original photo-text project of the century: the highly controversial civil rights era volume *Nothing Personal*. Chased out of print by scandalized reviewers, excoriated as politics and as art on the grounds of both images and text, *Nothing Personal* is a signal achievement for each of its authors, and deserves recognition as such. More to the point here, the story of its making is revelatory of the shifting life and afterlives of documentary, in which Harlem remains a touchstone, resource, and crossroads.

In one small but significant way, *Nothing Personal* resembled Wright and Rosskam's *Twelve Million Black Voices*: its very coming into being was made possible by a nexus of immigrant and migrant, Jewish and African American, Talented Tenth and bourgeois uplift schemes located existentially, and sometimes institutionally, in Harlem. Indeed, Harlem served as a point of departure not only for its native son Baldwin but for the work he shared with Avedon, often in ways that enabled (or enforced) meditation on the conditions of that work's making and meaning—that is to say, in ways that promoted each contributor's allegiances to the aesthetic as a site of political engagement, to cultural politics with equal inflection on both of those terms. Further still, Baldwin and Avedon's photo-textual invocations of Harlem and of histories for representing it enabled the novelist and the photographer alike to revisit and dramatically repudiate key tenets of postwar representation—fictive, photographic, racial, and other. The asymmetries in their investments are obvious: Baldwin's corrosive, self-scrutinizing accounts of Harlem as prison and scourge ("I despised [black people], possibly because they failed to produce Rembrandt") against Avedon's sometime puzzlements over Harlem as a photographic object resistant to originality and the directorial will.[13] But their attempts to put the force of these encounters in dialogue made remarkable, even revolutionary, use of photo-text, of Harlem as a symbolic object in the popular mind, and of the entwined afterlives of the two.

Certain highly vocal critics of *Nothing Personal* and its thumb-in-the-eye provocations charged that the volume did nothing more than capitalize in timely fashion on the notoriety of two figures known for their literary or photographic exploits. (These had included, most recently, Baldwin's publication of "The Fire Next Time" in 1962 in the *New Yorker* and Avedon's first exhibition, at the Smithsonian the same year, featuring radically unconventional portraits of figures such as Charlie Chaplin, sporting devil's horns as he left America for good, It girl and heiress Gloria Vanderbilt in the nude, and a shockingly haggard Duke and Duchess of Windsor, responding to Avedon's inspired fiction about witnessing the death of a dog of a breed they particularly adored.[14] But such critics had it wrong. *Nothing Personal* was in fact the long-delayed achievement of a partnership that had begun in earnest a quarter of a century earlier, at the very inception of its makers' careers. From 1938 to 1941, Baldwin and Avedon were classmates, "inseparable" friends, and coaspirants to literary fame at the no less than famous institution of DeWitt Clinton High, then a nationally celebrated school—"one of the best-known public secondary schools in the United States," hailed as a successful experiment in top-flight education on a public basis.[15] However different their experiences of its culture (Baldwin commuted to the pastoral campus in the north Bronx from Harlem; Avedon from the Upper East Side), both quickly attached themselves to Clinton's storied and remarkable literary journal, the *Magpie*, a semiannual publication featuring original fiction, journalism and reportage, poetry, and graphic arts, read widely in New York City.[16] By 1941, Avedon, still styling himself a poet, had been appointed *Magpie* editor in chief, during which tenure he won a citywide poetry competition for high school students and was named High School Poet Laureate of New York; Baldwin served as his literary editor; from his earliest days on the *Magpie* staff, Avedon published regular poetry entries under the title "Observations"—the same title he would retain for his first published book of photographs.[17] On Avedon's departure from Clinton in January 1941, Baldwin took over as editor, with the future novelist, leftist, and literary editor for the *Nation*, Emile Capouya, as his second in command.[18]

The constellation of so many formidable cultural figures in the making warrants attention, and not only to their literary juvenilia.[19] The broader culture of Clinton, beyond the pages of *Magpie*, registered and shaped a set of intersecting histories crucial to Baldwin and Avedon's projects and definitive of the development of postwar cultural practices. Founded in 1897 at 60 West Thirteenth Street, soon spilling over into an annex on East Twenty-third Street (then an assimilated extension of the Lower East Side), DeWitt Clinton High School moved in 1906 to Fifty-ninth Street at Tenth Avenue, and again in 1929 to its current home in the Bronx, on Mosholu Parkway.[20] Each of these locales reflected the largely Jewish, immigrant, and/or leftist or progressive background of students, faculty, and administrators, from the Yiddish-speaking strivers of the first waves of Eastern European migration to the alrightniks and members of the second generation.[21] Indeed, Clinton's siting roughly reflects the trajectory of Jewish American, and more broadly immigrant, assimilation in New York during the era.

By way of unscientific evidence for this history, the rolls of Clinton alumni during its first four decades include (among many others) Elias Lieberman, a member of the first graduating class (1901) and author of the widely circulated proimmigration poem "I Am an American"; Waldo Frank (1906), whose radical writings in the *Liberator* and *New Masses* paved the way for his landmark work of cultural criticism, *Our America* (1919); Nathanael West (ca. 1921), born Nathan Weinstein, son of German-speaking Lithuanians with a distinctly apocalyptic heritage who made their living building tenement houses on the Lower East Side and luxury apartments in Harlem; Lionel Trilling (ca. 1923); Henry Roth (ca. 1924), whose *Call It Sleep* (1934) reflects his family's tenure in the "virtual Jewish mini-state" of the Lower East Side, as well as those of Brownsville and prewar Harlem; Abel Meeropol (1926), son of Russian immigrants to the Bronx, schoolteacher, activist, lyricist for the song that would become Billie Holiday's anthem, "Strange Fruit," and the adoptive parent of the children of Ethel and Julius Rosenberg after their electrocution; Jack Greenberg (1941), Columbia Law School professor, future director of the NAACP's Legal Defense and Educational Fund, and chief spokesman in the argument before the Supreme Court in *Brown v. Board of Education*; and—not coincidentally—the soon-to-be New York Photo League member and Harlem documenter Aaron Siskind (1931).[22] Brought to birth on New York's East Side, in the very cradle of bohemian progressivism and of immigrant activism, Clinton in all its manifestations remained a proving ground for the mode of response that, on the literary field, Trilling would come to embody: a mix of articulate leftism, high-flying aestheticism, and strenuous self-invention.

Intrinsic to this culture, as to the immigrant histories on which it so lavishly drew, was a commitment to and fascination with the sometimes parallel, sometimes intersecting, sometimes opposed history of African Americans. From the outset, Clinton had been a racially integrated institution, and not just in theory; it prided itself (sometimes ostentatiously) on its progressive racial politics.[23] More to the point, Clinton made part of its powerful mythology a set of connections with Harlem and with the emergent, then dominant, then receding phenomenon of the Harlem Renaissance. Jesse Redmon Fauset taught at Clinton beginning in 1927, shortly after she left her position as literary editor for W.E.B. DuBois's *Crisis* and shortly before publication of her second novel, *Plum Bun*, in 1928. Countee Cullen, scion of Harlem's Salem M.E. church, graduated from Clinton in 1921, and his first published poem appeared in the pages of the *Clinton News*—a key event in the school's self-imagination; student interviews with Cullen were a recurring feature of the *Magpie*, including a prescient one conducted in 1942 by Baldwin (who had previously encountered Cullen during the latter's stint as a teacher at Baldwin's Harlem junior high school).[24] The Renaissance-era photographer James Latimore Allen, whose uplift-style portraits of well-to-do Harlemites rivaled those of James VanderZee, graduated from Clinton in 1924. Fats Waller, Bud Powell, and Romare Bearden—all legendary sons of Harlem—attended Clinton briefly before leaving for the greener pastures of their respective arts.

De facto, the vast majority of Harlem students was barred from admission into academic programs by tracking that relegated black youths, particularly boys, to vocational institutions. But for the Talented Tenth and chosen few, Clinton nonetheless provided "an adventure," escape into what one Harlemite called "a far, far away land."[25] In so doing, it sutured Renaissance-inflected paradigms for uplift onto the dynamics of progressive, immigrant, and Jewish striving, and made Harlem, real and symbolic, intrinsic to its institutional self-imagination. Nowhere is this fact more pointedly evidenced than in the portrait section of *The Clintonian*, the school yearbook, for 1941. Taking "Great Books" as its theme, the volume introduces its roster of graduates under the banner headline *UP FROM SLAVERY*; it concludes with the title of Caldwell and Bourke-White's quintessential progressive photo-text, so influential for both Wright and Ellison: *YOU HAVE SEEN THEIR FACES*.[26] However sophomoric these allusions, they exemplify the interpenetration of racial progressivism, immigrant aspiration, and liberal confidence that defined the school's culture in the interwar era.

The latter allusion also points to the ways in which Clinton's self-imagination as an urban institution was entangled with the ideology of documentary observation. An earlier graduate, Max Schuster—class of 1913, son of Jewish immigrants, and cofounder in 1924 of the upstart publishing house of Simon and Schuster—remarked of Clinton's Tenth Avenue location, in the notorious San Juan Hill district, that it "was an excellent place for a school to be" because it afforded "actual contact with the 'real' New York," with "unembellished glimpses of elements as they really were."[27] Openness to the "elements"—criminal, foreign, radical, nonwhite, rough trade, and otherwise other—remained part and parcel of the school's ideology, or at least its aesthetic culture as evidenced in the *Magpie*. With remarkable consistency, the pages of the journal throughout the 1930s and into the 1940s, long after the heyday of the Harlem Renaissance and of socially conscious fiction alike, revisit Harlem and the Lower East Side as resonant, and by implication metonymic, sites for registering the felt reality and aesthetic possibilities of metropolitan experience.

For example, R. Blackburn's "Block Dance 1937" invites the reader to "Come with me to One Hundred Forty-Fifth Street and Bradhurst Avenue"—a significant distance from the vestigial sites of sex tourism and entertainment clustered on Seventh Avenue between 125th and 132nd Streets—to be "jostl[ed]" within a "whirling blur" of "Lindy Hoppers" and "Roughcutters," whose fantastic moves transform the "vacant pavements" into a space of collective affirmation, and in so doing, defy detached observation.[28] A similarly participatory ethnographic text on the East Side describes its writer as "fortunate enough to have become acquainted with the Bowery" (the same beat pounded by Jacob Riis, Lewis Hine, Weegee, and Aaron Siskind's Feature Group) "by contact rather than by reputation." In particular, the document dwells on its distinctive economy of services: barber shops, tattoo parlors, and gin mills, which the author reviews and recommends ("the Vaughn . . . the La Rosa") by establishment.[29] The afterlives of the Renaissance and of immigrant striving become, we might say, methodologically entangled, in an enterprise both shaped by and aspiring to metropolitan bravado, documentary authenticity, and progressive politics in one.

It is this dense matrix that yielded the collaboration of Baldwin and Avedon: boy preacher struggling against the harsh conditions of extreme poverty and the sanctified Harlem life; son of the Jewish bourgeoisie (Avedon's family had owned an eponymous Fifth Avenue women's specialty store before the stock market crash; his first photographic excursions were made with the Young

Men's Hebrew Association), decades removed from an old country, and all the more fascinated by metropolitan glamour and the possibilities it afforded for self-invention.[30] Drawn with equal intensity by the heady culture of the *Magpie*, they conducted their shared schoolboy venture in a Gothic tower that was already "a romantic anachronism," experimenting with voices, genres, and personae.[31] Avedon would ultimately decide that he was, as he once wrote dismissively of Dorothy Parker, "merely an excellent versifier"; Baldwin would lose his faith.[32] But the Clinton gestalt, with its designs on progressive politics and Harlem as object, inaugurated a collaboration that exemplifies the logic of each figure's subsequent career—and their ongoing uses of Harlem, documentary, and photo-text as aesthetic and political resources.

Standard accounts of both Baldwin and Avedon's work invariably include a footnote to their first joint venture beyond *Magpie*, a photo-text book project titled "Harlem Doorways." In fact, the project was aborted from its inception, for reasons that are suggestive. According to Avedon, the book was essentially intended as an opportunity for each contributor to experiment with the possibilities of his chosen medium: photography, as wrested from socially conscious imperatives, for himself, and something like memoir, or literary journalism (or perhaps even public intellectual status) for Baldwin. Absent actual texts, the title suggests something self-consciously metaphoric: the exploration of Harlem as a symbolic space, an orphic landscape, a margin or threshold. Such a treatment would comport not only with Baldwin's later preoccupations but with the robust, enduring Orpheus motif in black cultural expression after the Renaissance (powerfully summed up, for example, in Nathan Mackey's linking of literal and cultural orphanage with the allure of art and the power of the past).[33] But Baldwin, who proposed the "Doorways" project, apparently had something more literal in mind: a photo-text study of the streetscape of his native grounds on the lines of Agee and Evans, whose starkly frontal images of rural cabins, churches, and small-town shop fronts had already become categorical (figure 4.1). According to Avedon, "Harlem Doorways" "was all Baldwin's idea. The name came from him. The thought came from him. And I thought: doorways. That's not where I'm going. Walker Evans I'll never be."[34]

The suggestion that Baldwin imagined himself, however briefly, a black Agee in search of his own Evans is one I will pursue later. First, however, it is worth considering the sole image connected with the project that Avedon actually printed and circulated (in limited fashion): a portrait of Baldwin in his mother's Harlem apartment, his small sister Paula seated on his lap (figure 4.2).[35] However unintentionally, the image resonates with respect to Baldwin's intentions: it hijacks the documentary project out from under the rubric of horta-

Figure 4.1. Walker Evans, Grocery Store, Moundville, Alabama, 1935–36. Farm Security Administration/Office of War Information Collection, Library of Congress.

tory photo-text and installs a very different kind of logic, one dependent on the context of Harlem for its generation. Unlike Aaron Siskind's frontispiece for *Harlem Document* (see figure 1.1), Avedon's shot is resolutely interior; there is nothing—no darkened background, no hint of a threshold that must be crossed—to suggest the photographer's hesitancy or doubt about his presence within the represented space. Shot at relatively close range in Avedon's early signature format (the square, precise, unflinching Rolleiflex), the image bespeaks an intimacy it also qualifies. Its subjects' gazes are lowered and directed to the left of the frame, just discernibly asynchronous with one another, toward some event or eventuality unavailable to the viewer.

Rosskam's portrait of the meditative Black Belt boy (see figure 2.12), as it appears in *Twelve Million Black Voices*, achieves its most powerful effects through photo-text sequencing and juxtaposition. By contrast, Avedon makes the problem of the look, or rather the staging of something we can only call vision, the point of the image as such. His shot frames a profoundly introspective Baldwin at center, between a glass tumbler in the right foreground and a

Figure 4.2. Richard Avedon, James Baldwin and Paula Baldwin, Harlem, October 15, 1946. Courtesy The Richard Avedon Foundation.

table mirror at background left, and thereby creates a kind of visual pun. Neither the glass (part of a domestic clutter bespeaking haste and privation) nor the looking glass (badly smudged and tilted in its frame, reflecting the mere sliver of open sky visible through a nearby window) seems sufficient to the felt quality of Baldwin's presence; both objects belong, the shot suggests, to a documentary iconography that has long been superseded. The relevant optic here is instead that of the subject, arrayed in a pose (finger grazing his upper lip, chin on thumb) that mimes meditation only to communicate withdrawal, an effect intensified by the intimate presence of the young girl. What the subject sees, in the privacy of his isolation, can only be a matter of speculation, the directed reading of gesture and incident. In this way, the question of optics also implicates the photographer, whose presence and way of seeing have transformed a familiar site of documentary work—the Harlem interior—into a new kind of camera obscura: a bounded, improvisatory space, defined not so as to "reflect" an evidentiary reality but to allow for free play with paradoxes of nearness and distance, visibility and insight (and perhaps, by way of suggestion, with black and white).

That Avedon would make such an image in 1946 tells us something about Baldwin's career as well as his own, and the place of Harlem and photo-textuality in both. By that time Avedon had been a professional photographer for just two years, but had already joined the staff of *Harper's Bazaar* at the invitation of its legendary art director, Alexey Brodovitch.[36] Avedon's early innovations in fashion work had earned him considerable credibility (he would be dispatched by *Bazaar* to Paris the following year, at the unlikely age of twenty-four, to cover the all-important collections). He had also recently shot his first signature independent project: images of the Roman street performer Zazi, interacting in the Piazza Navona with observers and hangers-on to produce impromptu tableaux of postwar (and barely postfascist) Europe. The turn—or perhaps, given the Clinton context in which Avedon's relationship with Baldwin initially developed, return—to Harlem for the "Doorways" encounter thus raises a key question. What would Harlem and the figure of Baldwin in it have to offer such a rising star, whose own celebrity career, oscillating between Fifth Avenue and the Place Vendôme, would soon become the stuff of Hollywood film, celebrity journalism, and legend?[37]

Like that of other Jewish American and émigré photographers before him, Avedon's work suggests that he encountered Harlem as an exemplary site of photographic trial and error. It was also, by the mid-1940s, a site of bracing engagement with the protocols of photographic predecessors. Close observers of his career have noted an ongoing strain of documentary interest, and not only in Avedon's infamous images of asylum inmates and napalm victims. Throughout his work can be traced an insistence—always lyrical rather than didactic—on the specific truth of the photographic encounter, however shaped and ephemeral. But Avedon's past masters were hardly agency officials like Rosskam or even, as his response to Baldwin's invitation emphasizes, the reigning iconoclast Evans. The most powerful analogue for his developing work was that of a very different documentary photographer, Helen Levitt; in this, Avedon shared a source of suggestion with Richard Wright.[38] Like Siskind, Rosskam, Shahn, and innumerable others of the FSA generation, Levitt too had become a photographer in the ambit of Jewish culture (in her case, the immigrant neighborhood of Bensonhurst, home to the Jewish baseball legend Sandy Koufax); the extraordinary street work with which she made her mark during the late 1930s and 1940s, documenting the dynamics of Harlem and East Harlem children's cultures as lived, contested, and observed, depended utterly on her defining sense of belonging to the bustling, frictional sidewalks of the city and its tenement worlds (see figures 2.4, 2.5).

Linked, in this body of work, to the affective complexity that inspired Wright to plot a Harlem-based collaboration with Levitt are two specific features of critical relevance to Avedon's engagements: its uses of the fluid, uneven theatricality of the Harlem street, with all its improvisatory and contending everyday practices, as a resource in the composition—or more accurately choreographing—of individual photographs; and their earned insistence on the conduct of this culture across various boundaries (including the divide between subjects and photographer). If Levitt suggested to Wright imaginative possibilities for reclaiming the territory of black manhood in the making as a subject of nuanced representation, her work taught Avedon how to find and create a certain dynamism, one dependent not only on camera angles or cropping or the creative use of focus but also on the photographer's understanding of street work as an inherently theatrical enterprise. But where Levitt's images eventually achieve a kind of invisibility for the camera, foregrounding what she reads as the inherent theatricality of the streetscape, Avedon urges the photograph to behave as the record of a mutual performance. At a key point in his early career, Harlem appears to have offered itself as one kind of proving ground for this aesthetic. What better place to test the possibilities and limits of image making that prizes both the specific tensions and the social implications of the photographic encounter?

Avedon remarked retrospectively that what he rejected from the earliest stages of his career was not photojournalism per se but its characteristic subject matter—what he calls "the man on the street"—in favor of another set of concerns: "the confusing nature of beauty, the uses of power, and the isolation of creative people."[39] Even absent any contribution by Baldwin to "Harlem Doorways," we can begin to see how their ongoing collaboration enabled Avedon to focus on these concerns. Although his commercial portfolio and his "art" projects have often been read as antithetical in context and intention, the "Harlem Doorways" shot palpably connects these two bodies of work via the resonances of Harlem. The clutter and disarray of the Baldwin family home is thoroughly familiar as a social landscape from two decades of documentary images of urban poverty, not least Wright and Rosskam's representations in *Black Voices* of the foul kitchenette. (The opening chapters of *Go Tell It on the Mountain* presuppose such imagery, as they limn the dirt and dust and "filth" of the Harlem tenement as the setting for John's spiritual crisis [20]). In the image of Baldwin, however, setting is drained of any informational content or use value, treated as an incidental fact or even a distraction rather than an indexical landscape. Already Avedon has exerted what one critic describes as the "pressure toward weightlessness, [the] gradual filtering out . . . of atmosphere itself" that characterized his use of the signature white background—a device he would employ for the first time, in his portrait of a Western Union messenger whose mode of self-expression particularly struck him, a mere five weeks after making the Harlem portrait of Baldwin.[40] At the same time, the context of mid-1940s Harlem (read: poverty, disaffection, the Negro problem) is itself a kind of portal or doorway through which perforce we view Baldwin, who remains distinctly isolated from everything that postwar, second-ghetto Harlem connotes. The vestigial presence of that context, the evidence of a form of identity evaded by the subject and the camera alike, heightens Baldwin's self-presentation as an existential hero. The future public intellectual, dominating postwar public culture, is here adumbrated as spiritual exile and racial refusenik in one.[41]

If this representation of Baldwin owes a good deal to Avedon's friendship with him, it is nonetheless shrewd. In 1946, the writer whose distinctive gimlet eyes and unconked hair—"so very Negro"—would become household icons was as yet a fledgling; his first professional publication still six months away, he was reworking a draft of *Go Tell It on the Mountain* (then called *Crying Holy*), which had been rejected by both Harper and Doubleday despite the intervention of Wright.[42] Yet Baldwin's self-presentation in the "Harlem Doorways" image already suggests, in essence, his terms for dissent from Wright's vocabulary, stance, and resources, insofar as it collaborates in prizing the performance of subjectivity over its exposure, the mystery of identity over the force of fact.[43] Avedon's portrait might well be set in photo-text conjunction with Baldwin's later comment about the discovery of "my role—as distinguished, I must say, from my '*place*'—in the extraordinary drama which is America."[44] Embodying the artist whose prescribed context—Harlem, the ghetto of black exemplarity, perhaps even the nation—is insufficient to his aims and experience, the Baldwin of Avedon's photograph already enacts a version of what Baldwin, after his fictive avatar John Grimes, would call witnessing. Avedon's Baldwin is, in other words, a resonantly equivocal figure, reflecting on the existential isolation from a home he can leave but never abandon.

In a later essay, Baldwin would describe himself at the very moment of the "Harlem Doorways" portrait as "a survivor . . . with murder in his heart," someone who "knew that there was no question any longer of his *life* in

America."[45] Retrospectively, the "Doorways" episode can be seen to provide an opportunity for Baldwin's redirection of the "rage and misery" that he had framed as resources for a mode of literary expression after Wright and Agee.[46] Here, in profound relief, Baldwin's alienation is registered not as an organic fact, a matter of social and sociological "conditions," but as a potentially chosen form of self-expression—one that would come to be "mysteriously indispensable" to his writing life and even his existence.[47] Wrested out from under the sign of Harlem, the ghetto, and the Negro, alienation as a condition and posture of response can be disentangled from documentary, with its binding "American image of Negro life," and from identity logic, writ as a prescribed set of "ways of being black"; it can, in other words, be embraced as a modernist ethos.[48] As Henry Louis Gates has noted, most of Baldwin's subsequent career was spent in a dizzying swerve between alternate conceptions of the writer as Gramscian organic intellectual and as modernist observer from the borders and limits of collective experience.[49] Real and symbolic Harlem, the "Doorway" image suggests, offered a powerful resource for Baldwin's early generation of this opposition.

This turns out to be true not only in the obvious way—that is, in the ongoing centrality to Baldwin's work of Harlem as birthplace and synecdoche for black America—but with respect to the shape of Baldwin's career and his entry onto the cultural field. His first professional publications were reviews of Maxim Gorki and Shirley Graham (the biographer of Frederick Douglass and wife of W.E.B. DuBois) that appeared in 1947 in *The Nation*; the former was published cheek by jowl with a standard leftist appeal for Zionism. At the same juncture, Baldwin also became a regular contributor of reviews to the Trotskyite *New Leader* at the behest of its literary editor, the Russian émigré Saul Levitas. During the following year, Baldwin's first published essay and work of short fiction appeared in the journal *Commentary*, house organ of the anti-Stalinist American Jewish Committee.

From the outset, in other words, Baldwin's negotiation of literary culture and institutions was perforce a matter of engagement with what one biographer calls, with the delicate force of quotation marks, "literary 'liberals'"[50]—a more or less polite euphemism for Jews, specifically for the Jewish American and Jewish émigré writers who had first coalesced around *Partisan Review*, were defining U.S. public culture through intellectual journalism, and were styling themselves as the New York Intellectuals. In the received story, Baldwin's engagement—that of a twenty-two-year-old Harlemite whose formal education ended with high school—with heavy hitters and canon makers such as Sidney Hook, Daniel Bell, Robert Warshow, Philip Rahv, Irving Kristol,

Elliot Cohen, Saul Bellow, Diana Trilling, and Mary McCarthy reads as both lopsided and "somewhat freakish."[51] But Baldwin's negotiation of the Jewish American left—of its distinctive politics, stylistics, and investments in the Negro—allowed him to make productive use of the overdetermined alienation suggested by the "Doorways" portrait.[52] Entering the overlapping precincts of the literary and of Jewish America, Baldwin was empowered to exploit at least some of his own multiple liminalities: as black writer resisting the role of court Negro downtown; as cosmopolitan intellectual defying the constraints of identity logic and Harlem.

Baldwin's inaugural essay, "The Harlem Ghetto," exemplifies both the limits imposed and the possibilities opened by this engagement on the grounds of his status as Harlem phenomenon. Published in February 1948, the piece was commissioned by *Commentary* coeditor Robert Warshow, who was eager to connect the anticommunist rhetoric of the post-Stalinist left with expressions of concern about civil rights at home. Warshow had invited the Harlem sociologist Kenneth B. Clark, whose statistical data and analysis would later undergird the plaintiff's successful case in *Brown v. Board of Education,* to contribute a piece on relations between blacks and Jews to the second number of the journal (a notable invitation, as what Warshow called "the delicate and perplexing problem of Negro-Jewish relations" cropped up in *Commentary*'s pages infrequently).[53] More locally, an editorial sidebar to Baldwin's essay emphasizes both the strategic and symbolic value of the uptown ghetto to the New York Intellectuals' project: "Whenever one ponders the progress of the American ideals of freedom and equality in the framework of today's realities, one inevitably thinks of the South—and of Harlem."[54] For the Intellectuals, well beyond the reign of socially conscious reportage and documentary, Harlem as historical ghetto evidences the logic of relations between Jewish and African Americans as metonymic (rather than, say, exploitative), founded on the grounds of shared marginality. Investing in Harlem as a form of symbolic capital, the *Commentary* left asserts a strategic distance from the equivocal accession to whiteness of American Jews during the cold war era. Thus the import of Warshow's leading editorial question: "How is it in Harlem in the winter of 1948?"

That Baldwin's piece should have been tailor-made to serve such interests is hardly surprising (and serve them it does, with acuity). But the context of *Commentary* and the Jewish-inflected left is in turn conducive to Baldwin's aims. Put in conjunction with the likes of Edmund Wilson, Oscar Handlin, and Thomas Mann, whose work accompanies his in the February number, Baldwin appears inspired to give free rein to a distinctive voice—the one that would dominate later texts such as *The Fire Next Time*—in which close observation, arid detachment, and honed passion get equal play. In it one hears an awareness if not an echo of the collective tone defining what Randall Jarrell had dubbed the Age of Criticism, whose strident exigency was well suited to Baldwin's developing gifts and temperament. What one critic pegs as the typical mode of the new Jewish intelligentsia—"aphoristic, allusive, polemical, prone to ironic syntheses of the high and the low . . . and passionately engaged in making discoveries and registering judgments that went beyond the particular books or authors under discussion"—aptly describes the style to which Baldwin, at this early stage, clearly aspired and here begins to achieve.[55] Appearing under the auspices of *Commentary*'s regular feature "From the American Scene," Baldwin is sutured not only to Jewish-inflected leftism but (again like John Grimes) to the key figure legitimating its claims on culture via modernism, Henry James. If "Harlem Ghetto" was inexorably framed by *Commentary*'s cultural directives, it was also assimilated to a tradition of robust cultural engagement that Baldwin embraced as his own.

Straddling Harlem and the institutional space of the Jewish American left, Baldwin in "Harlem Ghetto" has a little something for everyone: a scathing account of black institutions, particularly the church and press, for their self-serving meliorism; an incisive anatomy of black anti-Semitism that implicates Jewish disingenuousness about whiteness and race. One of the most cited passages in the text, which Eric Sundquist has called a "locus classicus" of narratives of black-Jewish relations, is the grim flourish with which Baldwin closes.[56]

> Both the Negro and the Jew are helpless; the pressure of living is too immediate and incessant to allow time for understanding. I can conceive of no Negro native to this country who has not, by the age of puberty, been irreparably scarred by the conditions of his life. All over Harlem, Negro boys and girls are growing into stunted maturity, trying desperately to find a place to stand; and the wonder is not that so many are ruined but that so many survive. The Negro's outlets are desperately restricted. In his dilemma he turns first upon himself and then upon whatever most represents to him his own emasculation. Here the Jew is caught in the American cross-fire. The Negro, facing a Jew, hates, at bottom, not his Jewishness but the color of his skin. It is not the Jewish tradition by which he has been betrayed but the tradition of his native land. But just as a society must have a scapegoat, so hatred must have a symbol. Georgia has the Negro and Harlem has the Jew.[57]

With this assessment Baldwin accomplishes the signal work he intended for "Harlem Doorways." He fashions himself in print as a successor to and repudiator of Agee, a witness unsparing and self-implicating, privileged by his experience of regional histories but unbound by them. Above all, his jeremiad seems designed to reject Wright's closing images in *Black Voices* of progressive rising; no amount of liberal fellow feeling will alter the structural conditions of Jewish and African American (or indeed of more broadly American) identity formation.[58] This fact is enacted as a paradox within this very text, in Baldwin's singular turn to the personal toward the close of "Harlem Ghetto": "And *my* Jewish friends in high school were not like that, I said, they had no intention of exploiting *me*, we did not hate each other. (I remember, as I spoke, being aware of doubt crawling like fog in the back of my mind.)"[59]

Absent the textual condition and presence of images, Baldwin's inaugural work is nonetheless shaped by the productive logic of photo-text, specifically by practices of documenting Harlem and the Negro under the sign of shared or continuous experience. Producing notes on culture for a Jewish (or perhaps "Jewish") audience, Baldwin can dispense with Wright's collective, unitary first-person plural and the burden of representativeness it implies. Writing from within the precincts of "literary 'liberals,'" he can appropriate the stance of principled marginality, the ethos of witnessing, and the privileging of authorial sensibility structural to their practice. From within the pages of *Commentary*, *The Nation*, the *New Leader*, *Partisan Review*, on the field of culture being reshaped by Jewish America, Baldwin thus achieves something like the collaboration he sought in the form of photo-text. Far from a deterrent to the eventual completion of *Go Tell It on the Mountain*, the early work he shaped to the informing contexts of Jewish American culture making was its condition of possibility.

In and Out of the Picture: Documentary Stances and the Making of *Nothing Personal*

After the "Doorways" episode, Avedon and Baldwin would each try—differently and unsuccessfully—to use Harlem as a subject for photo-text production. In 1947–48, backed by a $1,500 grant from the Rosenwald Fund, Baldwin collaborated with the photographer Theodore Pelatowski (to whom he had been introduced by Avedon) on a photo-text project they called "The Blood of the Dying Lamb."[60] Together Baldwin and Pelatowski visited Harlem storefront churches, including the one in which Baldwin had come up as a boy preacher, and dance halls; Baldwin appears to have found an Evans to play to his rendition of Agee. As described by Baldwin's biographer James Campbell, the resulting photographs stress the continuity between the expressive cultures of black religion, music, and dance; in all the represented venues, "the same anguish and joy is visible . . . , the same hands and feet responding to the same rhythm, the same embrace, the same call-and-response . . .—even, it seems, the same pianist."[61] The sheer insistence on sameness suggests that the images echo not only one another, but the weighty body of photojournalistic, commercial, and otherwise documentary images of African American culture that they reprise. Black congregants "roused to dance and sing," offering themselves up "in ecstasy," "rolling on the floor" and striking up a "pattern of rejoicing"[62]: these photographic subjects had been long familiar as such in the work of Wright and Rosskam, Bourke-White and Caldwell, Siskind and the Photo League (figure 4.3).

Missing from this visual archive is the framing and directive energy of the prose that would have been sutured to it—that is, Baldwin's characteristic oscillation between journalistic detachment and experiential intimacy. With respect to these images, Baldwin's intended move from Harlem doorways to Harlem spiritual practices as rubric reads as a deft attempt to wrest the activity of "witnessing" out from under the sanctified context and into textual space, the practice of his own authorial activity. Becoming a photo-textual witness— a function of his own invention and appropriation—to forms of African American witnessing, Baldwin potentially frees himself to transform the cultural practices that limn group identity as art. That, we might surmise, was the logic of "Blood of the Dying Lamb"; surmise we must, since Baldwin never actually produced the text for the volume. Biographers have suggested that he failed to attract a publisher in a tight commercial market, but Baldwin's difficulty was perhaps more fraught. There remained the ongoing problem of distinction from the work of Wright, whose section in *Black Voices* on "our blues, jazz, swing, and boogie-woogies" as "our 'spirituals' of the city pavements," the "expression of our bewilderment and despair in a world whose meaning eludes us," is a precursor if not the instigation for Baldwin and Pelatowski's project.[63] Baldwin's attempt in the rubric of photo-text to take back Harlem, from Wright and from his own experience, seems ultimately to have been untenable as such.

A very different logic governs Avedon's post-"Doorways" rapprochement with Harlem. In 1949 he made a series of images, shot on an aborted commission for *Life* magazine, of iconic sites of photographic encounter in New York. Among the most memorable (and among the very few Avedon chose to reproduce in any form) are a series made in Harlem. The series includes a characteristically witty shot of two men—a uniformed soldier and a civilian—on Lenox

Figure 4.3. Margaret Bourke-White, College Grove, Tennessee, 1936. By permission. Margaret Bourke-White Collection, Special Collections Research Center, Syracuse University Library.

Avenue, sporting with a lithe and elegant Dalmatian; the shot of an arrestingly beautiful woman crossing a vacant avenue; the portrait of a small boy kneeling on a Harlem sidewalk behind an overturned fruit crate and brandishing a large knife, which may or may not be real; the image of a woman at a Harlem lunch counter, her protective gaze—clearly averted from the camera—at odds with her jaunty hat (figure 4.4).[64] Although Avedon was responding to *Life*'s invitation to represent "New York" at large, and thus also trawled the photographi-

Figure 4.4. Richard Avedon, Anonymous Woman, Harlem, New York, 1949. Courtesy The Richard Avedon Foundation.

cally freighted precincts of Central Park, the Lower East Side, El stations, and automats, the Harlem shots embody what Avedon himself understood as the failure of this entire body of work, in the face of which he returned a five-figure advance and buried his contact sheets for more than forty years. "In those pictures," he asserted, "you can see the war within myself, as I was coming onto the territory of Walker Evans."[65] *Life* had convinced him, as Baldwin had not, to explore that territory: a certain strain of documentary put in service of *Life*'s glossy version of photo-text, for which Harlem as a photographic site was a powerful metonymy. The logic of this link, and of his dissatisfaction, is highlighted by Avedon's explanation of his subsequent investment in fashion work. The latter, he noted, was a project that allowed him to exercise his training and gifts "as a spy in the other country."[66] If Harlem's allure as another other country was palpable, the prospect of racial espionage there was signally repugnant. Instead, what Avedon already sought was the opportunity to "direct" the photographic encounter, based on a certain mutuality and will to performance. The territory of documentary after Evans, and of Harlem after the Renaissance, conduced for other-than-black photographers to allegories of social distance and unknowability, and thus to relatively static representations of alterity, racial or otherwise. The *Life* images, Harlem and all, fell for Avedon precipitously into this category: "I know that it's a kind of work. But I don't call this photography."[67]

Neither Baldwin nor Avedon, then, succeeds in creating a postdocumentary photo-text of Harlem as such. But their engagements on the territory Harlem opens are extraordinarily generative, and they culminate in the extended meditation on the conditions of social encounter across cultural divides that is *Nothing Personal*.[68] Far from a narcissistic rant or the opportunistic embrace of a zeitgeist (charges leveled against Baldwin and Avedon, respectively), *Nothing Personal* allows each to resolve certain structural impasses via the form of photo-text. In this collaboration, Harlem as literal subject and synecdoche for otherness disappears, to be succeeded by the dynamic of confrontational encounter that Harlem historically necessitates, and that the collaborators' experiences have opened. Within the text of *Nothing Personal*, Avedon and Baldwin each turn this dynamic to specific and unprecedented uses.

To begin with, the volume's orchestration of the relation between images and text makes a pointed departure from conventional photo-text apparatus. The latter works to suture narrative content and tone to specific images; by contrast, *Nothing Personal* eschews captions, narrative titles, and any other directive linkages.[69] Having produced their contributions more or less independently, Avedon and Baldwin cordoned them off in self-contained alternating sections. (These include four portfolios devoted respectively to weddings; avowed racists and "those fighting against the problem"; patients in a Louisiana mental institution; and a small group of images of racial and human solidarity, including a couple of mixed race with their child. The portfolios are interspersed with four episodic textual meditations on the national condition of despair, racial profiling and identity logic, the American failure of self-invention, and the redemptive possibility of love, writ as a form of witnessing.)[70] Trained to expect and respond to conventional photo-textual cues, many readers in the moment found the sequencing strategy mannered, self-consciously provocative, disconcerting—and rightly so. It has the effect not only of provoking hermeneutic activity—Why this juxtaposition? What connection between narrative and text locally and at large?—but of making the reader complicit in the creation of a felt reality that counts both as art and as the truth of the social. Hence the purposively documentary resonance of the boldly oversized "1964" that stands in as title on the volume's title page. At large, the physical dimensions and properties of the finished book—a formidable 11 × 14¼ inches, housed in a stark white box and full of startlingly oversized images, assertive croppings and bleachings, and dramatic emphasis in both photo and text sections on white space—adamantly displace the causal logic and knowability implied by the photo-text tradition from Bourke-White and Caldwell, and even Agee and Evans, through Rosskam and Wright and *Life* itself, on the brink of the protest era.

Avedon described these effects of format as part of a calculated attempt to conjoin the audience for his fashion work with a mass public attuned to Baldwin's international fame, awakening both to the realities of impending conflagration via the appeal of the "coffee-table book."[71] Yet in a moment when the commercial was itself being refitted as a cutting-edge aesthetic category— Andy Warhol's first exhibition of oversized silkscreens, the Campbell's soup cans, had been mounted just two years previously—their redirection of photo-text can be more judiciously read as a contestatory response to the new stylistics of the cool. In the context of Pop's increasingly dominant notion of art as a "record of the condition of being an uninvolved spectator," *Nothing Personal* is an intentioned take on detachment, provincialism, and magical thinking as endemic conditions of American culture—precisely the reality that Baldwin and Avedon aim in their own fashion to record and redress.[72] The critical dismissal of the volume as a shameless, even obscene, commercial project badly misreads its investments in an aesthetic diametrically opposed to Pop's affectless veneration of surface.

Consider, for example, Warhol's iconic "Marilyn" screenprint series of 1962 in relation to the 1957 portrait of Monroe in *Nothing Personal*, included as a quarter-page image in a series of full-page blowups of prominent cultural figures (including, in a disjunctive metonymy, Monroe's ex-husband, the playwright Arthur Miller). Warhol's image, which was made in direct response to Monroe's suicide, extols the reign of banality and false intimacy (figure 4.5). Delighting in the newly discovered screenprint process, with its capacities for flattening both affect and the visualized object, Warhol's image is, as one art historian puts it, "fascinated and yet indifferent."[73] By contrast, Avedon's portrait has been said to anticipate Monroe's tragic status (figure 4.6). Its insistence on its subject's weariness and deflation—her eyes averted, her fabulous platinum hair dimmed, her body exhausted, the world-famous cleavage not enhanced but obscured by the sequin sparkle of her halter dress—hardly restores a lost interiority, but it insists on the complexity of "image" as a lived and manufactured form. Unsparing, decisively unsentimental, Avedon's image nonetheless contests the "cool opacity of creatures who were already pictures before the picture was made"—that is, of Pop subjectivity, coalescing not only as an art world trend but as the predominant form of collective identity.[74]

The distinction between the Monroe images usefully frames the *Nothing Personal* aesthetic: here, tragedy itself remains a defining possibility, both existential and broadly social. That possibility is what yokes Baldwin's episodic meditations to Avedon's images, enabling the latter to intensify Baldwin's expressive gestures and social concerns. Juxtaposed with Avedon's initial portfolio of wedding portraits of assorted couples, from socialites to enlisted men, shot in the Marriage Bureau of lower Manhattan's City Hall (where the photographer literally becomes a witness), Baldwin's opening response redirects the potential irony attendant on Avedon's monumentalizing of the wedding snapshot into a mode of witnessing with its own expressive form:

> I used to distract myself, some mornings before I got out of bed, by pressing the television remote control gadget from one channel to another. This may be the only way to watch TV: I certainly saw some remarkable sights. Blondes and brunettes and, possibly, redheads—my screen was colorless—washing their hair, relentlessly smiling, teeth gleaming like the grill-work of automobiles, breasts firmly, chillingly encased—packaged, as it were—and brilliantly uplifted, forever, all sagging corrected, forever, all middle age bulge—MIDDLE AGE BULGE!—defeated, eyes as sensous [*sic*] and mysterious as jelly beans, lips covered with cellophane, hair sprayed to the consistency of aluminum, girdles forbidden to slide up, stockings defeated in their subversive tendencies to slide down, to turn crooked, to snag, to run, to tear, hands prevented from aging by incredibly soft detergents, fingernails, forbidden to break by superbly smooth enamels, teeth forbidden to decay by mysterious chemical formulas, all conceivable body odor, under no matter what contingency, prevented for twenty-four hours of every day, forever and forever and forever.[75]

Born of the critically detached look ("the only way to watch"), Baldwin's sustained parataxis approximates the agency of Avedon's camera, creating metonymic links between objects and subjects that remain, in everyday social life, irrevocably divided. The point of Baldwin's stream of consciousness is to parse his fellow citizens' "despair"—particularly that of "those homeless Europeans who now call themselves Americans and who have never been able to resolve their relationship either to the continent they fled or to the continent they

Figure 4.5. Andy Warhol, Marilyn, 1964. The Andy Warhol Foundation/Corbis.

conquered" (NP, 1:2). Unified only by the determination "to forget their pasts" (and in so doing "to make money"), these ancestors bequeath all Americans— race, region, and identity aside—the status of "betrayed exiles" (NP, 1:3). Blind to the history that has made them, these "remarkable creatures" embody a radical estrangement from desire and agency that, as Avedon's portraits complexly affirm, continues to be "proved by our faces" (NP, 1:3). To the force of Avedon's disciplined, revelatory photographic performances, Baldwin juxtaposes his stance as a subjective documentary observer; in tandem, text and images deploy the tragic sensibility as a form of political agency.

In retrospect, what seems most striking about *Nothing Personal* is the driving designs of both contributors on such an aesthetic, modernist yet situated decisively outside the originating contexts of modernism. Created out of the

Figure 4.6. Richard Avedon, Marilyn Monroe, New York City, May 6, 1957. Courtesy The Richard Avedon Foundation.

tension between "the provisional self" and "the undiscoverable self" (NP, 1:4), it is at play in the "irreducible gap" between the power of the mass image and the auratic force of human being (NP, 2:2); it hovers between apocalypse and redemption. This constellation of tropes and imperatives characterizes both Baldwin and Avedon's work at every phase, and not merely on generational lines. It extrapolates from a stance and set of commitments defining the freighted intersection of Jewish and African American claims on culture; it is tellingly named by one Baldwin biographer as "literariness."[76]

To date, the most probing account of *Nothing Personal* as a photo-text collaboration has been given by Joshua L. Miller, whose treatment helps us parse this identification. In his reading, *Nothing Personal* creates a rich dialogue between Baldwin's observations on the sterility, emasculation, and silencing effect of contemporary visual culture and Avedon's portraits, which "re-present" public figures so as to "subvert our received notions of personality and fame."[77] Further, the volume invites us to connect Baldwin's "passionate intimacy" on the dangers of American rhetoric and its unexamined myths with Avedon's visual explorations of their sustained power.[78] Against documentary texts— those of the FSA, or Wright and Rosskam's—that are inherently shaped as progressive narratives, Miller argues, Baldwin and Avedon attempt "to detach photographic images from the evidentiary purpose," to "evoke more than they express in the images and words set on the page."[79] For Miller, the ultimate aim of *Nothing Personal* is that of Barthesian excess, a drive to "regain for photography [a] premechanical state of nondidactical meaning."[80] But this logic is more than merely textual. Its venture in photo-text form conduces to each contributor's explorations of the uses of a broadly modernist sensibility— or, more precisely, of its afterlife in the specific context of incendiary identity logic, commodified angst, waning affect, and failed collective will.

More specifically, the "literariness" in which the history of Baldwin and Avedon's collaboration is embedded, along with the social histories of camera work and cross-racial encounter that helped define documentary practice, allows each artist to confront impasses structural to his work and reception. Allied with Baldwin's jeremiads, Avedon's celebrity portraits and location shots (City Hall; mental institution; the beach at Santa Monica) suggest a powerful continuity across the divide between "fashion" and "art" into which his projects have been almost inevitably sequestered. In dialogue with Baldwin's stridency, Avedon's images reveal the degree to which their own effects depend on a confrontational or frictional stance, both as the condition of their production and as the grounds for their aesthetic and social charge. *Nothing Personal*'s twinned portraits of a grimly unrepentant, then eerily confident George Wallace; an out-of-focus, overexposed Malcolm X, eyes hooded beneath his rimless spectacles, performing his own terrifying unreadability for white America (figure 4.7); the image of "William Casby, Born in Slavery," rendering with auratic precision the impress on its subject's face of an unimaginable past (figure 4.8); the oversized image of an anonymous mental patient, his body contorted with rigidity, his leg shackled to a metal pipe, who gazes at the camera with what appears to be alarmed recognition: all exemplify Baldwin's aperçu that Americans in the American century are "made uncomfortable and probably hostile" when "forced to look"—really look—"on another human being" (NP, 3:3). It is the singular achievement of the *Nothing Personal* images to have compelled such a look from their subjects, who appear to

Figure 4.7. Richard Avedon, Malcolm X, New York City, March 27, 1963. Courtesy The Richard Avedon Foundation.

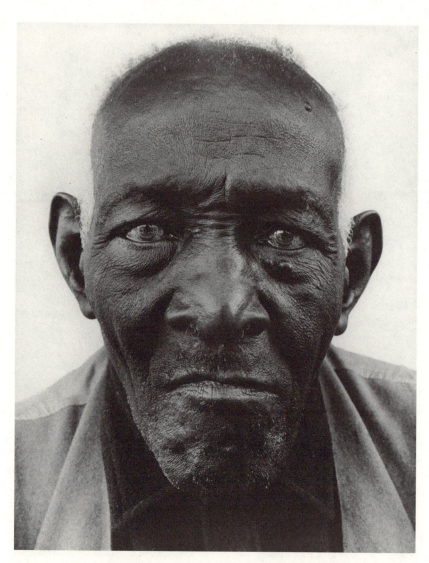

Figure 4.8. Richard Avedon, William Casby, Born in Slavery, Algiers, Louisiana, 1963. Courtesy The Richard Avedon Foundation.

Figure 4.9. Richard Avedon and Civil Rights Demonstrators, Atlanta, Georgia, 1963. Courtesy The Richard Avedon Foundation.

anticipate the limits of their self-representations, and to make this fact the condition of our engagement with them.

Whether the result of this engagement turns out to be the salutary "apprehension and acceptance of one's own identity" for which Baldwin proselytizes (NP, 3:2), Avedon's deployment of his images in the civil rights context can be seen as a remarkable refashioning of the conventions of site-specific (not just socially conscious) representation. Here, the structural conditions of Harlem photographic encounter, across divides addressed and created by documentary practice, extrapolate metonymically to certain thematic categories ("civil rights demonstrators," "racists," "the South") even as they undergird Avedon's controversial portrait aesthetic: the compelled performance of authentic selfhood.[81] That Avedon embraces these conditions is evidenced in a photograph made not by Avedon but of him, during his extensive travels during 1963 in Georgia, Mississippi, Louisiana, and other Southern states for the *Nothing Personal* project (figure 4.9). In the left foreground of the image, an African American man and woman wearing placards protesting the segregation of a public skating rink stand single file; in the right foreground, just feet or even inches away, a resigned Avedon gazes at the camera, one hand in his pocket, the other cradling his own ever-ready but now withdrawn Rolleiflex. While the man, whose sign reads "Let us roll along," looks deliberatively into the distance, the woman levels a cool and steady gaze at Avedon. There will be no rolling, at least for his camera; whatever kind of permission or engagement he has sought has been for the moment refused.[82] At the same time, the fact of the denied request distinguishes his work unequivocally from the documentary conventions that govern this record of the failed transaction.

Meanwhile, in the background and at the center of the image, a group of white bystanders occupies—more likely blocks—the sidewalk by the entrance to the rink; their tight proximity to one another and sameness of dress index, at the very least, a commonality of protective interest. Among them is a woman who appears to be gazing with equal hostility at Avedon and the protesters alike. Her posture and positioning, at the apex of an elongated triangle, suggest the equivalence she assumes between black protestors and photographic inter-loper; her assumption highlights the unbridged distance between Avedon and his desired subjects. This, it would seem, is the scenario par excellence of Ave-don's mode of production: white New York camera-wielding Jew mediating and embodying palpable social divides, operating as self-acknowledged "spy in the other country"—not of fashion, or the blithe, erotically charged worlds of women and celebrity, but of the land America has become.[83]

The context of civil rights culture, the socially pressing, even tendentious figures embodying its stridencies and challenges, enable Avedon's fullest ex-plorations of key, and entangled, convergences: between celebrity or notoriety and the private self; between the directorial energies of the camera and the felt urgencies of documentary; between the aesthetic and the political as sites of experience. No wonder that he has identified the images included in *Nothing Personal* as "some of my very best work."[84] Under the sign of photo-text, in conjunction with the collaborator who functions as a kind of mirror image, Avedon's work appropriates the energies of photography as a record of en-counters in the contact zone. Drawing on the very history of documentary production it resists, his work for *Nothing Personal* is the realization of a mod-ernist sensibility at the limits of its uses as an aesthetic and social resource.

If this achievement is paradoxically visible only in light of a documentary image that puts Avedon himself in the picture, an analogous case can be made for Baldwin. In Miller's reading, the thrust of Baldwin's narrative in *Nothing Personal* is a sustained "claim that he is a part of the phenomenon he exam-ines," in distinction to the "anxious outsider" of ethnographic documentary practice.[85] Baldwin's uses of the first-person—oscillation between singular and plural; rapidly shifting references for the collective (black Americans, men,

Americans, those who seek "the miracle of love," those who profess freedom as watchword)—do sharply distinguish his narrative from Wright's in *Black Voices*, whose first-person "we" remains essentially static and affirmative by implication. But while Baldwin is "a part of" the narrative, he also remains in a crucial sense apart from it. Contra the portrait work associated with "Harlem Doorways," and unlike Truman Capote (who authored a textual accompaniment to Avedon's first published book, *Observations*), Baldwin is never imaged in the volume on which he collaborates.[86]

Given his notoriety by the time of its publication, the omission is striking. Indeed, the framing condition of Baldwin's collaboration is nothing less than his meteoric rise to prominence as an iconic figure for civil rights activism, what F. W. Dupee called "the Negro *in extremis*, a virtuoso of ethnic suffering, defiance, and aspiration."[87] Between 1962 and 1964, Baldwin's image was exploited throughout the U.S. mass media under a number of predictable evidentiary rubrics: Harlem homeboy made good; exhibit A in the noble question of what *Life* would call "human dignity" versus the altogether more inconvenient question of what it called "any 'rights' for Negroes which can be legislated"; edifying voice of the Negro people.[88] His publication in the *New Yorker* in December 1962 of the "Down at the Cross" section of *The Fire Next Time*, reprising racial conflagration and black nationalism through the prism of his Harlem boyhood, had caused a serious firestorm. The ironic result was that Baldwin became precisely what he intended to avoid—a figure like Wright, made ineluctably to bear the burden of representativeness and spokesmanship. (As early as "Harlem Ghetto" Baldwin had cannily described the fate of the "Negro leader" as "the nicely refined torture a man can experience from having been created and defeated by the same circumstances.")[89] In an interview for (of all things) *Mademoiselle*, Baldwin agreed with his interlocutor that "stealing from the artist to pay for the Negro" was "one of the prices for my success."[90] At this juncture, Baldwin himself—provocateur and icon, civil rights celebrity and emblem—becomes a walking battleground between identity logic and existential freedom, between socially conscious representational functions and the urge to the individual talent.

Baldwin was hardly a stranger to this conflict. But the conditions of his celebrity in 1963–64 recreated him as, in essence, a subject for photo-text exploitation at a critical juncture in the nation's civil rights crisis. It is this context to which his participation in *Nothing Personal* most deeply responds. By way of producing *Nothing Personal*, Avedon conducted a photographic tour of the South as cultural battlefield that yielded images defying the limits of documentary expression; at the same moment, Baldwin was conducting his own tour of the Southland, aka "history's ass-pocket"; in so doing he himself inescapably became a subject of journalistic and documentary interest.[91] In May 1963, his portrait was featured on the cover of *Time* as a synecdoche for the issue's lead story on the swelling racial violence and protests in Birmingham.[92] During the same month, he starred in a public television documentary titled *Take This Hammer*, which featured Baldwin as a kind of tour guide to San Francisco as a site of racial segregation, violence, and unrest. Among the scores of photo-essays, journalistic reports, interviews, and reels of journalistic footage covering Baldwin's activities during these months was a *Life* feature also published in May 1963, under the title "Telling Talk from a Negro Writer," which suggests how fully his celebrity was made to conform to conventional photo-text paradigms.[93]

The two-part text by the *Life* reporter Jane Howard covers Baldwin's "whistle-stop tour" of the South (Congress of Racial Equality–sponsored stints at rallies, university forums, and church pulpits, where he appeared with activists such as Medgar Evers and James Meredith), as well as the chaotic frenzy of Baldwin's activism and after-hours sociality in Harlem.[94] Notably, Howard is introduced in the volume's "Editor's Note" as a fearless recorder, someone who "can scribble legible notes while smiling sweetly and looking dead into the eyes of her subjects."[95] She is thus framed as a documentary observer whose power rivals that of Baldwin, and of the "protruding eyes" that "gaze unwaveringly and for record lengths of time into the eyes of whomever he is talking to."[96] But this *Life*-enhancing gaze is utterly fungible; thus the editor's list of "busy, interesting people" whom Howard has pinned under it (including "author-scientist Rachel Carson, A & P heir Huntington Hartford, opera soprano Anna Moffo, city planner Robert Moses"). If Baldwin was a "most cooperative" subject, his "tough, eloquent" pronouncements "on the racial crisis" are no more or less suitable for framing than the lifestyles of the rich and famous.[97]

Illustrating Howard's text is a series of captioned photographs by documentary photographer Steve Schapiro, a self-admitted disciple of Walker Evans, W. Eugene Smith, and Robert Frank whose early documentary projects included work on East Harlem drug addicts, the Apollo Theater, migrant workers in Arkansas, and rural black poverty in North Carolina—that is, defining sites and themes of photo-text production.[98] Schapiro's contributions to the *Life* feature include shots of Baldwin comforting a black boy abandoned by his parents; talking with children in front of a ramshackle house on Dumaine Street, in a historically black neighborhood of New Orleans; posing in Jackson with the desegregation hero and Ole Miss student James Meredith; hobnobbing with the celebrity activists Geraldine Page and Rip Torn; posing with notebook in hand outside Black Muslim headquarters in Durham; and performing the latest dance craze, the Hitchhike, with an attractive female CORE worker. Although affectively complex, Schapiro's photos as sequenced here inevitably reprise the representational conventions of photojournalistic treatments of America in black and white, from FSA documentation of rural poverty through picture magazine exposés.

The ultimate effects of this visual styling become apparent in the photo-essay's closing image of Baldwin, whose caption reads: "In kitchen of his New York apartment Baldwin has 3 a.m. phone conversation." Huddled against the wall of a narrow, tiny kitchen, framed by its stark white walls and the detached range on which kettle and coffeepot sit, Baldwin is portrayed as a figure neither of bohemian insouciance nor of intimacy—and a far cry from the existential protagonist of Avedon's early portrait. The coiled cord of the telephone seems not to connect him with an unseen interlocutor so much as to imprison him within his own immediate surroundings, whose narrowness and poverty appear to have occasioned his protective crouch. The image is juxtaposed with narrative material that emphasizes Baldwin's insistence on freedom from economic security: "I didn't become a writer to earn a Cadillac or a split-level ranch house. . . . Evidence would indicate I come from a long line of what we call field niggers."[99] But it also ineluctably recalls the vast archive of images of black want and ghetto squalor (the same archive on which his own account of Harlem life in *Go Tell It on the Mountain* self-consciously draws). In this photograph, Baldwin becomes inseparable from the subjects of Wright's kitchenettes; his authenticity "both as one Negro and as his race's voice" raised against white America is purchased via his consignment to categorical documentary subjectivity. In fact, this culminating image puts Baldwin irrevocably in his "*place*" in the most literal way; it misidentifies the locale in question as "Harlem" rather than the apartment on West Eighteenth Street where Baldwin actually stayed.[100] This metonymic linking has, of course, an added charge in a moment in which another household name for civil rights, Lena Horne, could confront Attorney General Robert F. Kennedy to suggest that he "go to Harlem" with the Kennedy administration's record on civil rights; "*we* ain't going," she noted acerbically, "because *we* don't want to get shot."[101]

Life's photo-text framing of Baldwin thus clarifies the aims and achievements of *Nothing Personal*, in whose narrative an African American writer for the first time fully articulates the conditions for his own participation—exhortatory, confessional, proprietary—as a subject of photo-text. In Baldwin's uses of the genre, the very history of photo-text as an instrument for creating and recreating the Negro problem (to say nothing of the problem of the Negro intellectual) is little short of exploded. Still a figure for Harlem and all it connotes, Baldwin nonetheless makes good on the title of the volume; he is freed in the guise of unseen witness from the constraints of iconicity and authorial integrity alike. Juxtaposed with Avedon's work, his familiar stance as a subjective documentary observer allows Baldwin perhaps his most fully expressed claims on the literary heritage he seeks to command. Nowhere in Baldwin's considerable oeuvre does his prose more resonantly recall the affective complexities and rhythms of Henry James, turned to trenchant critical observation—specifically, James as the watchful observer, "restless analyst," and returned "alien" of *The American Scene*, meditating on the possible futurity of a polyglot, mass-mediated democracy and on the complex fate of the novel and the literary artist therein.[102] Like James, Baldwin transforms the fact of his own celebrity into an evasion of its most disabling constraints, an opportunity to generate a new kind of expressive form. Throughout *Nothing Personal*, Baldwin's narrative blurs categorical distinctions, shades modernist and activist commitments into one another, sutures the stances of the provocateur and the passionate defender of the power of art. Read against other artifacts of the celebrity he manufactured, including the *Life* profile, Baldwin's work in *Nothing Personal* offers itself as a key text—perhaps the singular work of the civil rights era in which Baldwin achieves a convincing resolution between social commitments and his chosen voice and genre.

Within the text, Harlem as an urban fact and national symbol makes only residual or metonymic appearance, as in Baldwin's account of walking "uptown, along the river" so as to "watc[h] strangers" in whom some possibility for recognition can yet be discerned (NP, 1:4), or in Avedon's studio images of the Harlem celebrities Adam Clayton Powell, Joe Louis, and Malcolm X. But Baldwin's authority as a subjective documentary observer, a writerly witness, turns on his status as a Harlem icon, an embodiment of the defining experience of the ghetto. Analogously, Avedon's extraordinary achievements at the intersection of portraiture, socially conscious art, and documentary extrapolate in their method and conception from the structure of photographic encounter that his work in Harlem presupposes. The resounding achievement of their collaboration is to exploit, in a newly fraught social context, Harlem's mobility as a signifier for racial experience, and the photo-textual histories and conventions it has generated, at the vanishing point of the genre their work revises. However unsuccessful in its imagined life as a commercial object, *Nothing Personal* achieves a dramatic departure from the canonical uses of photo-text, opening possibilities for productively frictional, affectively complex responses to the turbulence that would coalesce in (and as) "1964." In one of the reversals or deflections that characterize the genealogies of Harlem and documentary and their entangled afterlives, *Nothing Personal* would help bring home to Harlem felt possibilities for photo-textuality and documentary stylistics in the post-1964 era. In the reception of Baldwin's testimony, and his art, by Harlem writers struggling to respond to the tumultuous energies and urgent imperatives of the era, the face-off with photography and its histories would become again and newly a productive form of contention, stealth, and self-fashioning.

Chapter Five

Dodging and Burning:
The Writer and the Image after
the Civil Rights Era

I f Baldwin and Avedon's *Nothing Personal* formed the apex, in 1964, of a
modernist photo-text tradition, it was hardly the only engagement with
the genre undertaken in the face of the calls to love and hate and revolution
we have come to know as the 1960s. In the wake of the riots, demonstrations,
sit-ins, love-ins, outlaw celebrities and pop phenomena comprising the national culture, photographic images acquired new urgencies and intensities.
Photo-text and photographic narrative proliferated, from the pages of *Life* and
Time to the visual artifacts of Robert Rauschenberg and Romare Bearden;
icons in the making abounded, from the World's Fair in Queens, with its
futuristic Unisphere and City of Tomorrow, to Sproul Plaza in Berkeley, where
the Free Speech movement was being born. On this heightened visual landscape, Harlem in 1964 remained a resonant icon, a sign of the times and a
specific challenge to meaningful representation.

The challenge was, once again, embodied by an outbreak of violence. On
July 18, a massive wave of civil unrest gathered and broke in response to the
murder by an off-duty police officer in Yorkville of an unarmed fifteen-year-
old Harlem boy. The violence resulted in alarming death tolls, injuries, and
property damage over several days, as it spread throughout African American
communities in New York City and Rochester; this mass response commenced

the burning summers that would devastate inner cities in forty U.S. cities coast to coast. As one journalistic observer noted, "After Harlem exploded, every-thing was different. . . . Harlem started something."[1]

The visual and documentary records of this epochal, incendiary Harlem dif-fered in one crucial respect both from earlier accounts of African America's capital and from the imaging of contemporaneous sites of upheaval. Whereas the 1935 episode offered a fertile ground for developing the representational conventions of the photo-story as exposé, and the 1943 outbreak enabled the existential, alienated perception of social crisis developed by cultural outsiders, Harlem in 1964 occasioned a stance other than objective yet insistently docu-mentary. Photojournalistic images of that summer focus almost exclusively on the preemptive violence and threat of the police; in lieu of surreal parades of looted finery or collages of material objects torn from their everyday contexts, readers of mainstream news organs—including the *New York Times*, Associated Press and UPI reports, the *New York Post*, *Newsweek*, and *Time*—were con-fronted with shots of heavily armed police officers surrounding hapless detain-ees or chasing obviously terrified civilians, nightsticks at the ready (figure 5.1).

The causal logic for this change is clear, although it has gone generally unre-marked. For the first time in history, the coverage of inner city unrest was being conducted almost wholly by African American photographers and writ-ers, who by 1964 had become so much in demand for the new "ghetto beat" at mainstream publications that they set up a collective command post at the famed Theresa Hotel and traded stories of "riot duty" over drinks at the Red Rooster on 138th Street or Wells's down-home chicken restaurant on Seventh Avenue.[2] Collectively, these documenters produced images for the record that reactivated a photographic ontology discredited, or at least challenged, by the aspirations of postwar photography: an insistence on the image as an indexical object, a form of witnessing, a trace of the bloody truth. Yet they also recog-nized the instrumentality of identity logic to their work. Returning to the données of straight documentary, refusing (or at least struggling) to filter out the participation of their makers in the events they record, images of the 1964 Harlem outbreak attest to the mixed and ongoing uses of documentary con-ventions, from exposé and alternative history to witnessing and self-conscious negotiation of the history of image making.

For writers in and of this moment, the photo-text tradition in its many avatars—modernist, experimental, retrofitted, socially conscious—continued to exert a centripetal pull. By all accounts, the novel in the era of burning summers was undergoing death throes, or perhaps growing pains, of its own. Undercut, outpaced, overwhelmed by the intensity and rapidity of social

Figure 5.1. Photographer unknown, Girls Fleeing from Police during Riot, 1964. Corbis.

change, the novel as a form struggled, as influential readers have argued, on several fronts: the diminishing market for conventional realist fiction; the burdensome legacies of protest-era fiction; the impasses of a modernism that had purchased aesthetic complexity at the cost of its suppressed investments in Eurocentric or falsely colorblind notions of culture.[3] In the emerging institutions and communities that would coalesce later in the decade as a Black Arts movement, the commitment to auratic performance, collective experience, or community building and vernacular expression produced a powerful emphasis on antinarrative forms—jazz, experimental drama, stand-up performance, and spoken word.[4] Novelists of all stripes, particularly those who had come of age as writers during the dawning of the civil rights era, shared a critical problem: finding resources to respond to the confusing, devastating, sometimes exhilarating challenges of an incendiary history in the making.

In this context, the tradition of photo-text, the stances and modes of address it enabled, offered itself as an adaptable resource for a variety of writers. The 1960s were, in a double sense, an era of dodging and burning: a period of increasing and newly definitive militant activity, and a time of pronounced prominence for images that experimented, via such photographic techniques as dodging and burning, with the interface between documentary reportage and subjective witnessing, between realism or mimetic fidelity and the camera as an instrument of the expressionistic, abstract, and surreal.[5] In what follows, I explore episodically but in some depth the engagement of specific writers with photo-text at a critical juncture in the history of culture as politics—and at critical junctures in their own careers.

For example, Lorraine Hansberry's hands-on production of the 1964 photo-text *The Movement* allows for an intentioned redirection of her work (and her success) as civil rights era America's Negro playwright. Although not a published novelist, Hansberry used *The Movement* to experiment with narrative devices, associative logic, and ekphrastic resonances in ways that begin to depart from the modalities of well-made drama, bourgeois agency, and heterosexuality alike; in her work on photo-text it is possible to trace the beginnings of a new and experimental narrative stance. In the fiction of the Harlem noir master Chester Himes, documentary photo-montage serves as a critical and narrative touchstone. *Cotton Comes to Harlem*, a key text in his Harlem series also published in 1964, makes strategic use of documentary images as a device or emblem to shape a deliberately anachronistic narrative logic, via which Himes excoriates liberal pieties, evades formulaic identity logic, and frames his own work as a mode of vernacular modernism. For the novelist John Oliver Killens, often heralded as the spiritual father of Black Arts, an apparently incidental opportunity to comment on photo-text representation in the 1965 photo-text *Harlem Stirs* became a blueprint of sorts for his most experimental novel, *The Cotillion* (1971). Responding to the stylistic energies and the modes of address of *Harlem Stirs*, Killens develops a productive strategy both for expressing his commitment to black experience and expressive modes and for parrying the most straitening, self-destructive thrusts of identity thinking. Collectively, these very different figures suggest the labile appeal of photography for the novel, and for narratives of the nation, in a moment of radical involution if not revolution.

"People do not always need poets and playwrights": Hansberry, *The Movement*, and the Uses of Narrative

In the summer of 1964, Lorraine Hansberry—already, at the age of thirty-four, afflicted with the cancer that would cause her death the following January—

spent considerable time meditating on documentary photographs. The context for her interest is worth considering. *The Sign in Sidney Brustein's Window*, the second (and last) of Hansberry's plays produced during her lifetime, would preview in September. Like her celebrated 1959 text, *A Raisin in the Sun* (which had made her the youngest playwright and the first African American to win the New York Drama Critics Circle Award for best play of the year), *The Sign in Sidney Brustein's Window* was shaped as a living room drama, but set this time in the Beat-era Greenwich Village that Hansberry—and, until their consensual breakup, her white, Jewish husband Robert Nemiroff—had called home. Originally titled "The Sign in Jenny Reed's Window" and modeled on Hansberry's Village compatriot, the photographer Gin Briggs, *Sign* tracks a leftist Jewish intellectual disillusioned with the good fight, spent with knowledge that the promises of social reform ring hollow.[6] Although Hansberry put the photographer and her documentary commitments under erasure in the text's final versions, the resonant question remained. Whither, in these epochal times, goes the honorable tradition of liberal (aka downtown Jewish) dissent via the documentary mode?

As this very question was making its way from page to stage, another of Hansberry's texts remained unfinished, and perhaps unfinishable: her play *Les Blancs*, whose Kenyan protagonist, Tshembe Matoseh, returns to his homeland only to face the historical necessity of a choice between revolutionary violence, flight, and nonviolent struggle.[7] In the literally explosive context of U.S. civil rights activism and racist violence—marked, in 1964, by the use of police dogs in Birmingham and cattle prods in North Carolina, the gassing of student protestors by National Guard troops in Cambridge, Maryland, and the murders in Neshoba County, Mississippi, of the activists James Chaney, Andrew Goodman, and Michael Schwerner—the shared preoccupations and limits of these two dramas are thrown starkly in relief. Indeed, *Les Blancs* reads as something of a shadow text to *Sign*, on the order of a photographic negative, as it raises questions urged by history in the making. What modes of subjectivity and intersubjectivity are called for in these raddled times? What expressive forms, beyond traditional dramatic realism, might shape a commitment to collective experience—black; revolutionary; American?

Hansberry's work on photography not only spans the two dramatic texts, finished and unfinished, it also mediates her responses to these questions, and the evolution of her aesthetic and cultural commitments. During what was shaping up as a decisive moment in the civil rights struggle, Hansberry herself was at home in New York, where she struggled (often literally, in a wheelchair) to triangulate the considerable psychic distance between the Village as her home place, Broadway as her showcase, and Harlem as her imaginative battle-ground, the place where she had carried on her public life (however staged) as writer, activist, and editor, "mak[ing] streetcorner speeches," "talk[ing] to my people about everything on the streets."[8] All the while, she was looking at "photos from the front lines" crammed into "a new initialed dispatch case" beside her portable typewriter.[9] Thus casting herself in the role of wartime correspondent, Hansberry was writing and organizing the photo-text that would be titled *The Movement: Documentary of a Struggle for Equality.*

Published in the fall of 1964 by Simon and Schuster, *The Movement* was the first full-scale publication, commercial or otherwise, dedicated to youth activism, in particular the work of the grassroots radical group the Student Nonviolent Coordinating Committee (SNCC). Long a supporter of SNCC ac-tivities (she had, among other things, helped raise the money to purchase the station wagon from which Chaney, Goodman, and Schwerner were taken to their deaths), Hansberry either agreed or offered to fashion a narrative based on archival images of its work.[10] Even in the absence of commentary about the origins of the project, the published volume makes it clear how fully Hansberry entered into the conventions of photo-text, and the degree to which she used the occasion to explore her interest in image-text or narrative—that is, other than dramatic—possibilities. Although *The Movement* could hardly resolve the kinds of dramaturgical standoff embodied by *The Sign in Sidney Brustein's Window* and *Les Blancs*, it enabled Hansberry to reframe her dual commit-ments to liberationist projects—Africanist, globalized, or homegrown—and to the differently unfinished project of writing the American nation.

Unlike Richard Wright and her friend and contemporary James Baldwin, who (naturally) figures as a photographic subject in the pages of *The Move-ment*, Hansberry undertook photo-text not as a mode of collaboration with a specific interlocutor but as a kind of extended meditation in response to documentary images and iconography. *The Movement* includes the work of some twenty photographers, including agency photographers for UPI and Black Star, anonymous and archival image makers, and the canonized high-art practitioners Roy DeCarava and Robert Frank, but the majority of its im-ages were shot by the then unknown Danny Lyon.[11] In 1962, at the tender age of twenty, Lyon had become SNCC's first (and for a long while only) staff photographer, a kind of participant-observer who "ran along" with his camera as fellow activists marched and was arrested with them, but "could not hold hands and sing" Movement anthems at demonstrations because he always "had to step out and make a picture."[12] Hansberry appears not to have known Lyon personally; she is unmentioned in his detailed 1992 memoir, *Memories*

Figure 5.2. Danny Lyon, IRT 2, New York City, 1980. Magnum Photos.

of the Southern Civil Rights Movement, and her own posthumous collection of manuscripts and personal writings, *To Be Young, Gifted and Black* (1969), names Lyon only in marginal credits for several of his images. In any case, whether Lyon and Hansberry knew each other, the paths that led to their convergence are strikingly familiar. Described by his fellow SNCC activist Julian Bond as "inquisitive, New York-y, rumpled"—clearly euphemisms for "Jew"—Lyon was a self-taught photographer hailing from Forrest Hills, Queens, and a high school with "4,000 students, 90 percent of whom were Jewish and two of whom were black."[13] At age seventeen he took up the camera by way of exploring New York's iconic sites of photographic production and racial contact. Camera work, like his ensuing SNCC activism, drew Lyon as a mode for self-conscious enactment of "the middle-class trauma of breaking the law"; the streets and subways of Harlem, Brooklyn, and the South Bronx—enclaves of bracing encounter, "the spiritual heart of our democracy"—preoccupied him throughout his career (figure 5.2).[14] That career began in earnest when an image Lyon shot during his undergraduate stint at the University of Chicago was awarded a prize in a university art festival; one of the judges was none other than the former Harlem documenter Aaron Siskind (*Pictures*, 6).

Whatever the force of this serendipitous connection, Lyon began photographing local civil rights activism during his junior year at Chicago, in homage to his idol Mathew Brady. But Lyon's self-conception as a latter-day "historian with a camera" was far more self-consciously literary than Brady's had ever been (*Pictures*, 20). When Lyon lit out as a hitchhiker the summer after his junior year for a Mississippi already riven by radical activism and brutal state reprisals, he insisted on being driven "out to old Route 66, because that is the road Jack Kerouac used" (*Memories*, 20). His first foray into Movement photography came that summer in Cairo, Illinois, for which he made a beeline because the town "once marked the spot between freedom and slavery across the river in Missouri," the place "Huckleberry Finn and the runaway slave Jim were heading to on their raft but sailed by in the night" (*Memories*, 23). The following summer, as Lyon was being body-searched by police (who found his hidden film) in the aftermath of a vicious police attack on demonstrators at prayer, he "kept thinking of Camus's description of the execution of French resistance workers, who were told to run into a field, where the Nazis shot them" (*Memories*, 68). And after the makeshift coalition of Northern and Southern, black and white, Protestant, Jewish, and other radicals comprising SNCC had collapsed under the exigencies of black nationalism, and Lyon was searching for "a subject that had meaning for me," he made a pilgrimage to Knoxville, Tennessee, the birthplace of the storied collaborator of *Let Us Now Praise Famous Men*—not the legendary photographer Walker Evans, but the writer James Agee (*Pictures*, 60).[15] Crisscrossing the South, moving between his home in New York, the urban Midwest, and the unmapped back-roads towns that were making history, Lyon styled himself a latter-day adventurer in the mode of Whitman, powerful, rough-hewn, open-handed. "A Leica feels like a pistol in your pocket," he later wrote, "and there is something comforting about a view camera, which across my shoulder feels like an ax" (*Pictures*, 106).[16] From sober large-format compositions to snapshooting on the run, the aptest way to describe the photographic ideology that produced *The Movement*'s images might well be by citing "Song of Myself": "I am the man, I suffer'd, I was there."

Lyon's aspirations and pedigree, as distinct from his stylistics, frame him as heir both to Whitman and to that ethos of photographic encounter after Siskind, forged in the heat of lived histories of conflict and steeled to produce not evidence so much as the more complex effects of what Lyon called "mystery and reverence" (*Pictures*, 6). If his literary sensibilities allowed him, as Julian Bond put it, to "t[ake] that function" of propaganda and "ma[k]e it art," Hansberry's interest in visuality enabled her to exploit richly the narrative possibilities suggested by Lyon's images.[17] Hansberry was, in fact, well situated to make sense of Lyon's art as such. During her comfortably bourgeois youth in South Side Chicago she had taken visual arts classes at the Art Institute; during her two years as an undergraduate at the University of Wisconsin she majored in art, and went on to study painting in Guadalajara during her family's brief residence in Mexico. Although published materials offer no obvious evidence that Hansberry studied photographic history or techniques, her ready familiarity with broader iconographic traditions and visual idioms clearly informs her shaping of *The Movement*. With that work, Hansberry rethinks the possibilities of significant form in a context of social crisis, making use of photo-text narrative to press beyond the expressive limits of conventional realist drama.

From its opening pages, *The Movement* announces its displacement of the conceptual frame of the living room drama—in particular, *A Raisin in the Sun*, which begins with a long stage direction describing what Baldwin called the "claustrophobic terror" of the domestic space in which the Younger family is confined.[18] Here, Hansberry chooses to begin with a Lyon image of the open road, empty save for a single car approaching the viewer, barely visible in the distance (figure 5.3). But the mode of mobility implied here is not, in spite of the camera's angle, upward. Against the powerful vertical thrust of the composition, with its dramatic use of planar perspective and the road's receding broken line, the image opposes the force of horizontality: cracks densely scoring the road's surface; long shadows cast across it from sources somewhere within the lush landscape but not readily identifiable. Hansberry's introductory text—"This is the road from Jackson to Yazoo City, leading into the Mississippi Delta country, the heart of the Deep South"—confirms what Lyon's iconography implies. The American heartland is a battlefield; movement on this front will be an uphill battle. Such movement, under the auspices of the Movement, belongs to the animating traditions of American self-liberation: Huckleberry Finn lighting out for the territories; the adrenalated odyssey of Sal Paradise for freedom from deadening cold war pieties; the poet of "Song of the Open Road" stopping somewhere in wait for his countrymen. Exploiting the resonances of Lyon's image, Hansberry opens by equating the laboring of civil rights with unimpeded freedom of movement and self-invention, America's waking dream.

Hansberry also exploits the tension between mobility as a symbol "conjured up" by the camera and the structural fact of immobility, temporal and otherwise, that attends the photograph as a blink, a trace, a moment of experience frozen.[19] The opening sequence of *The Movement* deftly exploits that tension. Immediately following Lyon's shot of the road, Hansberry conjoins two stock images. One, by the documentary activist and sometime SNCC photographer

Figure 5.3. Danny Lyon, Yazoo, Mississippi, 1962. Magnum Photos.

Matt Herron, features an aged white pony grazing against the backdrop of a moldering, soot-darkened Mississippi plantation destroyed by fire; the second, shot by the photojournalist Norris McNamara, shows a Delta mansion dwarfed by a stand of new trees and surrounded by land gone to seed (8–9).[20] Such images of "the Old South" of "the countryside, between the towns," are "familiar" precisely in their emphatic stasis and anachronism (8). What Barthes calls the *"intense immobility"* of the photograph as object squarely frames the felt reality of the South as a land of primitive survivals, dead ends, failures to adapt to the exigencies of modernity and thus to thrive. Perhaps no other subject so consistently exemplifies photography's power of "arrest," the projection of the immobility of the captured image onto its once animate and living subjects.[21]

This Barthesian adhesion of photographic properties to the photographed subject—the segregated South—renders period photo-texts like Bourke-White and Caldwell's *You Have Seen Their Faces* intensely problematic. Here, however, it serves Hansberry's exploration of urgent paradoxes of mobility and constriction. For the final shot of *The Movement*'s opening sequence she chooses an archival lynching photo of a sort that is all too "familiar" (10–11). Two men's corpses, marked in such a way as to suggest their previous whipping and dragging, dangle from a tree in the background, surrounded by a thick knot of white onlookers who fill the foreground frame, triumphant, gleeful, grim, and titillated by turns. In sharp contrast to Wright, who incorporates a lynching image into *Twelve Million Black Voices* at the apex of a carefully shaped narrative arc tracing the "hateful web of cotton culture," Hansberry invokes lynching dead at the outset: her narrative, we understand, will bid to resist both the chronological order on which Wright relies and the familiar effects of dramatic climax and denouement.[22] Instead, Hansberry seeks to shape a more complex rhythm of aesthetic and social response. The lynching image indeed functions as a kind of caesura; the all too human bodies that hang, lifeless and motionless—in chilling contrast with the moved and moving bodies of their murderers, one of whom is caught, in the center foreground, only as a blur—index the immobility segregation both enforces and requires.[23] But Hansberry's text refuses to stop there. Offered up with the force of both eulogy and evidence, the image of the lynched, lifeless bodies becomes newly animated, made to point to another form of stasis: the economic immobility attending "the coming of industry into the Southland," which "has not changed the problems of many of its people—white or black—for the better" (13).

The force of Hansberry's metonymy, her substitution of one form of immobility for another, becomes clear on the pages following the lynching photograph. There, in a prominent double spread, she places Lyon's shot of a squalid Panama City, Florida, shack, its windows and doors incompletely covered by a length of fabric, its only visible occupant a small girl, apparently white, huddled in the doorframe. Far from rural in its setting, the shack clings to the bank of a waterway across which looms a full-scale industrial plant, smokestacks churning, construction debris littering the landscape. At the center of the image stands a budding tree, silhouetted against the smoke-filled sky, from which some article of clothing—perhaps a man's jacket—dangles. Placed in sequence and in this narrative frame, Lyon's image is made to rhyme with the lynching photograph; the audacious conjunction presses Hansberry's driving concerns. Segregation's practices, racism's law, long predate industrialization, but their undoing, she implies, will require recognition of the links (still powerfully repressed in 1964 by and for white Americans) between "the Southland" (13) and "the ghettos of the North" (14), between oppressive everyday realities and the allure for the spectator of "local color" (19), between economic inequality and pervasive habits of perception and representation.

Invisible, unanticipated, or transformative connection, in other words, is both the subject of the text and its shaping formal principle. Just as "the New South slams up against the Old" (13), "the South's chief exports"—"people"— batter against the hard facts of "the ghettos of the North" (14): so attests a brief portfolio of Roy DeCarava's Harlem images, including a shot of a young girl posed stiffly against a frame-filling brick wall (14) and another of a woman, baby in arms, crossing a vacant, rubble-strewn lot bounded by soot-darkened tenement brick (18). Just as the Movement marches directly at the set ranks of police, attack dogs, National Guard troops, and "the old order" (77), the directed "look upon the turbulence in men's eyes" (32) aims to counter the deadly force with which some "whites across the South observe and react" to the clamor for change (71): so argue the frequent portrait images by Lyon and others, including the famed art photographer David Heath (figure 5.4), orchestrated so as to create a complex play of gazes. If, as Susan Sontag argues with asperity, celebrated instances of postwar photo-text muster the effect of historical argument through the rote force of collage, Hansberry's text reverses that logic.[24] Employing unexpected, even aleatory juxtapositions, the text moves rapidly among traditional evidentiary captions ("This man earns about $2.50 a day"), bold headlines ("*WE SHALL OVERCOME!*"), lyrical passages, and extensive citations (from, among others, DuBois, Lyon, the abolitionist Theodore Parker, and the Nation of Islam organ *Muhammad Speaks*). Throughout, photo-text sequences are orchestrated in such a way that their contribution to the text's design becomes evident only in retrospect. Collectively, these strategies work to communicate the force of history as lived struggle—not least the struggle to connect daily choices and absent causes across the varied yet continuous landscapes of segregation in law and custom, in the nation's past and in its now.

Hansberry's interest in metonymy and its effects resonates in the section following the Harlem portfolio, as the text trains its attention once again on the South as the site of SNCC's rising. As if to emphasize her investment in metonymy, Hansberry begins a series of observations with the conjunctive "And": "And if a man's family is hungry, he may steal, and if he steals he can

Figure 5.4. David Heath, Untitled, from *A Dialogue with Solitude*, ca. 1964. By permission of the artist. Courtesy of Howard Greenberg Gallery, New York.

be sentenced to years of hard labor. . . . And then there is all the complicated silliness that a system took so much trouble to create" (22–24). These brief assertions are yoked not only to one another but to a series of sequenced images. The first, a conventional documentary portrait of an elderly black man, shows the subject posed in a rough cloth pullover pocked with holes and an old-fashioned wide-brimmed straw hat against a cotton field in flower. That image is succeeded—dwarfed, in terms of image size and layout—by Lyon's shot of a prison overseer, back to the camera, towering from his perch atop a railroad track above a crew of indistinguishable white-clad, African American inmates, whose analogous labor—digging rows for planting—is now openly forced and criminalized. But in lieu of a continuing brief against the criminalization of the disempowered, the text goes on to image "all the complicated silliness" of segregation, both "the silly . . . . . . and the unspeakable" (24–25, ellipses original).

The double-page spread linked to this text features a small inset image, top left, of segregated drinking fountains: an opulent floor model with a foot pump and gleaming drinking spout marked "WHITE," flanked by a tiny, waist-high

Figure 5.5. Photographer unknown, The Lynching of William Brown, Omaha, Nebraska, September 28, 1919. Nebraska State Historical Society Photograph Collections.

ceramic fountain with a tiny drainpipe for a spout marked "COLORED." Overshadowing this image, much as the guard towers above the work gang, is another lynching photograph, if anything more gruesome than the one the reader has previously encountered (figure 5.5). In the foreground lies a charred, dismembered male body, still locked into the posture of crucifixion on a fallen wooden frame, while a circle of white men in the background rings the site of the murder, many self-consciously posing for the large-format camera. The recrudescence of lynching in Hansberry's narrative, at a moment when the reader believes the text to have broached and (in effect) covered that subject, is in itself shocking. Conjoined with the gleaming floor tiles and ceramic bowls of the courthouse facilities, the eviscerated, still smoking remains of the lynching victim become even more disturbing, more intensely obscene. That the social logic of the drinking fountains underlies the fact of the smoldering corpse—that water, in effect, makes fire—militates against nature at its most elemental. In this brief narrative arc, the unanticipated movement from the dehumanized black laborer to the grotesque labor of dehumanization underscores segregation as both a mode of production and a social relation that is, via conformity as well as brutality, continuously reproduced. Hansberry's use of jarring conjunctions and associative logic not only subdues the predictable didacticism of conventional photo-text (oppression results in poverty results in theft results in prison culture). It also urges the presumptively white reader to understand its associative aesthetic as the means to a self-knowledge necessary in the face of impending, even violent, change.

Like Ellison, with whose social commitments hers are routinely contrasted to critical effect, Hansberry seizes on the metonymic properties of photo-text and postwar photography in response both to social exigencies and to the felt limits of literary form.[25] In Hansberry's case, those properties are productively at odds with the imperatives of dramatic naturalism, the working conditions she inherits and exploits to dated effect in *A Raisin in the Sun* and *The Sign in Sidney Brustein's Window*. The hallmarks of these "socio-realist drama[s]" so roundly derided by the post-1964 Black Arts dramatists Paul Carter Harrison, Amiri Baraka, and Ed Bullins—the commitment to coherent action narratives, sequential clarity, and a Euro-American "investment in individual destiny"; the embrace of an "objective" perspective on selfhood and social structures as evolving entities—are notably undercut, or at least displaced, by the protocol of *The Movement*.[26] Exploring the effects of contiguity and iconic linkage made available by the photo-text form, Hansberry breaks equally free of what Kimberly Benston has described as her early "neoAristotlean[ism]" and her later posture of "self-deprecating . . . alienation."[27] While her completed dramas exemplify the limits of dramatic naturalism—its understanding of "randomness, disorder, anarchy, and simultaneity in experience as . . . threateningly unnatural"[28]—*The Movement* takes no such understanding for granted. In the wake of Freedom Summer, and in the closing days of her own life, Hansberry tests the modes of serendipitous association, antilinearity, and ekphrasis opened by photo-textuality.

To be sure, *The Movement* presses these modes in continued service of a cross-racial—or what would come disparagingly to be called a liberal—enterprise, and of "America's much touted sense of fair play" (83). Dead a month before the assassination of Malcolm X, Hansberry completed her photo-text work in the brief moment before the rising tides of black nationalism and state counterinsurgency swept the grassroots activism of SNCC, writ as "the Movement," from historical center stage. Read in retrospect, the very text of *The Movement* seems presciently designed to meditate on the contending claims of radicalism and liberalism, nonviolent action and armed struggle, radical nationalism and the ideology of the indivisible American nation. On close inspection, the reader realizes that its longest arc (pages 46–117 of the

Figure 5.6. Danny Lyon, Cairo, Illinois, 1962. Magnum Photos.

published text) constitutes an extended exploration—precisely by way of metonymic gestures, frictional juxtaposition, and an emphasis on random yet exemplary detail—of the possibilities of sustaining cross-racial alliances and resisting the allure of militant identitarian claims.

Hansberry addresses the latter issue, of liberation struggles as an Africanist rather than an American project, most powerfully by indirection. Following a brief portfolio of images of marching and chanting youths, the text appears to sum up the state of activist art by noting that "the movement toward freedom" (in distinction to "the Movement") "has varied faces" (46). Notably, however, this portfolio (36–46) exclusively features black Americans: the variety in question concerns not race but the ideological purchases on it afforded by "the devotions of our culture": "traditional Christianity" and "more recently, Islam" (46). Exemplifying the former, Hansberry offers what is perhaps the best-known image of Lyon's career: a shot of soon-to-be SNCC chairman John Lewis, kneeling in prayer at the Cairo, Illinois, city hall beside an adolescent girl, head deeply bowed, her slim body supported by the index finger of her right hand against the pavement (figure 5.6).[29] Shot at close range and at the level of the kneeling figures, Lyon's image emphasizes the extraordinary inwardness—the protest-ant grace—of the subjects, thereby inflecting political will as a form of unimpeachable moral commitment. By contrast, the following pages are densely spread with images, shot by the Nation of Islam house photographer Don Charles, of the Nation as a disciplinary project: a Nation speaker at a podium flanked by ordered rows of guards, outside Michaux's bookstore in Harlem ("The House of Common Sense and Home of Proper Propaganda" [47]); rows of Nation women seated at a service or rally in an auditorium, made literally indistinguishable from one another by their white robes and headscarves (47); the limousine of Elijah Muhammad, circled by identically suited members of the Fruit of Islam standing at attention, their backs to the camera (48–49).

With this sequence, Hansberry meditates on the force—not only of arms—required to accomplish the Nation's goal of "separation of the so-called negroes and the so-called white Americans" (cited 46). Underpinning that project, she argues, is "a pot-luck nationalism" that "looks backward," not even to black Africa but "to Arabic cultures," and not generatively or productively (so she argues) but merely as "an accommodation to American racism" (48). Against these forms of "dedicat[ion]" and "intimidati[on]," Hansberry poses the Movement's homegrown and distinctly American history, which "began in the seventeenth century when Africans being transported to the New World mutinied on the high seas" (52). In its shifting shapes across the life of the nation—the escape and insurrection of unnamed slaves; the military service of Republican troops; the sabotage committed by oppressed workers; the "new methods" of the "'new Negro'" (52)—the Movement offers its own powerful record of revolutionary commitment. Absent photographs, Hansberry exemplifies them in a collage of citations: antebellum freedom fighters; Nat Turner; Frederick Douglass—"I urge you to fly to arms and smite with death the power that would bury the government and your liberty in this same hopeless grave"; an unnamed Jim Crow era preacher—"We want to live in peace with all mankind, and especially with the whites of the South. . . . But we do not want the peace of the lamb with the lion" (52).

It is this history, not the invented tradition of the Nation of Islam, Hansberry goes on to argue, that will stand most powerfully against the grim might of the old order, imaged in a sequence of shots of increasingly militarized guardians of the peace: local cops massed in Danville, Virginia (58); federal troops, rifles aloft and gas masks in place, blockading a street in Cambridge, Maryland, as young children look on (59); state troopers, with hard hats and combat gear, nonchalantly leaning against a car, the day after the firebombing of Birmingham's Sixteenth Street Baptist Church on September 15 (67). The latter event inevitably produces "a new urgency" of critical assessment about nonviolence as "the way" (94). With text reading "The responsibility for an answer lies heavily on the hearts and shoulders of the men who lead" (96), Hansberry pairs Lyon's shot of Martin Luther King at a press conference in the courtyard of a motel near the bombed church. In contrast with the familiar meditative look that characterizes so many of his portraits, King here scowls, training his gaze downward and off the page, away from the ranks of eager reporters making notes behind him, breathing literally down his neck.

The portrait of King, throned yet wracked, is countered by two Norris McNamara images on the facing page. In both images, young men—including a preadolescent boy—are shot in profile, casually dressed, and out of doors (in one case, astride the roof-level limb of a tree). As arrayed in this layout, the young men stare across the white space of the page break, holding rifles aloft in self-confident fashion. Yoked to an epigraph from the revolutionary broadside "The Riflemen of Bennington"—"Why come ye hither, redcoat? / Your mind what madness fills? / In our valleys there is danger! / And there's danger in our hills!"—the two images orchestrate a face-off between the embattled King and those free and determined to take up revolutionary arms. Unfolding through a metonymic logic, the sequence opens a middle ground between rank accommodationism and Nationalist proscription against "fraternization with 'white devils'" (106), and seizes that space in the name of what Hansberry now calls "the Negro Movement" (99). Refusing the status of the Negro as stranger in a strange and brutal land, Hansberry insists on his (and her: a point to which I will return) history as the "'old stock' America[n] in every sense: by blood, culture and temperament": even as the nation was being made by European migrations, "We were here" (99). Rejecting "the berets and dark shirts of Black Nationalists" and "the assertion of a newfound West African past" alike (105), Hansberry frames the Movement as rightful heir to the American tradition of "the drawn sword within reach of my right hand," defending a liberty that is "the eternal law of God" (98). Hansberry's Movement is second to none in its will to radical change. Profoundly indebted to the experiences and iconography of black life in America, it is nonetheless committed to the mutual interdependence of "my freedom and . . . yours" (104).

The explicit call to arms sits uncomfortably astride a reiterated claim to the power of "freedom songs" that the Whitmanian author and "you, my countryman" (by implication white) might in concert sound (104). No wonder, then, that the closing sequences of the text (104–24) draw notably back from some climactic statement of revolutionary will—the moral equivalent, on the one hand, of Baraka's revolutionary "thrash and moan," his resounding "muthafucka," or, on the other, of Richard Avedon's searing *Nothing Personal* images of subjects wracked by mental illness.[30] But on a closer reading, the narrative-

image play of *The Movement*'s final sequences appears so obviously anticlimactic as to suggest that anticlimax has become Hansberry's strategy. Returning
to SNCC's photographic archive, Hansberry notes that "[some of our people]
still find it in themselves to continue to work at voter registration and the
teaching of nonviolent tactics" (107). Under the rubric "Leaders for many
years" follows a series of portrait images of civil rights luminaries such as
A. Philip Randolph, Roy Wilkins, Bayard Rustin, Ossie Davis, SNCC's point
man Bob Moses, Doris Latner, Fannie Lou Hamer, and more (108ff). The
ostensible logic of this gallery of images is to instance the richness with which
"the Movement thrusts up new, energetic leadership" (112). But the reappear-
ance here of Malcolm X, featured for the first time at close range and directly
facing the camera, his chiseled face and charismatic presence fully registered
(115), suggests otherwise. The apparent redirection of the narrative into a roll
call of civil rights leaders is in some sense Hansberry's cover for another kind
of argument, pressed in less than straightforward fashion.

What strikes the reader in the closing gallery of images is the felt friction
between representations of male leaders—invariably suited and jacketed, or
clothed in the mantle of a romanticized solitude—and those of the Movement's women. (That effect would arguably be more powerful for culturally
conversant readers in 1964, those for whom Hansberry's 1961 confrontation
with Norman Mailer on the subject of the white Negro in the pages of the
Village Voice and her 1963 face-off with Attorney General Robert Kennedy at
the White House came readily to mind.)[31] A full-page candid portrait by Lyon
of Gloria Richardson, the radical SNCC field leader in Cambridge, Maryland,
is shot in an intimate setting and from below; barefoot, her head thrown back
in apparent laughter or pleasure and haloed by natural light, Richardson confronts us with a beauty and expressive complexity that defy the straightforward
honorific function (113). A portrait by the documentary photographer Marion
Palfi of the "tall, black-skinned, and beautiful" SNCC activist Annelle Ponder,
shot at close range in conversation with a fellow activist (figure 5.7), appears
above a citation from the radical historian Howard Zinn, who recounts a visit
to Ponder in a Mississippi jail after she had been severely beaten by police:
"they found her sitting there, her face swollen and marked, barely able to
speak. She looked up at them, and just managed to whisper one word: 'Freedom'" (117). In the sequence Hansberry establishes, Palfi's image subtly redirects the force of Zinn's reading. In this context, it is the anonymous—and
male—African American figure, silhouetted and dominating the far right of
the image, whom Ponder appears with all her depth of feeling to confront.
Austere yet affirmative, *The Movement*'s closing sequence of women's portraits

Figure 5.7. Marion Palfi, Annelle Ponder, Greenwood, Mississippi, 1963. Center for Creative Photography, Tucson, Arizona.

is Hansberry's rebuttal by indirection to the allure of Malcolm X and the Nation, to increasingly strident rhetorics of militant masculinity.[32]

Reading retrospectively, it becomes clear that Hansberry is invested via the play of photo-text in the possibilities for an imagination of radical change suggested when women—rather than lynched male bodies, or white military bodies, or even living and powerful black speakers of the Word—become figures for radical change. Throughout the text, photographs of women thread together its disparate portfolios and narrative arcs, allowing Hansberry a broader iconographic and allusive range. From the initial DeCarava portraits, luminous in their use of found light and their subjects' presence, to David Heath's evocative studies of women adrift in the eddying currents of desire and solitude, through the celebratory photojournalism of Jill Krementz (trained here on women participating in the 1964 March on Washington), through Palfi's portraits in the book's penultimate sequence, Hansberry orchestrates a secondary rhythm—not quite a counternarrative—that underlies the narrative of Movement history. At virtually every turn, images of women

Figure 5.8. Danny Lyon, Leesburg, Georgia, 1963. Magnum Photos.

secure yet redirect local claims for the Movement's power and meaning. A sequence devoted to the imprisonment of activists, anchored by a letter (written by Bob Moses from a Mississippi jail) that "became a movement legend," concludes with Lyon's photograph of some dozen young girls, imprisoned for more than three weeks in a single cell without furniture, blankets, clothing, a working toilet, or a reliable water source, shot through the jagged glass of a broken cell window (figure 5.8).[33] Punctuating the segment focused on the Birmingham church bombing are a list of the names and ages of the four victims—all, of course, girls—and an image of mourners, chiefly women, attending one of the funeral processions. Here, and for the text as a whole, the community's rage, outrage, grief, and grim determination are embodied not by official Movement or Nation leadership but in the person of a single unnamed woman, who confronts Lyon's camera with shocking ferocity, as if it were the living nemesis itself (figure 5.9; 90–91).

This investment of expressivity—what we might call the power of movement—in African American women is firmly linked with Hansberry's attempt to rethink her own modes of expressivity. It is, for example, no accident that the closing sequence of portraits includes by way of caption the bald assertion: "People do not always need poets and playwrights to state their case" (118). Neither poet nor playwright in this space, Hansberry labors as a producer of

Figure 5.9. Danny Lyon, Birmingham, Alabama, 1963. Magnum Photos.

meaningful narrative, an archivist collating images, evidence, citations, and voices from the nation's past. In the process she works iconographically, making central to an imagination of radical commitment images of the black woman unchained from mammydom, the martyrology of racial endurance, and conventional (or, more accurately, heterosexual) femininity alike.

The three final portrait images of the text testify, as a sequence, to this aim. From Marion Palfi's image of an elderly laborer—"*I worked for three dollars a day. I want freedom*" [118])—with her hair tied back in a neat kerchief, her hands thrown up, palms outward, in a traditional gesture of testifying, we move to Lyon's tight head shot of an adolescent girl, hair closely cropped and unstraightened, bare of the clips, braids, and bows that adorn the conspicuously dressed-up children in previous images (figure 5.10). Here, by way of testimony to the subject's will to political expression, the caption reads: "*A pickup truck came tearing down the street and drove straight into the crowd. We all scattered, except this girl, who wouldn't move. The truck slammed on its brakes, then hit her. She got up after that. She wasn't hurt too badly*" (118). In the final image of the sequence and of *The Movement*, Hansberry places Lyon's even tighter portrait, strikingly off-center, of an unnamed subject whose gender in this context resonates with uncertainty (figure 5.11; 123). Hair closely cropped, features beautifully modeled, the subject resembles the stoic young

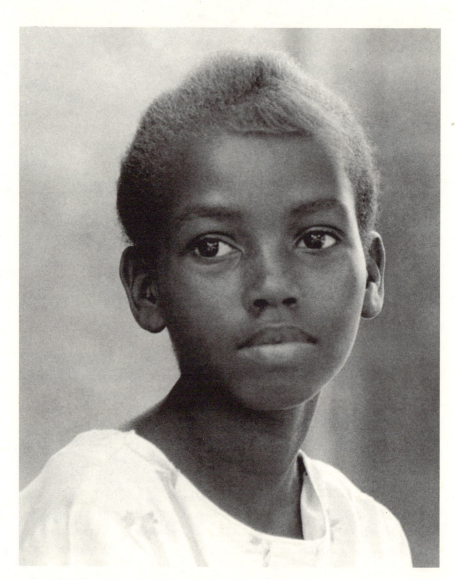

Figure 5.10. Danny Lyon, Hattiesburg, Mississippi, 1964. Magnum Photos.

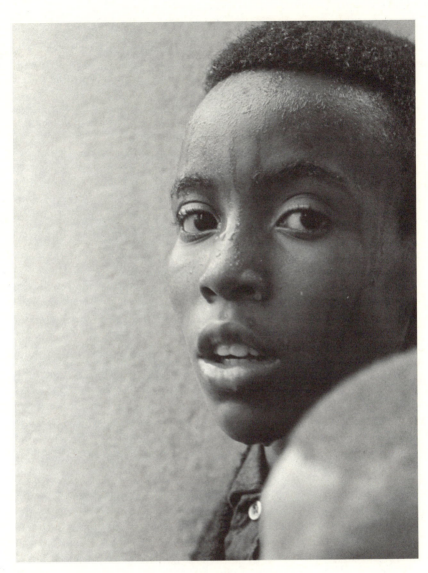

Figure 5.11. Danny Lyon, Cairo, Illinois, 1962. Magnum Photos.

girl whose image precedes this; a single button and the lap of the fabric at the subject's shirt collar suggest male attire, but the placement of the figure and the iconography of teardrops—indexed in Hansberry's caption as "hose fire" or "rain"—are distinctly feminizing (122). In conjunction with this image, Hansberry concludes:

> They stand in the hose fire at Birmingham; they stand in the rain at Hattiesburg.
> They are young, they are beautiful, they are determined.
> It is up to us to create, now, an America that deserves them. (122)

By this point, the generic referent of the third-person plural is shadowed by particularity—in other words, by gender uncertainty. What does a revolutionary (or indeed a black American woman) look like? What would it take for radical politics itself to create a place for other than militantly masculine determination and self-determination?

It is possible to read *The Movement*'s concluding drift by association and photo-text linkage as a gesture toward the radical lesbian-feminist politics claimed for Hansberry, based on her involvement in the fledgling San Francisco–based movement.[34] Of pointed interest here is Hansberry's use of photo-textual possibilities—the force of metonymy, a simultaneity of purpose and implication—to remake herself as a writer, and specifically a writer of narrative forms. Critical accounts of her life inevitably tend to emphasize the pathos of her unfinished work, and in particular her aborted plays, of which Hansberry wrote in a journal entry of September 16, 1964, "I sit at this desk for hours and sharpen pencils and smoke cigarettes and switch from play to play—Sidney, Toussaint, Les Blancs, and—nothing happens."[35] But she had also begun an autobiographical (and apparently less constricted) piece of work, a novel titled "All the Dark and Beautiful Warriors." On the strength of the brief excerpts published by Nemiroff, the concluding images of *The Movement* might well serve as that novel's photographic accompaniment.[36] Although the relative slightness of Hansberry's published work necessitates caution about the possible shapes of her lost post-1964 career, the evidence of *The Movement* indicates that photo-text enables her, at a critical moment in the iconicity of black intellectuals, to begin imagining herself differently on the stage of public culture: as a writer of formally indeterminate texts rather than conventional well-made drama, experimenting with voice even as she gives voice to labile erotic and political desires. Ironically, it is Hansberry's work on photo-text that allows her to make trial of narrative forms beyond the dramatic naturalism that, in her words, "tends to take the world as it is . . . [and] simply photograph the garbage can."[37] If her dramatic texts evidence the expressive limits of naturalism in an epoch of heightened political consciousness and crisis, Hansberry appears to have exploited photographic images and photo-text narrative as a way of moving beyond that settled territory. At its farthest reaches, her work on photo-text can be seen as her own response to the felt crisis of mimesis driving later Black Arts drama. In the movement through images, Hansberry becomes a secret sharer in the fortunes of African American dramatic art—and a telling figure on the broader landscape of art and revolution.

Reverting to Form: Chester Himes and the Moment of Photo-Text

In 1964, at just the time *The Movement* was making its way into print, the expatriate novelist Chester Himes published the seventh in his series of "Harlem Domestic" noir fictions, titled *Cotton Comes to Harlem*.[38] Himes's slick novel, which tells the tale of competing gangs of hustlers staking out Harlem as a territory ripe for flight-from-the-ghetto schemes, has nothing obvious to do with Hansberry or the photo-text form. Absent photographic images or obvious aspirations to experimental status, *Cotton* hews to the hard-boiled formula developed in Himes's previous Harlem-centered thrillers, from *A Rage in Harlem* (1957) through *The Heat Is On* (1961). Biographically, Himes himself would also appear to be a mismatch for Hansberry. Born in 1909, he wrote not only from the remove of expatriate Paris but about a Harlem in which he had never "worked . . . , raised children," or been "hungry, sick or poor"; in his own estimation he remained "as much of a tourist [there] as a white man from downtown changing his luck."[39] Unlike Hansberry and Baldwin (or indeed, Ralph Ellison and sometime Paris compatriot Richard Wright), Himes never took up photography as an adjunct mode of production or source of suggestion. Perhaps his most notable engagement with the camera was as the subject of a police mug shot in 1929, when he was arrested for armed robbery and began serving eight years of a twenty-five-year sentence in the Ohio State Penitentiary.

But at the epicenter of his formula tale of 1964 stands an invocation of photo-text history that speaks to Himes's aims as a writer in the emergent post–civil rights context. Embedded in noir stylistics, Himes's apparently casual reference to photo-textuality provides a key to the temporal scheme of *Cotton Comes to Harlem* and of his Harlem noir fiction at large. Read against the developing genealogy of photo-texts from Wright through Hansberry, with their implicit claims to newness and the living present ("It is for us to create, now, an America that deserves them"), *Cotton's* photo-textual moment exemplifies a strategy of willed anachronism, founded in Harlem's multiple histories and exploited to make a different kind of place for the African American novelist and the everything-but-colorblind postwar novel. Undeniably local, Himes's invocation of photo-text nonetheless attests to the aims and limits of the novel as it enters the post–civil rights era.

The scene in question, like so many of Himes's brilliant set pieces, appears unconnected with the byzantine plot already unfolding in preceding chapters (beginning with the theft by white gate-crashers of money collected in Harlem for a spurious Back to Africa scheme; the money is hidden in the eponymous bale of cotton, which then zigzags its way through Harlem's underground economies). One summer day, the morning after the heist, a newly remodeled storefront in the heart of Harlem's business district on Seventh Avenue is unveiled. Around it gathers an ever-thickening crowd of "Harlemites, big and little, old and young, strong and feeble, the halt and the blind, male and female, boys and girls," all of whom—the "blind" included—"star[e] in pop-eyed amazement."[40] Their gazes are arrested by the ultra-modern "plate-glass windows, trimmed with stainless steel," over which hangs "a big wooden sign glistening with spotless white paint upon which big, bold, black letters announced:

HEADQUARTERS OF
B.T.S. BACK-TO-THE-SOUTHLAND
MOVEMENT B.T.S.
Sign up Now!!! Be a 'FIRST NEGRO!'
$1,000 Bonus to First Families Signing! (80)

Himes's emphasis on visuality as a mode of hustle and byplay, sustained in the very typography of the text, links with a certain oxymoronic quality: the "shining steel" of the storefront mismatches the lettered wooden sign, as if Berenice Abbott's images of Manhattan's bridges, girders gleaming, or Lisette Model's glittering shop fronts, had been juxtaposed with the artisanal signage so favored by Walker Evans (80). In the advertisements emblazoning Back-to-the-Southland's windows, a similar dissonance reigns. Pulling out all the minstrel stops—cakewalking, jiving, chicken-licking, grinning—while renewing them for postwar prosperity, the ads feature images of "conk-haired black cotton-pickers" clad in overalls that "resemble Italian-tailored suits" (80). More "bright" images of "happy darkies" show celebratory workers singing what "surely must be spirituals" yet simultaneously "dancing the twist" (80); the approving "elders" who look on are "bobbing their nappy white heads" as they "cla[p] their manicured hands" (81). Literally central to this riot of updated reversions is "a blown up photomontage" contrasting drawings of "*The Happy South*" of modern plenty—churchgoers in Brooks Brothers suits and Saks Fifth Avenue dresses—with photographs "of famine in the Congo, tribal wars, mutilations, depravities, hunger and diseases, above the caption, '*Unhappy Africa*'" (81).

The moral equivalence, in Himes's purview, of latter-day minstrelsy with the mass image, trained on decolonizing, newly darkest Africa, is hardly surprising. But Himes's invocation, as "the center of all this jubilation," of the definitive technology of the New Deal—photo-text and photomontage—should give us pause (81). The *Life*-style spread in BTS's windows frames itself as a reversion to type: it presses Reconstruction-era white supremacist ideals—embodied in the person of the novel's foremost anachronism, BTS's Colonel Calhoun, clad in "a black frock coat and black shoestring tie," sporting "snow-white hair," a "drooping white moustache" and goatee, flaunting a "solid gold signet ring" with the initials of the vanished Confederacy (82)—under cover of a wholly outmoded economic formation. "You're thinking about the First World War," a junk dealer tells the elderly grifter, Uncle Bud, who tries to sell him the abandoned bale of cotton he has found; "Nowadays they're giving cotton away" (94).[41]

Such blatant anachronism is all the more striking in a novel that—unlike earlier Harlem Domestics—takes some pains to locate itself not only in postwar America but in the new or second ghetto, in the throes of a postindustrial havoc wreaked by civil rights backlash, high-rise renewal, and white flight.[42] The originating Back to Africa con, which has its Renaissance-inflected genesis in "a biography of Marcus Garvey" (34), is viable only because dense blocks of slum tenements in Harlem's notorious Valley are being "razed for a new housing development" in the signature fashion of postwar urban renewal, leaving the neighborhood "more overcrowded than ever due to relocation of families from the site of the new buildings to relieve the overcrowding" (2, 3). In another mode of relocation, this Harlem has again become, after a decade of post–*Brown v. Board* violence and harassment, a destination for black Americans "sent north by the white southerners in revenge" (33). Himes's symbolic object, the cash crop of a feudal productive mode, thus circulates in a Harlem pulsing with high-rise squalor, hard bop cultural energies, and postindustrial decline, all thinly laid over the infrastructure of earlier failed migrations. In this Harlem, "architects and bankers c[o]me at night" to boarded-up tenements in their limousines "to plan the construction of new buildings" (140); saxes swap fours in what is definitively postwar, post-Renaissance Big Wilt Chamberlain's Small's Paradise (45); Nation of Islam exhorters converge with Africanist sloganeering and "Communist Christian" propaganda, all facing off against the truncheons of antiriot police (5).

In the context of 1960s-era Harlem, readers have judged Himes's anachronisms careless, his chosen genre ill-suited to the cultural imperatives of the Movement and the moment. (Why, after all, employ such an atavistic figure as the "Colonel" when there are so many real-life Theodore Bilbos, George Wallaces, and Bull Connors to choose from?) But Himes's primary aim as a novelist is not to engage a contemporary micropolitics of race. His private letters and unpublished materials from the 1960s—nothing less than an extended Mississippi goddamn—make it clear that he could and did engage from his redoubt in Paris with the shifting tactics of a whole array of political figures: "pretentious, indescribably ignorant whiteys," "chickenshit" intellectuals, limp liberals, high-minded cold warriors, self-serving pan-Africanists, and black nationalist "loudmouthed leaders urging our vulnerable soul brothers on to getting themselves killed."[43] Why then his insistence on a Harlem that, as his biographer James Sallis puts it, "seems patently to date from earlier years"?[44] Far from nostalgic for his youthful experience of a Renaissance-inflected Harlem, Himes's fictive landscape is a willed reversion to outmoded form, whose meaning the central figure of photo-text clarifies. The provocation of the Back-to-the-Southland display accrues not, finally, to the so-called Colonel with the cheroot and the "calculated" Southern drawl (82). Rather, it is Himes who limns Harlem as a kind of "photomontage," a collage of arresting juxtapositions whose competing rhetorics and frames—uplift and delinquency, Africa and Southland, minstrelsy and the rhetorics of black power—are all at his writerly disposal.

Photo-text is, in other words, a powerful trope for Himes's attempts to seize on second-ghetto Harlem, roiling with racial dissent and its own histories of accommodation, and thereby to stake his claims as a postwar writer negotiating varied literary genealogies, militancies, and aspirations. Whatever the force of Harlem as a heterotopia or site of dissent, in *Cotton* it becomes the imaginative province for the writer wary of all the available stances. Layering primitivist, bebop, gangster, and Great Migration Harlems onto one another, Himes assembles a bodacious collage of icons not unlike the one mounted by Calhoun; he thus voices an idiosyncratic radicalism, skeptical of all and beholden to none. Back-to-the-Southland's elaborate display of images—brilliant showmanship, outrageous con, slick ruse for attempted recovery of the vanished goods—might well stand for Himes's aims under cover of formula fiction.

To put it comparatively, Harlem and hard-boiled stylistics, figured via photo-text, serve Himes toward the end of his career much as that genre serves

Hansberry at the truncated apex of hers: as an agency for shrugging off determinative writerly burdens. In Himes's case, they were labeled "protest, high seriousness," and "autobiography," the conventions consistently foisted on that trammeled postwar being, "the black American writer."[45] Two and a half decades beyond the cultural matrix around *Native Son*, Himes understood himself as struggling anew to find a generic alternative to "the old, used forms," a way to "break through the barrier that labeled me as a 'protest writer' ... [and] the victim of racism."[46] The context of that imperative had, of course, shifted considerably; by 1964, the last word on the fire next time was being delivered by a new cadre of "ghetto" writers, among them the overexposed Baldwin, the memoirist Claude Brown, Malcolm X, and the sociologist Kenneth Clark. Collectively, their "guided tour[s] to hell" were celebrated or feared, or both, for nation-stirring accounts of a postwar dystopia rife with delinquency and despair.[47] For Himes, who labored in the shadow of Wright and battled to the end of his life to alter the terms of his own reception, the hallmark stylistics of the new ghetto writing must have been déjà vu all over again: the first-person impulse—what Clark would call, with respect to his own landmark study of Harlem crime, "the anguished cry of [the] author"; reflexive "descent into the documentation" of white racism and revolutionary anger; the rejection of traditional formalisms for a raw, essentially "sociological import."[48] Committed to the novel as an expressive form, eschewing raddled interiority for slick surface and "strange shit," Himes explores the freedom to remain mordantly skeptical, to refuse a response to various calls—liberal, black aesthetic, or nationalist—for identification and belonging.[49]

Just as the work of photo-text enables Hansberry to work outside the reach and limits of a constricting theatrical realism, Himes's Back-to-the Southland photo-text figures his determination to press a writerly freedom from both identity claims and identification. This aim animates *Cotton*'s most outrageous—and anachronistic—set piece, the description of a riot brewing as the era's defining antagonists threaten to go head-to-head in the streets. Once again, the action unfolds at Harlem's center, the corner of 125th Street and Seventh Avenue, crossroads and intersection for white-owned department stores (like the real-life Kress's, ground zero for the 1935 riot) and black shoppers, sex tourism and vice cops, legitimate and criminal enterprises. Here, a self-ordained Bible thumper staking out a postwar landmark, the Chock Full O' Nuts, "exhort[s] the passersby to take Jesus to their hearts," while across the street the Harlem branch of the Nation of Islam—Temple Number Seven, Malcolm X's post—holds a mass meeting in front of Michaux's National Memorial Bookstore, where (just as in Hansberry's photo-text) the accouterments of identitarianism—African flags, posters proclaiming "WHITE PEOPLE EAT DOG . . . ALLAH IS GOD," a coffin marked "*The Remains of Lumumba*"—are on display (174–75). Toward this intersection marches a grim parade of mercenaries toting knives and sporting Back-to-the-Southland regalia, led by Calhoun with "all the indifference of a benevolent master" (175–76).

Coming head to head, then, in Harlem's defining crossroads are all the eddying currents of black life in America, from the failure of Reconstructionist, progressive, and liberal schemes for black modernization through industrial Jim Crow poverty, up to postindustrial (if not postcolonial) crisis. But the obvious payoff—a racial free-for-all that would confirm the worst fears of white America, the heady fantasies of Black Power advocates, and the hard-boiled code of excess in one—never materializes. Instead, Himes gives us the now weary heroes of the Harlem Domestic series, Coffin Ed Johnson and Grave Digger Jones, who stave off conflagration with a stylized routine familiar to series readers. Jones, drawing his long-barreled .38 special, stands at the northern edge of the melee and yells, "Straighten up!" while Johnson, from downtown, fires his matching .38 into the air and echoes, "Count off!" (176). When Calhoun ignores their signature warning, Jones responds by sending Calhoun's hat flying out of reach, transforming him from menacing white demagogue into comic buffoon. The denouement of the riot is thus the easy—too easy—restoration of local control. The paid agitators, uplifters, consciousness raisers, and hangers-on all march to the orders of the two cops, past a Colonel left standing "with three bullet holes in his hat" and surrounded by "the jeers and laughter of the colored people" (177).

Himes's hard-boiled veterans enact neither a resolution of real-life political crisis nor an apotheosis of hard-boiled cool but a fantasy of image management. Holding disparate, violently unstable formations in check, redirecting the vectors and energies of their social expression, Jones and Johnson become true Renaissance men, emblematic figures of Himes's photomontage Harlem. Their performance accomplishes no more than eliciting "the envious awe" of white cops and sending their own sorry selves, in a resonant phrase, "back to cotton" (178). But it also suggests Himes's investment in the mastery of competing historical and stylistic resources. Able to mobilize the disparate histories and codes of Harlem cultures spanning the century, and thus to create temporary forms of order, Jones and Johnson are bound by none of them. Thus liberated, Himes's surrogates pave the way for their author, in the face of incendiary violence from Harlem to Watts and back again, to produce "a kind of story where I could accuse everyone of inhumanity."[50] The expressive form that enables this "kind of story" is still, for Himes, despite all evidence and claims to the contrary, the novel. *Cotton*'s figures of photomontage announce his renewed commitment in the final trio of Harlem Domestics, written from 1964 to 1969, to a syncretism that declares him the self-styled successor to Wright and Faulkner, to Dostoyevsky and Chandler: a precise anatomist of black self-delusion no less than white brutality and greed.

Ironically, the force of Himes's commitment to the novel through the era of burning summers can best be judged via a final invocation in *Cotton* of the photo-text tradition. By way of conclusion, the insouciant narrator remarks retrospectively: "Now a week had passed. Harlem had lived notoriously on the front pages of the tabloids. Saucy brown chicks and insane killers were integrated with southern colonels and two mad Harlem detectives for the entertainment of the public. Lurid accounts of robberies and killings pictured Harlem as a criminal inferno" (244). The status quo, in other words, has been reestablished; the conventions of sensationalist photo-text are the only mode of "integration" visible from the vantage point of overcrowded, underserved, strife-ridden Harlem. Beyond that fact, Himes's parting shot implicitly provides a description of *Cotton* itself. What else have the last 240-odd pages been but a mad, lurid account of saucy brown chicks and insane killers (and "sexpot lesbians" and nappy-headed junk dealers and an iron-fisted Colonel to boot)? But Himes's brief blurb parts company, in the end, with the mass photo-textual conventions it names: while "Iris screamed in bold black print that she had been double-crossed by the police," the "Back-to-Africa movement vied with the Back-to-the-Southland movement for space and sympathy" (244). For good and all, Himes's exploitation of the noir form and of the force of Harlem's contending cultural histories evacuates the possibility of "sympathy," writ either as liberal engagement (or pseudo-engagement) or as identity-based claims to political unity.

The force of this achievement for an African American writer of this generation and moment is, paradoxically, blunted by canonical readings of Himes as "one of the angriest writers in the black protest movement"; such readings render invisible his mercurial evasions of blackness as a manifesto, badge of honor, or requirement for cultural citizenship.[51] However potent or generative his rage, Himes as a writer—"Foremost a writer," he asserted; "Above all else a writer"—resembles nothing so much as the unnamed character in *Cotton* who enables the novel's limited denouement by providing Jones and Johnson with a photograph that places Calhoun at the scene of a murder.[52] Confronted with the photographic evidence of their guilt, Calhoun's sidekick involuntarily replies: "Impossible! There was only a blind man there!" (235). Hiding in plain sight, working under cover—literally, the "dumb, sleazy covers"—of mass formula fiction, Himes works Harlem's iconicity like the master of a shell game. Manipulating the codes of the Renaissance, New Deal, protest, civil rights era, hard-boiled fiction, cultural nationalism, and more, he orchestrates a mode of "absurdity" that outdoes the realism—naturalist as well as socially conscious—whose constricting histories Himes means to evade.[53] For this high-stakes game, Calhoun's photo-text is the most resonant tell of the entire Harlem Domestics enterprise. Reverting to photo-text form, Himes exposes his own authorial designs; recognizing his maneuver as such, we develop a clearer picture of the cultural landscape for black writers, and of their strategies for using the novel to survey it.

"Can anybody . . . conjure up a picture?": John Oliver Killens and the Burden of Nationalism

In 1966, as part of its burgeoning Prometheus paperback book line on "the Negro Movement," the radical publishing house Marzani & Munsell released a photo-text titled *Harlem Stirs*, a documentary account of activism inspired by civil resistance below the Mason-Dixon line. Far more pointedly than *The Movement*, *Harlem Stirs* insists on what has come to look like the inevitability of a violent if not armed insurrection. Its graphic cover shows a larger-than-life black fist—the soon-to-be infamous Black Power salute—in which a copy of the Constitution, its "We the People" prominently visible, is being crushed. The images within, however, are far more familiar. Focusing on the Harlem rent strike of 1963–64 and the Harlem school boycott of 1964, ending with a brief nod to the civil unrest beginning in Harlem and spreading to other communities in July 1964, the text juxtaposes the heady, vertiginous, high-rise view of the city and its modernity opened by wealth and racial privilege with the density, poverty, and material squalor of the spaces afforded black Harlemites. Making the most of photo-textuality—grainy prints, full-page spreads, image density, effects of tonality and ekphrastic contrast—*Harlem Stirs* presses a definitive "contradiction" between "the lives white people lead" and the subjects' own.[54]

Although unmistakably postlapsarian in mood, *Harlem Stirs* descends from the New Deal–rooted, socially conscious tradition of documentary, as its roster of contributors suggests. One of its two key photographers was Don Charles, whose documentation of the Nation of Islam figures so pointedly in Hansberry's framing of a response to Nation ideology.[55] The bulk of the text consists of quotations from the *New York Times*, city Housing Commission reports, mayoral press conferences, the U.S. Census, and stirring speeches by Baldwin, SNCC's John Lewis, and CORE officials. The minimal linking text was written by Fred Halstead, a point man in the pro-Castro Socialist Workers Party who became, in 1968, the SWP candidate for president (and the author, in the radical antiwar classic *Out Now!*, of statements about the returning Vietnam veteran John Kerry that were widely exploited by the political right during the 2004 presidential campaign). The publisher, Carl Marzani, an Italian American immigrant who had worked as a Party organizer on the Lower East Side and later served three years in prison for it, was himself a former maker of agitprop films, including *The Great Swindle* (1947) and *Our Union* (1949). Given the pedigree of its contributors, *Harlem Stirs* offers itself as something of a test case for the durability and afterlife of documentary traditions—not least the cross-racial history of photo-text production—in the context of emergent cultural nationalism.

In one sense, the volume suggests how visual conventions long associated with liberal, progressive, and state-sponsored paradigms for redress or uplift (including the "all deliberate speed" of the desegregation era) are irredeemable for radical uses post-1964. The very terms in which the volume is framed, at least in back-cover plugging by the likes of Kenneth Clark ("How long can our society permit these shocking conditions to prevail? What will it require before the voices of justice and decency are heard?") and Ossie Davis ("The book is a life-giving experience, for it . . . instructs [us] to open our hearts to hope") suggest the insufficiency both of shock value and of the presumption of redress on which documentary image making, at least since Jacob Riis's *How the Other Half Lives*, had been founded. But in at least one specific case, *Harlem Stirs* opens a view to the suggestive play of photo-visuality. If photo-text seemed increasingly overexposed, outdated, bound by its earlier lives in the service of integrationist liberalism like Hansberry's, its uses in *Harlem Stirs* would animate the work of a writer struggling to make the novel form responsive to the urgencies of the mid-1960s moment, with all its violent threat, performative excesses, and utopian longings.

To make that play visible we have first to remark what is distinctive rather than readily familiar about *Harlem Stirs* as a photo-text. Although it hews closely to the overlapping traditions of exposé, protest, and consciousness raising, it also experiments with emerging visual modes. Notably, the volume was produced not by a cross-media collaboration (Evans and Agee; Bourke-White and Caldwell; Wright and Rosskam; Hughes and DeCarava; Baldwin and Avedon) or even an auteur (Hansberry), but by a commercial firm, Davis/Aviles Graphics, whose work on "visual design" receives top billing in the volume's acknowledgments. Explicitly shaped to "dramatize the suffering"—and gathering militancy—of Harlem's hemmed-in, overcrowded, underserved residents, still aiming to "force [white landlords and city officials] to act," *Harlem Stirs* not only avails itself of photo-text's defining shocks of juxtaposition, made and found contrast, and graphically magnified social circumstance, it also partakes of new strains of defamiliarization, variously indebted to developments in postwar photography and visual art.[56] At its most effective, *Harlem Stirs* abjures the sober evidentiary logic of documentary for a calibrated excess and willed stylization, a stance that partakes of and challenges representational realism, political gradualism, radical separatism, and unanchored pastiche in turn.

This fleeting and variable possibility is staked out, or at least suggested, in images that block the anticipated narrative trajectory of rising frustration, activism, and confrontation. An early shot by Anthony Aviles of the world of Manhattan's haves, paired with Baldwin's account from *The Fire Next Time* of the stark contrast between Harlem's Park Avenue and the same street downtown, avoids obvious commentary (figure 5.12). Shot or cropped tightly to frame the gilded letters spelling out "Tiffany & Co.," the image offers a study in contrasts: the bright clarity of the left side of the image gives way to both shadow and blur on the right; the bid for materiality—smooth limestone, against which the angularly sculpted lettering stands in high relief—is trumped by a manipulation of perspective and focus that results in a flattening effect, as if documentary rendering itself were yielding to an insistence on the artifice of the photograph as a surface and an object. However serendipitously, the image can be read as enacting the drift of straight photography beyond the imperatives of its New Deal services. Writ here are traces of Walker Evans and his influential interest in what he called "signs of the times," which put documentary and formalist visual modes simultaneously in play; of Aaron Siskind's postwar, post-Harlem images of wall art and graffiti, rendered with meditative estrangement; of Robert Frank's *The Americans* (1958), trained on the relations between anomie as a definitive condition and found abstraction as its expressive idiom.[57] Other images throughout *Harlem Stirs*—perhaps the preponderance of them—show readier, more obvious responses to white indifference and greed: sleek slumlords, impeccably dressed; businessmen suited up for power lunches; brokers advertising dispossession and foreclosure—"Apartment Houses Wanted Bought and Sold/Fast Action"—as their specialty (29). But the Tiffany shot functions differently. Abandoning clarity of purpose for a play with surface and depth so as to probe the social logic of racial and class estrangement, the image testifies to the surreal effects of inequality in a

Figure 5.12. Anthony Aviles, Untitled, from *Harlem Stirs*, 1964.

way that no amount of statistical fact ("Only 5.4% [.1 nonwhite] make over $15,000.00 a year") can do (12).

A later sequence on rats in Harlem tenements similarly frames the high incidence of infection and disease ("salmonella ..., leptospirosis, rickettsiaplex, rat-bite fever ... hepatitis and food poisoning") resulting from the unchecked spread of rodents in Harlem tenements, the subject of a 1964 public health campaign. But the visual materials assembled for a two-page spread emphasize not the animal menace so much as human hypocrisy. A tight, dramatically lit close-up of a rat, every whisker and strand of fur visible, fangs bared and eye glittering, is juxtaposed with a shot of Health Department brochures featuring cartoonish graphics (figures 5.13, 5.14). Listing "Things You Should Know to Get Rid of Rats," the latter lay the onus on ghetto tenants not

Figure 5.13. Anthony Aviles, Untitled, from *Harlem Stirs*, 1964.

In 1963 there were 684 reported cases of rat-bite in New York City...

Rats spell fear to mothers. Most of the rat-bite cases are young children. Rat bites cause salmonella infection, leptospirosis, rickettsiaplex, rat-bite fever. Rat droppings cause hepatitis and food poisoning —200 reported cases in 1963.

Rats also cause fires by gnawing on matchheads and through electric insulation. Periodically the city declares a campaign, such as the one in January 1964, which was supposed to spend one million dollars and add 26 new building inspectors to deal with estimates which ran as high as eight million rats in the slums. In any case, inspectors don't get rid of rats. The only way to get rid of them is to wipe out the slums.

The "anti-rat" campaign of 1964 petered out and no one knows what, if anything, was accomplished. Harlem residents point with bitter humor at the *one* activity the city did perform: the distribution of leaflets enjoining the slum dweller to "cooperate . . . to get rid of this nuisance."

LET'S GET RID OF RATS

EVERY TENANT MUST HELP

- Keep your house clean.
- Keep your food in covered jars or cans.
- Keep your garbage pail tightly covered.
- Do not throw garbage in the yard, hallway or dumbwaiter shaft.
- Keep your baby's crib clean.
- Wash your baby's face and body before putting him to bed. Rats follow the smell of milk.
- Watch your baby afterward.

Your landlord has been notified by the Health Department that he must exterminate the rats in your building. You can help get rid of rats in your own apartment. If we all cooperate, we can get rid of this nuisance.

DEPARTMENT OF HEALTH • CITY OF NEW YORK
GEORGE JAMES, M.D.   ROBERT F. WAGNER
Commissioner   Mayor

Figure 5.14. New York City Department of Welfare, Health Campaign Brochure, from *Harlem Stirs*, 1964.

Figure 5.15. Don Charles, In God We Trust (detail), from *Harlem Stirs*, 1964.

only to "Keep your house clean" but to "Wash your baby's face and body before putting him to bed" and "Watch your baby afterward"—an implicit admission of the magnitude of the infestation. Here, via play with kitsch idioms and ephemeral materials and the juxtaposition of competing representational registers, the book's graphic designers draw on a pop sensibility reigning, via Warhol, Rauschenberg, and Lichtenstein, in New York's art world. They thus inflect straight documentary representation ("In 1963 there were 684 reported cases of rat-bite in New York City . . .") with decidedly surrealist effects.

In what is arguably the controlling image of *Harlem Stirs*, didactic aim is wholly subordinated to visual stylistics. Two-thirds of the way through, at the apex of the narrative as such, the text chronicles the activism, confrontation by police, and arrest of Harlem rent strikers demonstrating against slumlords' failures to adhere to housing codes and the city's refusal to prosecute them. A sequence of images follows the arc from dangerously dilapidated apartment, tenants' barricade, and eviction to arrest and sentencing. But the sequence is interrupted by an image that appears extraneous to the visual narrative. Working with a small handheld camera as he was led toward a judge's bench from a holding cell, Don Charles shot a prominently displayed plaque—"In God We Trust"—so as to record and heighten felt tensions between arrest and mobility, both legal and photographic (figure 5.15). Something other than "one more piece of irony," the image aims to pose a visual challenge. However serendipitous or forced the conditions of its production, its dynamics—its low light, blur, underexposure, and graininess—not only recall the visual ethos of

Figure 5.16. William Klein, Candy Store, Amsterdam Avenue, New York, 1954–55. By permission of the artist. Courtesy of The Howard Greenberg Gallery, New York.

Weegee's *Naked City* (1945); they also rhyme with the stylistics of postwar photographers such as William Klein, whose *Life Is Good and Good for You in New York* (1954) seized on outlawed technical properties—grain, blur, contrast, accidents, cockeyed framing—as the only tools adequate to an appropriately Brechtian, constructively estranging representation of "the city I hated and loved" (figure 5.16).[58] When Klein's prospective editors initially rejected this work out of hand, claiming that "this is shit . . . too black, too one-sided, this is a slum," they were bridling not only at its content (racial and otherwise) but at its stylistics of excess, described by one critic as "half dada, half nightmare."[59] At its most inventive—for example, in the shot of a cop standing over the prone body of a fallen protestor, its high grain, blur, and austere composition recalling Frank's *Americans*; in Charles's portrait of a woman with a large rubber rat pinned to her chest, tightly cropped in the manner of work after Lisette Model; in arresting layouts juxtaposing PR materials for city housing projects and for the 1964 World's Fair—*Harlem Stirs* turns these widening possibilities of postwar photography to surprising and powerful account.

But as the text's conclusion suggests, no amount of photodocumentary imaging, however bracing or inventive, can picture the kind of liberation to which the text aspires. Following a sequence on the 1964 riots, the volume concludes with a by now predictable visual gesture: a series of portraits of Malcolm X, the one figure who "could articulate the heartbreak" and whose own rebirth as a leader of freedom movements "from Harlem to Hanoi" was aborted by his assassination in January 1965 (128). In the brief but yawning gap between *The Movement* and *Harlem Stirs*, a new world disorder had lurched into being: riots not only in Harlem and Watts, but Chicago, Detroit, and forty other U.S. cities; white backlash against the riots; mounting evidence of the inadequacy of federal civil rights legislation (trumpeted, in 1964, as a national victory) to ensure equal opportunity or due process; the coalescence of cultural nationalism and Black Power, which had, by 1966, radically remade organizations such as CORE and SNCC via the driving premise that "*Before a group can enter the open society, it must first close ranks.*"[60] Photo-text, with its deep roots in crossracial activism and ideologies of remediation, would appear by definition to be inadequate to this newly raddled context. To a large extent, cultural nationalists rejected the photographic as an expressive possibility altogether in favor of oral forms—for example, Baraka's "poems / like fists beating niggers out of jocks / or dagger-poems in the slimy bellies of the owner-jews"—more readily tagged as authentic, incendiary, and black.[61]

Paradoxically, however, *Harlem Stirs* figured in the work of a founding father of cultural nationalism, and its stylistics appear to have enabled his novelistic aims. By way of a general introduction, and as a selling point for left-leaning readers, the producers of *Harlem Stirs* invited the well-known novelist and cultural activist John Oliver Killens to contribute a prologue to the volume. At the time Killens was a reigning heavyweight on the Harlem cultural scene.[62] Having begun his career as a staffer at the National Labor Relations Board and an organizer for the Congress of Industrial Organizations, he became (like Lorraine Hansberry) a writer during the early 1950s for Paul Robeson's ill-fated *Freedom*; it was in a famously negative review of *Invisible Man* published there that Killens began to outline the literary credo that "a Black work of art helps the liberation or hinders it."[63] At the same time, Killens became the founding chairman of the Harlem Writers Guild, whose members included future eminences such as Paule Marshall, Maya Angelou, and Audrey Lorde. In 1964 he partnered with Malcolm X to cofound the Organization for Afro-American Unity, and in the following year he published a collection of political writings titled *Black Man's Burden*, whose variously socialist and cultural nationalist commitments made him "the spiritual father" (or the "ideological orchestrator," depending on one's point of view) of black writers coming of age post-1964.[64] Killens was, in short, uniquely suited not only to comment on Harlem activism as a participant-observer—he is a subject in at least one image in *Harlem Stirs*—but to embody its historical avatars, from Popular Front consensus and civil rights institution building to coalescing nationalism.

Killens's intersection with photo-text at this fraught juncture also significantly shaped his own development as a novelist. His two previous novels, *Youngblood* (1954) and *And Then We Heard the Thunder* (1962), firmly rejected the existentialist mode of Ellison and Wright in favor of epic tales of collective struggle in the Jim Crow context.[65] Both tilt toward noble characters and their achieved black manhood; both move toward an apex of shared triumph: the founding of an NAACP branch over the body of a murdered laborer in the rural South; the rejection by a black soldier mobilized into the white man's army of his own bourgeois "illusion," in favor of a racial solidarity to be expressed in writings dedicated to the untold stories of his black comrades in revolutionary arms.[66] On the basis of these and similarly motivated writings—including the hard-hitting essays of *Black Man's Burden* and the epic civil rights novel, *'Sippi* (1967), composed largely of material extended from *And Then We Heard the Thunder*—Killens was canonized as a writer of protest novels that, if not "second-rate," made of black history and expression a familiar saga of heroic triumph and agon.[67] In other words, the authorial stances that gave Killens his bona fides as a practitioner of Black Art were also seen as limiting the reach and energies of his fiction.

The reception of Killens, both by admirers and detractors, tends to inflect the didactic strain of his work, which reaches an apex in his post-*Cotillion* fiction—accounts of figures such as Denmark Vesey, Alexander Pushkin, and John Henry collectively known as the "Black heroism project."[68] Such a reading persists at the expense of Killens's most anomalous and inventive novel, a text that bridges Black Arts and emergent postmodernist stances in an unprecedented way: *The Cotillion, or One Good Bull Is Half the Herd*, published in 1971. With *The Cotillion*, the coming-of-age tale of a young woman in Harlem negotiating the lure of bourgeois "ladyship," Killens for the first time develops a narrative mode fully adequate to the vitality of African American expression as such, yet productively evasive of the representational conventions of protest and the constricting imperatives of nationalism. Although numerous projects (including work on drama, film scripts, critical essays, and journalism) intervened between *Harlem Stirs* and *The Cotillion*, Killens's photo-text engagement left a recognizable impress on his most complex novel. Aside from his contribution to *Harlem Stirs*, the brash comic energy of *The Cotillion* is without precedent in Killens's work. In the former, however, we can trace his interest in the cultural stances photo-textuality opens—and the uses he makes of them to further his own mixed designs on Black Power and a black aesthetic.[69]

As *The Cotillion* opens, its central figure, the "black and comely . . . Harlem princess" Yoruba, has been selected by members of a dicty black women's club called the Femmes Fatales (or, by her father, the "Fems Fat Tails") to participate as a deserving hardship case in the group's annual debutante cotillion at the Waldorf hotel.[70] Spiritually aligned with her father, a Penn Station porter and cultural nationalist, but reluctant to cross her mother, a West Indian Anglophiliac (she tells Yoruba, "I don't hold your father's color against him. . . . It's just that, just because he was born Black, he insist on living a Black life" [49]), Yoruba jives and meditates and sashays her way through various trials—waltz instruction with a "crosseyed fairy godfather" dance teacher (119), deportment sessions with the "Fat Asses" (139), street exchanges with Harlem's "gamers of the boulevards" (82)—all the while seduced and instructed by a writer and singer of "wild Black notes of/Love and hate and revolution" (55), Ben Ali Lumumba. In the novel's climactic scene, with Lumumba proudly at her side, Yoruba struts the stage not as a proper debutante but, complete with an Afro and African robes, as "the first natural woman in the annals of cotillions" (237). In the ensuing melee, even her mother joins her in a walk-out, as the nonplussed members of the black-tie orchestra strike up a rendition of "Dixie" (238).

This comic apotheosis, the text's generic payoff, is made possible by the presence of Lumumba not only as love interest but as the author of the very tale in question, a writer who has "just finished the novel that I'm forwarding to you, dear readers" (foreword). Seaman, wanderer, yarn-spinner, "liar," Lumumba has set aside his first book—a documentary account of his world travels titled *All the Way to Timbuktu*—in order to write a new kind of text: "halfly autobiographical and halfly fiction, all based on facts as I have gathered them," expressed in the surging rhythms of "Afro-Americanese" (foreword). Eschewing truisms about "objectivity, universality, composition, author-intrusion"—all the "craft shit"—Lumumba aims to serve up "a Black black comedy" and "do myself some signifying" (foreword). The result is an incisive skewering of all comers to the party: "Self-appointed. Self-anointed" black nationalist leaders (8); black bourgeois wannabes comforted by rituals of propriety in "these days of strife and strain and race riots and mini-skirts" (40); hustlers wrapped in the colors of nationalism ("If you going to be my baby, sister, you going to have to get out there on the block and sell it, while I'm organizing the revolution" [60]); eager participants in "the World Individual Champeenship of Blackness," who flock to buy Afro wigs, rabbit feet, and darkening skin creams "made primarily from minstrel lampblack" (65, 67); white bohos who indulge in sexual revolution, "plunk guitars and howl sad songs" (81); miserly West Indian landlords; raucous debaters over the politics of hair ("It's a simple question of do-process" [124]); debauched white debutantes and white women "spanking the plank" in imitation of black women miming white ones (174); even Lumumba himself, who is not above brandishing the banner of "the Nation" as a mode of seduction and self-aggrandizement—and who occasionally breaks the action he ostensibly narrates precisely so as to record it.

The Cotillion ultimately cleaves to the conventional logic of the coming-of-age novel, itself a powerful expression of bourgeois sensibility. But its forays into a kind of self-referentiality usually associated with contemporaneous novelists such as Donald Barthelme and Thomas Pynchon serve a critical function. Releasing the distinctive expressive energies of an "Afro-Americanese" embodied by Lumumba yet floating freely throughout the text, the framing fiction of Lumumba's authorship allows for the achievement of a collective protagonist and the generation of a stylistic excess that slips, unfettered, between expressive codes: from "down-home Baptist preach[ing]" and rhythm-and-blues (56) to the "poetic thing in the 'Roi-Jones-Dante-Graham-Archie-Shepp-Askia-Muhammad-Touré fashion" (55); from "Shakespeare in the park" to "snakeshit on the avenue" (201); from the "high-bred" to the "hybrid" (201), with "New York phrasing" and "down-South-up-South clashing and blending" (53). The brash, uncontainable voice Killens fashions, via the fiction of Lumumba's fiction, achieves more than the calculated send-up of black bourgeois mores with which he is generally credited. In an era of hardening convictions and racial loyalty tests (to say nothing of radical skepticism about the adequacy of the novel to "the urgency of the problem confronting the Negro American"), Killens exploits that form so as both to explore and to evade identity logic.[71] In the play between conventional novelistic structure and freewheeling, radically shifting voice, Killens moves fluidly through an impressive variety of cultural stances but remains fixed in none of them— a striking departure from the (pre)determined arcs of his earlier fiction. The voice of The Cotillion, speaking through Lumumba, is committed to global liberation struggles ("I got a closet full of African identity, like authentic from the source and jive") yet insistent on the primacy of "Black USA-ans" (91), alive to the affective power of revolutionary rhetoric but critical of its uses, trenchant (but not untender) in response to all desires—black bourgeois, white hipster, black revolutionary—for the "really real thing" (195).

As I have noted, such bold orchestration of the resonant notes of racial pride, pan-Africanism, cultural nationalism, and skepticism of all of these is unprecedented in Killens's fiction; even cursory readings of his earlier novels attest to the difference. Critics have accounted for its emergence by noting his indebtedness to the late 1960s work of Black Arts versifiers such as Baraka and Haki Madhubuti.[72] But The Cotillion partakes of their high-wire, fast-paced, loose-jointed signifying mode with the effect of undercutting its ethos of menace (at least in Baraka's case) and its implicit privileging of the decidedly masculinized poet-revolutionary. For the imagination of the cultural collective in the making that animates *The Cotillion*, Killens's prologue to *Harlem Stirs* is a more telling precursor. There, responding to the image of collectivity generated by the photo-text format and to the stylistic energies gathered by its visual design, Killens begins to sketch an outline for the conduct of his later novel.

By way of opening *Harlem Stirs*, Killens proclaims: "This [photo-text] is about a hero, a hero in the epic tradition and of profound proportions, a hero capable of acting out great tragedies. The name of the hero is Harlem."[73] For Killens, such representation "breaks sharply from the current trend of books about this much maligned community," which not only "have made Harlem the anti-hero, forever the villain," but have "literarily" exploited its history and iconic status (5). Killens's interest in this Harlem is itself a sharp break from the commitments of *Youngblood*, *Thunder*, and *'Sippi*, which insist on social transformation as the property of singular heroic men, the effect of their dawning inspiration. Although his prologue singles out specific Harlem activists, it accounts for the meaning of the images collected in *Harlem Stirs* by emphasizing not just a class consciousness or a racial solidarity but a collective agency—one that is too various and too dynamic to be easily organized or led. "Harlem," in other words, turns out to name not a traditional hero, epic or otherwise, but something like its antithesis: an organic social will, a force sweeping "the surrounding landscape like the sands of the insatiable Sahara" (3). And the stirring of this force displaces the coming-to-consciousness of the heroic individual; in the wake of its transformational agency, "things are never quite the same again, which may be classified as the understatement of the Twentieth Century" (3).

This figuration of Harlem, responsive to the alternately moody, didactic, and surreal visual effects of *Harlem Stirs*, might well be applied to the world of *The Cotillion*, and thus made to clarify its achievements. Like a force of nature, Lumumba and Yoruba's Harlem—"YMCA, Countee Cullen Library. Cockroaches. Schomburg. Love. Langston Hughes. Jesse B. Simple. Race riots. Pot. Laughter. Adam. Horsing around. Rats. Tears. Apollo. Hate. Blacks. Sounds. Folks. Funeral parlors. Liquor stores. Jackie Robinson. *Amsterdam News*. Jones. Wine. Jews. . . . Pimps. Pussy. Whores. Church. Charley. Home!" (61)—exceeds the grasp of any single participant-observer, including Lumumba, "son of Harlem" himself (foreword). The text's unity results not just from the seductive rhythms of Afro-Americanese but from a sequential inhabitation of vastly different iconic Harlem spaces—a strategy that echoes the carefully plotted mapping in *Harlem Stirs* of white and black New Yorks, from Fifth Avenue and the World's Fair to the welfare office, tenement, and picket line. Indeed, Killens's virtuoso display of vernaculars (folklore, jive, oral history, political rhetoric, seduction patter, the dozens) is predicated on the profound lability, the uncontainability, of that "hero . . . of profound proportions." In the end, the story is, as Lumumba notes, "not really about me," or even about the "fox named Yoruba," but about that stirring Harlem of mood and riff and flow, whose energy both inspires and defies the ideal of a really real world of black identity and expression (foreword).

Figuring Harlem as such "surging" pulsing movement (2), *The Cotillion* implies the insufficiency of any representational project, political or cultural, to contain it fully. Against the hortatory, prescriptive mode of nationalist leadership, Killens poses a certain participatory strain, one that echoes the invitation he tenders in *Harlem Stirs* (7) to "face these people in this book honestly and hear their stories." In the context of a black cultural free-for-all, in which protestors are "picketing pickets picketing pickets, who were picketing" until "you had to be some kind of genius to figure out who was picketing whom" (*Cotillion*, 7), what Yoruba and the reader alike require is not another exhorter but a guide to the inferno. Although Lumumba is well versed in "fine wailing" and the anthems of revolution (55), his courtship of Yoruba (who, as one reader aptly notes, embodies the possibilities of black liberation as a cultural project) is conducted in a series of invitations to see in tandem, as during their first shared walk through Harlem's familiar streets.[74] "Dig," Lumumba tells her; "Observe the guardian of law and order . . . consorting with the dusky lady of the very oldest profession"; "Follow the noble one in blue . . . and dig him saunter down the avenue and get his Sunday payoff from the junkman"; "Cognize the fine brown Black leggy sister in her natural state of being underneath that clean Afro"; "Now then, take notice of the cat in the flaming yellow El Dorado" (61–62). Atwitter with the romance of "the sweet and awful Harlem silence they had shared," Yoruba initially resents the instruction: "She had eyes. Didn't need him to spell things out for her" (62). But the act of mutual observation is proof against a host of illusions, those of black self-righteousness and demagoguery no less than bourgeois ladyship.

In this avatar, as mentor and self-implicating observer, Lumumba evolves from the stance Killens takes as acerbic tour guide to the world of *Harlem Stirs*, recalling the traditions of the Renaissance era when "white men . . . put white songs in black men's mouths and bade them sing. Remember? Oh what wonderful idiotic lyrics those 'happy colored people' sang Underneath the Harlem Moon. Remember?" (*Harlem Stirs*, 4). Armed with bitter certitude and rhetorical questions, that Killens commands the reader to "face it"; on the subject of police brutality, he asks, "Can anybody imagine New York's Finest participating in a civil rights demonstration on the side of the Negro demonstrators? Can anybody with the wildest and most vivid imagination conjure up a picture of a New York cop whipping a landlord's head?" (*Harlem Stirs*, 6). Absent this political fantasy, *The Cotillion* nonetheless responds to a landscape of cultural chaos—when everything is "topsy-turvey [*sic*] compared with what it used to be" and the world is "turning upside down, the bottom coming to the top, and erupting like Mount Etna" (66)—with the fantastic act of conjuring up pictures. Its stylistic excess, its comic inversions, its insistence on a multifarious "people" as its protagonist: all guard against the literalism of the ideological mode at its most straitening.

Finally, *The Cotillion* offers itself not only as a critique of bourgeois aspirations; it is also a bid for contestatory participation in the nationalist fray. Taking his cue from the most striking feature of *Harlem Stirs*—whose achievement he sums up in his conclusion by asserting, "I repeat, this book pictures Harlem as the protagonist" (*Harlem Stirs*, 7)—Killens fashions a narrative stance that celebrates that collective protagonist while defying the logic of more militant purchases on its "Soul" (1). If the controlled excesses of *Harlem Stirs*—its gestures toward pop, radical shock, and anomie—provide a precedent for picturing Harlem as protagonist, *The Cotillion*'s stylistic excess and self-consciousness indemnify the novel against self-destructive stridency, the revolutionary mode as mere style, performance, will to demagogic power. While Killens celebrates its heroine's "grand debut into the maturation of her Blackness" (210), the very nature of that blackness has become less clear, less prescriptive as the narrative unfolds. Dashikis and boubous and unprocessed hair—all the seasonable "masks" and accessories—aside, the world of the "'natural'" and the "really real" lies all before Yoruba, the community, and the form of the novel too, yet to be determined and made new (59). For this open view, Killens's engagement with photo-text and the photograph provides a powerful frame. His novel is exemplary of the history of engagement that precedes it, and suggestive of new textual forms after Black Arts that make photographic experience central to the work of looking back.

Harlem on My Mind: Revolution and the Look Back

I have argued for the importance to specific writers in the post–civil rights era of photographic practices and histories—in particular, for the powers of reinvention afforded by their engagements with documentary imaging. By way of concluding my episodic survey, I want to consider a broader context for their uses of the image and its cultural power. Freighted with its own histories of instrumental aims, descended from New Deal era practices, the form of documentary they invoke would seem irrelevant to the urgency of burning summers—part of the problem, in the idiom of the day, rather than the solution. But the invocation of documentary histories via Harlem, by way of shaping expressive forms adequate to movement, resistance, and change, turns out to be far from anachronistic. In retrospect, it can be seen as an important strategy in the creation of alternative usable pasts, or alternative uses of an iconography that has come to serve as the past, for black America and for America at large.

Nothing clarifies the stakes for this strategy so dramatically as the 1969 exhibit at the Metropolitan Museum of Art titled Harlem on My Mind, which attempted (to very different effect and on a far grander scale) a project not unlike those of The Movement or Harlem Stirs. Often described as the most controversial U.S. exhibition ever mounted, the show managed to infuriate virtually every sizable ethnic community in New York City, inflame artists and art critics alike, and catapult black nationalists, the Jewish Defense League, and the John Birch Society all at once onto genteel Fifth Avenue in protest.[75] A long overdue recognition by the Met (that grand dowager) of the zeitgeist, Harlem on My Mind was intended as what the museum's director called "a creative confrontation between white and black communities"; it was conceived as "a documentary exhibition without original works of art"—in other words, a photo-textual survey, whose interest would lie in the kinds of juxtapositions and visual experiences it created.[76] Commanding fifteen galleries—the entire temporary exhibition space of the museum's sprawling second floor—the show featured seven hundred images ranging from 11 × 14 inches to a monumental (and unprecedented) 18 × 50 feet, along with another five hundred projected photographs, text panels, and accompanying soundtracks.[77] In effect a history of documentary imaging in Harlem, the exhibit included photographs spanning turn-of-the-century photo agencies, the newly rediscovered work of James VanderZee, project photos by Aaron Siskind and other members of the Photo League, work by FSA photographers, images by postwar street photographers and photojournalists such as Helen Levitt and Gordon Parks, and more contemporary urban documentary by Lee Friedlander and Jay Maisel (whose Harlem photographs had accompanied an essay of Ralph Ellison's on the 1964 civil unrest).[78] With this panoply of images, the curator, Allon Schoener, aimed for what he called an "orchestrated information environment"; in the words of more skeptical reviewers, it was "as if Life magazine had suddenly gone 3-D," or Henry Luce's newsreel documentaries, *The March of Time*, had put on blackface.[79]

These contending purchases on documentary suggest both the robust afterlife of its earlier uses and its lability (to which Hansberry, Killens, and other writers were alert) in the context of rising battles over the politics of cultural ownership and representation. On the one hand, "documentary" as marshaled by Harlem on My Mind signifies a long-discredited investment in what Schoener calls "information," the neutral or disinterested "organiz[ation]" of images "into a pattern of experiences recreating the history of Harlem as it happened."[80] However misplaced, this very faith in a representational practice marked by ethnographic designs was Schoener's weapon of choice for mounting an assault on the sanctity of the museum and on modernist ideologies of significant form.[81] Insisting on the power of documentary images as agents of "confrontation," he argued that "the era of museums as places for silent contemplation of works of art ha[s] ended"—a point hardly lost on conservative critics such as Hilton Kramer, who labeled Schoener's effort to "politicalize" the "subtle transaction of the mind and the emotions" writ as Art as "totalitarian."[82] Although critics of the exhibit—and they were legion—decried Schoener's McLuhanesque rhetoric and the effect of a show "put together . . . to format" so as to emphasize its own communications techniques, the choice of Harlem as its subject was hardly irrelevant.[83] When the Metropolitan's flamboyant director, Thomas Hoving, first announced plans for a Harlem on My Mind show, his chief curator (an aficionado of Dutch art) noted, "I've got some wonderful paintings. Which Harlem did you mean?"—to which his boss replied, "The one north of us."[84] In 1969, in the new disorder of the post–civil rights era, the conjunction of Harlem with documentary imaging again and anew signified for white America the force of "confrontation" with the realities of power and impending change.

In Harlem itself, a mere twenty city blocks north of the Metropolitan, the category of "documentary" also resonated with old and new force. The artist Reginald Gammon of the Black Emergency Cultural Coalition, an activist group organized in response to Harlem on My Mind, summed up the first line of response among African American artists in Harlem: "They always pick somebody else to do your life."[85] The reviewer for the *New York Amsterdam News*, reporting in a far lower key than establishment journals, rejected not the presumptions of documentary imaging but the failed objectivity of the white man; the assembled images "portray truth, but there are other truths which are missing."[86] By contrast, the noted (and, notably, Jewish) photography critic A. D. Coleman pilloried Harlem on My Mind as "a staggering display of honky chutzpah," in part on the grounds of its suppression of unpictur-esque—or, we might say, iconic—realities: "How come . . . not a single cock-roach or a rat?"[87] And in the most dramatic gesture of protest against the show's yoking of Harlem, black life, and documentary, an unidentified person or persons defaced ten paintings—including a Rembrandt—in the galleries adjoining the exhibit by scratching small "H's" into their varnished surfaces. Whether the mark stood for "Harlem" or "Hoving," the perpetrator(s) seem to have expressed resistance to the consignment of African American experi-ence to the realm of documentary representation rather than "original art."[88]

Ironically, a good number of images included in the show—for example, Helen Levitt's complex, dynamic shots of Harlem youths that moved Richard Wright to imagine collaborating with her; Gordon Parks's taut images of the psychic effects of failed opportunity that inspired Ralph Ellison to create a shooting script for a joint photo-text project; Jay Maisel's tightly focused street portraits of real-life invisible men and Tod Cliftons; Lee Friedlander's sensitive portrayals of postbop jazz musicians—originated in contexts in which they evaded the restrictive force of Schoener's documentary frame, offering them-selves up as nuanced, indeterminate, subjective responses to Harlem and the history of documentary imaging.[89] To note this fact is not simply to emphasize the promiscuity of all photographic meaning or the willed blindness of Schoener's "objective" view to its own presumptions (both familiar themes). More important, the prominence in Harlem on My Mind of the images and photographers I have previously considered emphasizes the ways in which the exhibit as event recapitulates key histories of encounter and crossing. In its production and reception, a historical and imaginary convergence of Jewish American and African American experience breaks decisively down, but in so doing reveals its centrality to the development of documentary practice. Within this matrix, the power of Harlem as symbol, myth, and icon is reacti-vated and newly contested, in ways that both recall and sharply diverge from the model of the Renaissance. And the conflicted responses of black visual artists to the exhibition's uses of the documentary archive suggest why the latter remains a resource for writers like Hansberry, Himes, and Killens in the context of identitarian struggles and empowerment.

This framing of Harlem on My Mind as a culminating event for a genealogy of Harlem-centered imaging is warranted by the nature of the controversy it sparked. The most strident boycott of the show—in particular of its cata-logue—was not by Harlem artists or intellectuals or even an African American public (black viewers attended in record numbers), but by Jews.[90] Led by Meir Kahane (who had begun his political career by founding the Jewish Defense

League months earlier, in 1968, ostensibly in response to threats by Black Panthers), Jewish nationalists picketed on the very steps of the museum, shouting "No more Auschwitz!" A more muted chorus of observers across the political spectrum charged that an introductory essay to the catalogue written by a then-seventeen-year-old African American high school student from the Bronx, Candace Van Ellison, was explicitly anti-Semitic.[91] (The most often-cited passage from her essay, remarking on "Harlem riots between Afro-Americans and policemen" and "white America's tradition of hatred for Blacks," and culminating in the not unastute observation that "our contempt for the Jew makes us feel more completely American," would hardly have been startling to readers of DuBois, Wright, Ellison, Baldwin, or virtually any contemporary black writer; the clientele of the Metropolitan Museum was clearly another matter.)[92]

Ironically, Van Ellison's essay was expressly solicited by Schoener, whose credibility as a producer of "ethnic-environmental" shows had been forged in an acclaimed 1966 exhibit at the Jewish Museum, The Lower East Side: Portal to American Life, and whose very idea for Harlem on My Mind was born during the visit of two Harlem ministers to that earlier show.[93] Premised on Schoener's own identity as a Jewish American, his engagement with civil rights activism, and his experience as a curator of tenement life, Harlem on My Mind recapitulated the logic that had shaped the documentary tradition it reprised. Schoener was hardly unself-conscious about that history. The novelist John Henrik Clarke (a member of the consultant Harlem Cultural Council, which withdrew its support for the show, and the editor of a 1968 anthology of black writers' responses to William Styron's controversial *Confessions of Nat Turner*, whose contributors included Killens) initially approached Schoener with tales of his own experience as a *shabbas goy* working for Jews on the Lower East Side, along with an ultimatum: "If you're another downtown Jew who has come up here to rip us off, go away."[94] Nonetheless, Schoener's faith in the history (or myth) of a shared purchase on Harlem and in the self-evident power of documentary images of that site, both to inform and to move viewers, buoyed his sense of the enterprise—so much so that he even gave away copies of the exhibition catalogue, which would soon be withdrawn from publication at the behest of the mayor's office on the grounds of its "racism," as Hanukkah presents.[95]

Outside the Metropolitan's august facade, members of the Black Emergency Cultural Coalition were enacting their own response to the same history of documentary production.[96] The placards they carried had messages like "On the Auction Block Again," "That's White of Hoving," and "Soul's Been Sold Again," but most telling may have been the sign hoisted by the BECC cofounder and painter Benny Andrews, which proclaimed "Visit the Metropolitan Museum of Photography."[97] Not only had another downtown Jew come uptown, this time to commandeer the image and legacy of Harlem for a white institution, he had done so by distantiating African Americans from art, consigning their experience to "[nothing] more than a photographic exposition."[98] The implied equation of the "photographic" with "documentary" (i.e., spuriously objective, merely evidentiary, instrumental representation) must surely have proven uncomfortable for one of the most stalwart of the BECC protestors: Roy DeCarava. Invited to contribute a major portfolio to the show, including some of the intimate shots of Harlem families that had been published in *The Sweet Flypaper of Life*, emotionally complex portraits from *The Movement*, and a number of his lyrical street images, DeCarava had withdrawn his work with a statement charging that Schoener and company "have no great love or understanding for Harlem, black people, or history."[99]

To the extent that he employed the reigning nationalist idiom, DeCarava's statement was fully continuous with the public face of the BECC. But his most powerful responses to the show differ from those of his coactivists, in that they were staked on his fervent belief in the value as art—rather than mere "documentary"—of photographic work. Persuaded by fellow (nonblack) photographer David Vestal to view the exhibit so as to contribute to a collective review in the journal *Popular Photography*, DeCarava focused less on the fact of appropriation, "downtown" or all-purpose white, than on the show's insufficiencies as a vehicle for any photographic aesthetic or experience. The core design of Harlem on My Mind, a "labyrinth" structure, "is not a good way to exhibit photographs—even bad ones," he notes, and the scale and pacing of the images (of which there are "too many") leave one "feeling that one must not spend too much time on any one picture." The considerable technical achievement represented by the show's room-sized murals is for DeCarava "a waste" because "there is no room" to view them properly; even the less monumental photos are poorly served because this is "an impossible show to light." Finally, the exhibit is not only "bad" for DeCarava but "a horror," in no small part on aesthetic terms: "You cannot see the pictures. You cannot see the pictures for the hanging. You cannot see the pictures for the lack of space. You cannot see the pictures because of the pictures."[100]

In the cohort of the BECC, then, DeCarava is something of an anomaly, protesting not for a categorical distinction between photography and art but for a new understanding of the photographic as art. If sympathetic white people or downtown Jews in the Old Left mode cannot tell the story of Harlem and its cultures, photographic images that take documentary stylistics and practices as an aesthetic point of departure—like his own—are another matter. DeCarava's stance outside the Metropolitan Museum embodies his complex cultural positioning: in solidarity with calls for African American cultural ownership and inclusion, resistant to Renaissance-style patronage, insistent on the value to art (rather than documentation alone) of black subject matter, in service of more nuanced modes of documentary representation that are, as DeCarava claims of himself, "not objective."[101] The complexity of this stance, and its inadvertent continuity with the same social history underlying Schoener's identifications with Harlem, is suggested by the placard that DeCarava wore during the BECC's protest. Its legend—which DeCarava never explicated for public consumption—read: "The foreigners reveal the real nitty gritty."[102]

This aphorism brings us back to the similarly enigmatic statement with which my initial chapter began: that of Aaron Siskind, whose "Harlem Document" work, including images such as "Girl by Dressmaker's Dummy" and the sleeping man (see figures 1.11, 1.12), was hanging inside the museum even as DeCarava and the BECC circled outside. However distantly, DeCarava's invocation of "foreigners" echoes Siskind's remarks about the "sort of foreign" subjects, both like and unlike their documenters, who inspired the Feature Group's distinctive photographic ethos.[103] And the conjunction of the two clarifies the implications of DeCarava's post–civil rights era stance. Quite obviously, "foreigners" refers, in the context of Harlem on My Mind, to unwanted outsiders: Jews trading on long-spent affective investments; white people barred from citizenship in a new republic of images chartered by Black Power. But the "foreigners" in question are also artists, whose status as strangers, sojourners, those owing their allegiance to stances beyond consensus or party line, enables a view of unbidden possibilities and truths: "the real nitty-gritty." "Foreigners," in this sense, are image makers like DeCarava, but also like Siskind: those whose representational practice is predicated both on embeddedness in social contexts and a willed distance from them; on an awareness of the social history that shapes such practice, and a belief in the alchemy by which some revelatory experience can be made of "the real."

DeCarava's protest thus brings us full circle, gesturing back to the origins of the trajectory I have been tracing, in which the afterlives of Harlem and its Renaissance and of documentary image making are entwined. It also returns us to the matter of the viability of documentary as a cultural stance, and of photography's history and practices, as a resource for such differently situated writers as Hansberry, Himes, and Killens. Even as they seek, in distinctive ways, to document the past or remake it in the image of the present—that is, to embed contemporary African American experiences and responses in the long history of their formation and suppression—they also seize on the dual nature of the photograph image: not just its baseline relation to the real, but its own irreducible foreignness. For the writers I have considered, the strangeness of the photograph is manifold: its uncanny ability to collapse, and reinstate, historical distance; its power (highlighted and appropriated by Killens) to frame the real as the surreal; its tendency, as it floats between referents, to signify both literally and metonymically (as in Hansberry's uses of Lyon's images); its dual existence (shrewdly framed by Himes) as self-evident truth or tautology and the stuff of riotous excess. In all these and other ways, the photograph as document, the documentary image as resource, enables nuanced play between evidence and invention, between art and protest, between testimony and signifying.

On the landscape of hardening cultural nationalism, what we might call the ontological strangeness of the photograph conduces to foreign status of another kind, which DeCarava's proclamation recalls. The engagement with images and with an evolving documentary practice that is variously expressed by post-Renaissance writers—in Wright's work with Rosskam, his interest in Levitt, and his own photo production, in Ellison's textual redactions of Cartier-Bresson and Model, in Baldwin's responses to Avedon, and so on—employs the problematic duality of the image, its simultaneous specificity and universalizability of reference, as a pull against identitarian logic, or any logic of categorical or deterministic inclusion. Mobilizing this duality, writers at the crossroads of Harlem and documentary practice confront and activate, in the nationalist context, what Paul Gilroy calls "the tension between the claims of racial particularity on one side and the appeal of those modern universals that appear to transcend race on the other."[104] Sutured to novelistic, collectively autobiographical, and other formally self-conscious narratives, documentary images enable the creation of willed forms of friction and disjuncture from within black institutions and nationalist idioms, even as they mount powerful, varied claims on history and the real. Whatever the impact of Harlem on My Mind in histories of art and museum practice (and it was, ultimately, considerable), the exhibit was in an important sense precisely the "active crossroads" Schoener described, a site of strident confrontation over the uses and meaning of the photographic image.[105] In this signal effect, it most powerfully documented not Harlem or even an iconography of Harlem but crossroads Harlem; it became another, if not a final, chapter in the charged history of photographic engagements embedded there, to which writers and literary forms had become so richly indebted.

Coda

Looking Back:
Toni Morrison and the
Return to Plato's Cave

◈

However misguided or ill-fated, the Metropolitan's Harlem on My Mind exhibition marked a new era in the increasingly sensational New York art gestalt. Raising heated debate about the uses of photography, in particular the documentary image and its histories of edification, crisis management, and uplift, Harlem on My Mind embodied a turn to extended visual languages, combinatory aesthetics, and "environmental" experience that increasingly characterized the artifacts of postmodernism. Over the next two decades, in the varied practices of New York's art world ran a quickened interest in the photographic image and in conjunctions and assemblages of image and text. (Even those indifferent to that world are likely to recall Jenny Holzer's "truisms," often scripted in LED displays as a new form of light writing, or Barbara Kruger's photo-text montages, layering found photojournalistic images with her trademark admonitions: "your body is a battleground"; "your fictions become history.")[1] African American artists, variously positioned with respect to identity projects, had their own purchases on this renewed experimentation with image archives and icons. Their work probed the photograph not first (or not only) as a resource for appropriation, citation, or pastiche—stylistic hallmarks, on all accounts, of visual postmodernism—but as a signal object for exploring dialectical relations between the look and the look back, between the experiencing body or self and the past that mysteriously conditions it.[2]

In the work of black novelists of the same era, a heightened skepticism about the photographic image (sutured, in cultural effect, to the stereotype and the racial image repertoire) can be traced well beyond the founding of Black Studies programs and empowerment idioms. Such skepticism informs a wide range of novels: Ishmael Reed's *Mumbo Jumbo* (1972), which incorporates photographs into its percussive collage stylistics only so as to oppose their implied claims for fixity of reference; Paule Marshall's *The Chosen Place, The Timeless People* (1969), whose tale of identity and motherland reclamation in the Caribbean features, among other characters, a Jewish American anthropologist whose attempts to provide new images of modernity for the subjects of his study end in personal disaster; Alice Walker's *The Color Purple* (1982), in which the photograph is linked with repressive regulation of black women or with radical obstacles to their freedom of expression. Not until the last decade of the century, at a juncture that has been identified as "post-Black" with respect to visual culture, would the renewed interests of visual artists in photo-text and in the history of imaging black America come fully to bear on the end-of-century novel as such.[3] In what follows, I want briefly to consider a photo-text produced by a prominent visual artist, set in conjunction with a novel inspired, even provoked, by photographs. Both are centrally preoccupied with the problem of the look back; their respective responses to that problem afford me an opportunity to look back in conclusion on the history I have traced.

By 1995, the photographer and visual artist Lorna Simpson (b. 1960) was at the height of her reception as a maker of cutting-edge political art. In that year, she produced a photo-text project rooted in her extensive early experience of documentary imaging.[4] Titled "9 Props," the piece consists of nine 14 × 11 inch photographs, arranged in grids and identical in printing values and scale (figure C.1). In each, Simpson has photographed an everyday object or objects—a vase, teacups, a tumbler—made of black glass, entirely opaque; the images are reproduced not on light-reflective photographic paper or indeed any kind of paper but rather on felt cloth, whose dense, napped surface heightens the effect of opacity.[5] Beneath each image, reproduced directly on the felt, is a caption written by Simpson. Rather than addressing the object before us, each "caption" describes an iconic studio portrait made by the Renaissance-era Harlem photographer James VanderZee, from which the imaged prop has been copied, as for example his "Woman with Goldfish Bowl" (figure C.2). With her multiple pairings of mimetic objects and descriptive narratives,

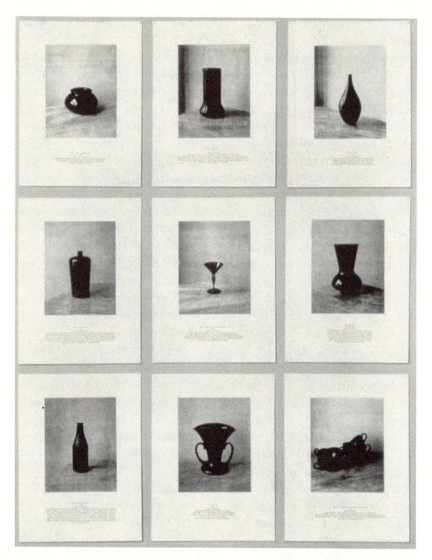

Figure C.1. Lorna Simpson, 9 Props, 1995. Courtesy of the Sean Kelly Gallery, New York. Used with permission. 2006.

Figure C.2. James VanderZee, Woman with Goldfish Bowl, 1923. © Donna Mussenden VanderZee.

Simpson invites the viewer to engage with a play of displacements. The familiar genre of the exhibition or photojournalistic caption—writ under the sign of the evidentiary or taxonomic—has been transformed as aesthetic meditation, used to reference a visual object and a portrait subject that remain unavailable. At the same time, the banal everyday object we see is elevated to the status of high art, even as the conventions of the still life are troubled by Simpson's narrative gestures toward the human figure.[6]

Suggestive as they are of the defining gestures of postmodernism—appropriation, generic hybridity—these displacements are hardly ends in themselves; "Props" presses them in service of a more specific problem. Referencing the foremost photographic chronicler of the Harlem Renaissance, Simpson marks VanderZee as a cultural predecessor whose sustaining archive of race images cannot be overcome via the practice of the camera alone. Exemplifying the Renaissance ideology of uplift so powerfully recorded and shaped by his portraits, VanderZee can only be addressed by way of a double displacement: into narrative, and into images that evacuate the human figure, with its material codings of class, racial consciousness, and racial pride, altogether. Finally, Simpson's photo-text presses even further. Imaging a series of variations on the vase, urn, or glass, her conjoined shots link their own meditations on VanderZee to the representational crisis of the Grecian urn, and the founding Western tradition of ekphrastic anxiety. In "9 Props" the object of representation is not only (or primarily) mute; it is most conspicuously opaque, blackened, blind. The artist's driving anxiety attends not the attempt to create narrative that might approach the immediacy and authority of visual experience, but the problem of recovering visual representation—in particular, the imaging of everyday black life—from the agencies in which it has become embalmed (not least a history of identity-based narratives in which women subjects have remained invisible or absent).[7] Looking back on the Harlem Renaissance as an originary source, confronting the iconicity of its generative images, Simpson seeks to transform the instrumental force of documentary and uplift, and the record of their presence in Harlem, into a resource for a latter-day photographic practice, one that stakes its claims both on modernist commitments and on the power of socially contestatory art.

In this respect, Simpson's "Props" makes a suggestive analogue for Toni Morrison's *Jazz*, published concurrently with Morrison's hard-hitting *Playing in the Dark: Whiteness and the American Literary Imagination* (1992) and shortly before her selection in 1993 as a Nobel laureate. Like Simpson's "Props," *Jazz* marks its author's first direct confrontation with the phenomenal precedent of the Renaissance and its iconic power. Morrison's readers have long noted the methodical precision of her attempts to chronicle African American history from within, from the Middle Passage, enslavement, and Reconstruction through interwar, postwar, and civil rights cultures. But the experience of what has been canonized as a high-water mark of black cultural achievement in America remains (at least until *Jazz*) conspicuously absent from her work. In Morrison's previous novels, the Renaissance figures much as VanderZee's portraits do in Simpson's photo-text: as a kind of omphalos, a mysteriously originary force whose meaning is too powerful (or too fragile) to be named as such.

This figuration animates Morrison's work from the outset. Her first novel, *The Bluest Eye* (1970), which partook with gusto in the era's skepticism of the image, implicitly links the devastating force of racial fantasies in black and white with the moment of the Renaissance. If Pecola Breedlove's mother, Pauline, "absorb[s]" her horrifically consequential notions of beauty and worth "from the silver screen" during the heyday of the New Negro era, its vaunted cultural productions have been useless to alter or mediate them.[8] In *Song of Solomon* (1977), where a careful chronological exactitude underlies Morrison's bravura play with folk, generational, and experiential temporalities, the Renaissance era is marked by its premature decline. The act with which the novel opens, the attempted flight of North Carolina Mutual Life Insurance agent Robert Smith from the cupola of Mercy Hospital in February 1931, stirs only incidental interest among passersby, who wonder whether "one of those things that racial-uplift groups were always organizing was taking place."[9] In the North country of the American Midwest, straddling the historical boundary between fugitive slavery in the United States and freedom in Canada, the recent history of the Renaissance is irrelevant to the realities of lived experience; at most it constitutes a brief interruption in the urgent transmission of deeper histories of identity, struggle, and survival.

Most dramatically, *Sula* (1973) literalizes the sustained depiction of the Renaissance as an absence or unmarked place—like the unfathomable space in the water into which Chicken Little disappears—in the writer's generative history. The crucial years between Sula's departure from the Bottom in 1927 and her return a decade later unfold outside the narrative's purview, in the emphatically blank pages that lie between the end of Part One and the start of Part Two. When Sula returns to Medallion adorned in "movie star" finery— "A black crepe dress splashed with pink and yellow zinnias, foxtails, a black felt hat with the veil of net lowered over one eye"—she embodies New Negro modernity in (as it were) spades; indeed, she might well be one of VanderZee's supremely confident, self-creating portrait subjects.[10] But the upshot of the modernity Sula exemplifies, Morrison wryly suggests, is just a dangerous license of self-invention and the sea of "pearly shit" wrought by the "plague of robins" heralding its effects.[11] Absent origin, blank page, raft of shit, the Renaissance remains in Morrison's fiction a monitory point of departure and a place of no return.

Little wonder, then, that Morrison's self-conscious invocation of the Renaissance as a fictive site in *Jazz* feels overdetermined. Throughout the novel, her virtuosity is mustered to rescue Renaissance-era culture on the ground, and Harlem as "the City" that nurtures it, from official—that is, literary and cultural—histories. No writers, or representative race men or women, feature here, or even uplifted figures of the sort that might populate VanderZee's images; there are only hairdressers, beauty products salesmen, street sheiks, the unacknowledged poets of everyday life, whose experience pulses with the complex, strident, swinging rhythms of the City.[12] Bewildered by the new mood of desire and "appetite," the straitlaced Alice Manfred contends in her own yearning with the seductive call to erotic release, and to arms, of the parade drums of Harlem's new marching blacks—music that "made her hold her hand in the pocket of her apron to keep from smashing it through the glass pane to snatch the world in her fist and squeeze the life out of it for doing what it did and did and did to her and everybody else she knew."[13] The same rhythms play inside the head of Joe's wife, Violet, accompanying her anguished fantasies of Joe's adulterous life with Alice's niece, the acne- and trauma-scarred Dorcas:

> Take her to Indigo on Saturday and sit way back so they could hear the music wide and be in the dark at the same time, at one of those round tables with a slick black top and a tablecloth of pure white on it, drinking rough gin with that sweet red stuff in it so it looked like soda pop, which a girl like her ought to have ordered instead of liquor she could sip from the edge of a glass wider at the mouth than at its base, with a tiny stem like a flower in between while her hand, the one that wasn't holding the glass shaped like a flower, was under the table drumming out the rhythm on the inside of his thigh, his thigh, his thigh, thigh, thigh, and he bought her underwear with stitching done to look like rosebuds and violets, VIOLETS, don't you know, and she wore it for him thin as it was and too cold for a room that couldn't count on a radiator to work through the afternoon, while I was where? (95)

Such adroit uses of parataxis do more than mimic the complex expressive structures of Renaissance-era jazz. Returning the era of the Renaissance to the purview of everyday life, Morrison implies the necessity of locating its effects in the longer arc of social experience after Reconstruction, from which vantage point its celebrated energies appear both more organic to mass African American culture and more baldly compensatory for the privations of its social context.[14] The driving motif of *Jazz*, its self-analogy with the art that Louis Armstrong called "that music," can thus be seen as an attempt to forestall the exceptionalist iconography of the Renaissance and the force of its most enduring images.

Paradoxically, the antivisual stance implied by this linking—as Morrison would elsewhere name it, a pronounced "weariness" in face of the flood of "photojournalism that comes pouring into our living rooms via newspapers, magazines, television and film documentaries"—obscures, if not belies, her career-long investment in photographic history, particularly the documentary record.[15] During the same year in which *Sula* was published, Morrison, a onetime textbook editor who specialized in materials for teaching African American culture, was shepherding into print at Random House a documentary photo-text project titled *The Black Book* (1974). A compendium of newspaper articles, family photos, trading cards, letters, dreambooks, and more, *The Black Book* arrayed its documentary materials on graphically rich pages designed to highlight its unprecedented archive of images of African America, including hundreds of photographs shot by a wide range of studio and agency photographers, photojournalists, and well-known *Life* and Magnum documentarians such as Henri Cartier-Bresson and George Rodger. The result was a visually complex collective family album, "a genuine Black history book" that "recollect[s] Black life as lived."[16] Although Morrison's name appears nowhere in the volume, she was in effect its ghost writer: the primary collator of materials, which included several of her own family photographs; and it was her considerable prestige as a Random House editor—"*the* black editor" in the world of New York publishing—that made *The Black Book* possible in the first place.[17]

Nor was Morrison's interest in photography confined to the archival historical record. A year earlier, she had contributed a brief foreword to the groundbreaking *Black Photographers' Annual 1973*, the first non-commercially produced anthology of African American photography. Its exceptionally high-quality reproductions spanned street documentary, photojournalism, commercial art, and experimental images, from archival studio work by VanDerZee through the Harlem portfolio of Roy DeCarava to the storied civil rights era images of Moneta Sleet Jr. Intended to "confron[t] . . . the correlation between image and destiny," the *Annual* also suggested the ongoing power of Harlem-inflected documentary conventions—found subjects, available light, self-conscious attention to the social relations that produce images—for black photographers forging a wide array of styles.[18] By 1978, when Morrison contributed a foreword to a collection of James VanDerZee's early mortuary portraits titled *The Harlem Book of the Dead*, she had become well recognized in black cultural circles for her commitment to photography as a resource for such aesthetic self-invention, in black art across media that inflected both "necessity and beauty."[19] For the possibilities of such art, the photo-textual world assembled in *The Black Book* is a signal precedent: "it is alive, it is visual, it is creative, it is complex, and it is ours."[20]

This more or less unremarked project on Morrison's part, the attempt to wrest photographic histories and effects from the constrictive grip of racial iconography for the ownership of black readers, is precisely what generates *Jazz*. For the first time addressing the burdensome precedent of the Renaissance, Morrison turns to its images as an imaginative point of contestation and departure. More specifically, *Jazz*—much like Simpson's "Props"—begins with Morrison's response to an iconic photograph by VanderZee, a photograph over which she had long meditated during the production of *The Harlem Book of the Dead* (figure C.3).[21] Lying in state in her casket, the anonymous subject of the image has, like Morrison's troubling protagonist Dorcas, been "shot by her sweetheart at a party with a noiseless gun" and died after refusing to reveal "who deathed [her]."[22] VanderZee's image displays the signature photographic strategies he devised for his mortuary documents—carefully wrought composition; the Sleeping Beauty motif; the use of overprinting (here, in the form of a welcoming white Jesus) to create a sense of multiple temporalities—but what strikes Morrison is the degree to which his documentation of mourning practices comprises a distinct aesthetic "vision," not that "of the camera but of the photographer." Signifying beyond the limits of the documentary mode, his images achieve an "intimacy" and "humanity"—indeed, a "narrative quality"—that makes them "*sui generis.*"[23] If Simpson's work seizes on VanderZee's so as to limn the problem of ekphrasis in reverse, as a matter of generating images that evade the power of cultural narratives, Morrison revisits his image so as to explore the problem of generating a novelistic response—definitively black, lyrical, and postmodernist—that can by turns rival, redirect, and intensify the "narrative quality" of such epochal images. Taking VanderZee's portrait of the departed woman as her point of departure, Morrison aims to rewrite the relation of the novel at the end of the century to the Renaissance as a limiting cultural model and to the image as the bearer of African American life.

Numerous readers have noted Morrison's use of VanderZee's image as a precedent. But their exploration of that link generally ends with the citation of an early passage in which an image of the dead girl's face, prominently displayed in the Traces' apartment, haunts them as they take turns gazing "at what seems like the only living presence in the house: the photograph of a bold, unsmiling girl staring from the mantelpiece" (11–12). Whether they find Morrison's invocation of the image dehumanizing or animating, critical readers have failed to note that Dorcas's photograph is not the only one invoked by the narrative.[24] In the distance between Morrison's invocation of VanderZee and her gesture toward an entirely fictive photograph, the primary urgency of the novel becomes clear. Beyond the act of giving the unnamed woman-child, framed as an exemplary protagonist of the real-life Renaissance, a story, Morrison wills the novel form to become a primary agency of collective memory.

This second, shadow photograph enters the narrative at what has often been identified as its least swinging, least jazzlike moment: during the fateful quest

Figure C.3. James VanderZee, I'll Tell You Tomorrow, 1926. © Donna Mussenden VanderZee.

of that absurd yet inevitable product of the peculiar institution and its legacies, the "radiantly golden" Golden Gray, to find his black father (139). Enfolded into the narrative of his journey is the account of yet another quest: Joe Trace's parallel attempt to make contact with his mother, the semimythical Wild, a cautionary figure of myth and folk wisdom—at once lost, unknown homeland of the African diaspora, and the haunting, elusive past of a nation lurching into modernity. In each of his three attempts to find Wild, Joe enacts (and Morrison rejects) a different mythic scenario of her loss. On his first attempt, he discovers "a sheltering rock formation" above the river Treason, its entrance "blocked by hedges of old hibiscus" (176). What draws him to the spot is a peculiarly beautiful sound: "the music the world makes" (176). Rather than struggle to enter the rock formation, Joe calls out, only to hear silence and "a snap like the breaking of twigs"; "disgusted" by the fragrance of "honey and shit" that wafts up to him, he departs (177). Here the ubiquitous orphic myth is both inverted and forestalled: the lure of the song occasions no look back; the mythic space in which the seeker might encounter the lost beloved remains an undiscovered country.

By the time of his second return, Joe has penetrated Wild's secret habitation—now empty, "the vestiges of human habitation . . . cold," marked only by a white-oak tree that preternaturally suggests the absent Wild (178). Pleading for "a sign," desperate for a fleeting glimpse of "her hand," Joe becomes a version of Apollo beseeching the transfigured Daphne, whose terror of intimacy puts her forever beyond reach or the power of human touch (178). But the fitness of this myth to Joe's desires is rendered equally suspect: in response to the "nothing" that follows his pleas, he aims a series of shotgun blasts at the limbs of the white-oak. Although he keeps his shells in his pocket, his gesture indicates that the mythic tropes Morrison has invoked are insufficient to Joe's search, to the national history it intersects and informs, and to the narrative that contains them (indeed, this very insufficiency is part of the story the novel seeks to tell).

Only when Joe returns for a third and final time to Wild's habitation does he penetrate to its inmost recess, a secret chamber buried "beyond the tree," "behind" the boulder they shelter (183). Forced to "crawl" and "squir[m]" backward to enter it, in a reenactment of his own birth, Joe finds himself in a "natural burrow" made of stone, in which "light hit him so hard he flinched": "It was like falling into the sun" (183). But Joe is no Icarus. This secret, unimaginable place, at once Hades and a site of transcendence, "pitch dark" yet flooded with a light that "follow[s] him like lava," is not so much a mythic space as a version of the camera obscura: a place where Joe can image the past, "rummage" among its artifacts, "touch and move" and be moved by them (183, 184). Wild herself is absent, but her trace—her status as trace, as Joe's Trace—is visible and palpable in the form of the objects Joe encounters; the state of heightened "watchfulness" and receptivity in which he does so rhymes with that of Ellison's invisible man confronting the artifacts of eviction. Here, as on that Harlem sidewalk, a world of objects—"Jars, baskets, pots; a doll, a spindle, earrings, a photograph, a stack of sticks, a set of silver brushes and a silver cigar case"—arrays itself "as though . . . wait[ing]" for an observer to give them new life in words, a tale, "History" (*Jazz*, 184; *Invisible Man*, 285).

But in this cave the photograph, literally central to the catalogue, goes conspicuously unremarked; the narrative shows not a trace of interest in what it might reveal. Instead, the narrator's attention, if not Joe's, trains itself on the apparent evidence of Golden Gray's presence. The unrecollected photograph, unlike the image of Dorcas displayed on the Traces' mantel, tells nothing; it offers us no face, no subject, no returning gaze. Inside the narrative's camera obscura, the space of human encounters "closed to the public" in which undiscovered history consists; inside Wild's burrow, the photograph as index, evidence, trace, gives way to the power of narrative to image forth a more fully realized experience of the past, lost and found, made usable as it is "change[d] . . . to a way it was never meant to be" (184). The only real mirror of the secret confluences between Joe's story and Golden Gray's—and thus between black and white experience, between rural Virginia and Harlem—is not the photograph, which itself in effect "disappear[s] without a trace," but the fragmentary, self-correcting narrative that unfolds as we read, "caught midway between was and must be" (124, 226).

Read as such, this allegory of what we might call Morrison's cave suggests that the title of *Jazz* is both overdetermined and misleading. The novel's deepest aim, in other words, is not to mimic jazz rhythms or sound in its admirable formal complexities but to harness, and cut off, the power of the image as a historical force and a rival for the novelistic imagination. Only in this context can we make the fullest sense of the novel's unifying strategy, its use of a subjective but disembodied first-person voice intended, Morrison claims, to register the narrative's status as a "talking book," a narrative "writing itself."[25] Consistently, "it" positions itself in the observational stance of the documentary observer or camera, stationed at "the window," "the hole I cut through the door to get in lives instead of having one of my own," taking "every opportunity I had to follow them" (220). The result is a series of found images—"pretty picture[s]" (8)—alternating with the fleeting private images that comprise its subjects' interiorities. The multiplicity and contestation of these images (so the narrative asserts) evade the fixity of the photographic record, do greater justice to the lives and experience frozen therein. Thus the talking book ends its meditation on its method by claiming for its own the image-making space of the camera obscura: "a place already made for me, both snug and wide open. With a doorway never needing to be closed, a view slanted for light" (221). Well beyond the agency of photo-textuality, its inhabitation of the secret chamber of the image and of history affords the caught subjects an ongoing life that prevails against the violence and arrest of the photograph: "not sepia, still, losing their edges to the light of a future afternoon. . . . For me they are real" (226).

Finally, Morrison's narrative comes to rest in a plangent appeal to the reader of the talking book to enter into that image- and history-making space:

> *I love the way you hold me, how close you let me be to you. I like your fingers on and on, lifting, turning. I have watched your face for a long time now, and missed your eyes when you went away from me . . .*
>
> But I can't say that aloud: I can't tell anyone that I have been waiting for this all my life and that being chosen to wait is the reason I can. If I were able I'd say it. Say make me, remake me. You are free to do it and I am free to let you because look, look. Look where your hands are. Now. (229)

Sight and the gaze are connected here—as they can never fully be in the case of that memento mori, the photograph—with touch; the book the reader literally holds allows (or so the voice urges us to believe) a fuller imaginative contact with the past, whose iconic images have been transfigured and made to move not just to the strains of Renaissance-era jazz but in time.

So framing her own project, thus aspiring, Morrison's novel brings us full circle: back to the entwined legacies of Harlem and the image, back to the complex play between word and image in which so much of the definitive work of the American novel of modernity and of African American cultural response is conducted. Miming the pulses and flows of the hot fives and big band era beat, *Jazz* gives us a clearer picture of the indispensability to literary figures of the image throughout the twentieth century as fact, as precedent, as history, and as aesthetic resource.[26] Read at the farther reaches of the history of engagement I have traced, Morrison's novel achieves for the richly varied texts comprising that history what her own novel may not fully have achieved for its protagonists: it makes "the space where the photo had been . . . real" (*Jazz*, 197). *Jazz* is thus a fitting text from which to look back, to frame for the record the power of the photograph, and of its Harlem lives and afterlives, as a provocation to love and rage, commitment and evasion, politics and art.

Abbreviations

ASA	Aaron Siskind Archive, Center for Creative Photography
ASA GEH	Aaron Siskind Archive, Harlem Document, George Eastman House
FGWM	Feature Group Weekly Minutes
LHP	Langston Hughes Papers
LMA	Lisette Model Archive
MPA	Marion Palfi Archive
REP, MS	Ralph Ellison Papers, Manuscript Division
REP, P&P	Ralph Ellison Papers, Prints and Photographs Division
RWP	Richard Wright Papers

Notes

Introduction

1. Powell, *Riots and Ruins*, 31–32. A considered account is given in *The Complete Report of Mayor LaGuardia's Commission on the Harlem Riot of March 19, 1935*. On the social logic underlying the outbreak, see Greenberg, *"Or Does It Explode?"* 3–5; Cohen, *Consumers' Republic*, 41–53, discusses economic conditions. For an accounting of Powell's activities and of the context of increasing white-on-black violence in which he responded, see Capeci, *Harlem Riot of 1943*, 70–75.

2. At the moment of the Harlem outbreak in 1935, the terms *riot* and *race riot* definitively signified white aggression against African Americans. DuBois (*Black North in 1901*, 46) refers to a 1900 outbreak on the West Side of Manhattan (bands of roving whites terrorized black residents for two days, with the sanction and participation of law enforcement) as "the police riot of New York"; of that same period, Cripps ("Introduction," i) notes that state responses to acts of vigilantism "effectively announced that white violence against blacks . . . would be organized, collective, in strength and in daylight, and against . . . blacks in their own city ghettos." Shapiro (*White Violence and Black Response*, 96) comments in detail on this too readily repressed history, noting that the term "urban race riot . . . hides more than it reveals." Many commentators on the 1935 episode in Harlem refer to it as "'riot,'" thus emphasizing its disruption of the historical logic of white supremacist violence and its status as the first spontaneous communal protest of African Americans on a mass scale. I have tried to preserve a similar emphasis.

3. This time nearly 1,500 stores—virtually all white-owned—were looted or destroyed, some five hundred participants arrested, and at least six people killed. See Gilje, *Rioting in America*, 157–58; Capeci, *Harlem Riot of 1943*; Clark, "Group Violence"; and White, "Behind the Harlem Riot."

4. On Harlem's second "great riot" as a template, see Gilje, *Rioting in America*, 144, 157; Shapiro, *White Violence and Black Response*, 261–62; and Myrdal, *American Dilemma*, 2:568.

5. A revealing view of the zoot suit riots (attacks by U.S. servicemen and civilians on Mexican American youths) in greater Los Angeles, culminating on June 3–7, 1943, is opened by the *Los Angeles Times* article "Zoot Suiters Learn Lesson in Fights with Servicemen." Discussions of these riots that suggest their structural difference from events in Harlem include Mazón, *Zoot-Suit Riots*, and Pagán, *Murder at the Sleepy Lagoon.*

6. By 1935, the black population in Harlem had increased by more than 800 percent; on the effects of this increase, see *Complete Report*, 53. The import of such material facts is central to Lewis's influential reading of the Renaissance as a heady but failed experiment by a misguided cultural elite; see Lewis, *When Harlem Was in Vogue.*

7. "Police End Harlem Riot," 1.

8. See Rotella, *October Cities*, 214–24, on Harlem as icon of the second ghetto, and De Jongh, *Vicious Modernism*, 145ff, on the uses of Harlem as a metaphor for urban crisis in writing of the 1960s.

9. Locke ("Harlem," 457) revealingly describes the first "great riot" in photographic terms.

10. Gilje, *Rioting in America*, 161.

11. Powell, *Riots and Ruins*, 55, 51.

12. Definitions of *documentary* are legion; the problem is worth addressing here. Generally, invention of the term is credited to British filmmaker John Grierson, writing on nonfictional film genres and visual strategies. But Grierson himself (*Grierson on Documentary*, 99, 100) declared that even though "the use of natural material has been regarded as the vital distinction" between documentary and other visual genres, the "array of species" exploiting such material is "unmanageable." Even without extending the term to comprise moving-image production, notes Carlebach (*American Photojournalism Comes of Age*, 107), "confusion over what constitutes documentary continues." As Bright (*Art Photography Now*, 157) sums it up, "The term 'document' is virtually synonymous with the medium of photography itself."

Among posited categories for studying New Deal era image making in particular are "social documentary" (see Carlebach, *American Photojournalism Comes of Age*, 103–42); "liberal documentary" (Margolis, "New Deal and Photography"); "documentary rhetoric," understood as a set of conventions broadly definitive of "popular forms of twentieth-century American culture" (Rabinowitz, *They Must Be Represented*, 77); "the document" as a photo-text mode designed to fulfill institutional agency aims (Hurley, *Portrait of a Decade*); and the documentary "mode of inquiry," aiming simultaneously to create "drama and emotion" and to record "objective" facts (Finnegan, *Picturing Poverty*, xv, 120–67). All of these have been influenced by the work of William Stott, who traces documentary assumptions, stylistics, and practices across a wide range of institutions; essentially, for Stott, documentary of the 1930s is a cultural genre in which "feelings come first" and "emotion," marshaled and directed, "count[s] more than fact" (Stott, *Documentary Expression and Thirties America*, 8–9).

After Stott, work on New Deal era documentary by prominent scholars such as Stange, Stein, Tagg, and Hurley has emphasized not the cultural logic of the category but institutional contexts in which it was developed. Distinguishing between photojournalism, social documentary, "straight" photography (i.e., images not technically manipulated at the printing stage), photo-essay, reportage, coverage, and myriad other forms of publication and production, these scholars have produced incisive accounts of a widely varied New Deal archive. But the very proliferation of such categories—as catalogued, for example, by Rosler, "In, around, and Afterthoughts," 271n1—suggests their provisionality; more to the point, the very exactitude of photo historical idiom fails to capture the labile power of documentary modes for literary figures responding to them, and not just as a matter of representational codes or institutional affiliation. In the history of black literary production, the predominance of realist and evidentiary traditions was long a given; as Petesch (*Spy in the Enemy's Country*, 8) notes, problems of authentication so powerfully defined that enterprise that it had become, by the mid-twentieth century, "the literary equivalent of the commissions of inquiry." In this context, notions of documentary and the document were bound to be more freighted and more labile than the precisely modulated categories of photo historical inquiry. For my own articulation of documentary as a cultural genre responding to this context, with varied and changing effects, an important model has been Rabinowitz (*Black & White & Noir*), who frames noir not as a film or textual genre but as "a leitmotif running through mid-twentieth-century American culture," a set of representational codes that "make sense of America's landscape and history" (14).

13. Model, LMA, AR6NB1, 2; "U.S. Minicam Boom," 160–64.

14. Hales (*Silver Cities*, 179) and Gandal (*Virtues of the Vicious*, 65–66) attempt to distinguish modern or twentieth-century documentary practices from earlier versions by pointing to the late nineteenth century as a critical moment. I concur that visual conventions and stylistics do dramatically change in this period, but the contract for image making—the logic governing relations between photographer and subject—does not. Not until the era of the New Deal does the essentially top-down and instrumentalist model for photographic production come under significant self-scrutiny, or itself become (in a kind of modernist effect) integral to photography's understanding of its project.

15. Gilje, *Rioting in America*, 150.

16. On the founding of *Life*, see Swanberg, *Luce and His Empire*, 15–24, and Wainwright, *Great American Magazine*. On *Life*'s appeal, see Tagg, "Melancholy Realism," 6.

17. Judging by pass-along readership rather than official circulation, more than 15 percent of all U.S. adults were regular readers; see Baughman, *Henry R. Luce and the Rise of the American News Media*, 92–94; DeVoto, "Report on Photography," 8.

18. Baughman, *Henry R. Luce and the Rise of the American News Media*, 97.

19. Stange, *Symbols of Ideal Life*, 111; see also Bezner, *Photography and Politics in America*, 6. For detailed accounting of the many other, often overlooked state-sponsored photographic projects, see Daniel and Stein, *Official Images*.

20. Luce, *Four Hours a Year*, quoted in Wainwright, *Great American Magazine*, 26.

21. *Complete Report*, 53–57; Osofsky, *Harlem*, 128–31, 141; McElvaine, *Great Depression*, 187–95; Ottley and Weatherby, *Negro in New York*, 265, 271.

22. Johnson, *Black Manhattan*, 3.

23. Watson, *Harlem Renaissance*, 3–4.

24. Adams, *Harlem Lost and Found*, 15.

25. "Police End Harlem Riot," 16.

26. "Italians Clash with Negroes," 10.

27. Powell, *Riots and Ruins*, 40.

28. Gurock, *When Harlem Was Jewish*, 66–73.

29. On earlier black photographers and the portrait tradition, see Willis, *Reflections in Black*. Parks ("Foreword," ix) describes the Smiths' desire "to zero in on what was left of the social and cultural enrichment of Harlem's Renaissance"; Miller ("The Smiths and Their Art," 9) describes their work as "striving all the time to present the community in a good light." Useful accounts of a national archive of racist stereotypes and their afterlives include Gates, "Face and Voice of Blackness"; Harris, *Colored Pictures*; and Stange, "'Photographs Taken in Everyday Life.'"

30. There is, of course, a rich body of work detailing the engagements of African American filmmakers, institutions, and audiences with the evolving history of motion pictures. But there is nothing like a comparable body of work with respect to still photography—in spite of the fact that its cultural effects and uses remained, for much of the twentieth century (and have done so, arguably, into the twenty-first), both urgent and distinct from those of film.

31. Shloss, *In Visible Light*, and Guimond, *American Photography and the American Dream*, offer admirably rich but similarly bounded readings.

32. Burgin, "Looking at Photographs," 131; Tagg, "Proof of the Picture," 11–12. Representative accounts of photography as an instrument of ideological inscription are given by Holland, Spence, and Watney ("Introduction," 2) and Stange (*Symbols of Ideal Life*, xiii).

33. Berger, "Understanding a Photograph," 294.

34. Samuels, *Facing America*; Smith, *American Archives*.

35. Wexler, *Tender Violence*. Much of this field-shaping work has been anthologized in Reynolds and Hutner, *National Imaginaries, American Identities*; this volume does not, however, register the more recent turn with respect to photographic practices that I note later.

36. Wexler, *Tender Violence*, 2. At this inaugural moment in her argument, it should be noted, Wexler is primarily concerned to counter previous notions of nineteenth-century photography as a widely democratic medium; her larger point—well taken—is that "the American family album was severely out of balance from the start" (2–3). But Wexler's own evidence suggests how critical to these excised Americans was the possibility of photographic self-representation, practice, and ownership. In what follows, I focus on various alternatives to "the American family album" created and explored by those who had been thus disserved.

37. Wallace, *Constructing the Black Masculine*, 7.

38. On lynching history as a primary ground for African American experience of visual culture, see Allen, *Without Sanctuary*. Among other readings, the volume contains a classically ambivalent response to photographs as documents (almost perforce of lynching) by Als. More broadly, Mitchell (*Picture Theory*, 162) articulates an understanding of photo-text production as driven by modes of "visual/verbal coding" that implicitly involve racial constructions. English (*Unnatural Selections*, 35–64) argues for a correlation between the uses of photography and uplift ideologies via eugenic thinking.

39. Baker, *Blues, Ideology, and Afro-American Literature*, 11; Edwards, *Practice of Diaspora*, 68. Edwards, I should note, emphasizes transnational print culture rather than music per se as a frame for the production and historical understanding of black internationalism; his "Literary Ellington" powerfully contests the key assumption "that music—more than literature, dance, theater, or the visual arts—has been the paradigmatic mode of black artistic production and the standard and pinnacle not just of black culture but of American culture as a whole" (1).

40. Wallace, *Dark Designs and Visual Culture*, 192.

41. These objections are largely staked by feminist scholars of African American culture, with an important recent exception. Warren, *So Black and Blue*, sharply contests the effects within a received history of African American cultural politics of the privileging of music as the exemplary folk, vernacular, or authentic racial form; I will have occasion later to engage with his readings. In general, however, the call for alternative frames—particularly visual contexts—in which to understand black cultural production has been a project of feminist scholarship. hooks, "In Our Glory," discusses women's uses of photography within domestic spaces, particularly under the reign of segregation. Willis painstakingly reconstructs the history of African American photographers from the inception of photographic technology through the present; see in particular *Reflections in Black* and *Family History and Memory*. Wall, *Worrying the Line*, embraces photographic images as instrumental—alongside music and other expressive modes—in the creation by black women writers of family genealogies lost, disrupted, and haunted by slavery. The relegation (in effect) of photography as a practice to the distaff side of African American studies has, it might be speculated, contributed to its relative neglect as a subject of scholarly inquiry. In any case, it has begun to inspire new thinking both by photo historians such as Stange, revisiting the effects and possibilities of FSA work in *Bronzeville*, and by African Americanists such as Baker and Benston, in new projects involving photographs in African American art and culture.

42. Pinney and Peterson, *Photography's Other Histories*.

43. My book is thus in dialogue with recent work such as Shawn Michelle Smith's study of W.E.B. DuBois's negotiation of the photographic archive and America's racial image repertoire, *Photography on the Color Line*, particularly "'Families of Undoubted Respectability,'" 77–112; Goldsby's argument (in *Spectacular Secret*) for literary form as a contestatory response to the visual regime of lynching; Lee's marvelous work (in

Picturing Chinatown) on vernacular portraiture and street photographs in San Francisco's Chinatown as an occasion for exploring not only the ethnographic gaze but also the social agency of those framed as others, and the power of their looks back; and Kaplan's study (in *American Exposures*) of photographic practice as a foundation for the creation of meaningful community. Other recent work with which I am in dialogue includes Willis's "Visualizing Political Struggle," on the affirmative power of civil rights era photography by black and nonblack photographers, and Raiford's account (in "Consumption of Lynching Images") of "antilynching" photography within the culture of civil rights activism.

44. For an illustration of the complexity of the camera and the cumbersome processes of image production before miniaturization, see Woodbury, *Encyclopaedic Dictionary of Photography*. Soby ("Art of Poetic Accident," 28) directly contrasts the view camera—"photography's formal instrument of expression," aiming "to record relatively fixed objects or scenes with forethought"—with "the hand camera" and its "spontaneity and motion, with the recording of the unforeseen and the quick."

45. A useful account of the presumed equation of documentary or street photography with middle- and leisure-class urges is given in Harvey, "Who Wants to Know What and Why?"

46. Coleman ("No Pictures," 4–5) considers the Jewishness of key practitioners; Kaplan (*American Exposures*, 131–54) argues for the relationship between photographic practice and the "not-oneness" of diasporic culture and being (132); Blair ("Jewish America through the Lens") explores the variety of photographic responses historically coded by immigrant, diasporic, and Jewish identity. Moore and Moore ("Observant Jews") discuss the uses by Jewish photographers of varied conventions for representing subjectivity; collectively, they argue, their body of work "has helped to renew photography as an endeavor requiring shared risk" (176). Within received photo history, Davidov (*Women's Camera Work*, 223–28) locates the development of the photographic ethos and stylistics of Dorothea Lange in her early experiences of life within the Jewish "ghetto" and its social networks and visual landscape.

47. This view has been most powerfully articulated in Kozloff, *New York*. I will have occasion later to dissent from his view, offering alternative genealogies and accounts of Jewish American photographic practice.

48. Pinney, "Introduction," 2, 1.

49. For recent photographic developments that challenge reigning models of appropriation or competition (as in Melnick, *Right to Sing the Blues*) and irreparably failed mediation (as educed by Sundquist, *Strangers in the Land*, particularly 311–80, 526), see Chevlowe, "Framing Jewishness," which describes the commissioning of new photographic work on the complex ethnoracial identity formation of Jews in the United States. In the same volume, projects by the African American photographer Dawoud Bey (48–55) and the Korean-born Nikki S. Lee (82–89) emphasize links between the lability of Jewishness and a strain of theatricality developing in postwar photographic projects.

50. On the "uncanny" and "magnetic" effects of these truth claims, see Trachtenberg, *Reading American Photographs*, 33; chapter 3, note 40 in this book; and Sandweiss, *Print the Legend*, 119–20, on the invention of daguerreotypean aura in twentieth-century contexts.

51. Barthes, *Camera Lucida*, 79.

52. Daniel Longwell, quoted in Wainwright, *Great American Magazine*, 21.

53. Sekula, *Photography against the Grain*, 56. Current versions of this skepticism—at work for at least two decades in the nexus of cultural theory and art history and recently exemplified by Elkins, "What Do We Want Photography to Be?"—have led to a recent turn against semiotics-based idioms for understanding photography's effects, in favor of phenomenological models grounded in the work of Jean-Luc Nancy (Kaplan, *American Exposures*), Walter Benjamin (Cadava, *Words of Light*), and Jacques Derrida (Batchen, *Burning with Desire*). Engagement with this body of scholarship is beyond my scope, but I would note that the work of Model, and the literary-photographic practices of figures such as Wright and Ellison, anticipate certain of these theoretical concerns.

54. Model, LMA, Notebook 5, 11b, 12b.

55. Model, LMA, Notebook 3, 1b; Notebook 5, 11b, 12b; Notebook 2, 15, 15.

56. Peirce, *Collected Papers*, 2:247, 264–65, 281, 320, 441. Elkins ("What Do We Want Photography to Be?" 938–39) notes with asperity how predominant are misreadings (or rather underreadings) of Peirce as a source for understanding photography. Even without engaging Peirce's notoriously elaborate terminology, I would call attention to his notion that "anything whatever, be it quality, existent individual, or law, is an Icon of anything insofar as it is like that thing and *used* as a sign of it" (2:247, emphasis added). Model's language of the analogue anticipates the skepticism about photographic presence I noted earlier, but her language emphasizes social experience, rather than discursive conventions or phenomenological process, as the ground of the image's effects.

57. Model, LMA, Notebook 19, 17b.

58. Model, LMA, Notebook 2, 15.

59. Model, LMA, Notebook 6, 21b.

60. Wall, "Marks of Indifference," 254.

Chapter One

1. Kao, "Personal Vision in Aaron Siskind's Documentary Practice," 15.

2. Useful information on the exhibition of "Harlem Document" can be found in *Photo Notes, February 1933–Spring 1950*. Although neither the "Harlem Document" book plan nor the exhibition materials written by Smith/Carter survive in full, several of the original exhibition boards are in the archives of the George Eastman House; a version of the project, including captions by Smith/Carter, was published as "244,000 Native Sons."

3. Milton Smith to Richard Wright, 20 May 1950, RWP, Box 106, Folder 1613; *Brooklyn Eagle*, Brooklyn Collection, Brooklyn Public Library; "Book-of-the-Month Author Talks for AFRO," in Kinnamon and Fabre, *Conversations with Richard Wright*, 53–56. For examples of Smith's photojournalistic work for *Ebony*, see "Day at Home with a Chorus Girl" and "Biggest Art Show." Both are attributed to Michael Carter; by October 1946, in Bontemps, "Langston Hughes," he is being credited as "M. Smith." None of the standard accounts of "Harlem Document" trace Smith's identity or work, an index either to his success in shifting identities or to the tight focus in photo historical work on specific photographic institutions and agencies.

4. Milton Smith to Richard Wright, 20 May 1950, RWP, Box 106, Folder 1613. On Smith's involvement with the activities of the Photo League, see Chiarenza, *Aaron Siskind*, 32.

5. Lewis, *When Harlem Was in Vogue*, 90.

6. The "Harlem Document" project was conducted between 1936 and 1939, and "The Most Crowded Block in the World" between 1938 and 1940. The protocols for the production of their images were continuous, and Smith "directed" and participated closely in both projects. Chiarenza (*Aaron Siskind*, 254n6) notes that Siskind himself "looked at all" his Harlem images—from his pre–Photo League work on—as "part of a continuing series," and framed them accordingly in the 1981 version of *Harlem Document*; I follow suit.

7. Kao, "Personal Vision in Aaron Siskind's Documentary Practice," 13. The best-known statement of the Photo League's documentary aims and of the project of "verism" was written by the influential photography critic (and lover of Berenice Abbott) Elizabeth McCausland; see "Documentary Photography," 6, 8.

8. A useful exception is Sandweiss, "Way to Realism." Focusing on the development of postpictorialist aesthetics among photographers on the West Coast, Sandweiss argues for the emergence of a distinctively American photographic realism, variously theorized and practiced but unified by its "dominant subject": "America"—a rapidly modernizing America—"itself" (38). Fleischhauer and Brannan, "Introduction," usefully emphasizes series production within the FSA canon so as to reconsider "the working photographer in the field" as an agent (over and against institutional aims and constraints); in the same volume, Trachtenberg, "From Image to Story," makes a powerful case for reading FSA work in the context of the project "file," which includes shooting scripts, negatives and prints, and the notes and accompanying text submitted by photographers. Conversely, Finnegan, *Picturing Poverty*, argues for the usefulness—and even the necessity—of reading FSA images in the context of their circulation within print culture and institutions, newly defining urban mass and visual cultures. None of these frames for reading, however, foregrounds the problem of urban representation as such. A nuanced and wide-ranging account of Harlem as a site for photographic representation more generally is given by Ings, "Street Ballet/Urban Drama." On the development of visual codes and experience in Harlem during the Renaissance era, and their importance in definitive texts of the Renaissance, see Balshaw's excellent study, *Looking for Harlem*.

9. Natanson, *Black Image in the New Deal*, 71; he also notes that the archive, with its emphasis on land management and rehabilitation programs, lacks the "urban accent" of Federal Writers' Project and other agency documentation. The one significant exception, Natanson notes, is Russell Lee's work on Chicago in 1941, which constitutes roughly a third of the entire FSA urban archive. Both Natanson, "Photo-Series," and Stange, *Bronzeville*, focus on Lee's work as a corrective lens through which to read the FSA project.

10. Susman writes definitively on the period's obsession with the "complex effort to seek and to define America as a culture" (*Culture as History*, 157); see also Susman, "Thirties," on the effort to "define the nature of culture" so as to "characterize, and adapt to an American Way of Life" (189, 188). Other indispensable accounts of the cultural landscape of the 1930s include Penkower, *Federal Writers' Project*, 2–4; Mangione, *Dream and the Deal*, 27–32; Harris's explorations of New Deal citizenry (*Federal Art and National Culture*); Aaron's classic study, *Writers on the Left*; and Denning's rich account, *Cultural Front*.

11. Chiarenza, *Aaron Siskind*, 27. On the notion of the "human document" associated with Lewis Hine and his ideal of participatory viewing, see Trachtenberg, *Reading American Photographs*, 190–209. Hines's work was rediscovered (and claimed as a precedent) during the 1930s by members of the Photo League and became central to its pedagogy and projects; Siskind's images reflect, more than many others produced in the same context, the power of Hine's example.

12. More ephemeral than "Harlem Document," these projects are difficult to document; the Feature Group's archival gestures were limited at best. In general, its work was treated as the property of the Photo League and often raided without permission for use by Communist Party organs such as the *Daily Worker* and commercial ventures such as *PM*. A letter by member Beatrice Koslofsky to Photo League president Eliot Elisofon makes formal complaint about lack of control over images; Koslofsky notes that the entire Bowery series—including all prints and negatives—had been pulled without permission from the Feature Group's files (Beatrice Koslofsky, 28 November 1939, ASA, AG 30 Photo League: Feature Group correspondence), and Feature Group weekly minutes for 4 April, 1939, indicate that the Park Avenue series had disappeared as well (AG 30 Photo League: Feature Group Weekly Minutes; hereafter cited as FGWM).

13. Siskind, "Feature Group," 28.

14. Ibid., 28, 27. On the Photo League's early ties to the American Communist Party, see Bethune, *New York Photo League*; on their lingering effects, see Bezner, "Aaron Siskind," 28–29.

15. Siskind, "Drama of Objects," 52.

16. Ibid.

17. See in particular Stephany, "Interview with Aaron Siskind," 41.

18. Siskind, "Feature Group," 28. As Siskind would retrospectively describe it, "What I was interested in . . . was the aesthetics of documentary photography. What kind of a

picture do you make when you are making what you call a 'documentary picture'? . . .
Do you express what you want to say, or do you say what it wants to say?" Siskind,
interview with Alan Cohen, Tom Cinoman, and Geoff Hughes, 6–7.

19. Stephany, "Interview with Aaron Siskind," 41.

20. Tagg, "Melancholy Realism"; Natanson, *Black Image in the New Deal*, 1–48, 85–
112; Galassi, "Introduction," in *Walker Evans and Company*, 10–37. Of special interest
to me is Kao, "Personal Vision in Aaron Siskind's Documentary Practice," 14, on the
"self-conscious relativism" of Siskind's documentary aesthetic. On recent exceptionalist
readings of Russell Lee, see note 9 in this chapter.

21. Tagg ("Melancholy Realism," 12) notes of Bourke-White's work for *Life* that "an
essential part of the story would always be an account of her pains to meet the challenge
of her assignment" at an "hour's notice." Such emphasis on the photographer's whirl-
wind relations with her subjects, Tagg argues, is matched by the formal qualities of her
images, which aim to be "as efficient, professional, and anonymous as the house-style
prose of the text" that accompanies them (13). Finally, for Tagg, the exemplary Bourke-
White image is quite the opposite of "documentary": "It does not demand the enactment of the viewpoint as a psychic space" (13).

22. Bethune, *New York Photo League*, 63.

23. This, at least, was the testimony of a former Photo League member turned House
Un-American Activities Committee informant during the League's waning years; Calomiris, *Red Masquerade*, 29.

24. *Photo Notes*, special issue (January 1948), n.p.

25. See Bethune, *New York Photo League*, 53.

26. Stephany, "Interview with Aaron Siskind," 41.

27. The Bowery, a riverfront neighborhood on the Lower East Side, remained an
iconic site of ethnic entrepreneurship, crime, and decline throughout the 1930s, when
Depression-era poverty gave its low history new life. As Sante (*Low Life*, 12) notes, the
Bowery had "always possessed the greatest number of groggeries, flophouses, clip joints,
brothels, fire sales, rigged auctions, pawnbrokers, dime museums, shooting galleries,
dime-a-dance establishments, fortune-telling agencies, lottery agencies, thieves' markets, and tattoo parlors, as well as theaters of the second, third, fifth and tenth rank,"
in addition to remaining "the only major thoroughfare in New York never to have had
a single church built upon it"; it remained a site in which Jewish American experience
and the representation and management of U.S. modernity were closely connected.
Harlow (*Old Bowery Days*, 1, 2) offers a roughly contemporaneous account of the
Bowery as "the most heterogeneous, the most chameleonlike . . . street" in New York—
and unfailingly a "notorious" one.

28. Chiarenza (*Aaron Siskind*, 27) argues that the tenement images "allud[e] to the
complex meaning of a kind of tenement life that contains the division of body and
spirit, of suffering and salvation"—an intention that makes this work "exceptional."

29. Stephany, "Interview with Aaron Siskind," 41.

30. Ibid.

31. McNeill (quoted in Natanson, "Robert H. McNeill and the Profusion of Virginia Experience," 113) describes the working conditions: "I had to be extremely stingy with film, because I didn't know whether I could get any more. There was never much time for stories; I'd be due at the next location in a matter of hours"; given these working conditions, McNeill and other agency photographers were compelled to "snap and run."

32. Stephany, "Interview with Aaron Siskind," 42.

33. Not only did FSA photographers visit the League and lecture there quite frequently, their published works and exhibitions also were noted and reviewed in the Photo League's journal, *Photo Notes*. In addition to photographic exhibitions and workshops, Roy Stryker spoke at the Photo League in 1939 and 1940; see *Photo Notes*, April 1939, 1; and March–April 1940, 1.

34. Vachon, quoted in Natanson, *Black Image in the New Deal*, 60.

35. On black responses to the developing institutions and genres of American mass media, see Willis, *Reflections in Black*; Gates, "Trope of a New Negro and the Reconstruction of the Image of the Black"; hooks, "In Our Glory"; and Lukasa, "Seeking a Cultural Equality."

36. Parker, "Views on Many Questions."

37. Marvel Cooke, cited in Willis and Lukasa, *Visual Journal*, 27.

38. Robert McNeill (quoted in Natanson, "Robert H. McNeill and the Profusion of Virginia Experience," 100) describes his dissatisfaction with the analogous work of the most prominent black portraitists of Washington, DC, the Scurlock brothers, in whose work "everything look[ed] so posed, so unreal. The photographer was so busy making sure that the pictures were flattering, that everything looked like everything else." Avidly seeking alternative models for his photographic practice, he "devour[ed] every photography magazine I could get my hands on" as well as the work of "Cartier-Bresson, Capa, *Life* stories, the FSA group."

39. Daniel and Stein, *Official Images*, viii; hooks, cited in Willis and Lukasa, *Visual Journal*, 3.

40. Stephany, "Interview with Aaron Siskind," 41; Kao, "Personal Vision in Aaron Siskind's Documentary Practice," 15. See also Chiarenza, *Aaron Siskind*, 17–24.

41. Stephany, "Interview with Aaron Siskind," 43; Roy Stryker, cited in Natanson, *Black Image in the New Deal*, 58; Bezner, "Aaron Siskind," 28; see also Natanson, "Robert H. McNeill and the Profusion of Virginia Experience," 99.

42. Natanson (*Black Image in the New Deal*, 47) charges that Siskind "sometimes overindulged a sense of the alluring poetry of Harlem life," but argues for the "educated visio[n]" of Siskind's "Harlem Document" work, as rooted both in hard facts and in "care and imagination"; Solomon-Godeau (*Photography at the Dock*, 79–82) makes Siskind exemplary of an abandonment of social consciousness consequent on the shift from social documentary to abstraction. Entin ("Modernist Documentary") offers a thoughtfully balanced reading that stresses the distinctive modernism of Siskind's formal and social negotiations. Raeburn (*Staggering Revolution*, 219–45) carefully details the circuits of production, exhibition, and publication defining the "Harlem Docu-

ment," with particular attention to the fate of several iconic Siskind images in *The New Masses*, *Look*, and other publications; more broadly, Raeburn powerfully redraws the frame in which the Photo League's work is viewed, juxtaposing Feature Group projects with such varied contemporaneous practices as celebrity portraiture, photographic journals for popular audiences, and landscape photography. None of these readings, however, takes fully into account the role of post-Renaissance Harlem as a social space in the evolution of Siskind's practice.

43. Kao, "Personal Vision in Aaron Siskind's Documentary Practice," 17; "Michael Carter's Statement" (Harlem Document), typescript, ca. 1940, Collection of the International Museum of Photography, 85:1028:1, George Eastman House. See also Kao, "Personal Vision in Aaron Siskind's Documentary Practice," 22.

44. Siskind, *Harlem Document: Photographs, 1932–1940*; hereafter cited as HD.

45. Siskind's observations in Stephany, "Interview with Aaron Siskind," 49, on the issue of print quality are worth noting, especially in light of Feature Group requests that he reprint his work: "I was really concerned with relating the print quality to the idea, the tones to the idea, rather than always getting a full range of tones and everything ... beautiful surface and toning and things like that. Which is very nice, but sometimes it's terribly irrelevant. Now I think that is a kind of dead end, making everything look beautiful."

46. Carter [Smith], "244,000 Native Sons," 8–9.

47. FGWM, 9 February 1939.

48. Aaron Siskind and Michael Carter [Milton Smith], "Toward a Harlem Document" (one-page exhibition catalogue), New School for Social Research, New York City, 1939. ASA GEH.

49. Siskind, "Drama of Objects," 52.

50. "U.S. Minicam Boom," 129. That Siskind owned or had access to 35 mm equipment is evidenced by a variety of his negatives, most recording his earliest, pre–Photo League work and images of family and close friends. Carl Chiarenza has noted that Siskind regularly borrowed camera equipment from Photo League property, which certainly included 35 mm cameras (email to author, 20 April 2006).

51. Siskind, "Credo," 56. Robert McNeill (quoted in Lukasa, "Seeking a Cultural Equality," 69) gives a suggestive account of the large-format process in his documentary practice: "We had to remember to open the camera; had to pull the lens out on a track until it was in proper position. [Then we would] open the back to look at the ground glass, and focus and set the diaphragm, cock the shutter, insert the film holder, pull the lid and compose the picture in the view finder. And then take the picture. I counted once: I think it was an 11-step process. I used to put a checklist on my camera [so that I would remember everything]." See also see Elisofon, "Types of Camera," 3. Intrinsic to the use of the large-format camera for Siskind was its "pedagogic" utility; during his tenure in the 1950s as a photography teacher at the Institute of Design in Chicago, he demanded that all students begin by working with a 4 × 5 view camera, whose use required not only specific kinds of technical mastery but a certain awareness of social

context and its framing relation to aesthetic production; see Traub, "Interview with Aaron Siskind," 76–77.

52. "U.S. Minicam Boom," 160.

53. Siskind, interview with Alan Cohen, Tom Cinoman, and Geoff Hughes, 6. Siskind's place of employment is indicated in a letter from the New York City School Board; see ASA Poems on envelopes (1928), AP 30:28.

54. At strategic points in the unfolding sequence, the reader of *Harlem Document* finds pointed remarks about the presence of outsiders in Harlem, specifically Jews. The drummer Jim Barber, interviewed by Ralph Ellison, talks at length about his encounters in segregated clubs with white patrons; his response to their blandishments—"What-in-the-world do you want to come up to *my* place for?" (HD, 50)—reads in context as a direct exchange with Siskind. It is, finally, open to the viewer to characterize the relations of Siskind's site-work to the kinds of cultural exchanges described by Harlem subjects, including the exploitation of "them what takes advantage of skin" (64); the outreach by do-gooders and thrill-seekers who demand that black acquaintances "take me up to Harlem and show me around" (50); the instrumental racism of landlords and proprietors who own "junk shops, second hand stores," and of whom various subjects insist, "I ain't giving these Jews my money" (51).

55. FGWM, 1 November 1939.

56. FGWM, 24 January 1939.

57. See, for example, Morgan Smith and Marvin Smith, "Ella Fitzgerald Performing with Chick Webb and His Orchestra at the Savoy Ballroom" (ca. 1938), and Robert H. McNeill, "A Couple Dancing at the Savoy Ballroom" (1937), both in Willis, *Reflections in Black*, 97 (plate 117), 99 (plate 121).

58. FGWM, 6 February 1939.

59. FGWM, 23 May 1939.

60. FGWM, 6 December 1939.

61. FGWM, 15 and 22 March and 4 October 1939.

62. FGWM, 23 May and 18 October 1939.

63. It is instructive to compare this image with earlier photos in the sequence: none features a direct gaze at the camera; the sequence consequently seems constructed to make that gaze the culmination of the montage. It is also instructive to compare the image with Siskind's more frequently reproduced photographs of entertainment venues; see Natanson, *Black Image in the New Deal*, 169–71, for "Amateur Night, Apollo Theater" and "Savoy Dancers."

64. FGWM, 20 September 1939.

65. Solomon-Godeau, *Photography at the Dock*, 182; Natanson, *Black Image in the New Deal*, 46–47.

66. Stephany, "Interview with Aaron Siskind," 43.

67. Ibid., 44.

68. Kao ("Personal Vision in Aaron Siskind's Documentary Practice," 15) is especially persuasive in her argument that Siskind cultivated a "'problematic' formalism"

as a mode for evading the appropriation and misuse of his images by contending documentary agencies.

69. Stephany, "Interview with Aaron Siskind," 46.

70. Ibid.

71. Siskind, "Credo," 57.

72. Stephany, "Interview with Aaron Siskind," 44.

73. Gee, *Photography of the Fifties*, 3. Motherwell referred to his fellow members of the New York School as "apolitical, like cats" (Kozloff, "Interview with Robert Motherwell," 37). The structural turn away from documentary may explain why the majority of critics locate Siskind's importance to the medium in his work of the early 1940s, which anticipates the coalescence of abstract expressionism in the New York School of painting; at that point (so the story goes), Siskind began single-handedly "to define an issue central to photography's leap from self-assigned functionalism" (Turner, "Aaron Siskind," 1). Kao ("Personal Vision in Aaron Siskind's Documentary Practice," 23) accounts for this shift with more contextual alertness: in her reading, it was the "complexity of collaborative Feature Group productions, coupled with the quagmire surrounding the manner in which different framing contexts transformed the photographers' theses," that led Siskind to produce "his highly personal independent photo-series."

74. Driskell, in "Evolution of a Black Aesthetic, 1920–1950," traces the force of this imperative as it descends from the Renaissance era, and argues that it essentially aborts the development of organic cultural institutions, as artists attempting to create new, hybrid, and experimental forms are rejected by cultural gatekeepers still committed to uplift or exposé. See also Stange, " 'Illusion Complete within Itself,' " 71.

75. See "Two Women, Mannikin's Hand," in Galassi, *Roy DeCarava: A Retrospective*, plate 144.

76. Natanson, *Black Image in the New Deal*, 46–47.

77. Alinder, "Chronology," and DeCarava, "Pages from a Notebook," give useful accounts of DeCarava's activities in Harlem and in support of Black Arts projects.

78. Galassi, "Introduction," in *Roy DeCarava: A Retrospective*, 20. Against such readings, Erina Duganne ("Looking In / Looking Out: Race and Subjectivity in Photography," PhD diss., University of Texas, Austin, 2004, 172–219) likewise emphasizes the complexity of DeCarava's responses to the imperatives of racial representation and to the institutional contexts in which he was exhibited (or not).

79. Galassi, "Introduction," in *Roy DeCarava: A Retrospective*, 20.

80. Roy DeCarava, application for Guggenheim Fellowship, cited in Galassi, "Introduction," in *Roy DeCarava: A Retrospective*, 19.

81. Ibid.; DeCarava, "Photography, Photographers, and a Gallery," DeCarava clippings file, Schomburg Center for Research in Black Culture; DeCarava, untitled, DeCarava clippings file, Schomburg Center for Research in Black Culture.

82. DeCarava, application for Guggenheim Fellowship, quoted in Galassi, "Introduction," in *Roy DeCarava: A Retrospective*, 19.

83. DeCarava's deft weaving of opposed aesthetic rhetorics, responsive to changing contexts of production, is a defining characteristic of his work. In the early 1980s, his negotiation of racial identitarianism becomes foremost in his interviews and public statements. At this point, the terms of raced cultural production have altered so profoundly that the rhetoric of documentary and of Lockean social instrumentality becomes newly powerful; "the black artist" is identified as one "whose concerns are about justice," in distinction to "the white artist," who "pursues an art that is not particularly relevant, in the sense that it deals with matters of form, matters of tonality, matters of shape" and "refers only to itself" (Miller, "'If It Hasn't Been One of Color,'" 847). Canonical readings of DeCarava's career—including Galassi's ("Introduction," in *Roy DeCarava: A Retrospective*) and Stange's ("'Illusion Complete within Itself'")—have not located his responses to questions about black aesthetics or his relations to socially conscious and formalist practices in changing contexts, from the emergent civil rights era through varied identitarian movements and visual postmodernism.

84. DeCarava to Minor White, quoted in Stange, "'Illusion Complete within Itself,'" 79.

85. So suggests Stange, "'Illusion Complete within Itself,'" 87.

86. Rampersad, *Life of Langston Hughes*, 2:249.

87. See Hughes, *Langston Hughes and the Chicago Defender*; Ottley, *Lonely Warrior*; Strother, "Black Image in the *Chicago Defender*."

88. Hughes, "Feet Live Their Own Life," in *Simple Omnibus*, 1. Perhaps the visual contexts of the sketches merely heightened the authenticity effects of Hughes's vernacular. Hughes himself noted retrospectively that "I cannot truthfully state, as some novelists do at the beginnings of their books, that these stories are about 'nobody living or dead'" ("Foreword: Who Is Simple?" in *Simple Omnibus*, vii), and Rampersad (*Life of Langston Hughes*, 2:173) suggests that certain turns of phrase, and more, were actually provided by Hughes's secretary, Nate White, another man of the streets; Hughes admitted that "Some of the Simple works . . . may be laid at his door," while White is quoted as claiming that Hughes "pretty much gave me a free hand" in composition.

89. Rampersad, *Life of Langston Hughes*, 2:66.

90. Hughes, *I Wonder as I Wander*, 200–201; Hughes, "Pictures More than Pictures: The Work of Manuel Bravo and Cartier-Bresson," 6 March 1935, LHP, Box 329, Folder 5369. Galassi (*Henri Cartier-Bresson*, 19) notes that this period in Cartier-Bresson's production is "one of the great, concentrated episodes in modern art."

91. Hughes, "Church for the Deaf"; Hughes, "Backstage"; Hughes and Alston, "Atlanta."

92. Meltzer, the son of Jewish immigrants from Austria, attended Columbia University beginning in 1932 and studied with Franz Boas, Ruth Benedict, and John Dewey; he remained friendly with Hughes for the remainder of the latter's life, and in 1967 they coauthored another picture book, *Black Magic: A Pictorial History of the African-American in the Performing Arts*.

93. Brewer, "Slavery Fills Many Pages in New Book," reprinted in Dace, *Langston Hughes*, 515.

94. Marion Palfi, letter to Sue Van Voorhies, 28 July 1973, MPP, AG46:2/25; Sorgenfrei, "Marion Palfi," 7–8. The networks linking Palfi to other projects with which I am concerned—her career as a portrait photographer in Berlin and Amsterdam during the 1930s; her work for the journal *Deutsche Illustrierte* in 1935, in the context of politically self-conscious uses of photo-text; her work at *Ebony* (including her cover shot for its first issue in December 1945; her contribution to "My Best Negro Picture" in 1947, also featuring Gordon Parks; and her work on an October 1946 photo-essay on Hughes to which Michael Carter/Milton Smith contributed); the Rosenwald Fellowship project for which Hughes wrote a recommendation; her inclusion in the Museum of Modern Art's exhibits In and Out of Focus in 1948 and Family of Man in 1955; and her membership and teaching at the Photo League through 1949—bear more consideration than I can give.

95. Langston Hughes, "Ups and Downs," MPA, AG46:3/62 (holograph MS). Rampersad, *Life of Langston Hughes*, 2:128, mentions Palfi only in passing as "a professional photographer" who "had been befriended by Hughes and other blacks after her arrival after the war as a refugee from Europe."

96. Hughes, "Ups and Downs," n.p.

97. Galassi ("Introduction," in *Roy DeCarava: A Retrospective*, 27) comments on the "available light revolution" in relation to DeCarava's aims. But as DeCarava's remarks in Miller, "'If It Hasn't Been One of Color,'" 848–49, make clear, his resistance to artificial light is both overdetermined and resistant to identitarian claims about the value of "blackness" per se: "There may be some black photographers who think in that one to one relationship, but I don't" (849).

98. The resonances of the Family of Man show, and of its status as a context for DeCarava's emergent work, are too complex to address here. Although attacked as cold war propaganda and an exercise in sentimentality, it remains, in terms of attendance records, catalogue sales, and popular influence, one of the most successful exhibitions in the history of U.S. photography. Sandeen, *Picturing an Exhibition*, 54–72, provides a balanced, comprehensive account both of critiques of the show and of its aims and achievements, and usefully frames some of its most consequential reviews, including Barthes's discussion of the exhibition's refusal of "the determining weight of History" in "Great Family of Man," 100–101, and Macdonald's belated but trenchant invocation of the exhibit in his influential jeremiad, "Masscult and Midcult II," 600n5, in which the show typifies "the Midcult mind" and its search for didactic authority.

99. DeCarava, untitled, DeCarava clippings file, Schomburg Center for Research in Black Culture.

100. DeCarava to Minor White, 21 November 1944, cited in Stange, "'Illusion Complete within Itself,'" 80.

101. Deschin, "Nineteen in Exhibit."

102. For a full list of shows at APG, see Galassi, "A Photographer's Gallery Schedule of Exhibitions," in *Roy DeCarava: A Retrospective*, 269–70. Rosenblum ("From Protest

to Affirmation") notes that the generation of Photo League photographers emerging in the postwar moment—including Bernstein, Weiner, Morris Engel, and Sol Libsohn—had been urged in their practice there to consider how photographs "convey their meanings through formal structure as well as subject matter, expression, and gesture"; at large, she suggests how interpenetrated the categories of "documentary" and "aesthetics" had become for photographers working in evolving documentary modes (50).

103. Miller, "'If It Hasn't Been One of Color,'" 851.

104. Galassi ("Introduction," in *Roy DeCarava: A Retrospective*, 20 and n. 12) offers Siskind as a foil—and perhaps a straw man—for his reading of the specific qualities and aims of DeCarava's work.

105. As virtually all of DeCarava's curators and readers have noted, he took a leadership role during the 1968 boycott by Harlem artists of the Metropolitan Museum of Art's photographic exhibition Harlem on My Mind. I discuss that show and DeCarava's response at the conclusion of chapter 5.

106. Galassi, "Introduction," in *Roy DeCarava: A Retrospective*, 20.

107. See Alinder, *Roy DeCarava, Photographs*, plate 11.

108. DeCarava, "Pages from a Notebook," 49. See, for example, "Two Boys in Vacant Lot" (1949), "Child in Window, Clothesline" (1950), "Woman Walking, Above" (1950), and "Boy Looking in Doorway" (1950), reprinted in Alinder, *Roy DeCarava, Photographs*, plates 2, 3, 5, 6.

109. Urban League of Greater New York, "The League Lens," in *Annual Report of the Urban League of Greater New York, 1947*, n.p. (microfilm), Schomburg Center for Research in Black Culture.

110. Halstead, *Harlem Stirs*, 57–59.

111. Stephany, "Interview with Aaron Siskind," 44.

112. See DeCarava, "Gittel," and Galassi, *Roy DeCarava: A Retrospective*, plate 71.

113. Miller, "'If It Hasn't Been One of Color,'" 853.

114. DeCarava to Minor White, 21 November 1955, cited in Stange, "'Illusion Complete within Itself,'" 80.

Chapter Two

1. Fabre, *Unfinished Quest*, 95, 116, 133.

2. Wallace, *Constructing the Black Masculine*, 135.

3. Ibid., 41, 44.

4. Wright, *Native Son*, 149. Hereafter, page numbers appear parenthetically in the text.

5. Fabre, *Unfinished Quest*, 25. This escapade, judged "amusing" by Fabre, cost the family its apartment; after an altercation between Wright's deeply religious mother and the owner of the building, who was also the proprietor of the brothel, they were evicted. On Wright's "career in voyeurism," Edith Anderson (*Love in Exile*, 32–33) insists on

Wright's activities in postwar Paris as a "Peeping Tom" who offers her a pair of binoculars to train on neighboring apartments and declares "gleefully" that he could "watch for hours."

6. Wright, "The Ethics of Living Jim Crow," in *Uncle Tom's Children*, xxii.

7. Ibid., xv.

8. Fabre, *Unfinished Quest*, 66, 58. Stepto shrewdly contrasts the version of this experience recounted in *Black Boy* with the theater scene of *Native Son*: for Stepto (*From Behind the Veil*, 133), *Black Boy* "revises a major moment in *Native Son* by affirming that arresting images of illiterate immobility and literate mobility may be contextualized in the same symbolic space." Stepto's emphasis is on "spatial expressions of social structure" (169); the play of visuality within these spaces is, I would argue, a crucial aspect of the experience and of its representations.

9. Wright, *Uncle Tom's Children*, 234.

10. Ibid., 383.

11. Such was the description given by *PM*'s founding editor, Ralph Ingersoll, quoted in Milkman, *PM*, 41.

12. Milkman, *PM*, 42–45. Wright had already been associated with fellow author and Southerner Caldwell. Fabre (*Unfinished Quest*, 130) notes that in February 1937 the editors of *Partisan Review* made Wright a member of the journal's editorial board, on which Caldwell also served. Although the position was honorary, the striving Wright would surely have been familiar with Caldwell's celebrity and his work. By 1940, Wright had become close to *PM*'s book review editor, Roger Pippett; according to Fabre (*Unfinished Quest*, 265), *PM* remained throughout the 1940s Wright's favored venue for reviews.

13. Wright, "Blueprint for Negro Writing," 48.

14. Federal Writers' Project of the Works Progress Administration, *New York Panorama*, "Fantastic Metropolis" portfolio, n.p.

15. *WPA Guide to New York City*, "Sugar Hill" and "Lenox Avenue," n.p. (following 364). Bold (*WPA Guides*, 112–15) argues for a marked difference in effect between the two guidebooks, evidenced in particular by one of the *Guide*'s Harlem images, which offers "comparisons" that are "much more complicated than the regulatory contrasts of *New York Panorama*."

16. Bold, *WPA Guides*, 115.

17. Walker, *Richard Wright*, 124.

18. Jurca (*White Diaspora*, 111–15) reads *Native Son* as an imaginative counterpart to Cayton's rebuttals of classic Chicago School sociological analyses of urban migration and expansion; produced in dialogue with Cayton's insistence on the inequality of mobility along racial lines, "*Native Son* was written during and responds to a crisis of geographical immobility" (113). Walker (*Richard Wright*, 122) claims to have provided Wright, at his request, with "every clipping published in the Chicago [daily] newspapers [including *PM*] on the Nixon case" for "over a year."

19. Rowley (*Richard Wright*, 189) is Wright's only biographer to mention this event; she identifies the photographer as Frank Marshall Davis, author of the critically esteemed poetry collections *Black Man's Verse* (1935) and *I Am the American Negro* (1937), editor of the *Atlanta Daily World* (the first financially successful African American daily newspaper in the United States), and executive editor of the Associated Negro Press of Chicago. Davis also founded a camera club of Chicago not unlike the Photo League in its organization and mission; his commitment to photojournalism as a cultural genre and to the camera as an instrument for exposure and expression is one index to Wright's developing interests. Wright's account of the visit is given in the unpublished manuscript "Chicago," RWP, Box 5, Folder 78.

20. Graham, "Photography: TLRs."

21. Wallace, *Constructing the Black Masculine*, 47.

22. "Negro Hailed as New Writer," in Kinnamon and Fabre, *Conversations with Richard Wright*, 28.

23. Rowley, *Richard Wright*, 190.

24. "Put Youth in Focus: National Photo Contest for Young People," brochure, 15 May–30 November, 1940, RWP, Box 118, Folder 1921. Denning (*Cultural Front*, 156–69) offers *Friday* as one example of a broadly "laborist" Popular Front culture; *Friday* was not only signally successful in representing the "common sense" of its second-generation working-class and ethnic constituency but also in yoking Popular Front politics to the forms and figures of mass culture (156). Although Denning meticulously documents *Friday*'s strong interest in Hollywood film (which was, he notes, "everywhere" [158]), he underreads the importance of photographic activity to the journal, and—given his attempts to reframe Popular Front culture outside the frame of the "depression documentary," as a set of activities that exceeds documentary and its (for him) defining "failures of narrative imagination" (119)—perhaps generally. *Friday* not only "adopted the pin-up aesthetic of the picture magazines" (94); it invited readers to submit images of their own locales and situations for reading the journal (thus suturing the image-world, collectivist practice, and photography), and it made investigative photojournalism central to its mission.

25. Wallace, *Constructing the Black Masculine*, 134.

26. In his notes on Levitt's show at the Museum of Modern Art, Wright refers to work by and on Levitt published in *Harper's Bazaar* (July 1944), *U.S. Camera* (May 1943), the *Magazine of Art* (May 1943), *VVV* (June 1942), *View* (January 1943), and *Minicam* (March 1943; January and September 1944); he may also have known the 1940 show at the Museum of Modern Art titled The Artist as Reporter, which was sponsored by *PM*, as well as commentary such as that by Steiner ("Wall and Sidewalk Drawings") and Soby ("Two Photographs by Helen Levitt"). That Wright actively desired to join his own work on Harlem youth and crime to Levitt's dynamic, allusive work suggests his ambition to develop the authorial and expressive vectors opened by *Black Voices*. For further discussion of Levitt's Harlem work, see Phillips and

Hambourg, *Helen Levitt*, 23–27; for Wright's notes on that work, see RWP, Box 86, Folder 1013.

27. See Wright, "A Recommendation," review of an exhibition of pictures of children by Helen Levitt, 1943, RWP, Box 86, Folder 1013.

28. Ibid. In particular, Wright directs his recommendation to those who may have reservations about photography as an art form, noting that Levitt's work provides a means of overcoming such reservations.

29. There is no extant record of the proceedings, but ACA's mission and history suggest Wright's involvement in fairly sophisticated discussions of photography at the crossroads of documentary and fine art, socially conscious representation and formalism, and more. ACA (undocumented, for example, in Denning, *Cultural Front*) was a major proponent of social realism in the visual arts; its second exhibition, Selections from the John Reed Club, not only defined the direction of the gallery but established its commitment to support immigrant, women, African American, Jewish, Latino, and non-U.S. artists by way of serving as "the people's gallery." ACA was also a motive force in organizing the earliest meetings of the American Artists' Congress, whose infrastructure would influence the Federal Arts Project and the WPA. On the exhibition and symposium in which Wright participated, titled "They Honor Their Sons," see Thomas, *Lisette Model*, 85.

30. Fabre, *Unfinished Quest*, 174.

31. Howe, "Black Boys and Native Sons."

32. Rosskam, "Introduction," in *Washington: Nerve Center*, n.p. See also Doud, interview with Edwin and Louise Rosskam.

33. Saretzky, "She Worked Her Head Off," 7. For discussion of Rosskam's work outside the FSA context and of the independence of his photographic practices at the apex of the FSA's power, see Saretzky, "Documenting Diversity."

34. Walker, *Richard Wright*, 119.

35. Munz, "New Negro."

36. For a useful survey of the photo-text tradition developing across national boundaries in the 1930s, see Parr and Badger, *Photobook*.

37. Eyman, *Print the Legend*, 214; Bristol, *Stories from Life*. Shloss (*In Visible Light*, 212–13) details Steinbeck's habit of "trailing" Dorothea Lange, making use of both the photographs and the documentation she and Taylor produced in shaping *Grapes of Wrath*.

38. Ward, "Representing Crisis"; Cayton, "Wright's New Book More than a Study of Social Status."

39. Davis, "Richard Wright's Powerful Narrative Beautifully Illustrated in New Book"; Thompson, "Books of the Times."

40. "March of the Negro."

41. Edwin Seaver, "Readers and Writers," transcript of radio broadcast, 23 December 1941, cited in Kinnamon and Fabre, *Conversations with Richard Wright*, 43.

42. See, for example, "March of the Negro," which claims, "If you have read Erskine Caldwell's *You Have Seen Their Faces* you will want this," and Reddick, "Negro and Jew," on Wright and Rosskam's as "a picture book of the Bourke-White type."

43. There are significant recent exceptions. Griffin considers *Twelve Million Black Voices* in the context of Wright's ongoing interests in migration experience and subjectivity; her relatively brief reading focuses in some detail on the play between literary and visual images throughout the text, which, she notes, alternatively "agree" with and "resist" one another (*"Who Set You Flowin'?"* 77, 76). In particular, she argues for a gap between images and text in which the specific qualities of Wright's narrative voice— critically distant, "of the people but beyond them" (78)—can be gauged. More broadly, Stange's brief but indispensable rereading of *Black Voices* (in "Black Chicago in Pictures," in *Bronzeville*, viii–xxviii) argues for the importance of the volume and for the power of exceptional FSA camera work (most notably Russell Lee's) to "stand out even now in our dense and pervasive visual culture," even as in the moment of its production it "signaled a new visual aesthetic at the dawn of mass-circulated photojournalism" (xv). Joseph Entin, "Richard Wright's Photo-Politics" (paper delivered at the American Studies Association, November 2004), offers a localized but suggestive argument for Wright's understanding of the affirmative possibilities opened by the photo-textual form and the artist's self-conscious manipulation of image-text relations. Jeff Allred ("From Eye to We") accounts persuasively for the text as one that exploits photo documentary conventions in part by way of critiquing the "emphasis on collective identity" that is characteristic of the era—and, it might be added, of black cultural production more generally (550); his reading also focuses on images such as the redoubled portrait of sharecroppers, with attention to Wright's complex negotiation of collective history, pedagogical authority, and representational practices for reimagining the distribution of cultural and other goods.

44. Wright, *Twelve Million Black Voices*, 12, 13; hereafter cited parenthetically by page number in the text.

45. See Stange, *Bronzeville*, xxiv, for detail on the volume's visual strategies.

46. Stange (*Bronzeville*, xxv) notes the consistency of *Black Voices*' visual strategies with those of other volumes produced by Rosskam; the same strategies have other implications, I am suggesting, in the context of Wright's concurrent projects.

47. Fabre, *Unfinished Quest*, 187; Walker, *Richard Wright*, 123–24.

48. Walker, *Richard Wright*, 171.

49. See *Twelve Million Black Voices*, 104. Wright's image, for whatever reason, was dropped from subsequent editions of the volume.

50. Walker, *Richard Wright*, 171.

51. Stange (*Bronzeville*, xxiv) notes that Rosskam sent Wright both images and dummies of page spreads to aid in his completion of the "urban chapters" of the text. The evidence of manuscript materials suggests that Wright thought extensively about image-text relations; up until the final stages of publication, he continued working with proof sheets sized at longer than normal length and absent page breaks, apparently so

as to facilitate discussions about the selection and placement of photos. See RWP, Box 62, Folders 731–32, and Box 63, Folder 733.

52. The so-called Black Belt thesis of the Communist Party, articulated at the Sixth Cominterm Congress in 1928, defined "the Negro question" as a matter of political nationalism, and became central (at least rhetorically) to the work of the Party in the United States. On the debate at the Congress, and the evolving fortunes of the nation-within-the-nation doctrine, see Solomon, *Cry Was Unity*, 68–91; on the policy viewed in the 1940s as a political failure, see Jonas, *Freedom's Sword*, 142–43.

53. Natanson, *Black Image in the New Deal*, 92; I have relied throughout on Natanson's incisive account (89–100) of Shahn's work in Pulaski County. Katzman ("Ben Shahn's New York," 26) links Shahn's work on "the 'Negro Question'" to a "Jewish empathy for blacks and their struggle for civil rights"; she also notes the scarcity of Shahn's work in Harlem—which might be read as an attempt on his part to image African Americans in less iconographically freighted sites of labor and experience.

54. Natanson, *Black Image in the New Deal*, 90, 92.

55. Ibid., 92.

56. Ben Shahn, cited in Natanson, *Black Image in the New Deal*, 93.

57. "Inheritors of Slavery," corrected typescript, RWP, Box 63, Folder 737.

58. As Griffin (*"Who Set You Flowin'?"* 75) notes, "The kitchenette is the dominant visual and literary image" in the central section of *Black Voices*, "a synecdoche for all the forces that act in the construction of a black urban dweller." Stange (*Bronzeville*, 23–27) reproduces Rosskam's working notes in the form of a "caption" as well as several kitchenette images by Rosskam and Russell Lee; the contrast between these images and the shot of the meditative youth in *Black Voices* is instructive. The sequence of images of children outside kitchenette tenements from which this shot is drawn is available in the Library of Congress Online Prints and Photographs Catalogue, Farm Security Administration/Office of War Information Black and White Negatives, posted online at http://lcweb2.loc.gov/pp/fsaquery.html.

59. Trachtenberg, *Reading American Photographs*, 26.

60. Federal Bureau of Investigation, "Richard Nathaniel Wright."

61. See, for example, Fabre, *Unfinished Quest*, 240, on the protagonist of the first novel Wright completed after *Black Voices*, featuring a "classic existential hero" whose "color [is] . . . no longer important."

62. Draft notes, *Twelve Million Black Voices*, RWP, Box 63, Folder 734.

63. Wright, quoted in Fabre, *Unfinished Quest*, 356.

64. Burns, "They're Not Uncle Tom's Children," 21, 22.

65. Ibid., 21.

66. Ibid.

67. Ibid.

68. Ibid., 22.

69. Cartier-Bresson, *Decisive Moment*, [14].

70. This group of texts included *The Color Curtain* (1956), *Pagan Spain* (1957), a compilation of essays, and a planned but uncompleted study, "French West Africa," of the peoples and cultures of West Africa. Virginia Whatley Smith, "Introduction," reads these texts as grounds for the claim for Wright as a pioneer of postcolonial thought. Hereafter, quotations from the American edition, *Black Power: A Record of Reactions*, will be cited parenthetically in the text.

71. Appiah describes Wright's reading of Gold Coast Africa as exemplary of a "paranoid hermeneutic" ("Long Way from Home," 181): because Wright rejects a logic of racial identification, his reactions "oscillate between condescension and paranoia" (180). Chiwengo ("Gazing through the Screen," 27) argues that Wright is guilty of historicizing "not his encounter with Africans but the development and rise to manhood of the African American." Shankar ("Richard Wright's *Black Power*") reads Wright's text as a travel narrative embedded in, and indebted to, the colonial context, whose rote assignment of value makes irremediable the gap between West and Other. Similarly, Cobb ("Richard Wright and the Third World," 230) describes Wright's initial responses to Africa as composed of "hostility, sympathy, repugnance, and condescension." Scholars grappling with broader histories of response to modernity, diaspora, and racial history tend to read Wright more sympathetically—most prominently Gilroy, who argues plangently for Wright's productive discomfort with his structural role as marginal figure (*Black Atlantic*, 151). Reilly argues that Wright's turn to travel writing enacts a productive rejection of his "individualist" philosophy, an "entry into conscious history" via the "Third World" ("Richard Wright and the Art of Non-Fiction," 519). Hakutani (*Richard Wright and Racial Discourse*) claims that Wright's account of Africa is balanced, predicated on a search for commonalities and points of convergence; Pratt argues that Wright "directly set himself to work parodying and reworking the inherited tropology" of colonial travel narrative, and thereby achieves a rich "ambivalent complexity" (*Imperial Eyes*, 222). Of particular interest to me is the work of Lowe, who argues that Wright's late travelogues "pionee[r] a new, hybrid kind of literary/scientific work" connected with cultural anthropology ("Richard Wright as Traveler/Ethnographer," 128), to which photographic images and evidence are important resources.

72. Wright, *White Man, Listen!* xvi–xvii.

73. An important recent rereading on these lines is that by Gaines (*American Africans in Ghana*, 52–68), who understands Wright's work on Africa as part of a collective effort to rethink "modernity" for black subjects, and argues that his often-critiqued political interpretations are nuanced by Wright's "speculative tone" (56–57). This speculative mode, I argue, is closely linked with Wright's photographic acts, and with a broader set of experiments with his own self-representation in various sites of encounter with uneven modernity.

74. For extended commentary by Wright on his own resistance to racial "feeling," see *Black Power: A Record of Reactions*, 119, 269, 275, 280. Wright emphasizes his disconnection on the grounds of spiritual practice (as in the moment when a cook in a suburban colonial household tells Wright, "I'm afraid, sar, that your ancestors do not

know you now," 215) and bodily hexis alike (as when he tries to imitate the virile spitting he encounters, "before my mirror in my hotel room with the door locked," and succeeds only "in soiling the front of my shirt," 316). Far from racial or political solidarity, Wright anticipates forms of evasion and resistance appropriate to West Africa writ as a "fifth column, a corps of saboteurs and spies of Europe" (cited in Fabre, *From Harlem to Paris*, 192).

75. According to Fabre (*Unfinished Quest*, 399), Wright boarded the ship that would bring him back to Paris from the Gold Coast with more than 1,500 photographic prints in hand; a number of them are available via the Beinecke's "Digital Images Online," posted online at http://beinecke.library.yale.edu/dl_crosscollex/.

The published text as well as Wright's travel notes suggest his numerous contrivances—including developing and printing negatives in makeshift equipment cobbled together from purchases in Accra's market—for producing images for use during his travels.

76. Lowe ("Richard Wright as Traveler/Ethnographer," 140–41) details the extent of Wright's work on images—their production, collection, captioning, and cropping—in connection with *Pagan Spain*, arguing that "photographic work was surely one of the mechanisms Wright proposed to use to counter his linguistic difficulty" (in this case, with Spanish). For Lowe, Wright's "fascinat[ion]" with "the interplay of words and images" (142) is explicitly connected with the late turn in his career, and with shifts in the discipline of cultural anthropology, in particular the rise of postcolonial modes of participancy-observation; this fascination, I argue, has a longer history for Wright, and links him with other cultural projects.

77. Wright apparently provided captions—many of them drawn from the text of *Black Power: A Record of Reactions*—to his British publishers; both the image selection and the captions tend to depart from the narrative's emphasis on failed encounters and the fragility of the documentary exchange. In the published image of a compound near Accra's market, for example, both the women and children of the group return the camera's gaze with friendly interest, but the image appears in the text just after Wright's account of an incident in the market in which he attempts to buy a pan for concocting "a chemical solution in which to develop" his film (*Black Power*, opp. 84). The economic exchange is short-circuited when Wright is asked, "What you do with pan, Massa? Women wanna know"; his denial that he will "buy it for wife," "cook chop," or even "make peepee in pan" results in an "outburst of laughter"—that is, another howl of black laughter (*Black Power*, 84). Throughout, with few exceptions, the images chosen for inclusion emphasize an evidentiary or illustrative function; the full range of images in Wright's archive, however, suggests other intentions.

78. For a full listing of prints, negatives, and contact sheets made in connection with Wright's travels to the Gold Coast, see RWP, Box 28, Folders 348–59, and Box 29, Folders 360–70.

79. Chiwengo, "Gazing through the Screen," 33.

80. Ibid.

81. On the editorial processes that resulted in the omission of images from the American edition, and Wright's involvement in producing images for the British edition, see Fabre, *Unfinished Quest*, 404, 406; Smith, "Richard Wright's Passage to Indonesia"; and Weiss, "Para Usted."

82. Nietzsche, *On the Genealogy of Morals*, 35–36.

83. Wright's implication in the force of such thrusts is made even more evident when the reader recalls how closely he has identified with the stool as a kind of poetic device; see particularly *Black Power: A Record of Reactions*, 229, 299, 314, 345.

84. See, for example, Moore, "'No Street Numbers in Accra,'" 59, which attempts to recuperate the open letter as "a revelation of Wright's own human condition," a "confess[ion]" of "what he tried to achieve in his own life as a writer."

Chapter Three

1. REP, P&P, Box 4, Folder "From wallet 1930s."

2. Jackson (*Ralph Ellison*, 178–81, 198–236) offers a detailed account of Ellison's indebtedness to Wright during this period.

3. Callahan, "Introduction," xv; Ellison, "'A Completion of Personality': A Talk with Ralph Ellison," in *Collected Essays of Ralph Ellison*, 797 (hereafter cited parenthetically as CE).

4. See, in particular, O'Mealley, *Jazz Cadence of American Culture*; O'Mealley, *Craft of Ralph Ellison*, 92–97; O'Mealley, *Living with Music*; Porter, *Jazz Country*, 74; Callahan, *In the African-American Grain*; and Callahan, "Frequencies of Eloquence."

5. Ellison's work, in this rendering, becomes the culminating chapter in a cultural genealogy that identifies vernacular music as a generative metaphor for democracy, or what Baker (*Blues, Ideology, and Afro-American Literature*, 13) famously calls "the *All* of American culture."

6. Negatives, contact sheets, and prints of Ellison's author portraits of Mary McCarthy, Frances Steegmuller, Langston Hughes, and others are included in the Ellison archive, along with portraits of McCarthy, Hughes, and Chester Himes. There are also substantial materials documenting Ellison's photographic work on exhibition and sale catalogues for museums and fine arts brokers, including numerous images of African sculptures and ceremonial objects. See REP, P&P, Boxes 4 and 5.

7. Never published in its intended form, "Harlem Is Nowhere" (CE, 320–28) became the penultimate essay of *Shadow and Act*. Ellison's notes and shooting script for Parks survive in REP, MS, Box 100, Folder "Harlem Is Nowhere." For an account of Ellison's collaboration with Parks, based on access to restricted archival materials, see Jackson, *Ralph Ellison*, 372–73. For an excellent account of Parks's work in the ambit of *Life*, and of the tension between his status as a participant within the African American communities he so powerfully imaged and his own ideal of "objectivity"—a tension we might see as analogous to that in Ellison's career between his commitment to deseg-

regation and his embrace of representational conventions aligned with the cultures of segregation—see Prosser, *Light in the Dark Room*, 89–122.

8. Ellison's private response to *Twelve Million Black Voices* suggests as much. A letter to Wright of 3 November 1941, RWP, Box 97, Folder "Ralph Ellison," strikingly appropriates the text's communal third-person voice to describe the distinctly personal sense of trauma and possibility occasioned by its images: "I think it [the sense of himself and Wright as 'brothers'] is because this past which filters through your book has always been tender and aching within us. We are the ones who had no comforting amnesia of childhood, and for whom the trauma of passing from the country to the city of destruction brought no anesthesia of unconsciousness. . . . We are not the numbed, but the seething."

9. Ellison, *Invisible Man*, 36; hereafter cited parenthetically in the text.

10. A judicious version of the received view on this issue is given by Sundquist (*Cultural Contexts*, 16): "Although Ellison shares with a number of novelists of the 1930s and 1940s an interest in photographic realism, he infused documentary fiction with a heightened sense that the writer's distortion of, and improvisation on, the observed world could bring out more effectively the moral and psychological density of its internal meaning."

11. Warren, *So Black and Blue*.

12. Warren's language, *So Black and Blue*, for naming the historically conditioned limitations of Ellison's work is itself strikingly dependent on metaphors of sight and insight. With respect to the body of essays that came to stand in for a successfully completed novel after *Invisible Man*, "what Ellison's work . . . demonstrated was that attempting to represent 'the Negro' outside of the political realm of direct representation—whether one did so literally, sociologically, philosophically, administratively, or philanthropically—was to enter a hall of mirrors" (20); short of more profound effects, the essays achieve probing attention to the ways "that race shaped and refracted American reality" (20). In summation, Warren argues, "each essay . . . constitutes a critical snapshot of the way that ascribed racial status refracts and is refracted through some of the central issues of particular historical moments" in such a way that "looking at and through Ellison" is "simultaneously a way of looking at and through ourselves" (23). Warren's argument reifies as metaphor a practice of looking, whose specific purchases on history and critical production are thus obscured. Ellison, I argue, understood these very tropes as historically conditioned; to recognize that he appropriated and developed them at a specific moment in the life of photographic response allows for a clearer sense of what such metaphors imply or commit us to—and what they perhaps evade.

13. Alternative, that is, to such foundational readings as Nadel, *Invisible Criticism*, 1–26.

14. Emerson, "Goethe; or The Writer," in *Works of Ralph Waldo Emerson*, 7:251, 252.

15. DuBois, *Souls of Black Folk*, 4. The ubiquitously cited passage on the Negro as "a sort of seventh son, born with a veil, and gifted with second-sight in this American

world," has become, as Lewis ("Introduction," xv) notes, almost rote—a "standard epistemic devic[e]" for making sense of racial experience in the United States. This very familiarity has obscured the actual photographic incident that gives rise to DuBois's trope. Such photographic calling cards, which Oliver Wendell Holmes described as "the sentimental 'greenbacks' of civilization," remained in wide circulation during the 1870s, the era of DuBois's initiation. For discussion of the social implications and uses of *cartes de visite* and cabinet cards (in which Holmes is cited), see Taft, *Photography and the American Scene*, 143, and on the extended vogue of card portrait exchange into the Reconstruction era, 140–50, 323–35.

16. Jacobs, *Eye's Mind*, 146, reads this lens as "a representative of American social science" in its particular purchase on black Americans; "the photographic lens can be understood to suggest a measure of the aspiring visual mastery and the attendant violence which Ellison associated" with American sociology. Such a reading, I suggest, moves too quickly from the material fact of photographic practice and artifacts to figurative resonances.

17. In Ellison's archive, numerous materials document the variety of darkroom and photographic services he employed, including LECO Photo Services, 47th Street Photo, Central Hardware, the United Camera Exchange, and the Graphic Arts Photo Service. Their disparate locations, ranging from lower to upper Manhattan and from the East to the West Side, suggest how far Ellison carried his apparatus and his project as photographer, both literally and imaginatively.

18. See Elisofon, "Types of Camera."

19. See Ellison and Murray, *Trading Twelves*, facing page 134 (n.p.).

20. REP, P&P, Box 2.

21. Ibid.

22. Ellison, cited in Ellison and Murray, *Trading Twelves*, 118.

23. The standard account of the camera and the interwar left is Bezner, *Photography and Politics in America*; richly detailed, it stops at precisely the juncture—that of documentary conventions and emergent civil rights culture—I consider here.

24. The phrase was borrowed from Ellison's notes during oral histories he conducted as a writer at the New York branch of the Federal Writers' Project. For the full text of the interview, see Siskind, *Harlem Document*, 54–55.

25. Ellison, "Introduction," in *Invisible Man*, vi–vii.

26. Ellison and Murray, *Trading Twelves*, 113.

27. See Agee and Evans, *Let Us Now Praise Famous Men*, 398–401.

28. See, for example, the street images published in the portfolio included in Ellison and Murray, *Trading Twelves*, n.p.

29. See Livingston, *New York School*.

30. In *New York: Capital of Photography*, Kozloff connects photographic stances and camera styles with facts of social and ethnic origin—particularly what he calls (71) the Jewish Americans' "lovers' quarrel with assimilation." For an alternative reading of the Jewish American presence in photography, one that stresses not identification as a vec-

tor of response but a dynamics of self-staging and theatricality, see Blair, "Jewish America through the Lens." Other critical accounts include Coleman, "No Pictures"; Gilbert, *Illustrated Worldwide Who's Who*; and Moore and Moore, "Observant Jews."

31. Of interest with respect to Ellison's self-positioning on the cultural field is the discovery by Jackson ("Ralph Ellison's Invented Life") that Ellison's actual birth date was a year earlier than Ellison reported it; Jackson argues persuasively for a considerable freedom of self-invention afforded Ellison as a writer via this gesture of rebirth.

32. For two quite different accounts of the continuing power of the document as a tool of analysis and a means of encounter with respect to black culture and traditions, see hooks, "In Our Glory," and Wallace, *Dark Designs and Visual Culture*.

33. Model, LMA, Box 14, Notebook 2, 15.

34. REP, P&P, Box 4.

35. Roosevelt, "The Forgotten Man," in *Public Papers and Addresses*, 624. Ellison's relationship to the rapidly changing rhetorics of U.S. communism and socialism has been variously represented and contested, notably by Foley, "Reading Redness"; Watts, *Heroism and the Black Intellectual*; Jackson, *Ralph Ellison*, 198–236, 326–48; and Arnold Rampersad, in numerous conference papers drawn from his forthcoming biography of Ellison.

36. It is likely that the woman cut off in (and from) the wallet photo was Wright's first wife, Dhima Rose Meadman; Ellison served as best man at their wedding in 1939. Her incomplete removal from the picture, apparently not long in advance of Wright's subsequent divorce and remarriage in 1941, suggests any number of motives, not excluding Ellison's desire to frame his relationship with Wright as a version of dozens swapped in the exercise of image making.

37. Tate, "Notes on the Invisible Woman," 164. Waligora-Davis, "Riotous Discontent," gives a suggestive reading on the issue of gender and the evasion of racial feminization.

38. Maxwell, "'Creative and Cultural Lag,'" 63. Maxwell distances himself from the phenomenon he so aptly names; his reading takes pains both to show the overdetermination of such readings and to argue for the power of Ellison's uses, critical and novelistic, of the conditions of belatedness and "lag."

39. Baker (*Blues, Ideology, and Afro-American Literature*, 195) argues that the Trueblood episode, and all it connotes and signifies, confirm Ellison's commitment to the black underclass; a contesting view and a pointed summary of the debate are offered in Warren, So *Black and Blue*.

40. Trachtenberg (*Reading American Photographs*, 13) describes this effect as follows: "A copper plate coated with highly polished silver, bearing a floating image developed in fumes of mercury and toned in gold, the daguerreotype contained within itself the alchemical hierarchy of metals, from low to high, from base to noble. It also resembled a looking glass, another object charged with magical associations. By a slight shift of focus from the image to the surface on which it appears, beholders see their own reflections. A doubling of image upon image: the viewer's image, mobile and immediate,

superimposes itself upon the fixed daguerrean image. The effect was apparitional in another sense as well: at the merest tilt of the plate, the photographic image flickers away, fades into a shadowed negative of itself while still entangled in the living image of the beholder." On the photographic miniature—in daguerreotype, tintype, and an array of other reproductive forms—as a mode of redoubling the troubled indexicality and memory function of the image, see Batchen's remarkable "Ere the Substance Fade."

41. The importance at Tuskegee of the photograph, in all its manifestations, as an agency in the struggle for economic and civil rights was paramount. By 1905, Booker T. Washington had already begun laying the groundwork for the donation by Kodak magnate George Eastman of funds to establish a chair and department of photography. The first student to enroll in the new photography division in 1916 was P. H. Polk, who would later join the faculty as a professor of photography and whose studio portraits made at Tuskegee exemplified both the uplift ideologies and the histories of image management that defined the institution's culture. For examples of the kinds and uses of portrait images that typified Tuskegee culture from the late nineteenth century well into the twentieth, see Thompson, *Tuskegee University Then and Now*; on connections between daguerreotype portraiture and uplift ideologies, see Shaw and Shubert, *Portraits of a People*, 111–12, 118–21.

42. On the connections among daguerreotypes, magic, and the "black" arts, see Trachtenberg, *Reading American Photographs*, 12–14; on the social meanings and affective power of the miniature as a scale of experience and desire, see Stewart's classic reading, *On Longing*, 37–69. Also of interest in this connection is the work of Orvell (*Real Thing*, 73–102) on the duality of late nineteenth-century camera practices, designed both to direct attention to historical fact or material evidence and "to estrange" viewers from themselves and "from reality" (77).

43. Jackson, *Ralph Ellison*, 170–71.

44. The very word *section* resonates with the nomenclature of New Deal era programs, which were divided and subdivided into "project," "units," and "sections"— most famously, the Historical Section of the FSA.

45. Warren, *So Black and Blue*, 38.

46. A prime example of the distinctly managerial tone is Park's essay, "Education in Its Relation to Cultures" (1918), in *Race and Culture*, 261–83, featuring his assertion about the Negro as "the lady of the races" (280)—an assertion that struck Ellison both privately and in print as outrageous in its very matter-of-factness. Warren (*So Black and Blue*, 86–90) implies a managerial tone or stylistics in his discussion of Park's role in problematic constructions of "Negro literature" as the appropriate object of sociological inquiry and in the warrant for claims, on the part of white and black elites alike, to speak for the Negro.

47. Bourke-White's influence, it should be noted, had some surprising (and not only contestatory) results. Gordon Parks, the first African American photographer hired under the auspices of the FSA, the first African American photographer on staff at *Life* magazine, and later the maker of iconic counter-representations such as the film *Shaft*

(1971), continued to credit *You Have Seen Their Faces* as a key text that "opened my eyes to the possibility of using my camera as an instrument or a weapon" (quoted in Goldberg, *Margaret Bourke-White*, 193); long after his initial encounter with the text, her images "stayed in my mind" (Parks, *Voices in the Mirror*, 87).

48. Caldwell and Bourke-White, *You Have Seen Their Faces*, 11.

49. Bourke-White, "General Notes for Journal-American Article," cited in Silverman, *For the World to See*, 80. What Mitchell (*Picture Theory*, 296–97n12) describes as the "manipulative" force of Bourke-White and Caldwell's "legends" is particularly strong in the case of this image, which features evidence of the power of documentary iconography in the form of the newspapers lining the cabin's walls. Bourke-White herself notes, in the retrospective *Portrait of Myself*, 128, that in such spaces as this one she has "the uneasy feeling that if I explored around enough, I would find advertisements I had done myself."

50. Ellison's framing of the invisible man as subject to documentary protocols is itself usefully read via "An Extravagance of Laughter," first published in *Going to the Territory* in 1985. There, he describes being taken by Langston Hughes, "just weeks after my arrival in New York," to the Broadway stage version of Caldwell's *Tobacco Road* (CE, 615), where Caldwell's genius at "plac[ing] the yokelike anti-Negro stereotypes upon the necks of the whites" reduces Ellison to such vociferous laughter that he himself becomes a spectacle: viewers in the balcony begin "getting to their feet to gawk at me," as he endures a "soul-wracking agony of embarrassment" (CE, 649). In other words, Ellison too becomes the mediating figure and excluded middle of a racialized drama. But whereas the invisible man can respond to that predicament only with abjection and rage, Ellison describes his own experience as "redemptive," one for which he is "eternally grateful to Erskine Caldwell": "In a flash, time was telescoped and the imaginary assumed the lineaments of past experiences" (CE, 655). In that epiphanic, figuratively photographic moment, art and history, subjective truth and social experience, coincide.

51. Baker (*Blues, Ideology, and Afro-American Literature*, 176) claims that the Trueblood episode is exemplary within the novel in that it "generates its meanings in a dialogic relation with various systems of signs"; among these systems, I argue, photography is powerfully at work.

52. Ellison may also have known of Evans's commissioned portfolio of images made at the museum's groundbreaking exhibition in 1935 of African sculpture, which it showcased as art objects rather than ethnographic artifacts. In an unpublished memoir, Walker Evans's first wife, Isobel Story, describes their frequent exchanges with Ellison as part of the overlapping circles of artists, intellectuals, and leftists in New Deal era New York; thanks to Albert LaFarge for sharing this information.

53. *Anti-graphic* was the term coined by cultural impresario Lincoln Kirstein in his review of the American Photographs exhibition; see Kirstein, "Photographs of America," 192.

54. REP, P&P, Box 2.

55. Barthes, *Camera Lucida*, 5.

56. Sontag, *On Photography*, 61.

57. For a persuasive reading of this scene as emblematic of Ellison's investments in the material object as a source of dialectical thought, see Conner, "Litany of Things," especially 177–84.

58. Quoted in Barthes, *Camera Lucida*, 38. Kertész, a leading and brilliant exponent of the small-format camera aesthetic, is an apt analogue for Ellison; eschewing the deliberate, analytic description that resulted from larger formats, Kertész developed a stylistics aimed at elliptical representation, or what Szarkowski (*Looking at Photographs*, 92) calls a "lyric truth," wrested from documentary and broadly social contexts.

59. Ellison, "Eyewitness Story of Riot." For a reading of Ellison's two accounts of the riot in their distinctive contexts, see Waligora-Davis, "Riotous Discontent," 388–89.

60. Ellison's contact with Cartier-Bresson's work is a matter of cultural conjunction as well as specific contact. For detailed accounts of Cartier-Bresson's friendship and collaboration with Langston Hughes (including accounts of his extended stay with Hughes in Mexico in 1934) and his "research" in Harlem clubs, social venues, and radical political organizations, see Hughes, *I Wonder as I Wander*, 293–95, and Nabokov, *Bagazh*, 200–201. Clippings and other materials indicate that Ellison may have attended (and was certainly aware of) Cartier-Bresson's first retrospective exhibition at the Museum of Modern Art in 1947; his clippings files on Cartier-Bresson begin in the mid-1940s and span Ellison's lifetime.

61. Among them are a number of Cartier-Bresson's images as reproduced in *Life*'s regular "Speaking of Pictures" feature, the very title of which suggests an ekphrastic frame for Ellison's engagement.

62. For one version of such criticism, see chapter 2, note 64.

63. For a reproduction of this image, see Galassi, *Henri Cartier-Bresson*, plate 55.

64. Galassi (*Henri Cartier-Bresson*, 16) describes Cartier-Bresson's extended travels in Africa as "a further step in his personal revolt" from bourgeois life and the studio apprenticeship system. But Cartier-Bresson was hardly immune to modernist mythologies; he himself noted that "the Africa he saw was the Africa of Joseph Conrad's *Heart of Darkness* . . . and of Louis-Ferdinand Céline's *Journey to the End of the Night*" (quoted in Galassi, *Henri Cartier-Bresson*, 16).

65. Like Cartier-Bresson's work, Model's appeared in numerous venues known to Ellison. Her mannequin shots appeared in 1940 in *Cue*, a popular weekly devoted to documenting New York's cultural goings-on; they were also included in her first group show, held that year at the Museum of Modern Art, and appeared at the Photo League in 1941. Beginning shortly thereafter, Model also did extensive work in Harlem, where she conducted a survey of black youth for *Look* magazine and pursued work on a long-term project on jazz musicians, culture, and performance—almost surely on Ellison's radar—in collaboration with various Harlem performers as well as Langston Hughes. For details of Model's projects, see Thomas, *Lisette Model*.

66. See Fabre, *Unfinished Quest*, 258–59, 265; and chapter 2 in this book.

67. For reproductions of these images, see Thomas, *Lisette Model*, 28–29, 38–39, 78–79, 86–89.

68. Model, cited in Thomas, *Lisette Model*, 101. See also ibid., 100, on Hearst's rejection of Model's images of dancer Pearl Primus, and more broadly of "anything that did not mirror middle White America."

69. See, for example, "Harlem after a Night of Rioting"; "Harlem Toll: 6 Dead, 543 Hurt, 500 Jailed"; "Looters at Work"; and "Some of the Damage in Harlem."

70. "Male and Female Vandals Blitz Harlem in Sunday [Melee]."

71. The *Amsterdam News*, 7 August 1943, 1, accompanied another of its mannequin images with the caption, "Fortunate is it that the above are not demolished human forms. But it could have been, because the 'mob on parade' last Sunday night spared almost nothing except human lives. . . . The above photo shows 'raped' dummy models in front of Blumstein, Harlem's largest department store."

72. I invoke the classic formulation of metaphor and metonymy as tropes—and indeed as organizing principles of cognition and expression—asserted in Jakobson's seminal 1956 essay, "Two Aspects of Language and Two Types of Aphasic Disturbances," reprinted in Jakobson and Halle, *Fundamentals of Language*, 69–96. In particular, Jakobson stresses the contiguity, the "existential connection," between signifier and signifier as a hallmark of metonymy, versus the quality of sameness as that of metaphor (95). Following Jakobson's lead, Lakoff and Johnson (*Metaphors We Live By*, 5) elaborate influentially on metonymy as the trope of indexicality, of a relationship of "direc[t] connection to reality"—counter to the logic of metaphor, whose "essence," they argue, "is understanding and experiencing one kind of thing in terms of another."

73. Such ascriptions are catalogued by Jackson, "Ralph Ellison's Invented Life," 16–17.

74. That aim helps explain the redoubling of a certain signal object: the chain, or more precisely, the chain link. Appearing first as an ornament on Bledsoe's desk as "a 'symbol of our progress'"—which Bledsoe brandishes at the very moment in which he tells the narrator, "'Boy, I'm getting rid of you!'" (141)—the link reappears in the form of a gift to the invisible man from Brother Tarp, this time bearing not the stamp of jealously guarded power but "the marks of haste and violence" that index Tarp's escape from the chain gang and his creative negation: "'I said *hell*, no! And I kept saying no until I broke the chain and left'" (387). Although obviously a "luck piece" and a kind of legacy, Tarp's chain accrues symbolic meaning that becomes so overdetermined and complex that it is virtually indecipherable. That it has "a heap of signifying wrapped up in it" (388) is true in part because the link comes to function as—in effect—a master metaphor for the very problem of metonymy, of a lived and meaningful connection to one's "people" and to collective experience.

75. Posnock ("Ellison, Arendt, and the Meaning of Politics") argues that Ellison's understanding of the political as a category of analysis and practice was strikingly similar to Hannah Arendt's; both, in his reading, are exponents of dynamism, division, and

the irreconcilability of available political stances. In a very different kind of argument, Allen ("Ralph Ellison on the Tragi-Comedy of Citizenship," 38) claims that Ellison's novel manifests its political interests not by performing protest but by "bring[ing] analytic pressure to bear on the interactions between strangers, whose only relation to one another is that of common citizenship"; "The politics in the novel lies," she argues, in its "account of what it is like, psychologically speaking, to be an individual in a democratic world of strangers."

76. Ellison, "Native Land"; Ellison, "Harlem Is Nowhere," in CE, 320; Ellison, "The Art of Romare Bearden," in CE, 686.

77. Paule Marshall, cited in O'Mealley, "Introduction: Jazz Shapes," ix.

78. O'Mealley, notes to "Richard Wright's Blues," in Living with Music, 101.

79. See chapter 2.

80. Ellison, "A Special Message to Subscribers," in CE, 350.

81. Ellison, "Address to the Harvard Alumni, Class of 1949," in CE, 419, 423.

82. Ellison, "Tell It Like It Is, Baby," in CE, 31; Ellison, "Art of Romare Bearden," in CE, 835.

83. Warren ("Chaos Not Quite Controlled") reads "Tell It Like It Is, Baby," and in particular its dream sequence, as a template for "the problems that plagued his famously unfinished" second novel (189)—that is, for Ellison's "unsuccessful attempts to negotiate the difference between writing about segregation and writing about desegregation" (189). The gist of the dream, in this reading, is an unanswerable question: "What effect could Ellison as a novelist, working in a form that many scholars had declared defunct, have on a nation still at war with itself over the status of the Negro?" (197).

84. Ellison, "Art of Romare Bearden," in CE, 835.

85. Ellison, Juneteenth, 314, 266.

86. Yukins, "An 'Artful Juxtaposition on the Page.'"

Chapter Four

1. Baldwin, Go Tell It on the Mountain, in Baldwin: Early Novels and Stories, 24; hereafter cited parenthetically as GT.

2. Wallace, Dark Designs and Visual Culture, 366.

3. Critical accounts of Johnson's text have focused on the passage immediately following the revelatory moment, in which the narrator examines himself in a mirror, staging his critical awareness, in Lacanian terms, of the specularity of his own identity. But the precipitating event, a literal scene of instruction (the narrator "d[oes] not quite understand" his principal, and even "question[s] her" about the racial distinction she presses), chimes more resonantly as such in the historical context of desegregation, when the schoolhouse becomes a newly fraught site of racial encounter and declaration. Johnson, Autobiography of an Ex-Coloured Man, 16.

4. Barthes, Camera Lucida, 3, 51. Other convergences between Barthes and Baldwin's narrator also assert themselves; John's heightened self-consciousness and the begin-

nings of his birthday quest turn out to involve a lost image of his mother, not unlike Barthes's famously withheld Winter Garden photograph: "the face that he gave her in his dreams, the face that had been hers in a photograph he had seen once, long ago, a photograph taken before he was born" (GT, 20).

5. Barthes, *Camera Lucida*, 51.

6. Baldwin's ongoing interest in James as a key source for his self-fashioning appears to have begun in 1945, as he read widely in European and American literature; during the late 1940s, as he significantly rewrote *Go Tell It on the Mountain*, Baldwin was reading James extensively. The novelist Ann Birstein, a fellow habitué of postwar literary Paris, has noted that, when members of their circle fantasized about unpublishable books, the one they imagined for Baldwin was "A Negro Looks at Henry James" (cited in Campbell, *Talking at the Gates*, 58). Moreover, Baldwin's resistances to, and public quarrels with, Wright were styled in the idiom of James (Campbell, *Talking at the Gates*, 70); and he began the novel that would become *Giovanni's Room* (1956) as a revision of James's *Portrait of a Lady*, out of which his first representation of an explicitly same-sex love affair emerged. For more extensive accounts of Baldwin's indebtedness to James, see Leeming, "Interview with James Baldwin on Henry James"; Leeming, *James Baldwin*, 61, 89, 104; Tóibín, "Henry James of Harlem"; Weatherby, *James Baldwin*, 96–98; and Miller, "'Maw of Western Culture.'"

7. Scruggs's lyrical reading of the novel, *Sweet Home*, is based on these closing phrases. Although Scruggs emphasizes the religious and institutional dimension of John's gesture—i.e., asserting John's acceptance of "the way of the black church," and "an inherited communal wisdom that could help people to survive in the earthly city" (149, 139)—his own language confirms the power of visual tropes and experience throughout the novel, from the figure of the "watchman upon the city wall" to the demands and opportunities of New York as the "unfinished" city of which forms of witnessing and second sight are born. In these inflections, I would argue, and not in an emphasis on spirituality alone, Baldwin "engaged the history of his time in such a way as to connect him to the experience and values of [Toni] Morrison's generation" (166).

8. Baldwin would characterize his own desire "to own a sixteen-millimeter camera and make experimental movies" as "morbid" ("Autobiographical Notes," in *Baldwin: Collected Essays*, 9). On Baldwin and film, see Ellis, "Black Boy Looks at the Silver Screen."

9. Baldwin, "Notes of a Native Son," in *Baldwin: Collected Essays*, 84. The vastly overdetermined quality of Baldwin's fictional conjunction of John Grimes's coming-of-age and the Harlem riot becomes clearer in light of other narratives of filiation associated with that moment—as, for example, the account of the photographer Gordon Parks (*Half Past Autumn*, 56–65) of his first interview with Richard Wright, scheduled in Harlem for the very day of the 1943 riot. When the two do meet the following morning, Wright presents Parks with a copy of *Twelve Million Black Voices*: just as in Baldwin's text, the riot, photographic response, and a genealogy of black intellectuals become mutually informing.

10. Baldwin, "Many Thousands Gone," in *Baldwin: Collected Essays*, 31.

11. See chapter 1.

12. Walker, *Richard Wright*, 119.

13. Baldwin, "Autobiographical Notes," in *Baldwin: Collected Essays*, 8.

14. The blistering *New York Review of Books* account by Brustein lambastes *Nothing Personal* as a "superfluous non-boo[k] . . . for the Christmas luxury trade," produced by "show-biz moralists" who are avatars of "an honorable tradition of revolt gone sour" ("Everybody Knows My Name," 10, 11).

15. Eckman, *Furious Passage of James Baldwin*, 76; Stein, *Stein on Writing*, 4.

16. Gerard J. Pelisson and James A. Garvey III, "DeWitt Clinton High School Goes to the Movies" (manuscript, DeWitt Clinton High School archive, Bronx, NY). Campbell, *Talking at the Gates*, 15–16, notes that *Magpie* was "a splendid production: well-printed, on high quality paper, with many of the contributions enhanced by illustrations, some of which are of a professional standard."

17. See, for example, Avedon, "Observations," *Magpie*, June 1939, 18, and January 1940, 20–21. *Observations* was published in collaboration with Truman Capote in 1959. See "Student Tops 32 in Poetry Contest"; the secondary headline reads, "Negro Girl Is Second."

18. Campbell, *Talking at the Gates*, 14.

19. Campbell (*Talking at the Gates*, 14–19) traces in Baldwin's *Magpie* work the origins of his voice and stylistics; Leeming (*James Baldwin*, 29–30) links it with Baldwin's exploration of his sexuality. See Avedon, *Evidence*, 123.

20. Gerrard Pelisson, interview with the author, Bronx, NY, 9 June 2003.

21. Leeming, *James Baldwin*, 26. For example, although the Bronx campus remained open to students citywide, it attracted a high proportion of students living in the Amalgamated Clothing Workers co-op directly across the street, almost entirely populated throughout the 1930s by left-of-center immigrant Jews.

22. Roth, quoted in Brawarsky, "Mystery of Henry Roth." Kellman (*Redemption*, 34–37) details the Roths' departure from the Lower East Side for Jewish Harlem. Martin (*Nathanael West*, 16–19, 20) describes the career of the Weinstein family as Harlem landlords.

23. Like all New York public schools of the era, Clinton was a same-sex institution. Whether its modes of integration were successful, experientially or sociologically, seems to be a matter of opinion. Campbell (*Talking at the Gates*, 14) notes that "of the fourteen graduates' portraits on the first page [of the yearbook for Baldwin's graduating class], only one—Baldwin's—is black." Leeming (*James Baldwin*, 26) notes that "in one history class, containing not only James Baldwin but boys with names like Capouya, Guerrero, and Cammaro, a perfectly pleasant but naïve young teacher revealed her 'terrifying innocence' by announcing that America was being ruined by the flood of immigrants from southern Europe." Eckman (*Furious Passage of James Baldwin*, 74–75) suggests that Clinton was only "partially integrated." In terms of harder numbers, whatever they may measure, Clinton's demographics were notable with respect to midcentury city

norms; in 1943, there were slightly more than ten thousand students enrolled (attending in double shifts), of whom nearly 20 percent were African American (Frank D. Gilroy, cited in Clinton High School Exhibition, DeWitt Clinton Library, June 2003).

24. Baldwin, "Rendezvous with Life," *Magpie*, Winter 1942, 19–20, DeWitt Clinton archive. The encounter was a key event in Baldwin's life as a writer; he would later admit in a letter to Langston Hughes, who had admired Baldwin's use of dialect and asked about his aspirations as a poet, that he had written a great deal of poetry while in junior high at Douglass and had shown some of it to Cullen, then Douglass's literary adviser; "All Cullen had said was, 'It's an awful lot like Hughes'" (Campbell, *Talking at the Gates*, 17).

25. Quoted in Eckman, *Furious Passage of James Baldwin*, 74.

26. *The Clintonian*, DeWitt Clinton High School yearbook, June 1941, DeWitt Clinton archive.

27. *Magpie*, January 1938, 32, DeWitt Clinton archive. More than one student would compare the San Juan Hill facility to "a Bowery flophouse"; see Martin, *Nathanael West*, 38. San Juan Hill had been, in the early decades of the twentieth century, an African American neighborhood, so named in commemoration of the contributions of black veterans to Roosevelt's victory in the Spanish-American War; its ongoing reputation as a site of race mixing, rough trade, and criminal activity persisted well into midcentury. On the tenor of Schuster's middlebrow publishing project, which powerfully reflected the cultural matrix of Clinton, Korda (*Another Life*, 71) notes: "Nobody was ever better at inventing books that filled a *need*. . . . [Simon and Schuster's books were] born from Max's passionate belief that you could learn anything, change anything, help yourself ahead in any way merely by reading the right book"—a religion of culture highly relevant, as I argue later, to Baldwin's self-fashioning.

28. *Magpie*, January 1938, 66, DeWitt Clinton archive.

29. S. Cloth, "Oh! The Bowery," *Magpie*, June 1938, 55–56, DeWitt Clinton archive. Also relevant are Robert Panara's dialect poem, "The Beaver and 'iz Tail," January 1938; and O'Neill Carrington, "In a Harlem Cabaret," January 1942.

30. Avedon, *Evidence*, 122.

31. Eckman, *Furious Passage of James Baldwin*, 79.

32. Avedon, "Speaking of Parker," *Magpie*, October 1941, 6, DeWitt Clinton archive.

33. Mackey, "Sound and Sentiment, Sound and Symbol," 603, rewrites the orphic moment as one virtually absent the fateful look: "Song is both a complaint and a consolation dialectically tied to [the historical] ordeal, where in back of 'orphan' one hears echoes of 'orphic,' a music that turns on abandonment, absence, loss. . . . Music is wounded kinship's last resort."

34. Avedon, interview with the author, New York, 17 October 2003.

35. Avedon, *Evidence*, 126. Avedon's proof sheets from his photographic sessions with Baldwin show that they experimented with several backdrops—in effect stage settings—for the portrait, including what appears to be an interior under construction whose saddle horses become a prop for Baldwin's poses. Avedon's interests in the value

of Harlem as a space of photo-textual encounter become clearer in light of a follow-up session of shooting in the Baldwin apartment, in which he records the varied responses of Baldwin's family members to the images they have collaboratively produced, and to the presence of his camera in their charged and intimate space. Negative folder "1946," Richard Avedon Papers, Richard Avedon Foundation, New York.

36. Brodovitch's status as a Russian Jewish émigré is not irrelevant here; Avedon has noted his own affinity, and that of other photographers of his generation, for figures "closer to the Europe from which our parents had come, out of pogroms, out of the Spanish Civil War," and describes midcentury photography itself as "a very close cultural wave beginning in that Europe that picked us all up." Avedon, interview with the author, New York, 17 October 2003.

37. On Avedon's work as visual consultant for *Funny Face*, and his own forays into television and film work, see *Evidence*, 136–37, 140–41.

38. Livingston, "Art of Richard Avedon" 37, notes: "Of all the quasi-journalistic photographers of that era, only Helen Levitt, whose film, *The Quiet One*, he saw in 1949 [the year of its release], and whose photographs he saw at the Museum of Modern Art as early as 1943 [at her first solo exhibition there], moved him to recognize new possibilities in the kind of photojournalism associated with *Life* or with the Photo League." Avedon's abiding interest in Levitt reminds us that he, too, developed a postdocumentary project out of early engagements with documentary culture and practice; at about the time he was encountering Levitt's film work, Avedon was exhibiting some of his own street images at the Photo League, then advertising itself as "a testing ground for values in face of the blandishments of the commercial world" and a venue for exploring "the problems of the photographer as a creative individual." See *This Is the Photo League*, "On the Exhibition," n.p., exhibition catalogue, Giesel Library, University of California, San Diego; Avedon's name is listed under "Member Contributors," whose ranks also included Berenice Abbott, Lou Bernstein, Eliot Elisofon, Morris Engel, Sid Grossman, Dorothea Lange, Sol Libsohn, Lisette Model, Marion Palfi, Walter Rosenblum, and Aaron Siskind (n.p.).

39. Avedon, cited in *Evidence*, 38.

40. Livingston, "Art of Richard Avedon," 70.

41. Ibid., 71.

42. Gates, "Welcome Table," 308.

43. Baldwin's filial revolt was not only literary. Paula Maria, the other subject of Avedon's photograph, was not only born on the day of his father's death but was "named by me"; when he "returned home—Harlem—in 1946 to do, with a white photographer, one of several unpublished efforts," he was surely aware of his various offenses against his father's law. Baldwin, *No Name on the Street*, 22.

44. Baldwin, *Price of the Ticket*, 172.

45. Baldwin, "Every Good-Bye Ain't Gone," in *Baldwin: Collected Essays*, 774.

46. Ibid., 775.

47. Ibid., 779.

48. Baldwin, "Many Thousands," in *Baldwin: Collected Essays*, 31; Baldwin, "Every Good-Bye Ain't Gone," in *Baldwin: Collected Essays*, 775.

49. Gates, "Welcome Table," 309.

50. Leeming, *James Baldwin*, 50.

51. Campbell, *Talking at the Gates*, 40.

52. Campbell (ibid., 38) notes that Baldwin's accounts of this early reviewing, as a trial of representativeness in which white editors presumed his expertise on the "Negro problem," were misleading, since Baldwin "more often than not left the office [of *Commentary* or *New Leader* or *Partisan Review*] with a different book from the one they had offered him," including an account of a Brooklyn Jewish street gang, a work on Catholic philosophy, an Erskine Caldwell novel, *The Portable Russian Reader*, and two volumes on the fiction of Robert Louis Stevenson. Baldwin, in other words, parlayed his cachet as found Negro spokesman for Jewish American cultural projects into a platform for his own self-exploration as writer. That the complex networks of Jewish American culture making continued to be crucial to Baldwin is made clear by Leeming (*James Baldwin*, 61), who follows Baldwin's career as a cultural "prophet" during his exile in Paris in the homes of "white, liberal, mostly Jewish middle-class Americans." As Harap (*In the Mainstream*, 21) notes, it was in these precincts that Baldwin first made the acquaintance of Saul Bellow, the reigning novelist of the so-called Jewish Decade of American literature, and was introduced to the works of his "new model," Henry James.

53. Clark, "Candor about Negro-Jewish Relations"; editorial sidebar, "Harlem Ghetto: Winter 1948."

54. "Harlem Ghetto" sidebar.

55. Longstaff, "New York School of Intellectuals," 1295. Leeming (*James Baldwin*, 51) cites an early review for the *New Leader* in which Baldwin begins to hone his signature mode of "cutting irony."

56. Sundquist, *Strangers in the Land*, 19. Sundquist's epic volume bracingly details the ongoing contestations, engagements, and face-offs that comprise the "interethnic partnership" of mutually mediating outsiders; from this record, the cultural field of photography, with its distinctive lives and afterlives, is absent.

57. Baldwin, "Harlem Ghetto," in *Baldwin: Collected Essays*, 165.

58. Baldwin, "Many Thousands Gone," in *Baldwin: Collected Essays*, 24–25.

59. Baldwin, "Harlem Ghetto," in *Baldwin: Collected Essays*, 165, italics original.

60. Baldwin's biographers have generally noted this collaboration only in the context of Baldwin's writerly "failures" (Leeming, *James Baldwin*, 43), or so as to identify Pelatowski as Baldwin's first significant love interest, "the man he loved better than anyone else in the world" (Campbell, *Talking at the Gates*, 180); of greater interest may be the utility of the project as such for Baldwin's development of the stance and stylistics of witnessing.

61. Campbell, *Talking at the Gates*, 36.

62. Ibid.

63. Wright, *Twelve Million Black Voices*, 128; on the link with Wright, see Campbell, *Talking at the Gates*, 37.

64. For these and other shots, see thumbnails in Avedon, *Evidence*, 131–33.

65. Avedon, interview with the author, New York, 17 October 2003.

66. Ibid. Ironically, Avedon here replicates the idiom of James Agee, whose notion of "spies" and "counterspies" is generated in response to Evans's photographic inexorability; a case in point is the anecdote, very early in Agee's text, of their attempt to gain permission from a young African American couple to make images of and inside a nearby black church. When their overtures predictably terrify (or annoy) the couple into a stalwart know-nothingness, Agee makes it clear that Evans will get the shot nonetheless (Agee and Evans, *Let Us Now Praise Famous Men*, 35–39). Avedon's self-description thus shrewdly underscores the distance of his project from the documentary context in which his career began.

67. Avedon, interview with the author, New York, 17 October 2003.

68. Avedon (telephone conversation with the author, 17 February 2004) stressed the continuity between these collaborations, noting that his work with Baldwin on *Nothing Personal* "was just the way it had been back in the *Magpie* days."

69. In this respect, it radically extends the defining gesture of *Let Us Now Praise Famous Men*, whose ethical imperative is framed—as Mitchell (*Picture Theory*, 290–390) argues—precisely through its formal principle of rupture, or "blockage," of image from text (292). But Evans's images and Agee's prose nonetheless retain the structure of the traditional ekphrastic dialogue, in the sense that they invite attempts to link competing representations, and to see the very multiplicity and contestation of images as proof of the representational fidelity of the enterprise to found realities and human subjects.

70. Avedon, telephone interview with the author, 5 March 2004.

71. Miller, "'Striking Addiction to Irreality,'" 173.

72. Hughes, *American Visions*, 540. Hughes's assessment of Warhol (*American Visions*, 539–41) is more broadly useful for assessing the *Nothing Personal* aesthetic.

73. Hughes, *American Visions*, 540.

74. Hickey, "In the Theatre of Innocence."

75. Avedon and Baldwin, *Nothing Personal*, 1:1; hereafter cited parenthetically as NP.

76. Campbell, *Talking at the Gates*, 51.

77. Miller, "'Striking Addiction to Irreality,'" 179.

78. Ibid., 180.

79. Ibid., 182.

80. Ibid.

81. These are the categories named in the project précis, Avedon, *Evidence*, 145.

82. Compare the force of this image with a shot of the same event, absent Avedon and the tensions that framed the encounter, "Civil Rights Demonstration, Atlanta, Georgia," in Avedon and Arbus, *Sixties*, 64.

83. The suggestion of Avedon's implication via practice in civil rights culture is buttressed by the records of the Student Nonviolent Coordinating Committee, which docu-

ment his fundraising on behalf of SNCC as well as his donation of equipment and time for training SNCC photographers; see *Student Nonviolent Coordinating Committee Papers*, Reel 36, A:XI: 1.

84. Avedon, interview with the author, New York, 17 October 2003.

85. Miller, "'Striking Addiction to Irreality,'" 175.

86. See Avedon, *Observations*. Avedon's first volume, it should be noted, was not a photo-text but a series of portraits framed more conventionally as such. Capote's portrait is placed as the final Avedon shot of the volume, and is followed by an image of Avedon's powerful mentor and editor, Alexey Brodovitch, taken by Avedon's own student, the photographer Hiro. Thus placed, Capote's image becomes part of a constructed genealogy of artists and intellectuals—a genealogy in which photo-textuality is also implicated.

87. Dupee, "James Baldwin and the 'Man.'"

88. Editorial, "Beyond Rights." On the FBI's imaging of Baldwin in its surveillance files, and the revealing acts of ekphrasis it constitutes, see Wallace, *Constructing the Black Masculine*, 135–42. Wallace concludes, 142, that Baldwin's very look "promises a final transcendence" of the "tragedy" of misrecognition; the larger archive of images documenting Baldwin's celebrity suggests the fragility of this promise.

89. Baldwin, "Harlem Ghetto," in *Baldwin: Collected Essays*, 166.

90. "Disturber of the Peace," 207.

91. Baldwin, *No Name in the Street*, 61.

92. *Time*, 19 May 1963.

93. Howard, "Telling Talk from a Negro Writer."

94. Ibid., 86.

95. "Editor's Note."

96. Howard, "Telling Talk from a Negro Writer," 86.

97. "Editor's Note."

98. Some of Schapiro's most powerful images, including shots from his earliest photographic essays on drug addicts in East Harlem and migrant workers in Arkansas that led to his appointment as a staff photographer for *Life*, and the Harlem images that were exhibited in the 1968 Museum of Metropolitan Art exhibit Harlem on My Mind, have recently been republished in *American Edge*. Schapiro's often-stated ambition to chronicle the "icons" of American life as such is clearly visible in his representations of Baldwin.

99. Howard, "Telling Talk from a Negro Writer," 86.

100. Leeming, *James Baldwin*, 219.

101. Cited in ibid., 224.

102. James, *American Scene*, 124.

Chapter Five

1. Caldwell, "Get Back Here Now!," in *Caldwell Journals*, posted online at www.maynardije.org/news/features/caldwell/Chapter12/.

2. Caldwell, "Harlem: The Colony Converges," in *Caldwell Journals*, posted online at www.maynardije.org/news/features/caldwell/Chapter9/.

3. The most authoritative version of this argument is made by Dickstein (*Gates of Eden*, 91–92). But his own wide-ranging, incisive readings of literary projects of the era partially undercut the argument, to the extent that they persuasively press claims that, as he writes of "the Jewish novel" of the 1950s, "the literature and politics of the period are one" (50), and "the sixties are as likely to be remembered through novels as through anything else they left behind" (92). On modernism's ostensibly neutral claims to an ideology of "culture" whose logic replicates racial essentialism in new forms, see Michaels, *Our America*.

4. The emphasis on antivisual forms is pronounced not just in African American cultural movements and their histories. Banes (*Greenwich Village, 1963*, 84ff) treats the emergence of vernacular visual codes in careful detail, but mentions photography only parenthetically. On the "proclivity" of Black Arts era cultural practitioners for popular cultural sources and aural/auratic effects, both closely linked to a vestigial or ongoing history derived from Popular Front activity, see Smethurst, *Black Arts Movement*, 23–37; of particular interest is Smethurst's account of new Black Arts and Black Power journals as products of "the influence of the cultural memory of the Old Left" (47)—a reading that invites further attention to visual objects and images in circulation in these contexts.

5. Dodging and burning are darkroom techniques for adjusting the tone, shadows, and highlights in specific areas of an image, by adding or reducing light to those areas during printing so as to increase or decrease the amount of detail or visual information visible in the final print. Such techniques—a matter of aesthetic sensibility as well as technical prowess—have long been associated with art photography, but they came to define photojournalistic and photo-essayistic work during the postwar period as well. See Warren, "Burning In," in *Encyclopedia of Twentieth-Century Photography*, 181–82, and "Dodging," in *Encyclopedia of Twentieth-Century Photography*, 410–11.

6. Hansberry, "Proposed Work—September, 1960," in *To Be Young, Gifted and Black*, 125.

7. Hansberry's ex-husband, Robert Nemiroff ("Critical Background," 43–46), discusses the vexed status of the play and its production in 1970, which met a largely critical reception, particularly among Black Arts proponents, who objected to the theatrical realism that had made *Raisin in the Sun* such a resounding liberal triumph during its nearly two years on Broadway.

8. Hansberry, *To Be Young, Gifted, and Black*, 77. Hansberry had moved to New York at age twenty to work for Paul Robeson's *Freedom*; she lived, she notes, 77, "(to my total dissatisfaction) on the lower east side" because "it is too damn crowded in the ghetto for even those who want to move in," but nonetheless insists on locating her life as an artist and activist in Harlem—particularly in its streets. Hansberry's critics have been quick to dismiss such claims as compensatory for her bourgeois upbringing; they are, however, no more or less self-serving than a host of other such claims on Harlem during this era.

9. Nemiroff, "Foreword," xv.

10. Materials in *The Student Nonviolent Coordinating Committee Papers*, suggest that staff members of SNCC's photography department—a volatile and piecemeal operation—were responsible for forwarding images to Hansberry, or at least to her editor at Simon and Schuster, for her consideration. An unsigned memo dated 17 January 1964 ("Photographers with Prints at S & S") lists more than two dozen photographers as contributors or possible contributors—including Bruce Davidson and Richard Avedon, both of whom were about to publish photo-texts of their own. Although the author of the memo speaks quite directively (s/he notes that "for personal reasons, I would like to have at least one picture by [Robert Frank] in the book," that David Heath "is a sort of friend of mine," and that the final book "must use 1–2 of [Joe Spieler's] pictures at least"), the final text reflects other choices—i.e., Hansberry's, not least with respect to the title; in the SNCC memo, the volume is still being referred to as "Freedom Now." See *Student Nonviolent Coordinating Committee Papers*, Reel 36, A:XI: 3.

11. Again, evidence suggests that Hansberry was responsible for organizing and editing the volume. Lyon notes, in a letter of 12 February 1964 to his parents, that he has "finished with his work for the book" (*Memories of the Southern Civil Rights Movement*, 135), but Nemiroff describes Hansberry as working with a steady stream of photographs throughout that spring and summer (Nemiroff, "Foreword," xv–xvi); further, Lyon retrospectively refers to *The Movement* as "SNCC's photo book" rather than his own (*Memories of the Southern Civil Rights Movement*, 128).

12. Lyon, *Memories of the Southern Civil Rights Movement*, 26, 84.

13. Bond, "Foreword," 6; Lyon, *Memories of the Southern Civil Rights Movement*, 9. The degree to which Lyon's person was itself an icon of that stock figure of civil rights activity, the radical New York Jew—and not only for Bond or other African American activists—is evidenced by Lyon's anecdotes (*Memories of the Southern Civil Rights Movement*, 150) about being typed by local Klansmen and even mistaken by FBI agents in 1964 for the then missing Michael Schwerner.

14. Lyon, *Memories of the Southern Civil Rights Movement*, 11; Lyon, *Pictures from the New World*, 136. Hereafter, these two works are referred to parenthetically as *Memories* and *Pictures*, respectively.

15. Carson ("Blacks and Jews in the Civil Rights Movement," 37) clarifies the terms of the work of non-African Americans in SNCC; while on-the-ground participation by white activists in the early 1960s amounted to "a handful of Northern Whites," the "small number of Jewish activists on SNCC's staff exerted an influence out of proportion to their numbers." In view of the facts and demographics of SNCC activity, Lyon's role in shaping the visual record of the movement and his uses of the opportunity to rethink documentary stylistics and meaning are all the more striking.

16. In this sense, the closest analogue for Lyon as a self-conscious performer of his role may have been Bob Dylan, whom Lyon photographed in 1962–63, performing in Mississippi cotton fields and at voter registration rallies and visiting SNCC outposts.

Throughout his career Lyon continued to wed embedded image making, photo-textual production, and postdocumentary performance. By way of introduction to *The Paper Negative*, his fictive (auto)biography of a photographer in the American Southwest, Lyon offers the following manifesto: "Photographers traditionally have worked in silence, putting everything into the picture, that small area, measured in inches, that they have staked out. I have never done that, but have usually presented my photographs in books with a text. In the texts I have spoken through other people's voices, sometimes out of respect for what they had to say, and sometimes as a disguise for myself" (n.p.). From the inception of his career, traveling with his Nikon and his portable Olivetti typewriter, Lyon self-consciously created himself as a producer of what he later called "photoliterature" (*Pictures*, 86).

17. Bond, "Introduction," in Lyon, *Pictures*, 6.

18. Baldwin, "Sweet Lorraine," x. For Hansberry's stage direction, see Hansberry, *Raisin in the Sun*, 3–4.

19. Hansberry, *Movement*, 8. Hereafter page numbers appear parenthetically.

20. It is worth noting that Herron's connections with SNCC and the civil rights movement—including work for the American Friends Service Committee and the organization in 1964 of the Southern Documentary Project, focused on civil rights activities in Mississippi—were mentored by Dorothea Lange. During the same period, however, Herron also pursued photographic studies in the mode of photographer and curator Minor White and Paul Strand: in the civil rights era South, Herron too found a photographic subject that activated both formalist and socially conscious stylistics and histories. On Norris McNamara's tempestuous relationship with SNCC's photo staff during his stint as a member, see *Student Nonviolent Coordinating Committee Papers*, Reel 36, A:XI: 1.

21. Barthes, *Camera Lucida*, 49, 78.

22. Wright, *Twelve Million Black Voices*, 43; the lynching image, credited to AP/World Wide, appears on 45.

23. The ideological and affective force of such juxtapositions—that is, between lifeless black bodies and moving white ones—is addressed by Goldsby (*Spectacular Secret*, 72) in connection with the circulation of lynching images as picture cards, stereographs, and other nineteenth-century forms—that archive, she argues, constituted a visual regime that "helped turn American modern"; and by Shawn Michelle Smith (*Photography on the Color Line*, 119–26) in a detailed account of the "fantasy of whiteness" as control—over racial hierarchy, black subjectivity, and gender as well as representational or symbolic activity—constructed in the scene and the archive of lynching.

24. Sontag, *On Photography*, 73.

25. See, e.g., Cheney, *Lorraine Hansberry*, 19; and Cruse, *Crisis of the Negro Intellectual*, 102, 220.

26. Harrison, *Drama of Nommo*, 200–202; Benston, *Performing Blackness*, 49–50, 73, 30.

27. Benston, *Performing Blackness*, 30.

28. Ibid.

29. Lyon (*Memories of the Southern Civil Rights Movement*, 26) notes that SNCC raised ten thousand dollars—a significant windfall—by reproducing this image as a poster for sale at the cost of one dollar.

30. Jones [Baraka], *Black Music*, 176, 175, cited in Benston, *Performing Blackness*, 213; Benston, *Performing Blackness*, 189.

31. Hansberry, "Genet, Mailer, and the New Paternalism"; Mailer, "Mailer to Hansberry."

32. Palfi's own genealogy is worth recounting: born in Berlin, where her father was a storied theater director, she worked as a freelancer for German magazines, then in the forefront of experimental photo-text stylistics. Fleeing the Nazis, like so many other documentarians of her generation, she arrived in the United States in 1940 and became a member of the Photo League; she used a Rosenwald Fellowship to travel across the United States photographing the effects of racism and segregation, published as a photo-essay on Jim Crow and lynching titled "There Is No More Time" (1949). In her photo-text projects, including "Georgia Study" (1949) and "In These Ten Cities" (1950–51), portraits of women feature prominently; perhaps her best-known image is "Wife of Lynch Victim" (1949). For reproductions of her work, see Palfi, *Marion Palfi*, and Palfi, *Invisible in America*.

33. Lyon, *Memories of the Southern Civil Rights Movement*, 16.

34. Hansberry's emergent lesbian engagements can be traced in letters she appears to have written (signing only her initials "L.H.N." and "L.H.") to *The Ladder*, the publication of the pioneering lesbian organization Daughters of Bilitis based in San Francisco. In two lengthy letters, she affirms her interest in and support of West Coast lesbian activism, meditates on the relations between lesbians and gay men, and links homophobic cultural norms with antifeminism. See letter, L.H.N., *The Ladder*, May 1957, 26–28; letter, L.N., *The Ladder*, August 1957, 26–30; Hansberry responds in part to Stephens, "Transvestism"; Bradley, "Some Remarks on Marriage"; and Osborne, "One Facet of Fear."

35. Hansberry, *To Be Young, Gifted and Black*, 169.

36. Nemiroff has not to date published a full version of "All the Dark and Beautiful Warriors" as he indicated in published statements that he planned to do; for a sense of the novel, see Cheney, *Lorraine Hansberry*, 30; and Hansberry, *To Be Young, Gifted and Black*, 36–38, 49–51, 132.

37. Hansberry, cited in Cheney, *Lorraine Hansberry*, 135.

38. For the often-recited story of the genesis of the Harlem Domestics, see Sallis, *Chester Himes*, 271–72.

39. Himes, *My Life of Absurdity*, 126.

40. Himes, *Cotton Comes to Harlem*, 80; hereafter cited parenthetically in the text.

41. The junk dealer, one Mr. Goodman, makes it clear that this is not only a postwar but a post–cold war context: "Who wants unprocessed cotton?" he asks. "Not even good for bullets no more. Nowadays they shoot atoms" (94).

42. On this representational work, Rotella (*October Cities*, 152) notes parenthetically, "Writing about the second ghetto, Himes later became a very different writer indeed." An index to this difference, I am arguing, is the newly self-conscious mode of his invocations of Renaissance-era cultural production, and particularly of photomontage.

43. Himes to John A. Williams, 16 July 1969, cited in Margolies and Fabre, *Several Lives of Chester Himes*, 152; Himes to Williams, 8 March 1969, cited in ibid., 149; Himes, "Preface," in *Blind Man with a Pistol*, 5.

44. Sallis, *Chester Himes*, 219.

45. Ibid., 274; Himes, *My Life of Absurdity*, 36.

46. Himes, *My Life of Absurdity*, 36.

47. Cover blurb, Brown, *Manchild in the Promised Land*.

48. Cited in Hentoff, "Urban Blight," 71; "Books"; "Year of the Fact."

49. Himes, *My Life of Absurdity*, 126.

50. Himes, quoted in Fabre and Skinner, "Introduction," xi.

51. Jacket blurb for Himes, *Plan B*.

52. Himes, *Quality of Hurt*, 117.

53. Himes's account of generating the Harlem Domestics (*My Life of Absurdity*, 109) is relevant here: "I thought I was writing realism. It never occurred to me that I was writing absurdity. Realism and absurdity are so similar in the lives of American blacks one cannot tell the difference."

54. Baldwin, cited in Halstead, *Harlem Stirs*, 30.

55. For an example of Charles's work, see *Umbra* 1, no. 2 (December 1963): 55.

56. Halstead, *Harlem Stirs*, 57, 62. Hereafter, page numbers will be cited parenthetically in the text.

57. Evans, cited in Galassi, *Walker Evans and Company*, 161.

58. Klein, quoted in Livingston, *New York School*, 314.

59. "William Klein."

60. Stokeley Carmichael and Charles V. Hamilton (italics original), cited in Saul, *Freedom Is, Freedom Ain't*, 303; Carson, *In Struggle*, 191–228; and Frederickson, *Black Liberation*, 286–97. On SNCC's role in this transformation, and in particular the rise of anti-Zionism as a defining aspect of Black Power, see Sundquist, *Strangers in the Land*, 314–15, 311–80.

61. See Neal, "Black Arts Movement." On the revolutionary project as the attempt to counter the dominant image-world and "construct . . . a particular way of looking at the world" through a genuinely dialectical art (i.e., music), see Stewart, "Development of the Black Revolutionary Artist," 3. In the same volume, Wilson's "Screens," 133, argues that African Americans who become tools for white America as it enforces "the established socio-economic system" (and the dominant racial regime) are properly understood as "screens": those who obscure the realities of power by wedding themselves to its image repertoires. A free-floating and labile skepticism of the image and of visuality, in other words, inflects much of the cultural nationalist idiom. On the uses

of graphic—rather than photographic—visual statements in Black Power (specifically Black Panther) culture, see Streitmatter, "*Black Panther* Newspaper."

62. See in particular Cruse's equal-opportunity jeremiad (*Crisis of the Negro Intellectual*, 498–519) on the poverty of black intellectual leadership.

63. Killens, quoted in Gilyard, "John Oliver Killens."

64. Gayle, *Way of the World*, 261; Gilyard, *Liberation Memories*, 1; Cruse, *Crisis of the Negro Intellectual*, 502. Against the view of Killens as a Stalinist purging the ranks of the Negro faithful stand assessments such as that of Macon ("John Oliver Killens," 420): "Killens's name will forever ring simultaneously with the bells of freedom." On Killens as "ideological orchestrator" in his powerful function as organizer of literary and cultural conferences during the mid-1960s, see Gilyard, *Liberation Memories*, 113.

65. In his review of *Invisible Man* for *Freedom*, "Books," Killens had famously denounced Ellison as perpetrator of "a modernized 'surrealist' anti-Negro stereotype"; "The Negro people need" *Invisible Man*, he concludes, "like we need . . . a stab in the back."

66. Killens, *And Then We Heard the Thunder*, 482.

67. Cruse, *Crisis of the Negro Intellectual*, 498.

68. Gilyard, *Liberation Memories*, 95.

69. On '*Sippi* as "virtually a sequel," see Gilyard, *Liberation Memories*, 22. A powerful alternative account of *The Cotillion*'s energies is given by Murray ("How the Conjure-Man Gets Busy"), who argues for *The Cotillion* as an exploration of the language politics of cultural nationalism, and specifically of Baraka, as confounding the need to draw "meaningful distinctions between charlatanism and activism," between practice and rhetoric (302). Murray is carefully attuned to the gender dynamics of Killens's representations of nationalist performativity; my reading offers an alternative account of his sources for their exploration.

70. Killens, *Cotillion*, 1; hereafter cited parenthetically in the text.

71. Participant, New School Negro Writers' Conference, April 1965, cited in Cruse, *Crisis of the Negro Intellectual*, 503.

72. See Gilyard, *Liberation Memories*, 92.

73. Killens, "Preface," in Halstead, *Harlem Stirs*, 3; hereafter cited parenthetically in the text.

74. Pate, "Foreword," xxi.

75. Dubin, *Displays of Power*, 37–38. See also Schoener, "Introduction to the New Edition," in *Harlem on My Mind*. On the catalogue as a flashpoint for protest and interethnic contestation, see Schoener, "Introduction to the New Edition," 10–11; Dubin, *Displays of Power*, 30–35; and Hoving, *Making the Mummies Dance*, 167–70. The catalogue sold a record-setting one thousand copies per day for two weeks before being withdrawn under political pressure from office of the mayor and the city council, in spite of the insertion of apologies by the museum's director and by the author of the introduction; the remaining twenty-six thousand copies were ultimately distributed to African American cultural organizations in Harlem.

76. Metropolitan Museum of Art press release, 16 November 1967, cited in Schoener, "Introduction to the New Edition," in *Harlem on My Mind*.

77. Schoener ("Introduction to the New Edition," in *Harlem on My Mind*) provides a useful account of the exhibition plan room by room. Among contemporaneous reviewers, Deschin ("Harlem's History") is singular in discussing the technical aspects—"a considerable achievement"—of the exhibit's monumental murals.

78. Ellison, "Harlem's America."

79. Glueck, "Art: 'Harlem on My Mind' in Slides, Tapes and Photos"; Goldin, "Harlem Out of Mind."

80. Schoener, "Editor's Foreword," in *Harlem on My Mind*, n.p. His rhetoric is echoed by the Met's director, Thomas Hoving, in "Director's Note," 243, on the new museology: "It doesn't interpret or explain. It sticks to the facts."

81. Although the influence of Schoener's example of exhibition practices has been duly noted in studies of museology and curatorial practice, the overdetermination of his rejection of the traditional museum and of modernist aesthetics has been largely ignored. Schoener was the nephew of the sculptor William Zorach, a commercially successful producer of monumental abstractions influenced by fauvism. Perhaps more than coincidentally, Zorach's death in 1966 coincides with Schoener's first "ethnic-environmental"—or what we might call postmodernist—exhibition.

82. Schoener, "Introduction to the New Edition," in *Harlem on My Mind*; Kramer, "Politicizing the Metropolitan Museum." The value of "confrontation" as a keyword for Schoener is evident in a pre-exhibition interview with Glueck, "Adam C., Mother Brown, Malcolm X," which cites him as noting that his design for the show ensures that "you really must confront" the subjects of the images, and proclaiming on the matter of scale as an exhibitional device that "I'd like to wipe out the walls and ceilings entirely—we'd be better off doing the show in a tent."

83. Glueck, "Art: 'Harlem on My Mind' in Slides, Tapes and Photos."

84. Quoted in Dubin, *Displays of Power*, 21.

85. Quoted in ibid., 38. Holmes, interview with Cliff Joseph.

86. Aldridge, "Exhibit on Everybody's Mind."

87. Coleman, "Latent Image."

88. Arnold, "Paintings Defaced at Metropolitan." The vandalism—"the most grave" in the history of the Met (Arnold, Ibid., 1)—was disavowed by members of the BECC; no one, apparently, thought to inquire of Kahane and the Anti-Defamation League or members of the John Birch Society whether they had been involved, and no one was ever apprehended or charged. The perpetrator(s) not only were canny about concealment—and this in the most popular galleries of the Metropolitan, directly adjoining the Harlem exhibition—they also used sharp instruments that left legible but reparable scratches on the varnish surfaces (rather than the actual pigment layers) of the canvases, and only in a corner of each canvas (presumably also with the desire to avoid irreparable damage). The most heavily scratched painting was a Christ attributed to Rembrandt, part of a series of acclaimed religious portraits made, as was his practice, from figures

in his everyday life—a not irrelevant fact, given the contestations raised by Harlem on My Mind over documentation and art, everyday black subjects and social allegory, and more.

89. Jay Maisel, b. 1931, and Friedlander, b. 1934, exemplify the lability of postwar documentary and photojournalistic projects and stylistics. Maisel, a Brooklyn-born yeshiva-student-turned-freelance photographer, achieved fame as a maker of urban images for commercial contexts; a more recent volume of his work is titled *On Assignment* (1990). But his first one-man show was mounted by none other than Roy DeCarava at A Photographer's Gallery in 1955, and his work—from early black and white through color and more recent digital technology—has consistently been premised, like DeCarava's, on the refusal of technical manipulation, including the use of added light or digital manipulation. Mayer and Berman, "Interview with Jay Maisel"; Weisgrau, "Jay Maisel."

90. African Americans accounted for some 15 percent of the record-breaking audience for the show—a nearly sevenfold increase in the museum's average. Schoener, "Introduction to the New Edition," in *Harlem on My Mind*; "Big Crowds Force Museum to Cut Off 'Harlem' Show Line."

91. On the informing context of an ongoing struggle for community control of schools in Brooklyn that pitted predominantly Jewish American teachers against predominantly African American parents, see Dubin, *Displays of Power*, 23–25.

92. Van Ellison, "Introduction"; see especially "Intergroup Relations," which discusses African American engagements with Irish American, Puerto Rican, and Harlem Jewish communities.

93. As Schoener ("Introduction to the New Edition," in *Harlem on My Mind*) framed it at the outset of the project, "if blacks are interested in the history of the Lower East Side, everyone will certainly be interested in the history of Harlem."

94. Ibid. On the context for nationalist responses to mainstream and aesthetic uses of black history, see Clarke's own contributions to Clarke, *William Styron's Nat Turner*.

95. Dubin, *Displays of Power*, 30.

96. Handler, "75 Artists Urge Closing of Museum's 'Insulting' Harlem Exhibit."

97. "Museum Pickets Assail Hoving over Coming Harlem Exhibition"; Dubin, *Displays of Power*, 39.

98. Holmes, interview with Cliff Joseph. A more recent version of this criticism is made by Michele Wallace ("Signifying Nothing," 84), who complains of the show's slighting of "such great artists as Romare Bearden and Jacob Lawrence" for mere "documentary history"—in effect, "an interactive Harlem theme park."

99. Roy DeCarava, quoted in Vestal, "Can Whitey Do a Beautiful Black Picture Show?" 122; DeCarava, quoted in Glueck, "Total Involvement of Thomas Hoving," 85.

100. DeCarava, quoted in Vestal, "Can Whitey Do a Beautiful Black Picture Show?" 80.

101. DeCarava, quoted in ibid., 122.

102. Ibid., 79.

103. See chapter 1.

104. Gilroy, *Black Atlantic*, 147.

105. Schoener, "Introduction to the New Edition," in *Harlem on My Mind*; Wallace, "Signifying Nothing," 85; *Harlem on My Mind*, back cover; Dubin, *Displays of Power*, 63.

Coda

1. Holzer, *Truth before Power* and *Laments*; see also Kruger, *Remote Control* and *Money Talks*.

2. For readings of African American artists and identity logic in the postmodernist context, see Bailey, "Rethinking Black Representations"; Bailey and Hall, "Vertigo of Displacement"; and Mercer, *Welcome to the Jungle*, 233–58. Against these views, Erina Duganne ("Looking In / Looking Out: Race and Subjectivity in Photography," PhD diss., University of Texas, Austin, 2004, 1–5) argues for the complex engagement with documentary traditions of African American photographers of the immediate postwar era, who anticipate the rejection of "objective truths while working within" the documentary tradition (5).

3. See, for example, Golden, *Freestyle*.

4. On the construction and exhibition of "9 Props," see Willis and Simpson, *Lorna Simpson*; Wright, Hartman, and Simpson, *Lorna Simpson*; and Golden, Jones, and Iles, *Lorna Simpson*. Jones ("In Their Own Image," 133) aligns Simpson with other visual artists who draw on documentary backgrounds and employ photo-textuality or inserted text as a way "to both delimit and expand the implicit meanings in standard 'straight' photography."

5. Simpson created "9 Props" as artist-in-residence at the Pilchuck Glass School; at her request, and to her specifications, artisans there replicated the "props" she chose from VanderZee's portrait work.

6. On the tension between figures and voice in Simpson, see Young, "Lorna Simpson."

7. On anonymity and female presence, see Willis, "Conversation"; Solomon-Godeau, "Mistaken Identities"; and Heartney, "Figuring Absence."

8. Morrison, *Bluest Eye*, 85.

9. Morrison, *Song of Solomon*, 3.

10. Morrison, *Sula*, 90.

11. Ibid., 89.

12. Griffin (*"Who Set You Flowin'?"* 194) was the first to argue in this vein; with its shift in focus, she contends, *Jazz* "reclaim[s] the Jazz Age" for African American modernity, as against Anglo-European modernism. To this act of reclamation, I suggest, contestation over the photographic image and its histories of use is central.

13. Morrison, *Jazz*, 59; hereafter cited parenthetically in the text.

14. For the displacement of "Harlem Renaissance" by "post-Reconstruction" as frames of reference, see Carabi, "Interview with Toni Morrison," 40.

15. Morrison, "Foreword," in *Harlem Book of the Dead*, n.p.

16. Morrison, "Behind the Making of *The Black Book*," 90.

17. Quoted in Als, "Ghosts in the House," 72. Wall (*Worrying the Line*, 90–92) details the history of Morrison's participation in the "build[ing]" of the project; for Wall, the "concept of the image" as a point of departure for modes of recollection forms a critical link between *The Black Book* and *Beloved*, which both aim to "provoke a kind of story-telling that is participatory, improvisational, and collective" (95). Of particular interest is Wall's reading of photographs as objects that "call the written text into being" (17)—in essence, a profoundly affirmative reading of what I call the ekphrastic problem in black and white.

18. Riley, "Introduction."

19. Morrison, "Foreword," in *Black Photographers Annual*, n.p.

20. Morrison, "Behind the Making of *The Black Book*," 89.

21. Naylor, "Conversation," 207.

22. VanderZee, Dodson, and Billops, *Harlem Book of the Dead*, 84.

23. On uses of the Sleeping Beauty myth in mortuary photography, see Burns, *Sleeping Beauty*. Morrison, "Foreword," in *Harlem Book of the Dead*, n.p.

24. See, respectively, McDowell, "Harlem Nocturne," 4; and Smith, "Blue Note."

25. Carabi, "Interview with Toni Morrison," 43, 44.

26. See, for example, Morrison's *Remember*, a photo-text featuring "a treasure chest of archival photos" by documentary photographers such as Bruce Davidson and Elliott Erwitt—ironically, reproduced in the same "sepia" mode that Morrison's talking book rejects. According to the volume, these photographs served as "the inspiration" for her fictive account of the responses of the imaged subjects (jacket copy, n.p.).

Bibliography

Archival Sources

Aaron Siskind Archive. Center for Creative Photography. Tucson, Arizona.

Aaron Siskind Archive. George Eastman House. Rochester, New York.

DeWitt Clinton Archive. DeWitt Clinton High School. Bronx, New York.

Langston Hughes Papers. James Weldon Johnson Collection, Beinecke Library. Yale University.

Lisette Model Archive. National Gallery of Canada. Ottawa, Ontario.

Marion Palfi Archive. Center for Creative Photography. Tucson, Arizona.

Ralph Ellison Papers. Manuscript and Prints and Photographs Divisions, Library of Congress.

Richard Avedon Archive. Richard Avedon Foundation. New York.

Richard Wright Papers. James Weldon Johnson Collection, Beinecke Library. Yale University.

Roy DeCarava Papers. Schomburg Center for Research in Black Culture. New York.

Published Sources

Aaron, Daniel. *Writers on the Left*. New York: Harcourt, Brace and World, 1961.

Adams, Michael Henry. *Harlem Lost and Found: An Architectural and Social History, 1765–1915*. New York: Monacelli Press, 2002.

Agee, James, and Walker Evans. *Let Us Now Praise Famous Men*. Boston: Houghton Mifflin, 1941.

Aldridge, Cathy. "Exhibit on Everybody's Mind." *New York Amsterdam News*, 1 February 1969, 38.

Alinder, James. "Chronology." In *Roy DeCarava, Photographs*, ed. James Alinder, 187–91. Carmel, CA: Friends of Photography / Matrix Publications, 1981.

———, ed. *Roy DeCarava, Photographs*. Carmel, CA: Friends of Photography / Matrix Publications, 1981.

Allen, Danielle. "Ralph Ellison on the Tragi-Comedy of Citizenship." In *Ralph Ellison and the Raft of Hope: A Political Companion to* Invisible Man, ed. Lucas E. Morel, 37–57. Lexington: University Press of Kentucky, 2004.

Allen, James, ed. *Without Sanctuary: Lynching Photography in America.* New York: Twin Palms Publishers, 2000.

Allred, Jeff. "From Eye to We: Richard Wright's *12 Million Black Voices,* Documentary, and Pedagogy." *American Literature* 78, no. 3 (2006): 549–83.

Als, Hilton. "Ghosts in the House." *New Yorker* 79, no. 32 (27 October 2003): 64–75.

———. "GWTW." In *Without Sanctuary: Lynching Photography in America,* ed. James Allen, 38–44. New York: Twin Palms Publishers, 2000.

Anderson, Edith. *Love in Exile: An American Writer's Memoir of Life in Divided Berlin.* New York: Steerforth Press, 1999.

Appiah, Kwame Anthony. "A Long Way from Home: Wright in the Gold Coast." In *Richard Wright,* ed. Harold Bloom, 173–90. New York: Chelsea House, 1987.

Arnold, Martin. "Paintings Defaced at Metropolitan; One a Rembrandt." *New York Times,* 18 January 1969, 1, 28.

Avedon, Richard. *Evidence, 1944–1994.* New York: Random House, 1994.

———. *Observations.* With comments by Truman Capote. New York: Simon & Schuster, 1959.

Avedon, Richard, and Doon Arbus. *The Sixties.* New York: Random House, 1999.

Avedon, Richard, and James Baldwin. *Nothing Personal.* Photographs by Richard Avedon and text by James Baldwin. New York: Atheneum, 1964.

———. Photos by Richard Avedon and text by James Baldwin. New York: Atheneum, 1964.

Bailey, David. "Rethinking Black Representations: From Positive Images to Cultural Photographic Practices." *Exposure* 27, no. 4 (Fall 1990): 37–46.

Bailey, David, and Stuart Hall. "The Vertigo of Displacement: Shifts within Black Documentary Practices." *Ten.8* 2, no. 3 (Spring 1992): 15–23.

Baker, Houston A., Jr. *Blues, Ideology, and Afro-American Literature: A Vernacular Theory.* Chicago: University of Chicago Press, 1984.

Baldwin, James. *Baldwin: Collected Essays,* ed. Toni Morrison. New York: Library of America, 1998.

———. *Baldwin: Early Novels and Stories.* New York: Library of America, 1998.

———. *No Name in the Street.* New York: Laurel, 1972.

———. *The Price of the Ticket: Collected Nonfiction, 1948–1985.* New York: St. Martin's / Marek, 1985.

———. "Sweet Lorraine." In *To Be Young, Gifted and Black: Lorraine Hansberry in Her Own Words,* by Lorraine Hansberry, ed. Robert Nemiroff, ix–xii. Englewood Cliffs, NJ: Prentice-Hall, 1969.

Baldwin, James, and Richard Avedon. *Nothing Personal.* Photographs by Richard Avedon and text by James Baldwin. New York: Atheneum, 1964.

Balshaw, Maria. *Looking for Harlem: Urban Aesthetics in African-American Literature.* London: Pluto Press, 2000.

Banes, Sally. *Greenwich Village, 1963: Avant-Garde Performance and the Effervescent Body.* Durham, NC: Duke University Press, 1993.

Barthes, Roland. *Camera Lucida: Reflections on Photography,* trans. Richard Howard. New York: Hill & Wang, 1981.

———. "The Great Family of Man." In *Mythologies,* trans. Annette Lavers, 100–102. New York: Hill & Wang, 1972.

Batchen, Geoffrey. *Burning with Desire: The Conception of Photography.* Cambridge, MA: MIT Press, 1999.

———. "Ere the Substance Fade." In *Photographs Objects Histories: On the Materiality of Images,* ed. Elizabeth Edwards and Janice Hart, 32–46. London: Routledge, 2004.

Baughman, James L. *Henry R. Luce and the Rise of the American News Media.* Boston: Twayne Publishers, 1987.

Benston, Kimberly. *Performing Blackness: Enactments of African-American Modernism.* London: Routledge, 2000.

Berger, John. "Understanding a Photograph." In *Classic Essays on Photography,* ed. Alan Trachtenberg, 291–94. New Haven, CT: Leetes Island Books, 1980.

Bethune, Beverly Moore. *The New York Photo League: A Political History.* Ann Arbor, MI: University Microfilms International, 1982.

Bey, Dawoud. Artist portfolio. In *The Jewish Identity Project and New American Photography,* ed. Susan Chevlowe, 48–55. New York: Jewish Museum / New Haven, CT: Yale University Press, 2005.

Bezner, Lili Corbus. "Aaron Siskind: An Interview." *History of Photography* 16, no. 1 (1992): 28–33.

———. *Photography and Politics in America: From the New Deal into the Cold War.* Baltimore: Johns Hopkins University Press, 1999.

"Big Crowds Force Museum to Cut Off 'Harlem' Show Line." *New York Times,* 27 January 1969, 35.

Blair, Sara. "Jewish America through the Lens." In *Jewish in America,* ed. Sara Blair and Jonathan Freedman, 113–34. Ann Arbor: University of Michigan Press, 2004.

Bold, Christine. *The WPA Guides: Mapping America.* Jackson: University Press of Mississippi, 1999.

Bond, Julian. "Foreword." In *Memories of the Southern Civil Rights Movement,* by Danny Lyon, 6–7. Chapel Hill: University of North Carolina Press, 1992.

Bontemps, Arna. "Langston Hughes." *Ebony* 1, no. 11 (October 1946): 19–22.

"Books." *New Yorker* 41, no. 39 (13 November 1965): 276.

Bourke-White, Margaret. *Portrait of Myself.* New York: Simon & Schuster, 1963.

Bradley, Marion Zimmer. "Some Remarks on Marriage." *The Ladder,* July 1957, 14–16.

Brawarsky, Sandee. "The Mystery of Henry Roth." *Jewish Week* 218, no. 15 (2 September, 2005): 27.

Bright, Susan. *Art Photography Now.* London: Aperture, 2005.

Bristol, Horace. *Stories from Life: The Photography of Horace Bristol.* Athens: University of Georgia / Georgia Museum of Art, 1995.

Brown, Claude. *Manchild in the Promised Land.* New York: Macmillan, 1965.

Brustein, Robert. "Everybody Knows My Name." *New York Review of Books* 3, no. 9 (17 December, 1964): 10–11.

Burgin, Victor. "Looking at Photographs." In *The Photography Reader*, ed. Liz Wells, 130–37. London: Routledge, 2002.

Burns, Ben. "They're Not Uncle Tom's Children." *The Reporter* 14, no. 5 (8 March 1956): 21–23.

Burns, Stanley. *Sleeping Beauty: Memorial Photography in America*. Santa Fe: Twelvetrees Press, 1990.

Cadava, Eduardo. *Words of Light: Theses on the Photography of History*. Princeton, NJ: Princeton University Press, 1997.

Caldwell, Earl. *The Caldwell Journals*. Robert C. Maynard Institute for Journalism Education History Project, October 2005. Posted online at www.maynardije.org/news/features/caldwell/.

Caldwell, Erskine, and Margaret Bourke-White. *You Have Seen Their Faces*. New York: Modern Age, 1937.

Callahan, John. "Frequencies of Eloquence: The Performance and Composition of *Invisible Man*." In *New Essays on* Invisible Man, ed. Robert O'Mealley, 55–94. Cambridge: Cambridge University Press, 1988.

———. *In the African-American Grain: The Pursuit of Voice in Twentieth-Century Black Fiction*. Urbana: University of Illinois Press, 1988.

———. "Introduction." In *Flying Home and Other Stories*, by Ralph Ellison, ix–xxxviii. New York: Random House, 1996.

Calomiris, Angela. *Red Masquerade: Undercover for the FBI*. Philadelphia: J. B. Lippincott, 1950.

Campbell, James. *Talking at the Gates: A Life of James Baldwin*. New York: Viking, 1991.

Capeci, Dominic J., Jr. *The Harlem Riot of 1943*. Philadelphia: Temple University Press, 1977.

Carabi, Angels. "Interview with Toni Morrison." *Belles Lettres* 10, no. 2 (Spring 1995): 40–43.

Carlebach, Michael L. *American Photojournalism Comes of Age*. Washington, DC: Smithsonian Institution Press, 1997.

Carson, Clayborne. "Blacks and Jews in the Civil Rights Movement: The Case of SNCC." In *Bridges and Boundaries: African Americans and American Jews*, ed. Jack Salzman, 36–49. New York: George Braziller / Jewish Museum, 1992.

———. *In Struggle: SNCC and the Black Awakening of the 1960s*. Cambridge, MA: Harvard University Press, 1981.

Carter, Michael [Milton Smith]. "Biggest Art Show." *Ebony* 1, no. 9 (August 1946): 49.

———. "Book-of-the-Month Author Talks for AFRO." In *Conversations with Richard Wright*, ed. Keneth Kinnamon and Michel Fabre, 53–56. Jackson: University Press of Mississippi, 1993.

———. "A Day at Home with a Chorus Girl." *Ebony* 1, no. 4 (February 1946): 18–23.

———. "244,000 Native Sons." *Look* 4 (21 May 1940): 8–12.

Cartier-Bresson, Henri. *The Decisive Moment*. New York: Simon & Schuster, 1952.

Cayton, Horace R. "Wright's New Book More than a Study of Social Status." *Pittsburgh Courier* 32, no. 16 (15 November 1941): 13.

Cheney, Anne. *Lorraine Hansberry*. Boston: G. K. Hall, 1984.

Chevlowe, Susan. "Framing Jewishness: Photography and the Boundaries of Community." In *The Jewish Identity Project and New American Photography*, ed. Susan Chevlowe, 1–26. New York: Jewish Museum / New Haven, CT: Yale University Press, 2005.

Chiarenza, Carl. *Aaron Siskind: Pleasures and Terrors*. New York: Little Brown / Center for Creative Photography, 1982.

Chiwengo, Ngwarsungu. "Gazing through the Screen: Richard Wright's Africa." In *Richard Wright's Travel Writings: New Reflections*, ed. Virginia Whatley Smith, 20–44. Jackson: University Press of Mississippi, 2001.

Clark, Kenneth B. "Candor about Negro-Jewish Relations." *Commentary* 1, no. 2 (February 1945): 8.

———. "Group Violence: A Preliminary Study of Attitudinal Patterns of Its Acceptance and Rejection, A Study of the 1943 Harlem Riot." *Journal of Social Psychology* 19 (1944): 319–37.

Clarke, ed. *William Styron's Nat Turner: Ten Black Writers Respond*. New York: Beacon Press, 1968.

Cobb, Nina Kressner. "Richard Wright and the Third World." In *Critical Essays on Richard Wright*, ed. Yoshinobu Hakutani, 228–39. Boston: G. K. Hall, 1982.

Cohen, Lizabeth. *A Consumers' Republic: The Politics of Mass Consumption in Postwar America*. New York: Knopf, 2003.

Coleman, A. D. "Latent Image: Christmas Gift." *Village Voice* 14, no. 15 (23 January 1969): 15.

———. "No Pictures: Some Thoughts on Jews in Photography." *Photo Review* 23, no. 1 (2000): 2–5.

The Complete Report of Mayor LaGuardia's Commission on the Harlem Riot of March 19, 1935. New York: Arno Press, 1969.

Conner, Marc C. "The Litany of Things: Sacrament and History in *Invisible Man*." In *Ralph Ellison and the Raft of Hope: A Political Companion to* Invisible Man, ed. Lucas E. Morel, 171–92. Lexington: University Press of Kentucky, 2004.

Cripps, Thomas R. "Introduction." In *Hanover*, by Jack Thorne, i–vii. New York: Arno Press / New York Times, 1969.

Cruse, Harold. *The Crisis of the Negro Intellectual*. New York: William Morrow, 1967.

Dace, Tish, ed. *Langston Hughes: The Contemporary Reviews*. New York: Cambridge University Press, 1997.

Daniel, Pete, and Sally Stein, eds. *Official Images: New Deal Photography*. Washington, DC: Smithsonian Institution Press, 1987.

Davidov, Judith Fryer. *Women's Camera Work: Self/Body/Other in American Visual Culture*. Durham, NC: Duke University Press, 1998.

Davis, Ben, Jr. "Richard Wright's Powerful Narrative Beautifully Illustrated in New Book." *New York Sunday Worker*, 9 November 1941, 22.

DeCarava, Roy. "Gittel." Posted online at www.masters-of-photography.com/D/decarava/decarava_gittel.html.

DeCarava, Sherry Turner. "Pages from a Notebook." In *Roy DeCarava: A Retrospective*, ed. Peter Galassi, 41–60. New York: Museum of Modern Art/Abrams, 1996.

De Jongh, James. *Vicious Modernism: Black Harlem and the Literary Imagination*. Cambridge: Cambridge University Press, 1990.

Denning, Michael. *The Cultural Front: The Laboring of American Culture in the Twentieth Century*. London: Verso, 1997.

Deschin, Jacob. "Harlem's History in Visual Survey." *New York Times*, 19 January 1969, D31.

——. "Nineteen in Exhibit." *New York Times*, 12 June 1955, 14X.

DeVoto, Bernard. "Report on Photography." *Saturday Review of Literature* 17, no. 12 (15 January 1938): 8.

Dickstein, Morris. *Gates of Eden: American Culture in the Sixties*. New York: Basic Books, 1977.

"Disturber of the Peace: James Baldwin." Interview with James Baldwin. *Mademoiselle* 57, no. 1 (May 1963): 174–75, 199, 201–7.

Doud, Richard. Interview with Edwin and Louise Rosskam, Roosevelt, NJ, 3 August 1965. Smithsonian Archives of American Art. Posted online at www.aaa.si.edu/oralhist/rosska65.htm.

Driskell, David C. "The Evolution of a Black Aesthetic, 1920–1950." In *Two Centuries of Black American Art*, 74–78. New York: Alfred A. Knopf for the Los Angeles County Museum of Art, 1976.

Dubin, Steven C. *Displays of Power: Memory and Amnesia in the American Museum*. New York: New York University Press, 1999.

DuBois, W.E.B. *The Black North in 1901: A Social Study*. New York: Arno, 1969.

——. *The Souls of Black Folk*. New York: Penguin, 1989 [orig. 1903].

Dupee, F. W. "James Baldwin and the 'Man.'" *New York Review of Books* 1, no. 1 (February 1963): 1–2.

Eckman, Fern Marja. *The Furious Passage of James Baldwin*. New York: M. Evans / Lippincott, 1966.

Editorial, "Beyond Rights: The Issue of Human Dignity." *Life* 54, no. 21 (24 May 1963): 4.

"Editor's Note." *Life* 54, no. 21 (24 May 1963): 3.

Edwards, Brent. "The Literary Ellington." *Representations* 22, no. 1 (Winter 2002): 1–29.

——. *The Practice of Diaspora: Literature, Translation, and the Rise of Black Internationalism*. Cambridge, MA: Harvard University Press, 2003.

Elisofon, Eliot. "Types of Camera." In *Photo Notes, February 1933–Spring 1950; Filmfront, December 1934–March 1935*, 3–4. Rochester, NY: Visual Studies Workshop, 1977. [Piece orig. published August 1938.]

Elkins, James. "What Do We Want Photography to Be? A Response to Michael Fried." *Critical Inquiry* 31, no. 3 (Summer 2005): 938–56.

Ellis, Cassandra M. "The Black Boy Looks at the Silver Screen: Baldwin as Moviegoer." In *Re-Viewing James Baldwin: Things Not Seen*, ed. Quentin L. Miller, 190–214. Philadelphia: Temple University Press, 2000.

Ellison, Ralph. *Collected Essays of Ralph Ellison*, ed. John F. Callahan. New York: Modern Library, 1995.

———. "Eyewitness Story of Riot: False Rumors Spurred Mob." *New York Post*, 2 August 1943, 4.

———. "Harlem's America." *New Leader* 46, no. 19 (26 September 1966): 31–32.

———. *Invisible Man*. New York: Random House, 1980 [orig. 1952].

———. *Juneteenth: A Novel*, ed. John F. Callahan. New York: Vintage, 2000.

———. "Native Land." *New Masses*, 2 June 1942, 29.

Ellison, Ralph, and Albert Murray. *Trading Twelves: The Selected Letters of Ralph Ellison and Albert Murray*, ed. John F. Callahan. New York: Vintage, 2001.

Emerson, Ralph Waldo. *The Works of Ralph Waldo Emerson*, ed. James Elliot Cabot. 14 volumes. Boston: Riverside Press, 1883.

English, Daylanne. *Unnatural Selections: Eugenics in American Modernism and the Harlem Renaissance*. Chapel Hill: University of North Carolina Press, 2004.

Entin, Joseph. "Modernist Documentary: Aaron Siskind's Harlem Document." *Yale Journal of Criticism* 12, no. 2 (Fall 1999): 321–56.

Evans, Walker. *Walker Evans: American Photographs*. New York: Museum of Modern Art, 2003.

Eyman, Scott. *Print the Legend: The Life and Times of John Ford*. Baltimore: Johns Hopkins University Press, 2001.

Fabre, Michel. *From Harlem to Paris: Black American Writers in France, 1840–1980*. Champaign-Urbana: University of Illinois Press, 1991.

———. *The Unfinished Quest of Richard Wright*, trans. Isabel Barzun. New York: William Morrow, 1973.

Fabre, Michel, and Robert E. Skinner. "Introduction." In *Plan B: A Novel*, by Chester Himes, v–xxx. Jackson: University of Mississippi Press, 1993.

Farm Security Administration/Office of War Information Black and White Negatives. Library of Congress, Online Prints and Photographs Catalogue. Posted online at http://lcweb2.loc.gov/pp/fsaquery.html.

Federal Bureau of Investigation. "Richard Nathaniel Wright." File 100-157464. Posted online at http://foia.fbi.gov/rnwright/rnwright1a.pdf.

Federal Writers' Project of the Works Progress Administration. *New York Panorama*. New York: Random House, 1938.

Finnegan, Cara A. *Picturing Poverty: Print Culture and FSA Photographs*. Washington, DC: Smithsonian Books, 2005.

Fleischhauer, Carl, and Beverly W. Brannan. "Introduction." In *Documenting America, 1935–1943*, ed. Carl Fleischhauer and Beverly W. Brannan, 1–14. Berkeley and Los Angeles: University of California Press, 1988.

Foley, Barbara. "Reading Redness: Politics and Audience in Ralph Ellison's Early Short Fiction." *Journal of Narrative Theory* 29, no. 3 (Fall 1999): 323–39.

Frederickson, George M. *Black Liberation: A Comparative History of Black Ideologies in the United States and South Africa.* New York: Oxford University Press, 1995.

Gaines, Kevin K. *American Africans in Ghana: Black Expatriates and the Civil Rights Era.* Chapel Hill: University of North Carolina Press, 2006.

Galassi, Peter. *Henri Cartier-Bresson: The Early Work.* New York: Museum of Modern Art, 1987.

———, ed. *Roy DeCarava: A Retrospective.* New York: Museum of Modern Art / Abrams, 1996.

———, ed. *Walker Evans and Company.* New York: Museum of Modern Art, 2000.

Gandal, Keith. *The Virtues of the Vicious: Jacob Riis, Stephen Crane, and the Spectacle of the Slum.* New York: Oxford University Press, 1997.

Gates, Henry Louis, Jr. "The Face and Voice of Blackness." In *Facing History: The Black Image in American Art, 1710–1940*, ed. Guy C. McElroy and Christopher C. French, xxix–xlvi. Washington, DC: Bedford Arts / Corcoran Gallery of Art, 1990.

———. "The Trope of a New Negro and the Reconstruction of the Image of the Black." *Representations* 24, *America Reconstructed, 1840–1940* (Autumn 1988): 129–55.

———. "The Welcome Table: James Baldwin in Exile." In *Exile and Creativity: Signposts, Travelers, Outsiders, Backward Glances*, ed. Susan Rubin Suleiman, 305–20. Durham, NC: Duke University Press, 1998.

Gayle, Addison, Jr. *The Way of the World: The Black Novel in America.* Garden City, NY: Anchor Press, 1975.

Gee, Helen. *Photography of the Fifties: An American Perspective.* Tucson: Center for Creative Photography / University of Arizona, 1980.

Gilbert, George. *The Illustrated Worldwide Who's Who of Jews in Photography.* Riverdale, NY: G. Gilbert, 1996.

Gilje, Paul A. *Rioting in America.* Bloomington: Indiana University Press, 1996.

Gilroy, Paul. *The Black Atlantic: Modernity and Double Consciousness.* Cambridge, MA: Harvard University Press, 1993.

Gilyard, Keith. "John Oliver Killens." *Chickenbones: A Journal*, May 2003. Posted online at www.nathanielturner.com/johnoliverkillens.htm.

———. *Liberation Memories: The Rhetoric and Poetics of John Oliver Killens.* Detroit: Wayne State University Press, 2003.

Glueck, Grace. "Adam C., Mother Brown, Malcolm X." *New York Times*, 12 January 1969, D26.

———. "Art: 'Harlem on My Mind' in Slides, Tapes and Photos." *New York Times*, 17 January 1969, 28.

———. "The Total Involvement of Thomas Hoving." *New York Times Magazine*, 8 December 1968, 47ff.

Goldberg, Vicki. *Margaret Bourke-White: A Biography*. New York: Harper and Row, 1986.

Golden, Thelma. *Freestyle*. New York: Studio Museum in Harlem, 2001.

Golden, Thelma, Kellie Jones, and Chrissie Iles. *Lorna Simpson*. London: Phaidon, 2002.

Goldin, Amy. "Harlem Out of Mind." *Art News* 68, no. 3 (March 1969): 53.

Goldsby, Jacqueline. *A Spectacular Secret: Lynching in American Life and Literature*. Chicago: University of Chicago Press, 2006.

Graham, Mike. "Photography: TLRs." 9 October 2001. Posted online at www.geocities.com/heidoscop/tlr.htm.

Greenberg, Cheryl Lynn. *"Or Does It Explode?": Black Harlem in the Great Depression*. New York: Oxford University Press, 1991.

Grierson, John. *Grierson on Documentary*, ed. Forsyth Hardy. New York: Harcourt Brace, 1947.

Griffin, Farah Jasmine. *"Who Set You Flowin'?": The African-American Migration Narrative*. New York: Oxford University Press, 1995.

Guimond, James. *American Photography and the American Dream*. Chapel Hill: University of North Carolina Press, 1991.

Gurock, Jeffrey S. *When Harlem Was Jewish, 1870–1930*. New York: Columbia University Press, 1979.

Hakutani, Yoshinobu. *Richard Wright and Racial Discourse*. Columbia: University of Missouri Press, 1996.

Hales, Peter B. *Silver Cities: The Photography of American Urbanization, 1839–1915*. Philadelphia: Temple University Press, 1984.

Halstead, Fred. *Harlem Stirs*. New York: Marzani and Munsell, 1966.

Handler, M. S. "75 Artists Urge Closing of Museum's 'Insulting' Harlem Exhibit." *New York Times*, 23 January 1969, 14.

Hansberry, Lorraine. "Genet, Mailer, and the New Paternalism." *Village Voice* 4, no. 32 (1 June 1961): 10, 14–15.

———. *Les Blancs: The Collected Last Plays of Lorraine Hansberry*, ed. Robert Nemiroff. New York: Random House, 1972.

———. *The Movement: Documentary of a Struggle for Equality*. New York: Simon & Schuster, 1964.

———. *A Raisin in the Sun*. New York: Random House, 1959.

———. *To Be Young, Gifted and Black: Lorraine Hansberry in Her Own Words*, ed. Robert Nemiroff. Englewood Cliffs, NJ: Prentice-Hall, 1969.

Harap, Louis. *In the Mainstream: The Jewish Presence in Twentieth-Century American Literature, 1950s–1980s*. New York: Greenwood Press, 1987.

"Harlem after a Night of Rioting." *New York Times*, 3 August 1934, 10–11.

"The Harlem Ghetto: Winter 1948." *Commentary* 5, no. 2 (February 1948): 165.

"Harlem Toll: 6 Dead, 543 Hurt, 500 Jailed." *New York Daily News*, 3 August 1943, C2 10–13.

Harlow, Alvin F. *Old Bowery Days: The Chronicles of a Famous Street.* New York: D. Appleton, 1931.

Harris, Jonathan. *Federal Art and National Culture: The Politics of Identity in New Deal America.* New York: Cambridge University Press, 1995.

Harris, Michael D. *Colored Pictures: Race and Visual Representation.* Chapel Hill: University of North Carolina Press, 2003.

Harris, Middleton, ed. *The Black Book.* New York: Random House, 1974.

Harrison, Paul Carter. *The Drama of Nommo.* New York: Grove Press, 1972.

Harvey, Sylvia. "Who Wants to Know What and Why?—Some Problems for Documentary in the '80s," *Ten.8* 23 (1986): 26–31.

Heartney, Eleanor. "Figuring Absence: Lorna Simpson, Photography: Sean Kelly Gallery, New York, New York." *Art in America* 83, no. 12 (December 1995): 86–87.

Hentoff, Nat. "Urban Blight." *New Yorker* 41, no. 24 (31 July 1965): 71–79.

Hickey, Dave. "In the Theatre of Innocence." In *American Edge*, by Steve Schapiro, n.p. New York: Arena Editions, 2000.

Himes, Chester. *Blind Man with a Pistol.* New York: Vintage Crime / Black Lizard, 1989.

———. *Cotton Comes to Harlem.* London: Cannongate, 2001 [orig. 1964].

———. *My Life of Absurdity: The Autobiography of Chester Himes*, vol. 2. New York: Thunder's Mouth Press, 1998.

———. *Plan B: A Novel*, ed. Michel Fabre and Robert E. Skinner. Jackson: University of Mississippi Press, 1993.

———. *The Quality of Hurt.* Garden City, NY: Doubleday, 1972.

Holland, Patricia, Jo Spence, and Simon Watney. "Introduction: The Politics and Sexual Politics of Photography." In *Photography/Politics 2: Photography Workshop*, 1–7. London: Comedia Publishing Group, 1986.

Holmes, Doloris. Interview with Cliff Joseph (1972). Smithsonian Archives of American Art. Posted online at www.aaa.si.edu/collections/oralhistories/transcripts/joseph72.htm.

Holzer, Jenny. *Laments.* New York: Dia Art Foundation, 1990.

———. *Truth before Power.* Bregenza, Austria: Kuntshaus Bregenz / New York: DAP, 2005.

hooks, bell. "In Our Glory: Photography and Black Life." In *The Photography Reader*, ed. Liz Wells, 387–94. New York: Routledge, 2002.

Hoving, Thomas. "Director's Note." *Metropolitan Museum of Art Bulletin* 27, no. 5 (January 1969): 243–44.

———. *Making the Mummies Dance: Inside the Metropolitan Museum of Art.* New York: Simon & Schuster, 1993.

Howard, Jane. "Telling Talk from a Negro Writer." *Life* 54, no. 21 (24 May 1963): 81–90.

Howe, Irving. "Black Boys and Native Sons." *Dissent* 10, no. 4 (Autumn 1963): 353–68.

Hughes, Langston. "Backstage: Entertainers Keep Busy with Hobbies and Friends between Acts." *Ebony* 4, no. 5 (March 1949): 36–38.

———. "Church for the Deaf: Choir Sings Hymns in Sign Language in Harlem Church." *Ebony* 4, no. 7 (May 1949): 47, 49–50.

———. *I Wonder as I Wander: An Autobiographical Journey*. New York: Hill & Wang, 1956.

———. *Langston Hughes and the Chicago Defender: Essays on Race, Politics, Culture, 1942–62*, ed. Christopher C. De Santis. Urbana: University of Illinois Press, 1995.

———. *The Simple Omnibus*. New York: Aeonian Press, 1961.

Hughes, Langston, and John C. Alston. "Atlanta." *Ebony* 3, no. 3 (January 1948): 19–24.

Hughes, Langston, and Roy DeCarava. *The Sweet Flypaper of Life*. New York: Simon & Schuster, 1955.

Hughes, Robert. *American Visions: The Epic History of Art in America*. New York: Knopf, 1999.

Hurley, F. Jack. *Portrait of a Decade: Roy Stryker and the Development of Documentary Photography in the Thirties*. Baton Rouge: Louisiana State University Press, 1972.

Ings, Richard. "Street Ballet/Urban Drama: Harlem Sidewalks in Photography, 1900–1960." 16 November 2000. Posted online at www.nottingham.ac.uk/3cities/.

"Italians Clash with Negroes." *New York Herald Tribune*, 4 October 1935, 10.

Jackson, Lawrence. *Ralph Ellison: The Emergence of Genius*. New York: John Wiley and Sons, 2002.

———. "Ralph Ellison's Invented Life: A Meeting with the Ancestors." In *The Cambridge Companion to Ralph Ellison*, ed. Ross Posnock, 11–34. New York: Cambridge University Press, 2005.

Jacobs, Karen. *The Eye's Mind: Literary Modernism and Visual Culture*. Ithaca, NY: Cornell University Press, 2001.

Jakobson, Roman, and Morris Halle. *Fundamentals of Language*. 2nd ed., rev. The Hague: Mouton, 1971.

James, Henry. *The American Scene*. New York: Horizon, 1967 [orig. 1907].

Johnson, James Weldon. *Autobiography of an Ex-Coloured Man*. New York: Vintage, 1989 [orig. 1927].

———. *Black Manhattan*. New York: Da Capo, 1991 [orig. 1930].

Jonas, Gilbert. *Freedom's Sword: The NAACP and the Struggle against Racism in America, 1909–1969*. New York: Routledge, 2005.

Jones, Kellie. "In Their Own Image," *Artforum* 29, no. 3 (November 1990): 133–38.

Jones, Leroi [Amiri Baraka]. *Black Music*. New York: William Morrow, 1968.

Jurca, Catharine. *White Diaspora: The Suburb and the Twentieth-Century American Novel*. Princeton, NJ: Princeton University Press, 2001.

Kao, Deborah Martin. "Personal Vision in Aaron Siskind's Documentary Practice." In *Aaron Siskind: Toward a Personal Vision, 1935–1955*, ed. Deborah Martin Kao and Charles A. Meyer, 13–25. Chestnut Hill: Boston College Museum of Art, 1994.

Kaplan, Louis. *American Exposures: Photography and Community in the Twentieth Century*. Minneapolis: University of Minnesota Press, 2005.

Katzman, Laura. "Ben Shahn's New York: Scenes from the Living Theater." In *Ben Shahn's New York: The Photography of Modern Times*, by Deborah Martin Kao, Laura Katzman, and Jenna Webster, 25–29. Cambridge, MA: Fogg Art Museum, Harvard University Art Museums / New Haven, CT: Yale University Press, 2000.

Kellman, Steven G. *Redemption: The Life of Henry Roth*. New York: W. W. Norton, 2005.

Killens, John Oliver. *And Then We Heard the Thunder*. New York: Alfred A. Knopf, 1964.

———. *Black Man's Burden*. New York: Touchstone, 1970.

———. "Books." *Freedom* 1, no. 7 (June 1952): 7.

———. *The Cotillion, or One Good Bull Is Half the Herd*. New York: Coffee House Press, 2002 [orig. 1971].

Kinnamon, Keneth, and Michel Fabre. *Conversations with Richard Wright*. Jackson: University Press of Mississippi, 1993.

Kirstein, Lincoln. "Photographs of America: Walker Evans." In *American Photographs/Walker Evans*, by Walker Evans, 189–98. New York: Museum of Modern Art, 1988 [orig. 1938].

Korda, Michael. *Another Life: A Memoir of Other People*. New York: Delta, 2000.

Kozloff, Max. "An Interview with Robert Motherwell." *Artforum* 4, no. 1 (September 1965): 33–37.

———. *New York: Capital of Photography*. New York: Jewish Museum / New Haven, CT: Yale University Press, 2002.

Kramer, Hilton. "Politicalizing the Metropolitan Museum." *New York Times*, 29 January 1969, D31.

Kruger, Barbara. *Money Talks*. New York: Skarstedt Fine Art, 2005.

———. *Remote Control: Power, Culture, and the World of Appearances*. Cambridge, MA: MIT Press, 1994.

Lakoff, George, and Mark Johnson. *Metaphors We Live By*. Chicago: University of Chicago Press, 1980.

Lee, Anthony. *Picturing Chinatown: Art and Orientalism in San Francisco*. Berkeley and Los Angeles: University of California Press, 2001.

Lee, Nikki S. Artist portfolio. In *The Jewish Identity Project and New American Photography*, ed. Susan Chevlowe, 82–89. New York: Jewish Museum / New Haven, CT: Yale University Press, 2005.

Leeming, David. "An Interview with James Baldwin on Henry James." *Henry James Review* 8, no. 1 (Fall 1986): 47–56.

———. *James Baldwin: A Biography*. New York: Knopf, 1994.

Lewis, David Levering. "Introduction." In *The Souls of Black Folk*, by W.E.B. DuBois, xi–xxxiii. New York: Modern Library, 2003.

———. *When Harlem Was in Vogue*. New York: Knopf, 1981.

Livingston, Jane. "The Art of Richard Avedon." In *Evidence, 1944–1994*, by Richard Avedon, 11–101. New York: Random House, 1994.

———. *The New York School: Photographs, 1936–1963*. New York: Stewart Tabori & Chang, 1992.

Locke, Alain. "Harlem: Dark Weather-Vane." *Survey Graphic* 25, no. 8 (August 1936): 457–62, 493–95.

Longstaff, S. A. "The New York School of Intellectuals." In *The Johns Hopkins Guide to Literary Theory and Criticism*, ed. Martin Groden and Martin Kreiswirth, 1295–96. Baltimore: Johns Hopkins University Press, 1997.

"Looters at Work and in Custody during the Rioting in Harlem." *New York Herald Tribune*, 3 August 1943, 6.

Lowe, John. "Richard Wright as Traveler/Ethnographer: The Conundrums of Pagan Spain." In *Richard Wright's Travel Writings: New Reflections*, ed. Virginia Whatley Smith, 121–43. Jackson: University Press of Mississippi, 2001.

Lukasa, Jane. "Seeking a Cultural Equality: The Visual Record of Robert H. McNeill." In *Visual Journal: Harlem and D.C. in the Thirties and Forties*, ed. Deborah Willis and Jane Lukasa, 61–95. Washington, DC: Center for African American History and Culture and Smithsonian Institution Press, 1996.

Lyon, Danny. *Memories of the Southern Civil Rights Movement*. Chapel Hill: University of North Carolina Press, 1992.

———. *The Paper Negative*. New York: Bleak Beauty, 1980.

———. *Pictures from the New World*. New York: Aperture, 1981.

Macdonald, Dwight. "Masscult and Midcult II." *Partisan Review* 27, no. 3 (Fall 1960): 589–631.

Mackey, Nathaniel. "Sound and Sentiment, Sound and Symbol." In *The Jazz Cadence of American Culture*, ed. Robert G. O'Mealley, 602–28. New York: Columbia University Press, 1998.

Macon, Wanda. "John Oliver Killens." In *The Oxford Companion to African American Literature*, ed. William L. Andrews, Frances Smith Foster, and Trudier Harris, 419–20. New York: Oxford University Press.

Mailer, Norman. "Mailer to Hansberry." *Village Voice* 4, no. 33 (8 June 1961): 11–12.

"Male and Female Vandals Blitz Harlem in Sunday [Melee]." *New York Amsterdam News*, 7 August 1943, 1.

Mangione, Jerre. *The Dream and the Deal: The Federal Writers' Project, 1935–1943*. Boston: Little, Brown, 1972.

"The March of the Negro." *New York World-Telegram*, 11 November 1941, 13.

Margolies, Edward, and Michel Fabre. *The Several Lives of Chester Himes*. Jackson: University Press of Mississippi, 1997.

Margolis, Eric. "The New Deal and Photography: Liberal Documentary Goes to School: Farm Security Administration Photographs of Students, Teachers and Schools." In *American Visual Cultures*, ed. David Holloway and John Beck, 107–15. London: Continuum, 2005.

Martin, Jay. *Nathanael West: The Art of His Life*. New York: Farrar, Straus and Giroux, 1970.

Maxwell, William J. "'Creative and Cultural Lag': The Cultural Education of Ralph Ellison." In *A Historical Guide to Ralph Ellison*, ed. Steven C. Tracy, 59–83. New York: Oxford University Press, 2004.

Mayer, Chris, and Larry Berman. "An Interview with Jay Maisel." BermanGraphics, 2001–2. Posted online at http://bermangraphics.com/press/jaymaisel.htm.

Mazón, Mauricio. *The Zoot-Suit Riots: The Psychology of Symbolic Annihilation*. Austin: University of Texas Press, 1988.

McCausland, Elizabeth. "Documentary Photography." In *Photo Notes, February 1933–Spring 1950; Filmfront, December 1934–March 1935*, 6–9. Rochester, NY: Visual Studies Workshop, 1977. [Piece orig. published January 1939.]

McDowell, Deborah. "Harlem Nocturne." *Women's Review of Books* 9, no. 9 (1992): 1–5.

McElvaine, Robert S. *The Great Depression: America, 1929–1941*. New York: Times Books, 1984.

Melnick, Jeffrey. *A Right to Sing the Blues: African Americans, Jews, and American Popular Song*. Cambridge, MA: Harvard University Press, 1999.

Meltzer, Milton, and Langston Hughes. *Black Magic: A Pictorial History of the African-American in the Performing Arts*. New York: DaCapo Press, 1967.

Mercer, Kobena. *Welcome to the Jungle: New Positions in Black Cultural Studies*. New York: Routledge, 1994.

Michaels, Walter Benn. *Our America: Nativism, Modernism, and Pluralism*. Durham, NC: Duke University Press, 1995.

Milkman, Paul. *PM: A New Deal in Journalism, 1940–1948*. New Brunswick, NJ: Rutgers University Press, 1997.

Miller, Elisse. "'The Maw of Western Culture': James Baldwin and the Anxieties of Influence." *African American Review* 38, no. 4 (Winter 2004): 625–37.

Miller, Ivor. "'If It Hasn't Been One of Color': An Interview with Roy DeCarava." *Callaloo* 13 (1990): 847–57.

Miller, James A. "The Smiths and Their Art." In *Harlem: The Vision of Morgan and Marvin Smith*, 1–13. Lexington: University Press of Kentucky, 1998.

Miller, Joshua L. "'A Striking Addiction to Irreality': *Nothing Personal* and the Legacy of the Photo-Text Genre." In *Re-Viewing James Baldwin: Things Not Seen*, ed. D. Quentin Miller, 154–89. Philadelphia: Temple University Press, 2000.

Mitchell, W.J.T. *Picture Theory: Essays on Verbal and Visual Representation*. Chicago: University of Chicago Press, 1994.

Moore, Deborah, and MacDonald Moore. "Observant Jews and the Photographic Arena of Looks." In *You Should See Yourself: Jewish Identity in Postmodern American Culture*, ed. Vincent Brook, 176–204. New Brunswick, NJ: Rutgers University Press, 2006.

Moore, Jack B. "'No Street Numbers in Accra': Richard Wright's African Cities." In *Richard Wright's Travel Writings: New Reflections*, ed. Virginia Whatley Smith, 45–59. Jackson: University Press of Mississippi, 2001.

Morrison, Toni. "Behind the Making of *The Black Book*." *Black World* 23, no. 4 (February 1974): 86–90.

———. *The Bluest Eye*. New York: Holt, Rinehart, and Winston, 1970.

———. "Foreword." In *Black Photographers Annual 1973*, n.p. Brooklyn: Black Photographers Annual, 1972.

———. "Foreword." In *The Harlem Book of the Dead*, by James VanderZee, Owen Dodson, and Camille Billops, n.p. Dobbs Ferry, NY: Morgan & Morgan, 1978.

———. *Jazz*. New York: Knopf, 1992.

———. *Remember: The Journey to School Integration*. New York: Houghton Mifflin, 2004.

———. *Song of Solomon*. New York: Plume, 1977.

———. *Sula*. New York: Vintage, 1973.

Munz, Charles Curtis. "The New Negro." *The Nation* 153 (13 December 1941): 620.

Murray, Rolland. "How the Conjure-Man Gets Busy: Cultural Nationalism, Masculinity, and Performativity." *Yale Journal of Criticism* 18, no. 2 (Fall 2005): 299–322.

"Museum Pickets Assail Hoving over Coming Harlem Exhibition." *New York Times*, 15 January 1969, 41.

Myrdal, Gunnar. *An American Dilemma*. 2 vols. New York: McGraw-Hill, 1964.

Nabokov, Nicolas. *Bagazh: Memoirs of a Russian Cosmopolitan*. New York: Atheneum, 1975.

Nadel, Alan. *Invisible Criticism: Ralph Ellison and the American Canon*. Iowa City: University of Iowa Press, 1988.

Natanson, Nicholas. *The Black Image in the New Deal: The Politics of FSA Photography*. Knoxville: University of Tennessee Press, 1992.

———. "The Photo-Series: Russell Lee, Chicago, and the 1940s." In *The Black Image in the New Deal: The Politics of FSA Photography*, 142–202. Knoxville: University of Tennessee Press, 1992.

———. "Robert H. McNeill and the Profusion of Virginia Experience." In *Visual Journal: Harlem and D.C. in the Thirties and Forties*, ed. Deborah Willis and Jane Lukasa, 97–147. Washington, DC: Center for African American History and Culture and Smithsonian Institution Press, 1996.

Naylor, Gloria. "A Conversation: Gloria Naylor and Toni Morrison." In *Conversations with Toni Morrison*, ed. Danielle Taylor-Guthrie, 188–217. Jackson: University Press of Mississippi, 1994.

Neal, Larry. "The Black Arts Movement." Reprinted in *The Black Aesthetic*, by Addison Gayle Jr., 272–90. New York: Doubleday, 1971.

Nemiroff, Robert. "A Critical Background." In *Les Blancs: The Collected Last Plays of Lorraine Hansberry*, ed. Robert Nemiroff, 35–46. New York: Random House: 1972.

Nemiroff, Robert. "Foreword." In *To Be Young, Gifted and Black: Lorraine Hansberry in Her Own Words*, by Lorraine Hansberry, ed. Robert Nemiroff, xiii–xviii. Englewood Cliffs, NJ: Prentice-Hall, 1969.

Nietzsche, Friedrich. *On the Genealogy of Morals*, trans. Walter J. Kaufmann and R. J. Hollingdale. New York: Vintage, 1967.

O'Mealley, Robert G. *The Craft of Ralph Ellison*. Cambridge, MA: Harvard University Press, 1980.

———. "Introduction: Jazz Shapes." In *Living with Music: Ralph Ellison's Jazz Writings*, ed. Robert G. O'Mealley, ix–xxxv. New York: Modern Library, 2001.

———. *The Jazz Cadence of American Culture*. New York: Columbia University Press, 1998.

———, ed. *Living with Music: Ralph Ellison's Jazz Writings*. New York: Modern Library, 2001.

Orvell, Miles. *The Real Thing: Imitation and Authenticity in American Culture, 1880–1940*. Chapel Hill: University of North Carolina Press, 1989.

Osborne, Nancy. "One Facet of Fear." *The Ladder*, July 1957, 6–7.

Osofsky, Gilbert. *Harlem, the Making of a Ghetto: Negro New York, 1890–1930*. New York: Harper and Row, 1965.

Ottley, Roi. *The Lonely Warrior: The Life and Times of Robert S. Abbott*. Chicago: H. Regnery, 1955.

Ottley, Roi, and William J. Weatherby, eds. *The Negro in New York: An Informal Social History*. New York: New York Public Library, 1967.

Pagán, Eduardo Obregón. *Murder at the Sleepy Lagoon: Zoot Suits, Race, and Riot in Wartime L.A.* Chapel Hill: University of North Carolina Press, 2003.

Palfi, Marion. *Invisible in America*. Lawrence: University of Kansas Museum of Art, 1973.

———. *Marion Palfi*. Tucson: Center for Creative Photography / University of Arizona, 1983.

Park, Robert Ezra. *Race and Culture: The Collected Papers of Robert Ezra Park*, vol. 1, ed. Everett Cherington Hughes, Charles S. Johnson, et al. Glencook, IL: Free Press, 1950.

Parker, F. "Views on Many Questions." *New York Amsterdam News*, 29 July 1939, 6.

Parks, Gordon, Sr. "Foreword." In *Harlem: The Vision of Morgan and Marvin Smith*, ix. Lexington: University Press of Kentucky, 1998.

———. *Half Past Autumn: A Retrospective*. Boston: Bulfinch Press / Corcoran Gallery of Art, 1997.

———. *Voices in the Mirror*. New York: Anchor Books, 1992.

Parr, Martin, and Gerry Badger. *The Photobook: A History*, vol. 1. London: Phaidon Press, 2004.

Pate, Alexs D. "Foreword." In *The Cotillion, or One Good Bull Is Half the Herd*, by John Oliver Killens, ix–xxi. New York: Coffee House Press, 2002 [orig. 1971].

Peirce, Charles Saunders. *Collected Papers of Charles Saunders Peirce*, vols. 1–6, ed. Charles Hartshorne and Paul Weiss. Cambridge, MA: Harvard University Press, 1931–35.

Penkower, Monty Noam. *The Federal Writers' Project: A Study in Government Patronage of the Arts*. Urbana: University of Illinois Press, 1977.

Petesch, Donald A. *A Spy in the Enemy's Country: The Emergence of Modern Black Literature*. Iowa City: University of Iowa Press, 1989.

Phillips, Sandra S., and Maria Morris Hambourg, eds. *Helen Levitt*. San Francisco: San Francisco Museum of Art, 1991.

Photo Notes, February 1933–Spring 1950; Filmfront, December 1934–March 1935. Rochester, NY: Visual Studies Workshop, 1977.

Pinney, Christopher. "Introduction: 'How the Other Half . . . .' " In *Photography's Other Histories*, ed. Christopher Pinney and Nicolas Peterson, 1–14. Durham, NC: Duke University Press, 2003.

Pinney, Christopher, and Nicolas Peterson, eds. *Photography's Other Histories*. Durham, NC: Duke University Press, 2003.

"Police End Harlem Riot; Mayor Starts Inquiry; Dodge Sees a Red Plot." *New York Times*, 21 March 1935, 1, 16.

Porter, Horace. *Jazz Country: Ralph Ellison in America*. Iowa City: University of Iowa Press, 2001.

Posnock, Ross. "Ellison, Arendt, and the Meaning of Politics." In *The Cambridge Companion to Ralph Ellison*, ed. Ross Posnock, 201–16. New York: Cambridge University Press, 2005.

Powell, Adam Clayton, Sr. *Riots and Ruins*. New York: Richard A. Smith, 1945.

Pratt, Mary Louise. *Imperial Eyes: Travel Writing and Transculturation*. New York: Routledge, 1992.

Prosser, Jay. *Light in the Dark Room: Photography and Loss*. Minneapolis: University of Minnesota Press, 2005.

Rabinowitz, Paula. *Black & White & Noir: America's Pulp Modernism*. New York: Columbia University Press, 2002.

———. *They Must Be Represented: The Politics of Documentary*. London: Verso, 1994.

Raeburn, John. *A Staggering Revolution: A Cultural History of Thirties Photography*. Champaign: University of Illinois Press, 2006.

Raiford, Leigh. "The Consumption of Lynching Images." In *Only Skin Deep: Changing Visions of the American Self*, ed. Coco Fusco and Brian Wallis, 267–73. New York: International Center of Photography / Harry N. Abrams, 2003.

Rampersad, Arnold. *The Life of Langston Hughes*. 2 vols. New York: Oxford University Press, 1986–88.

Reddick, L. D. "Negro and Jew." *Jewish Survey* 2 (January 1942): 25.

Reilly, John M. "Richard Wright and the Art of Non-Fiction: Stepping Out on the State of the World." *Callaloo* 9, no. 3 (Summer 1986): 507–20.

Reynolds, Larry J., and Gordon Hutner, eds. *National Imaginaries, American Identities: The Cultural Work of American Iconography.* Princeton, NJ: Princeton University Press, 2000.

Riley, Clayton. "Introduction." In *Black Photographers Annual 1973*, n.p. Brooklyn: Black Photographers Annual, 1972.

Roosevelt, Franklin Delano. *The Public Papers and Addresses of Franklin D. Roosevelt*, vol. 1, *1928–32*. New York: Random House, 1938.

Rosenblum, Naomi. "From Protest to Affirmation: 1940–1980." In *Decade by Decade: Twentieth-Century American Photography from the Collection of the Center for Creative Photography*, ed. James Enyeart, 48–61. Boston: Bulfinch Press, 1989.

Rosler, Martha. "In, around, and Afterthoughts (On Documentary Photography)." In *The Photography Reader*, ed. Liz Wells, 261–74. New York: Routledge, 2002.

Rosskam, Edwin. *Washington: Nerve Center.* New York: Alliance Publishing, 1939.

Rotella, Carlo. *October Cities: The Redevelopment of Urban Literature.* Berkeley and Los Angeles: University of California Press, 1998.

Rowley, Hazel. *Richard Wright: The Life and Times.* New York: Henry Holt, 2001.

Sallis, James. *Chester Himes: A Life.* New York: Walker, 2000.

Samuels, Shirley. *Facing America: Iconography and the Civil War.* New York: Oxford University Press, 2003.

Sandeen, Eric. *Picturing an Exhibition: The Family of Man and 1950s America.* Albuquerque: University of New Mexico Press, 1995.

Sandweiss, Martha. *Print the Legend: Photography and the American West.* New Haven, CT: Yale University Press, 2002.

———. "The Way to Realism, 1930–1940." In *Decade by Decade: Twentieth-Century American Photography from the Collection of the Center for Creative Photography*, ed. James Enyeart, 35–47. Boston: Bulfinch Press, 1989.

Sante, Luc. *Low Life: Lures and Snares of Old New York.* New York: Farrar, Straus, Giroux, 1991.

Saretzky, Gary D. "Documenting Diversity: Edwin Rosskam and the Photo Book, 1940–41." *Photo Review* 24, nos. 1–2 (2001): 6–16.

———. "She Worked Her Head Off: Edwin and Louise Rosskam and the Golden Age of Documentary Photography Books." *Photo Review* 23, no. 3 (2000): 2–10.

Saul, Scott. *Freedom Is, Freedom Ain't: Jazz and the Making of the Sixties.* Cambridge, MA: Harvard University Press, 2003.

Schapiro, Steve. *American Edge.* New York: Arena Editions, 2000.

Schoener, Allon, ed. *Harlem on My Mind: Cultural Capital of Black America, 1900–1968.* New York: New Press, 1995.

Scruggs, Charles. *Sweet Home: Invisible Cities in the Afro-American Novel.* Baltimore: Johns Hopkins University Press, 1993.

Sekula, Allan. *Photography against the Grain: Essays and Photo Works, 1973–1983.* Halifax, Nova Scotia: Press of the Nova Scotia College of Art and Design, 1984.

Shankar, S. "Richard Wright's *Black Power*: Colonial Politics and the Travel Narrative." In *Richard Wright's Travel Writings: New Reflections*, ed. Virginia Whatley Smith, 3–19. Jackson: University Press of Mississippi, 2001.

Shapiro, Herbert. *White Violence and Black Response: From Reconstruction to Montgomery*. Amherst: University of Massachusetts Press, 1988.

Shaw, Gwendolyn DuBois, and Emily K. Shubert. *Portraits of a People: Picturing African Americans in the Nineteenth Century*. Seattle: University of Washington Press, 2006.

Shloss, Carol. *In Visible Light: Photography and the American Writer, 1840–1940*. New York: Oxford University Press, 1987.

Silverman, Jonathan, ed. *For the World to See: The Life of Margaret Bourke-White*. New York: Viking, 1983.

Siskind, Aaron. "Credo." Reprinted in *Aaron Siskind: Toward a Personal Vision, 1935–1955*, ed. Deborah Martin Kao and Charles A. Meyer, 56–57. Chestnut Hill, MA: Boston College Museum of Art, 1994.

———. "The Drama of Objects." Reprinted in *Aaron Siskind: Toward a Personal Vision, 1935–1955*, ed. Deborah Martin Kao and Charles A. Meyer, 50–53. Chestnut Hill, MA: Boston College Museum of Art, 1994.

———. "Feature Group." Reprinted in *Aaron Siskind: Toward a Personal Vision, 1935–1955*, ed. Deborah Martin Kao and Charles A. Meyer, 26–31. Chestnut Hill, MA: Boston College Museum of Art, 1994.

———. *Harlem Document: Photographs, 1932–1940*. New York: Matrix, 1981.

———. Interview with Alan Cohen, Tom Cinoman, and Geoff Hughes. In *Columbia I Photography Interviews*, 1–8. Chicago: Columbia College, 1983.

Smethurst, James. *The Black Arts Movement: Literary Nationalism in the 1960s and 1970s*. Chapel Hill: University of North Carolina Press, 2005.

Smith, Marcelle. "Blue Note: Postmortem Photography and the Genesis of *Jazz* for Toni Morrison." *Philological Papers* 41 (1995): 146.

Smith, Shawn Michelle. *American Archives: Gender, Race, and Class in Visual Culture*. Princeton, NJ: Princeton University Press, 1999.

———. *Photography on the Color Line: W.E.B. DuBois, Race, and Visual Culture*. Durham, NC: Duke University Press, 2004.

Smith, Virginia Whatley. "Introduction." In *Richard Wright's Travel Writings: New Reflections*, ed. Virginia Whatley Smith, xi–xiv. Jackson: University Press of Mississippi, 2001.

———. "Richard Wright's Passage to Indonesia." In *Richard Wright's Travel Writings: New Reflections*, ed. Virginia Whatley Smith, 86–88. Jackson: University Press of Mississippi, 2001.

Soby, James Thrall. "The Art of Poetic Accident: The Photographs of Cartier-Bresson and Helen Levitt." *Minicam* 6, no. 7 (March 1943): 28–31.

———. "Two Photographs by Helen Levitt." *Harper's Bazaar* 78, no. 7 (July 1944): 32–33.

Solomon, Mark. *The Cry Was Unity: Communists and African Americans, 1917–1936*. Jackson: University of Mississippi Press, 1998.

Solomon-Godeau, Abigail. "Mistaken Identities." In *Mistaken Identities*, ed. Abigail Solomon-Godeau and Constance Lewallen, 19–65. Santa Barbara: University Art Museum, University of California, 1993.

———. *Photography at the Dock: Essays on Photographic History, Institutions, and Practices*. Minneapolis: University of Minnesota Press, 1991.

"Some of the Damage in Harlem." *New York Herald Tribune*, 3 August 1943, 7.

Sontag, Susan. *On Photography*. New York: Anchor / Doubleday, 1977.

Sorgenfrei, Robert. "Marion Palfi: A Biography." In *Marion Palfi Archive*, comp. Robert Sorgenfrei and David Peters, 7–10. Guide Series no. 10. Tucson: Center for Creative Photography / University of Arizona, 1985.

Stange, Maren. *Bronzeville: Black Chicago in Pictures, 1941–1943*. New York: New Press, 2004.

———. " 'Illusion Complete within Itself': Roy DeCarava's Photography." *Yale Journal of Criticism* 9, no. 1 (1996): 63–92.

———. " 'Photographs Taken in Everyday Life': *Ebony*'s Photojournalistic Discourse." In *The Black Press: New Literary and Historical Essays*, ed. Todd Vogel, 207–27. New Brunswick, NJ: Rutgers University Press, 2001.

———. *Symbols of Ideal Life: Social Documentary Photography in America, 1890–1950*. New York: Cambridge University Press, 1989.

Stein, Solomon. *Stein on Writing*. New York: St. Martin's Griffin, 2000.

Steiner, Ralph. "Wall and Sidewalk Drawings: What Goes on in the Minds of New York Children." *PM's Weekly* 1, no. 37 (2 March 1941): 48–49.

Stephany, Jaromir. "Interview with Aaron Siskind." In *Aaron Siskind: Toward a Personal Vision, 1935–1955*, ed. Deborah Martin Kao and Charles A. Meyer, 40–49. Chestnut Hill, MA: Boston College Museum of Art, 1994.

Stephens, Barbara. "Transvestism: A Cross-Cultural Survey." *The Ladder*, July 1957, 10–14.

Stepto, Robert. *From Behind the Veil: A Study of Afro-American Narrative*. Champaign-Urbana: University of Illinois Press, 1979.

Stewart, James T. "The Development of the Black Revolutionary Artist." In *Black Fire: An Anthology of Afro-American Writing*, ed. LeRoi Jones and Larry Neal, 3–10. New York: William Morrow, 1968.

Stewart, Susan. *On Longing: Narratives of the Miniature, the Gigantic, the Souvenir, the Collection*. Durham, NC: Duke University Press, 1993.

Stott, William. *Documentary Expression and Thirties America*. New York: Oxford University Press, 1973.

Streitmatter, Rodger. "*Black Panther* Newspaper: A Militant Voice, A Salient Vision." In *The Black Press: New Literary and Historical Essays*, ed. Todd Vogel, 228–24. New Brunswick, NJ: Rutgers University Press, 2001.

Strother, Ella T. "The Black Image in the *Chicago Defender*, 1908–1975." *Journalism History* 4, no. 4 (1977–78): 137–41, 156.

The Student Nonviolent Coordinating Committee Papers, 1959–1972. Microfilm. Sanford, NC: New York Times Microfilming Corporation of America, 1982.

"Student Tops 32 in Poetry Contest." *New York Times*, 24 May 1941, L13.

Sundquist, Eric. *Strangers in the Land: Blacks, Jews, Post-Holocaust America*. Cambridge, MA: Harvard University Press, 2005.

———. ed. *Cultural Contexts for Ralph Ellison's* Invisible Man. Boston: Bedford, 1995.

Susman, Warren I. *Culture as History: The Transformation of American Society in the Twentieth Century*. New York: Pantheon, 1984.

———. "The Thirties." In *The Development of an American Culture*, ed. Stanley Coben and Lorman Ratner, 179–218. Englewood Cliffs, NJ: Prentice-Hall, 1970.

Swanberg, W. A. *Luce and His Empire*. New York: Scribners, 1972.

Szarkowski, John. *Looking at Photographs: 100 Pictures from the Collection of the Museum of Modern Art*. New York: Museum of Modern Art, 1999 [orig. 1973].

Taft, Robert. *Photography and the American Scene: A Social History, 1829–1889*. New York: Dover, 1964.

Tagg, John. "Melancholy Realism: Walker Evans's Resistance to Meaning." *Narrative* 11, no. 1 (January 2003): 3–77.

———. "The Proof of the Picture." *Afterimage* 15, no. 6 (January 1988): 11–13.

Tate, Claudia. "Notes on the Invisible Woman in Ralph Ellison's *Invisible Man*." In *Speaking for You: The Vision of Ralph Ellison*, ed. Kimberly Benston, 163–72. Washington, DC: Howard University Press, 1987.

Thomas, Ann. *Lisette Model*. Ottowa, Ontario: National Gallery of Canada, 1990.

Thompson, Ralph. "Books of the Times." *New York Times*, 18 November 1941, 29.

Thompson, Tommy L. *Tuskegee University Then and Now*. Louisville, KY: Harmony House, 1993.

Tóibín, Colm. "The Henry James of Harlem: James Baldwin's Struggle." *London Review of Books*, 14 September 2001, 15–20.

Trachtenberg, Alan. "From Image to Story: Reading the File." In *Documenting America, 1935–1943*, ed. Carl Fleischhauer and Beverly W. Brannan, 43–73. Berkeley and Los Angeles: University of California Press, 1988.

———. *Reading American Photographs: Images as History, Mathew Brady to Walker Evans*. New York: Hill & Wang, 1989.

Traub, Charles. "Interview with Aaron Siskind." In *Aaron Siskind: Toward a Personal Vision, 1935–1955*, ed. Deborah Martin Kao and Charles A. Meyer, 70–79. Chestnut Hill, MA: Boston College Museum of Art, 1994.

Turner, Peter. "Aaron Siskind: Photographer." In *Aaron Siskind: Photographs, 1932–1978*, [1–6]. New York: St. Martin's Press, 1985.

Urban League of Greater New York. "The League Lens." In *Annual Report of the Urban League of Greater New York, 1947*, n.p. Microfilm in Schomburg Center for Research in Black Culture.

"The U.S. Minicam Boom." *Fortune* 14, no. 4 (October 1936): 125–29, 160, 164, 167–68, 170.

VanderZee, James, Owen Dodson, and Camille Billops. *The Harlem Book of the Dead.* Dobbs Ferry, NY: Morgan & Morgan, 1978.

Van Ellison, Candace. "Introduction." In *Harlem on My Mind: Cultural Capital of Black America, 1900–1968*, ed. Allon Schoener, 11–15. New York: New Press, 1995.

Vestal, David. "Can Whitey Do a Beautiful Black Picture Show?" *Popular Photography* 64, no. 5 (May 1969): 79–82, 122, 124–25.

Wainwright, Loudon. *The Great American Magazine: An Inside History of* Life. New York: Knopf, 1986.

Waligora-Davis, Nicole A. "Riotous Discontent: Ralph Ellison's 'Birth of a Nation.'" *Modern Fiction Studies* 50, no. 2 (Summer 2004): 385–410.

Walker, Margaret. *Richard Wright: Daemonic Genius.* New York: Amistad / Warner Books, 1988.

Wall, Cheryl. *Worrying the Line: Black Women Writers, Lineage, and Literary Tradition.* Chapel Hill: University of North Carolina Press, 2005.

Wall, Jeff. "Marks of Indifference: Aspects of Photography in, or as, Conceptual Art." In *Reconsidering the Object of Art: 1965–1975*, ed. Ann Goldstein and Anne Rorimer, 246–57. Los Angeles: Museum of Contemporary Art, 1995.

Wallace, Maurice O. *Constructing the Black Masculine: Identity and Ideality in African-American Men's Literature and Culture, 1775–1995.* Durham, NC: Duke University Press, 2002.

Wallace, Michele. *Dark Designs and Visual Culture.* Durham, NC: Duke University Press, 2004.

———. "Signifying Nothing." *Village Voice* 40, no. 35 (29 August 1995): 84–85.

Ward, Jeff. "Representing Crisis: A Timeline of Social Documentary Practice." 8 June 2004. Posted online at www.thispublicaddress.com/depression/timeline3.html.

Warren, Kenneth W. "Chaos Not Quite Controlled: Ellison's Uncompleted Transit to *Juneteenth.*" In *The Cambridge Companion to Ralph Ellison*, ed. Ross Posnock, 188–200. New York: Cambridge University Press, 2005.

———. *So Black and Blue: Ralph Ellison and the Occasion of Criticism.* Chicago: University of Chicago Press, 2003.

Warren, Lynne, ed. *Encyclopedia of Twentieth-Century Photography*, vol. 1. New York: Routledge, 2006.

Watts, Jerry Gafio. *Heroism and the Black Intellectual: Ralph Ellison, Politics, and Afro-American Life.* Chapel Hill: University of North Carolina Press, 1994.

Watson, Steven. *The Harlem Renaissance: Hub of African-American Culture, 1920–1930.* New York: Pantheon Books, 1995.

Weatherby, J. *James Baldwin: Artist on Fire.* New York: Laurel, 1989.

Weisgrau, Richard. "Jay Maisel: Legendary Photographer Speaks from Experience." American Society of Media Photographers, 2006. Posted online at www.asmp.org/culture/mentor_maisel01.php.

Weiss, M. Lynn. "Para Usted: Richard Wright's *Pagan Spain*." In *The Black Columbiad: Defining Moments in African-American Literature and Culture*, ed. Werner Sollors and Maria Diedrich, 212–25. Cambridge, MA: Harvard University Press, 1994.

Wexler, Laura. *Tender Violence: Domestic Visions in an Age of U.S. Imperialism*. Chapel Hill: University of North Carolina Press, 2000.

White, Walter. "Behind the Harlem Riot." *New Republic* 109 (16 August 1943): 220–21.

"William Klein." Posted online at http://en.wikipedia.org/wiki/William_Klein. Accessed 10 May 2006.

Willis, Deborah. "A Conversation: Lorna Simpson and Deborah Willis." In *Lorna Simpson*, by Deborah Willis and Lorna Simpson, 57–58. San Francisco: Friends of Photography, 1992.

———. *Family History and Memory: Recording African-American Life*. Irvington, NY: Hylas Press, 2005.

———. *Reflections in Black: A History of Black Photographers, 1840 to the Present*. New York: W. W. Norton, 2000.

———. "Visualizing Political Struggle: Civil Rights–Era Photography." In *American Visual Cultures*, ed. David Holloway and John Beck, 166–73. London: Continuum, 2005.

Willis, Deborah, and Jane Lukasa, eds. *Visual Journal: Harlem and D.C. in the Thirties and Forties*. Washington, DC: Center for African American History and Culture and Smithsonian Institution Press, 1996.

Willis, Deborah, and Lorna Simpson. *Lorna Simpson*. San Francisco: Friends of Photography, 1992.

Wilson, C. E. "The Screens." In *Black Fire: An Anthology of Afro-American Writing*, ed. LeRoi Jones and Larry Neal, 133–43. New York: William Morrow, 1968.

Woodbury, Walter E. *The Encyclopaedic Dictionary of Photography*. New York: Arno Press, 1979 [orig. 1898].

The WPA Guide to New York City: The Federal Writers Project Guide to 1930s New York. New York: New Press, 1992 [orig. 1939].

Wright, Beryl J., Saidiya V. Hartman, and Lorna Simpson. *Lorna Simpson: For the Sake of the Viewer*. New York: Universe / Museum of Contemporary Art, 1992.

Wright, Richard. *Black Power*. London: Dennis Dobson, 1954.

———. *Black Power: A Record of Reactions in a Land of Pathos*. New York: Harper, 1954.

———. "Blueprint for Negro Writing." In *Richard Wright Reader*, ed. Ellen Wright and Michel Fabre, 36–49. New York: Da Capo Press, 1997.

———. *Native Son*. New York: Perennial, 1987 [orig. 1940].

———. *Twelve Million Black Voices*. Photo direction by Edwin Rosskam. New York: Thunder's Mouth Press, 1988 [orig. 1941].

Wright, Richard. *Uncle Tom's Children.* New York: Harper and Brothers, 1938.

———. *White Man, Listen!* New York: Anchor / Doubleday, 1964 [orig. 1957].

"Year of the Fact." *Newsweek*, 27 December 1965, 73.

Young, Joan. "Lorna Simpson." In *The Hugo Boss Prize*, 84–95. New York: Solomon R. Guggenheim Foundation, 1998.

Yukins, Elizabeth. "An 'Artful Juxtaposition on the Page': Memory, Perception, and Cubist Technique in Ralph Ellison's *Juneteenth*." *PMLA* 119, no. 5 (October 2004): 1247–63.

"Zoot Suiters Learn Lesson in Fights with Servicemen." *Los Angeles Times*, 7 June 1943, A1.

Index

Page numbers in italics refer to figures.

Avedon, Richard, 11, 69, 121, 164, 165–75, *172, 183, 187, 189, 190, 191,* 193, 198, 215, 231, 251, 301n17, 308n10. *See also* Baldwin, James; *Nothing Personal*
Aviles, Anthony, 232, *233, 234*

Baker, Houston, 13, 113, 271n41, 296n51
Baldwin, James, 11, 94, 123, 160–97, 198, 203, 206, 223, 227, 231, 232, 248, 251; as subject of image-making, 170–73, *172,* 193–96; works of: "Blood of the Dying Lamb," 179–80; "The Fire Next Time," 166, 178, 193, 232; *Giovanni's Room,* 300n6; *Go Tell It on the Mountain* 160–64, 174–75, 179, 195; "The Harlem Ghetto," 177–79, 193; "Many Thousands Gone," 164; "Notes of a Native Son," 164. See also Avedon, Richard; *Nothing Personal*; photo-text, as resource for writers
Baldwin, Paula Maria, 170, *172,* 303n43
Balshaw, Maria, 274n8
Banes, Sally, 307n4
Baraka, Amiri, 212, 215, 238, 241, 312n69
Barthelme, Donald, 241
Barthes, Roland, 15, 136, 156, 162, 188, 207–8, 282n98, 299n4
Batchen, Geoffrey, 273n53
Bearden, Romare, 152, 168, 198, 314n98
Bell, Daniel, 176
Bellow, Saul, 177, 304n52
Benedict, Ruth, 281n92
Benjamin, Walter, 88, 273n53
Benston, Kimberly, 13, 212, 271n41
Bernstein, Lou, 283n102, 303n38. *See also* New York Photo League
Bey, Dawoud, 272n49
Bilbo, Theodore, 226
Birstein, Ann, 300n6
Black Arts, 18, 50, 212, 223, 239, 241, 243; aesthetics of, 200; and popular culture, 307n4; and postmodernism, 239, 241–42. *See also* Black Nationalism; Black Power
Black Emergency Cultural Coalition (BECC), 246, 248–49, 250, 313n88
Black Manhattan, 8
Black Muslims, 195. *See also* Nation of Islam

Black Nationalism, 10, 215. *See also* Black Power
Black Panthers, 248, 311–12n61
Black Photographers' Annual, 259
Black Power, 220, 228, 230, 238, 239, 250; print culture of, 307n4, 311n60, 311–12n61. *See also* Black Nationalism
Black Star Photo Agency, 203
Blair, Sara, 272n46
Boas, Franz, 281n92
Bond, Julian, 204, 205
Bontemps, Arna, 54, 274n3
Bourke-White, Margaret, 6–7, 65, 74, 75, 78, 81, 120, 132, 134, *135,* 136, 138, 168, 180, *181,* 184, 208, 231, 276n21, 287n42, 296n49. See also documentary; *Life*; photo-journalism; *You Have Seen Their Faces*
Bowery, the, as iconic site, 21, *22,* 23, 28, *28, 29,* 38, 169, 276n27, 302n27. *See also* Lower East Side
Brady, Mathew, 205
Brannan, Beverly W., 274n8
Bravo, Manuel, 281n90
Briggs, Gin, 202
Bristol, Horace, 75
Brodovitch, Alexey, 173, 303n36, 306n86
Brooklyn Eagle, 19
Brown v. Board of Education, 167, 177, 255
Brustein, Robert, 301n14
Bullins, Ed, 212
Bunche, Ralph, 53
Burns, Ben, 94–96

Cadava, Eduardo, 273n53
Caldwell, Erskine, 7, 65, 74, 75, 78, 81, 134, 138, 168, 180, 208, 231, 284n12, 287n42, 296n49, 296n50, 304n52. *See also* documentary, as resource for writers; photo-text; *You Have Seen Their Faces*
Callahan, John, 113
cameras, formats and types: camera obscura, as metaphor, 262–63, 264; daguerreotype, 15, 131, 155, 273n50, 294–94n40, 295n42; handheld, 272n44; Kodak, 14; large-format, 38, 41, 211, 278n51; Leica, 14, 87, 94, 117, 119, 205; medium-format, 69; miniature,

130–31, 295nn40 and 42; Polaroid, 117, 154; Rolleiflex, 42, 69, 171, 192; small-format, 14, 55, 197n58; 35mm, 38, 69, 117, 278n50; twin-lens reflex, 69, 70, 112; view, 38, 117, 118, 205, 272n44, 278–79n51. *See also* Leica revolution

Campbell, James, 179, 301nn16 and 19, 304n52

Camus, Albert, 205

Capa, Robert, 277n38

Capote, Truman, 193, 301n17, 306n86

Capouya, Emile, 167

Carson, Clayborne, 308n15

Carson, Rachel, 194

Carter, Michael. *See* Smith, Milton

Cartier-Bresson, Henri, 10, 53, 55, 56, 94–97, *95, 96,* 117, 142–44, *144,* 145, *145,* 251, 259, 277n38, 281n90; *The Decisive Moment,* 96–97. *See also* photo-text, as resource for writers

Casby, William, 188, *190*

Cayton-Warner research file, 69, 77. *See also* photography, and social science

Céline, Louis Ferdinand, 297n64

Chagall, Marc, 72

Chamberlain, Wilt, 225

Chandler, Raymond, 229

Chaney, James, 202, 203

Chaplin, Charlie, 166

Charles, Don, 10, 214, 230, 236, *236,* 237, 311n55. *See also Harlem Stirs*; photography, and civil rights

Chevlowe, Susan, 272n49

Chiarenza, Carl, 274n6, 276n28, 278n50

Chicago Defender, 52, 53, 94

Chiwengo, Ngwarsungu, 100, 289n71

Civil Rights Congress, 27

Clark, Kenneth B., 177, 227, 231

Clark, Tom C., 27

Clarke, John Henrik, 248

Clinton News, 168. *See also* DeWitt Clinton High School

Clintonian, The, 168. *See also* DeWitt Clinton High School

Cobb, Nina Kressner, 289n71

Cohen, Elliot, 172

Coleman, A. D., 246–47, 272n46

Commentary, 176, 177, 178, 304n52

Communist Party, 27, 31, 61, 76, 81, 93, 165, 231, 275n12, 288n52; and the New York Photo League, 275n14

Congress of Industrial Organizations (CIO), 238

Congress of Racial Equality (CORE), 194, 195, 231, 238

Connor, Bull, 226

Conrad, Joseph, 297n64; *Heart of Darkness,* 110, 297n64

Convention People's Party, 97

Crisis, 168

Croner, Ted, 121, *122. See also* New York School of photography

Cue, 297n65

Cullen, Countee, 97, 168, 302n24

Daguerreotype. *See* cameras, formats and types of; photo-text, as resource for writers

Daily News, 147

Daily Worker, 19, 65, 275n12

Davidov, Judith Fryer, 272n46

Davidson, Bruce, 308n10, 316n26

Davis, Frank Marshall, 285n19

Davis, Griffith J., 53

Davis, Ossie, 216, 231

DeCarava, Roy, 10, 49–60, 203, 209, 217, 249–50, 251, 259, 314n89. *See also* APG (A Photographers Gallery); *Sweet Flypaper of Life, The*

DeCarava, Sherry Turner, 57, 231

de Kooning, Willem, 48

Delano, Jack, 82–85, *83, 85,* 86. *See also* Farm Security Administration, Historical Section (FSA)

Denning, Michael, 285n24, 286n29

Derrida, Jacques, 273n53

Deschin, Jacob, 56, 313n77. See also *New York Times*

Deutsche Illustrierte, 282n94

DeVoto, Bernard, 6

Dewey, John, 281n92

DeWitt Clinton High School: and photo-text collaboration, 166–70, 173; and racial and

Harlem (*cont'd*)

graphic activity, 7–8, 9–10, 20–21, 37, 46–47, 57–60, 65–69, 71, 76, 95, 120–21, 163–64, 165, 170, 173–74, 179–83, 194, 204, 209, 226, 245–51, 259, 274n8, 288n53, 297n65, 302–3n35, 306n98. *See also* African Americans; documentary; photography, and African Americans

Harlem Cultural Council, 248

"Harlem Document," 19, 20, 21–49, 32–33, 37, 47, 48, 51, 56, 61, 65, 66, 68, 74, 164, 171, 250; exhibition and publication of, 23, 32, 273n2. See also *Harlem Document*; Siskind, Aaron

Harlem Document, 33–49, 52, 53, 56, 120, 121. *See also* "Harlem Document"; Siskind Aaron

"Harlem Doorways," 170, 173, 174, 177, 179, 180, 193

Harlem on My Mind, 245–51, 252, 283n105, 306n98; aims of, 306n98; 312n77; audience for, 306n88; catalogue for, 312n75; controversies over, 313–12n88

Harlem Renaissance, 4, 9–10, 17, 18, 48, 54, 143, 168, 169, 183, 247, 250, 255; as antimodel, 66, 230, 243, 250, 256–58, 259–60; and photographic practice, 31; as precedent, 9–10, 256; visual codes of, 38, 256

Harlem Stirs, 230–38, 239, 241, 243, 244, 245. *See also* Killens, John Oliver

Harlem Writers Guild, 238

Harlow, Alvin F., 276n27

Harper's Bazaar, 147, 173, 285n26

Harris, Michael D., 270n29

Harrison, Paul Carter, 212

Hartford, Huntington, 194

Harvey, Sylvia, 272n45

Hawthorne, Nathaniel, 92

Hearst, William Randolph, 38, 147, 298n68

Heath, David, 209, *210*, 217, 308n10

Hemingway, Ernest, 74

Herron, Matt, 207, 309n20

Himes, Chester, 118, 201, 223–30, 247, 250, 251, 291n6; and aesthetics of absurdity, 311n53; works by: *Cotton Comes to Harlem*, 201, 223–30; *The Heat Is On*, 223; *A Rage in Harlem*, 223

Hine, Lewis W., 28, *28*, 169, 275n11

Hiro, 306n86

Holiday, Billie, 167

Holland, Patricia, 270n30

Holmes, Oliver Wendell, 293n15

Holzer, Jenny, 252

Hook, Sidney, 176

hooks, bell, 271n41

Horne, Lena, 39, 195

Hoving, Thomas, 246, 247, 313n80. *See also* Harlem on My Mind; Metropolitan Museum of Art

How the Other Half Lives, 231. *See also* Riis, Jacob

Howard, Jane, 194–95. *See also* Baldwin, James, as subject of image-making; *Life*

Howe, Irving, 26, 73

Hughes, Langston, 50, 52–55, 94, 112, 118, 142, 231, 242, 291n6, 296n50, 297nn60 and 65, 302n24; and Simple stories, 52, 281n88. See also *Sweet Flypaper of Life, The*

Hurley, F. Jack, 268n12

Hurwitz, Leo, 151

Ings, Richard, 274n8

Jacobs, Jane, 57

Jakobson, Roman, 298n72

James, Henry, 92, 163, 178, 196, 300n6

Jarrell, Randall, 178

Jewish Defense League, 245, 247–48

Jews: and African Americans, 12, 163–74, 177–79, 187, 204, 238, 247–48, 249, 253, 308nn13 and 15; in Harlem: 8, 39, 58, 173–74, 249–50, 279n54, 301n22; as New York Intellectuals, 176–78; as practitioners of photography, 11, 14–15, 15, 58, 74, 140, 142, 192, 202, 204, 246–47, 272nn46 and 49, 288n53, 293–94n30, 303n36, 308n13, 310n32, 314n89. *See also* African Americans, and Jews; photography, and Jews

John Birch Society, 245, 313n88

John Reed Club, 286n29

Lower East Side (*cont'd*)
181–82. *See also* Jews, as practitioners of photography; photography, and Jews

Luce, Henry R., 6, 7, 16, 74, 120, 140, 246. See also *Life*

Lumumba, Patrice, 228

lynching, images of, 13, 208–9, 211–12, *211*, 271nn38 and 43, 309n23, 310n32

Lyon, Danny, 203–6; *204, 207, 213, 218, 219, 220, 221*, 251, 308n11; and "photoliterature," 309n16; in SNCC, 308n15, 310n29. See also *Movement, The*; Student Nonviolent Coordinating Committee (SNCC)

Macdonald, Dwight, 282n98

Mackey, Nathan, 170

MacLeish, Archibald, 74

Macon, Wanda, 312n64

Mademoiselle, 193

Madhubuti, Haki, 241

Magazine of Art, 285n26

Magnum, 259

Magpie, The, 166–67, 168, 169, 170, 305n68. *See also* Avedon, Richard; Baldwin, James; DeWitt Clinton High School

Mailer, Norman, 216

Maisel, Jay, 245, 247, 314n89

Malcolm X, 188, *189*, 196, 212, 216, 217, 227, 237, 238, 313n82

Mann, Thomas, 177

Manning, Jack. *See* Mendelsohn, Jack

Marshall, Paule, 152, 238, 253

Marzani, Carl, 231

McCarthy, Mary, 177, 291n6

McCausland, Elizabeth, 72, 274n7

McKay, Claude, 66

McNamara, Norris, 207, 215, 309n20

McNeill, Robert H., 41, 277nn31 and 38, 278n51, 279n57

Meadman, Dhima Rose, 294n36

Meatyard, Ralph Eugene, 56

Meeropol, Abel, 167

Melnick, Jeffrey, 15, 272n49

Meltzer, Milton, 53

Mendelsohn, Jack, 26, 42, 121. *See also* New York Photo League

Meredith, James, 194

metonymy: definition of, 298n72; as strategy for photo-text narrative, 185, 208–12, 215, 222, 298n74. *See also* photography, and metonymy

Metropolitan Museum of Art, 245–46, 248, 249, 250, 283n105, 306n98, 313n88. *See also* Harlem on My Mind

Michaels, Walter Benn, 307n3

Miller, Arthur, 184

Miller, James A., 270n29

Miller, Joshua L., 187–88, 192

Minicam, 285n26

Mitchell, W.J.T., 271n49, 296n49, 305n69

Model, Lisette, 10, 16–17, 69, 72, 121, 122, 124, 136, 144–46, *146*, 158, 237, 251, 273n56, 303n38. *See also* Ellison, Ralph; New York School of photography

modernism: literary, 11, 18, 75, 157 186–88, 200, 201, 307n3; photographic, 11, 18, 57, 70, 75, 76, 96, 186–88; visual, 49, 51, 60, 246, 281n83

Moffo, Anna, 194

Monroe, Marilyn, 184–85, *186, 187*

Moore, Deborah and MacDonald, 272n46

Morey, Hal, 66, 68, *68*

Morris, Vivian, 33

Morrison, Toni, 159, 256–64; and editorship of *The Black Book*, 259, 316n17; works by: *Beloved*, 316n17; *The Bluest Eye*, 256–57; *Jazz*, 256–64; *Playing in the Dark*, 256; *Remember: The Journey to School Integration*, 315n26; *Song of Solomon*, 257; *Sula*, 257, 258

Moses, Bob, 216, 218. *See also* Student Nonviolent Coordinating Committee (SNCC)

Moses, Robert, 194

Motherwell, Robert, 280n73

Movement, The, 201–38, 245, 249. *See also* Hansberry, Lorraine; Lyon, Danny; photography, and civil rights; photo-text; Student Nonviolent Coordinating Committee (SNCC)

Muhammad, Elijah, 214

Muhammad Speaks, 209

Murray, Albert, 113, 119
Murray, Rolland, 312n69
Museum of Modern Art, and photography, 55, 71, 136, 282n94, 285n26, 296n52, 297nn60 and 65, 303n38
Mussolini, Benito, 9

NAACP, 239; Legal Defense and Educational Fund of, 167
Nancy, Jean-Luc, 273n53
Natanson, Nicholas, 21, 86, 275n9, 277n42
Nation, The, 167, 176, 179
Nation of Islam, 214, 217, 218, 225, 227, 230. See also Black Muslims
National Labor Relations Board, 238
National Urban League, 19. See also Urban League, The
Nation's Business, 7
Negro Quarterly, 151
Nemiroff, Robert, 202, 307n7, 308n11, 310n36
New Deal, the, 5, 10, 12, 30, 37, 51, 60, 165, 225, 245; and documentary, 17; in Harlem, 31; photographic projects of, 66, 74; as precedent for uses of photographs, 230, 232; visual conventions of, 38. See also documentary; Farm Security Administration, Historical Section (FSA); Federal Arts Project; Federal Writers' Project
New Leader, 176, 179, 304n52
New Masses, The, 61, 151, 167, 278n42
New Negro Renaissance, 85. See also Harlem Renaissance
New Republic, 61, 151
New York Amsterdam News, 31, 147, 242, 246, 298n71
New York Herald Tribune, 147
New York Intellectuals, 176–78. See also Baldwin, James; Jews, as New York Intellectuals
New York Photo League, 7, 10, 23, 27–28, 32, 47, 56, 61, 65, 66, 71, 74, 165, 167, 180, 245, 274n3, 275n11, 282n94, 297n65, 303n38, 310n32. See also documentary; Feature Group, The; New Deal, the; photo-text
New York Post, 199

New York School of painting, 280n73
New York School of photography, 121, 123, 124, 139, 140, 142
New York Times, 19, 56, 61, 147, 199, 230
New Yorker, 165, 166, 193
Newsweek, 199
Nietzsche, Friedrich, 108
Nixon, Robert, 69
Nkrumah, Kwame, 97, 109, 110
Nothing Personal, 11, 164, 165, 166, 179–97, 198, 215. See also Avedon, Richard; Baldwin, James; photography, and civil rights; photo-text

O'Mealley, Robert, 113
Organization for Afro-American Unity, 238

Page, Geraldine, 195
Palfi, Marion, 54, 216, 217, 219, 303n38, 310n32. See also Hughes, Langston; phototext
Parade, 19
Park, Robert, 295n46
Parker, Dorothy, 170
Parker, Theodore, 209
Parks, Gordon, 113, 151, 245, 247, 270n29, 282n94, 291n7, 295–96n47, 300n9. See also Ellison, Ralph; Farm Security Administration, Historical Section (FSA); Life; photo-text
Partisan Review, 176–77, 179, 284n12, 304n52
Peirce, Charles Saunders, 17, 273n56
Pelatowski, Theodore, 179
Petesch, Donald A., 269n12
Photo League. See New York Photo League
photography: and African American studies, 12, 13, 62; and African Americans, 31–32, 51, 62–65, 70; and analogy, 16, 17; and civil rights, 53, 191, 191–92, 198–251, 207, 213, 217, 218, 219, 220, 221, 259; and film (moving images), 75, 113, 142, 152, 155–57, 258, 268–69n12, 270n30, 285n24, 295–96n47, 303nn37 and 38; and iconicity, 131, 150; and identity logic, 199, 201, 227, 229, 241, 281n83; and indexicality, 16, 17, 124, 263, 150–51, 199; and Jews (see Jews, as prac-

photography (*cont'd*)
titioners of photography); and metonymy, 139, 150, 251; ontology of, 6, 14, 15–17, 199, 251; phenomenology of, 273n53; and postmodernism, 252–53, 313nn81 and 82; and social science, 20, 51, 58, 63, 69, 77, 93, 117, 129, 289n71, 293n16; and surrealism, 236, 251; and witnessing, 163–64, 175, 179, 180, 185, 199, 304n60. *See also* cameras, formats and types; documentary; photojournalism; photo-text

photojournalism, 28, 52, 53, 62, 74, 96, 147, 152, 174, 180, 193–97, 199, 258, 285n24; in Harlem, 31; and photographic techniques, 307n5. *See also* documentary; *Life*; photo-text

photo-text: aesthetics of, 77, 92, 136, 171, 230, 245–46, 253–56, 270n38, 287nn43 and 51; history and example of, 7, 10, 11, 19, 21, 23, 63, 74–75, 151, 164, 179, 252, 253, 259, 282n94, 286n36, 310n32, 316n26; *Invisible Man* and, 137–40, 149; *Nothing Personal* as, 165–66, 187–88; as resource for writers, 53–54, 60, 63–64, 66, 70, 72, 76–77, 78–94, 138–39, 163, 165, 170, 179, 183–84, 187–88, 192, 195–97, 203, 206, 208–12, 217–19, 223–25, 226–30, 231–39, 242, 243, 264; *Twelve Million Black Voices* as, 76–84, 92–94. *See also* documentary; Farm Security Administration, Historical Section (FSA)

Pictorial History of the Negro in America, A, 53

Pinney, Christopher, 15

Pippett, Roger, 284n12

PM, 52, 65, 144, 284nn11, 12, and 18, 285n26. *See also* documentary; photo-journalism; photo-text

Polk, P. H., 295n41. *See also* Tuskegee Institute

Pollock, Jackson, 48

Ponder, Annelle, 216, *217*

Popular Front: as context for cultural production, 54, 61, 93, 285n24; as precedent and resource, 238, 307n4. *See also* documentary; Federal Arts Project; Federal Writers' Project; New Deal, the; New York Photo League

Popular Photography, 249

Porter, Horace, 113

Posnock, Ross, 298n75

postmodernism. *See* documentary, postwar contexts for; photography, and postmodernism

Powell, Adam Clayton, 1, 2–3, 196

Powell, Bud, 168

Preston, Hart, 70

Primus, Pearl, 298n60

Prom, Sol, 26. *See also* Feature Group, The; New York Photo League

Proust, Marcel, 137

Pushkin, Alexander, 239

Pynchon, Thomas, 241

Rabinowitz, Paula, 269n12

Raeburn, John, 277–78n42

Raiford, Leigh, 272n43

Rampersad, Arnold, 52, 281n88

Rahv, Philip, 176

Randolph, A. Philip, 216

Rauschenberg, Robert, 198, 236

Ray, Man, 66

Reed, Ishmael, 253

Reilly, John M., 289n71

Rembrandt, 247, 313–14n88

Richardson, Gloria, 216

Riis, Jacob, 28, 91, 169, 231

riots: definition of, 267n2; as photographic subject, 1–6, *2, 3, 4*, 9, 58, 141–42, 146–48, *148*, 163–64, 198–99, *200*, 227–29, 237–38, 267nn1, 2, 3, 4, and 5, 300n9. *See also* Harlem, activism in, riots in

Rivera, Lino, 9

Robeson, Paul, 238, 307n8

Robinson, Jackie, 242

Rodger, George, 259

Roosevelt, Franklin Delano, 23, 126–27, 302n27

Rosenberg, Ethel and Julius, 167

Rosenblum, Naomi, 282–83n102

Rosenblum, Walter, 121, 303n38. *See also* New York Photo League

Rosler, Martha, 269n12

Rosskam, Edwin, 10, 73–75, 77, 86, 88, 89, 90, *90*, 91, 92–93, 164–65,171, 173, 180, 184, 188, 231, 251, 288n58. *See also* Farm Security Administration, Historical Section (FSA); *Twelve Million Black Voices*; Wright, Richard

Rotella, Carlo, 311n42

Roth, Henry, 167

Rothstein, Arthur, 24, 26, 31, 132, *133. See also* Farm Security Administration, Historical Section (FSA)

Rowley, Hazel, 285n19

Rustin, Bayard, 216

Sallis, James, 226

Sandeen, Eric, 282n98

Sandweiss, Martha, 273n50, 274n8

Sante, Luc, 276n27

Saturday Review, 61, 151

Schapiro, Steven, 194–95, 306n98

Schoenberg, Arnold, 144

Schoener, Allon, 245–46, 248, 249, 251, 313n82, 314n93; influence of on curatorial practices, 313n81. *See also* Harlem on My Mind; Metropolitan Museum of Art; photography, Jews and

Schuster, Max, 169

Schwerner, Michael, 202, 203, 308n13

Scruggs, Charles, 300n7

Sekula, Allan, 16, 17

Shahn, Ben, 24, 86–88, *87, 80,* 121, 173. *See also* Farm Security Administration, Historical Section (FSA); photography, Jews and

Shakespeare, William, 241

Shankar, S., 289n71

Shepp, Archie, 241

Shloss, Carol, 270n31, 286n37

Simpson, Lorna, 253–56, *254,* 260, 315n5

Siskind, Aaron, 19, 21–49, *22, 34, 36, 40, 43, 45, 46,* 56, 59, 61, 66, 74, 86, 117, 120, 122, 165, 167, 169, 171, 173, 180, 204, 205, 232, 245, 250, 277n42, 303n38. *See also* Feature Group, The; Harlem, as site of photographic activity; "Harlem Document"; *Harlem Document*; Jews, and African Americans; Lower East Side; New York Photo League; photography, Jews and

Sleet, Moneta, Jr., 259

Smethurst, James, 307n4

Smith, Milton, 19, 20, 23, 32–33, 37, 44, 51, 52, 74, 164, 274n6, 282n94. *See also* Harlem, as site of photographic activity, "Harlem Document"; *Harlem Document*; Siskind, Aaron

Smith, Morgan and Marvin, 10, 41, 270n29, 279n57

Smith, Shawn Michelle, 271–72n43, 309n23

Smith, Virginia Whatley, 289n70

Smith, W. Eugene, 55, 194

Soby, James Thrall, 272n44

Socialist Workers Party, 231

Solomon-Godeau, Abigail, 277n42

Sontag, Susan, 137, 209

Southern Documentary Project, 309n20

Spence, Jo, 270n30

Spieler, Joe, 308n10

Stange, Maren, 268n12, 270nn29 and 32, 271n41, 287n43

Steegmuller, Frances, 291n6

Steichen, Edward, 55

Stein, Sally, 268n12

Steinbeck, John, 74, 286n37; and origins in documentary of *Grapes of Wrath*, 75

Stepto, Robert, 284n8

Stevenson, Robert Louis, 304n52

Story, Isobel, 296n52

Stott, William, 268n12

Strand, Paul, 72, 101, 117, 151, 309n20. *See also* documentary

Stryker, Roy, 32, 51, 277n33. *See also* Farm Security Administration, Historical Section (FSA)

Student Nonviolent Coordinating Committee (SNCC), 203, 204, 206, 209, 212, 213, 216, 231, 238, 305–6n83, 308nn10 and 11; photographic activities of, 203–4, 206–7, 216, 310n29; photography staff of, 309n20; role of non-African Americans in, 308n15, 311n60. *See also* Hansberry, Lorraine; Lyon, Danny; *Movement, The*; photography, and civil rights

300n9; as photographer, 100–107, *101, 102, 103, 105*, 110, 112–13, 273n53, 285n26, 287n42, 290nn75, 77, and 78, 291n81; works by: *Black Boy*, 71, 112, 153, 284n8; *Black Power*, 94–111; "Blueprint for Negro Writing," 66; *The Color Curtain*, 289n70; *Native Son*, 10, 61, 62–63, 65, 70, 72, 74, 75, 76, 78, 164, 284n8; *The Outsider*, 98; *Pagan Spain*, 289n70, 290n76; *Twelve Million Black Voices*, 73–94, 98, 99, 100, 107, 110, 139, 153, 164, 165, 171, 174, 179, 208; *Uncle Tom's Children*, 61, 64–65, 112. *See also* Rosskam, Edwin; *Twelve Million Black Voices*

You Have Seen Their Faces, 7, 74, 75, 77, 108, 132, 133–34, 139, 168, 208, 287n42,296n47. *See also* Bourke-White, Margaret; Caldwell, Erskine; documentary; photo-text

Young Men's Hebrew Association, 169–70

Zinn, Howard, 216
Zorach, William, 313n81